Crime and Punishment
in Western Countries, 1980–1999

Crime and Punishment in Western Countries, 1980–1999

Edited by Michael Tonry and David P. Farrington

Crime and Justice
A Review of Research
Edited by Michael Tonry

VOLUME 33

The University of Chicago Press, Chicago and London

The University of Chicago Press, Chicago 60637
The University of Chicago Press, Ltd., London

ISSN: 0192-3234

ISBN: 0-226-80869-6 (cloth)
ISBN: 0-226-80871-8 (paper)

LCN: 80-642217

Library of Congress Cataloging-in-Publication Data

Crime and punishment in western countries, 1980/1999 / edited by
Michael Tonry and David P. Farrington.
    p. cm.-- (Crime and justice : a review of research, ISSN
0192-3234 ; v. 33)
  Includes bibliographical references and indexes.
    ISBN 0-226-80869-6 (cloth : alk. paper) -- ISBN 0-226-80871-8 (pbk.
: alk. paper)
    1. Criminal justice, Administration of--Cross-cultural studies. 2.
Crime--Cross-cultural studies. 3. Punishment--Cross-cultural studies.
I. Tonry, Michael H. II. Farrington, David P. III. Crime and justice
(Chicago, Ill.) ; v. 33.
  HV6001.C672vol. 33
  [HV7419]
  364 s--dc22
  [364   2005024762

Contents

Preface

This is the twelfth thematic volume to be published as part of *Crime and Justice*. It is, in two respects, different from any other. First, it does not consist of the series staple, state-of-the-art reviews of knowledge on particular subjects, but instead consists of essays reporting original empirical analyses of criminal justice system data in a wide range of countries, to a common template, with very substantial efforts having been made to adjust data to make the findings cross-nationally comparable. This volume contains something more akin to original research reports than to review essays.

Second, the fruits of this labor appear in two versions. The Bureau of Justice Statistics (BJS), which sponsored the enterprise, has published *Cross-National Studies in Crime and Justice*, edited by David Farrington, Patrick Langan, and Michael Tonry, online and in hard copy. It contains chapters on all of the countries included in this book plus Sweden. They are more technically written and focus more on statistical and methodological questions than do the essays in this volume. The BJS versions of the essays contain many more tables and figures, and appendices provide supporting data.

The essays in this volume contain basic comparable data on crime, victimization, case-processing, and punishment over a twenty-year period for the seven countries represented. They also contain, however, much fuller descriptive and interpretive discussions than do the BJS versions.

Readers who are interested in reanalyzing data themselves to test hypotheses not considered by writers should consult the BJS versions. Readers more interested in a contextual understanding of the data presented, and in the authors' efforts to make sense of what they have found, will likely find this volume of greater interest.

Crime and Punishment in Western Countries has an intellectual history. David Farrington—alone, with Per-Olof Wikström, and several times with Patrick Langan—has undertaken analyses of crime and punishment trends for England and Wales alone and in comparison with Sweden and the United States. This volume extends those efforts to a much wider range of countries and has several major aims.

The first is to present as fully and reliably as can be, for purposes of comparative analyses, comparable data on crime and punishment over a twenty-year period from a variety of Western countries. Truly comparable data are not available anywhere else.

The second, both more and less ambitious, is to attempt significantly to advance efforts at cross-national research and analysis of data from justice system operations both methodologically and analytically. Few such efforts have been made. We hope that this one will stimulate efforts by others. By identifying weaknesses, or things that could have been done better, or estimation techniques that would have made solution of particular problems easier, others will be able to undertake projects in years to come that will stand on the shoulders of this one.

The project generally followed standard *Crime and Justice* procedures but, owing to its inherent difficulty and the importance of trying to adjust data from individual countries to make the final analyses as consistent as possible, the process was elongated. Papers were originally commissioned in 2000, and a small conference to discuss first drafts was held in Cambridge in September 2000. That conference was attended by the writers and by Gordon Barclay, Lars Dolmen, Uberto Gatti, Chris Kershaw, Helmut Kury, Theodore Ferdinand, Amanda J. Matravers, and Per-Olof Wikström.

In the aftermath of that meeting, David Farrington wrote lengthy and detailed letters to the writers of each paper, asking questions and suggesting ways the analyses might be altered and the data adjusted to make the results more comparable. Informed by David's advice, and the discussions at the initial meeting, second drafts were prepared. These were then discussed at a second Cambridge conference, convened in June 2001, attended by the writers and a somewhat broader set of people including Gordon Barclay, Alfred Blumstein, Philip Cook, David Downes, James Lynch, Pat Mayhew, and Per-Olof Wikström.

The then-current drafts were again closely and critically discussed. Fortified again by detailed written suggestions from David Farrington, writers prepared revised versions. These versions, edited and vetted in various ways, became the BJS versions of the essays.

The final BJS versions were, in effect, the first drafts for the *Crime and Justice* versions. Once they were complete, and submitted to BJS, we considered how the *Crime and Justice* versions should differ. Because *Crime and Justice* is written for a less specialized audience, we instructed writers that they need not include or discuss analyses which, for various technical reasons relating to the data systems of their own countries, did not provide strong findings or findings from which valid inferences could be drawn. For reasons of volume length, and their otherwise availability through BJS, we decided not to publish the data appendices. We did, however, ask the writers to develop much fuller introductions describing both the justice system of their country and the nature and characteristics of changes over time in data systems, to discuss much more fully the inferences and conclusions they draw from their analyses, and to set out research agendas identifying next steps in advancing this sort of work in their own country. Those revised and augmented essays, typically much longer than the BJS versions, make up the contents of this volume.

This initiative has been long, complicated, and arduous. We are enormously grateful to the writers for putting up with a process that required them to prepare four and sometimes five or six drafts. Without exception, writers seemingly cheerfully received numerous detailed suggestions and requests for changes and amplifications in their work and cooperated with sometimes nit-picking *Crime and Justice* editorial processes. We are grateful to the Bureau of Justice Statistics for funding so unconventional a project and in particular to Laurence Greenfeld and Patrick Langan for making the project possible and for overseeing publication of the BJS version. We are also enormously grateful to Vickie Sheridan, who oversaw the editing and production of both the BJS report and this *Crime and Justice* volume with her usual high standards, uncanny eye for detail, and good spirits.

Was all this effort worthwhile? Inevitably and inexorably, that bottom-line question is for others to answer.

Michael Tonry
David P. Farrington

Michael Tonry and David P. Farrington

Punishment and Crime across Space and Time

Crime rates rose in the United States from the mid-1960s through the early 1990s;[1] imprisonment rates began rising in 1973 and continued to do so through 2005. To the man on the street and many politicians, those patterns appear to tell a comforting story. As crime rose, more miscreants were arrested, prosecuted, convicted, and imprisoned, and imprisonment rates increased. After a long while, nearly twenty years, the deterrent and incapacitative effects of increased imprisonment took hold, and crime rates fell. "Prison works," as some politicians are quick to claim.

The logic is tidy but the conclusion is not necessarily right, as comparisons of the United States and Canada show (Tonry 2004, fig. 5.23). Crime rate trends in Canada have closely paralleled those in the United States since 1970. When America's crime rates rose, so did Canada's. When America's crime rates fell, so did Canada's. However, there is no resemblance between American and Canadian imprisonment trends. After a four-decade-long period of stable imprisonment rates (Blumstein and Cohen 1973), the American rate grew continuously after 1973, more than quadrupling to 700 per 100,000 population, and the absolute

Michael Tonry is Sonosky Professor of Law and Public Policy, University of Minnesota, and senior fellow, Netherlands Institute for the Study of Crime and Law Enforcement, Leiden. David P. Farrington is professor of psychological criminology, University of Cambridge. The authors are grateful to Darrick Jolliffe for preparation of the tables and figures.
[1] That is the simplest way to say it. More complexly, official rates of recorded crime rose through the early 1980s, fell for five years, rose again through 1990–91, and fell continuously thereafter. The trends shown by victimization data are slightly different but agree that crime has been falling since the early 1990s.

1

number of people imprisoned increased even more. Canada's total imprisonment rate has remained essentially flat for four decades, generally fluctuating around a narrow band of 100–110 prisoners per 100,000.

So, if the increasing volume of crimes and criminals inexorably caused American imprisonment rates to rise and prisons to bulge, why didn't the same thing happen in Canada? And if greatly increased severity of punishment and higher imprisonment rates caused American crime rates to fall after 1990, what caused the Canadian rates to fall? The story must be more complicated than the man on the street or most American politicians know.

Other pairs and sets of adjacent countries with similar cultures provide further demonstrations that the relations between crime and punishment rates are not inexorable.[2] Scandinavia provides the best. Crime rate trends in Denmark, Finland, Norway, and Sweden, as shown by official data, have moved in parallel for more than forty years. When rates in one country rise, they rise in all; when rates fall in one, they fall in all. Overall, for all four countries, crime rates rose substantially between 1965 and 2000, with lots of intermediate ups and downs.

Imprisonment rates in Denmark, Norway, and Sweden were broadly stable between 1960 and 2000, ranging between fifty and seventy per 100,000. Finland's fell by two-thirds, from around 180 per 100,000 in 1960 to sixty in 2000. If punishment affects crime, Finland's crime rate should have shot up, compared with crime rates in the rest of Scandinavia. To the contrary, Finland's crime trends closely paralleled the rest of Scandinavia, and, throughout, Finland held its initial relative position of having the second-lowest crime rates in Scandinavia (Lappi-Seppälä 2001, 2004).

So what happened in Finland? If harsher penalties and higher imprisonment rates should reduce crime rates, shouldn't a sustained long-term reduction in severity and in imprisonment rates increase crime rates?[3]

---

[2] Between 1950 and 1995, English crime rates increased much more than those in Scotland. From 1980 through 1995, crime rates in Scotland leveled off without any marked increase in punishment. English crime rates rose substantially between 1980 and 1993, reaching a peak from which they continue to fall. English imprisonment rates fell steeply in the late 1980s and nearly doubled between 1993 and 2005 (Smith 1999). Smith concludes, "at a minimum, these findings suggest that it is possible to have less crime without more punishment" (p. 316).

[3] A similar comparative question can be asked about the Netherlands, which has had continuously rising imprisonment rates since 1973, with a relative rise (fourfold) comparable to that in the United States, in contrast to Belgium, which had a much lesser increase in imprisonment rates but comparable crime trends over decades (van Rullers and Beijers 1995; Junger-Tas 2001).

Comparative and cross-national questions about crime and punishment have become easier to ask and answer in recent years because a comparative and cross-national literature on penal policy is beginning to accumulate. Language barriers, noncomparability of national crime data, and simple parochialism long conspired to make credible cross-national comparisons nearly impossible, but those problems are becoming more manageable.

Cross-national analyses traditionally have been based primarily on comparisons of official crime rates and imprisonment rates per 100,000. Official crime rates, however, are considerably less complete than are data from victim surveys and may be misleading because of changes over time in victim reporting to police, police recording of reported crimes, and police agency reporting to central data banks. It is important to investigate to what extent increases in imprisonment rates reflect increases in the number of crimes committed, increases in the probability of conviction given a crime, increases in the probability of custody given a conviction, increases in sentence lengths, or increases in the fraction of time served.

The project whose fruits are presented in this volume attempted to standardize crime and punishment data from eight countries so that we can begin to look meaningfully across national boundaries. It sought to obtain and present more sophisticated, valid, and informative data than are available anywhere else. The countries are Australia, Canada, England (and Wales), the Netherlands, Switzerland, Scotland, Sweden, and the United States. Although there are some well-known differences between inquisitorial civil law and adversarial common law systems and procedures, the criminal justice systems of the eight countries are much more similar than different.

The most challenging differences for our purposes are in the details of criminal law codification and the organization of information systems. There are substantial differences between countries in how offenses are defined. In some, for example, murder includes both completed and attempted killings. In others, only completed killings count.

Burglary is a separate offense in some countries, but not in others, and where it is a separate offense, it does or does not include both residential and commercial incidents. In some places, there is no separate burglary offense at all and crimes that would be counted as burglaries in the United States or England are counted under various other property offense classifications.

Some motor vehicle theft definitions distinguish between automobiles and other motorized vehicles; some do not. Some distinguish between thefts of and from vehicles; others do not. Sometimes, as in Switzerland, all motorized vehicles are classified together, which means that, as happened, a great reduction in theft of mopeds and light motorcycles can produce an enormous drop in "motor vehicle crimes." For an opposite phenomenon, Dutch recording practices do not include joyriding among motor vehicle thefts; this means that the offenses counted are mostly more serious organized "professional" vehicle thefts that are dealt with more seriously and punished more severely. What might otherwise seem unusually low Dutch motor vehicle theft rates and unusually severe sentencing practices may instead result from how offenses are classified.

None of the countries has a fully integrated, offender-based transactional information system, which means that aggregate data must typically be cobbled together from different sources. This is easiest in a sparsely populated country such as Sweden, with 9 million people, highly centralized governmental institutions, and unique national identity numbers for citizens. It is hardest in large or populous federal systems characterized by strong separation-of-powers doctrines and by criminal justice institutions organized at state or provincial levels.

Part of the process of developing this volume consisted of identifying significant ways in which offense definitions, recording practices, and information systems differed and developing techniques to adjust for the effects of those differences. This was easier to do for victimization and recorded crime data than for case-processing data.

For processing data it was easier to do for countries with smaller populations and unitary (nonfederal) systems of government (namely, the Netherlands [16 million], Scotland [under 6 million], and Sweden) than for more populous and federal countries (Australia, Canada, and the United States). England, a populous country (approximately 55 million), with centralized institutions, and Switzerland, a small (under 8 million people) federal country, fell in between.

It was most difficult for Canada and Australia because national data systems for judicial and correctional processes incorporating state and provincial data remain incomplete, underdeveloped, and often unreliable. The U.S. Bureau of Justice Statistics (BJS) has been working on solving these problems for more than thirty years, so though the United States potentially faces the same impediments as Canada and Australia, problems of data reliability are considerably less acute.

From each of eight countries, data on offending were drawn from victimization surveys and police records, and case processing data were drawn from police, court, and correctional sources.[4] We attempted to identify all relevant differences among the offenses we studied, as well as numerous differences between countries in the organization and completeness of data systems.[5]

In this introduction, we discuss current knowledge of cross-national patterns of crime and punishment. We rely primarily on data made possible by this project but try to provide contexts by referring to data drawn from other sources. Section I describes the methods employed in this project in some detail. Section II discusses cross-national comparisons of crime levels and patterns over time. Section III discusses cross-national comparisons of punishment levels, patterns, and trends over time. The conclusion summarizes major findings concerning crime and punishment trends cross-nationally and sets out methodological suggestions for improving future initiatives such as this one.

We draw a number of conclusions: According to both victim survey data and police records, burglary rates fell in most of the countries during the 1990s, with the steepest declines occurring in Canada, England, the Netherlands, Scotland, and the United States. The pattern for robbery was more mixed.[6] Homicide rates either fell substantially toward the end of the twentieth century or were essentially flat at low levels between one and two per 100,000 population. Except for Canada, where both survey and recorded rates rose, and Sweden, where there was no clear pattern, motor vehicle theft rates fell in every country during the 1990s and in several during the 1980s. These conclusions parallel those that would be drawn from data for 1995–2000 from the *European Sourcebook of Crime and Criminal Justice Statistics* (Council of Europe, Committee of Experts 2003): homicide,

---

[4] This volume contains essays on all those countries except Sweden, but Swedish data are used in this introduction and in three essays that draw on all eight (Cook and Khmilevska, in this volume; Farrington and Jolliffe, in this volume; Blumstein, Tonry, and Van Ness, in this volume). A more technical companion volume published by the U.S. Bureau of Justice (Farrington, Langan, and Tonry 2004), containing additional data, contains chapters on all eight countries.

[5] Each essay discusses definitions and problems in achieving cross-national comparability. The fullest discussion of definitional differences among European countries can be found in the *European Sourcebook of Crime and Criminal Justice Statistics, 2003* (Council of Europe, Committee of Experts 2003).

[6] Either discordant results for victim survey and official data, broad stability according to one or both, or volatility according to one or both.

burglary, and motor vehicle theft declines in most countries, with a more mixed pattern for robbery.

United States policies were the most punitive of the eight countries by every measure: probability of commitment given a conviction, expected days imprisonment per recorded crime, expected days imprisonment per conviction, and average times served by those imprisoned.[7] National punishment policies vary substantially not only in imprisonment rates but also in more complex ways: Sweden achieves low imprisonment rates by combining high probabilities of imprisonment given a conviction with relatively short sentence lengths. Switzerland achieves comparably low imprisonment rates for convicted offenders by combining low probabilities of imprisonment with relatively long sentence lengths. Across all eight countries, there were few distinct trends in commitment probabilities or average sentence lengths. In England there were clear upward trends in average time served in the 1990s for four of the six offenses studied. There were marked increases in Scotland in the probability of custody given a conviction and in Australia in average time served.

We draw no strong conclusions concerning the effects of national differences in punishment policies and practices on crime rates. However, we found no evidence that robbery or burglary rates are correlated with national differences in time served in prison. James Q. Wilson has rightly observed that "social scientists have made great gains in explaining why some people are more likely than others to commit crimes but far smaller gains in understanding a nation's crime rate" (Wilson 2002, p. 537). Cross-national differences in legal and political culture, institutional arrangements, and constitutional traditions and values shape both crime and punishment in ways that no one has yet figured out how to quantify (Zimring and Hawkins 1991; Young and Brown 1993).

I. Methods

It is not easy to explain trends in national crime rates, the probability and severity of legal punishment, and differences between countries. There are enormous problems of comparability over time and between countries, in laws, measurement methods, recording practices, and macrosocial, cultural, and political factors. However, the first step in moving toward explanations is to obtain comparable data over time and space. Writers from the

---

[7] The findings reported here are based on calculations shown in Blumstein, Tonry, and Van Ness (in this volume).

eight countries were asked to pull together crime and case processing data, when necessary to adjust and reclassify it to make it as comparable as possible across countries and time, and then to carry out a series of calculations prescribed by a common template (see the appendix).

A. Similar Prior Research

The essays in this volume build on a series of earlier efforts to characterize the operation of national criminal justice systems, initially in England alone and then in comparison with the United States and Sweden. The aim of those efforts was to estimate crime-specific numbers flowing through the criminal justice system at each stage, from crimes committed to crimes reported to the police, crimes recorded by the police, offenders convicted, offenders sentenced to custody, average sentence length, and average time served.

The best way to do this would be to conduct a longitudinal study that tracked offenders through the criminal justice system, using a unique identification number for each offender at each stage. National-level data tracking individual offenders are not available in most countries. Aggregate national data, however, are available for many key stages (e.g., crimes committed, persons convicted, persons sentenced to custody). These separate counts permit reasonably accurate estimates of the flows of offenders from one stage to the next.

In the first of the efforts to do this comparatively, Farrington and Langan (1992) estimated numbers flowing through the criminal justice systems of England and the United States and compared trends over time (between 1981 and 1987 in England and between 1981 and 1986 in the United States). The starting point for England was 1981 because that was the year of the first British Crime Survey.

Farrington and Wikström (1993) then compared trends between 1981 and 1987 in England and Sweden. Farrington, Langan, and Wikström (1994) compared all three countries, extending the previous analyses to 1981 to 1991 for England and Sweden and 1981 to 1990 for the United States.

The first three cross-national analyses reported changes between two widely separated times rather than trends over time, making it difficult to know when changes occurred and how to explain them. A fourth study (Langan and Farrington 1998) calculated all numbers and probabilities for seven years in the United States (1981, 1983, 1986, 1988, 1990, 1992, and 1994) and for six years in England (1981, 1983, 1987, 1991, 1993, and 1995). The American years were those in which the

National Judicial Reporting Program survey was carried out (1986, 1988, 1990, 1992, and 1994); it provided the numbers of adults convicted and sentenced to custody, plus 1981 and 1983, for which estimates of these quantities were derived. The English years were those in which the British Crime Survey was carried out, providing estimates of the numbers of crimes committed and reported to the police.[8] All of the needed information was not available for other years. The work reported in this volume is modeled on that fourth study and extends the analyses to encompass time trends in eight countries between 1981 and 1999.

B. Methods

The eight countries were chosen because large-scale representative national victimization surveys had been conducted in each at least three times between 1981 and 1999, and they otherwise appeared to have adequate criminal justice data. National victimization data from the separate countries were used rather than data from the International Crime Victims Survey (ICVS; Kesteren, Mayhew, and Nieuwbeerta 2000) because the sample sizes in the ICVS, typically about 2,000 per country, and the nonresponse rates, typically 30–50 percent, were unsatisfactory for our purposes (especially for estimating linking probabilities for particular crimes).

Six serious crimes were studied for the years 1980 through 1999: residential burglary, vehicle theft, robbery, serious assault, rape, and homicide. For each, the following information was obtained: the number of crimes committed (according to a national victimization survey), the number of crimes reported to the police (according to a national victimization survey), the number of crimes recorded by the police, the average number of offenders committing each crime, the number of persons convicted, the number of persons sentenced to custody, the average sentence length, and the average time served. These quantities are then compared in each country with the national population, and linking probabilities are estimated (e.g., the probability of an offender being convicted, the probability of a convicted person being sentenced to custody).

---

[8] The rationales for the two countries' coverage dates differ because the U.S. National Crime Victimization Survey is carried out continuously with each household interviewed at six-month intervals while the British Crime Survey was then conducted at longer and irregular intervals. Conversely, because England is a unitary governmental entity, routinely compiled statistics on sentencing and punishment are available for every year.

In order to relate crimes committed to persons convicted, the average number of offenders committing each crime must be known. If, for example, three persons jointly commit one crime, this can lead to three persons being convicted. In calculating the probability of an offender being convicted, it is important, therefore, to divide the number of persons convicted (in this example, three) by the number of offenders (the number of offender-crime pairs, which in this example is three), not by the number of crimes (in this example, one).

Because of problems of comparability, data were not collected on all possible stages of the criminal justice system or on all possible sentences. For example, while U.S. national data on arrests have been published annually for many years, national arrest data were not collected in England until 1999. In many continental European countries, police record suspects, not all of whom are arrested, rather than arrests. Consequently, the individual country analyses are based variously on crimes reported in victimization surveys or on offenses resulting in convictions. Concerning punishment, the individual country analyses focus on convictions and custody because the problems of comparability were much less daunting than if other sanctions such as suspended sentences, probation, fines, and other community penalties were separately considered.

The individual country analyses address the following key questions that any theory of crime or criminal justice should be able to explain: How has the crime rate changed over time? Has the probability of a victim reporting a crime to the police increased or decreased over time? Has the probability that the police will record a crime that is reported to them increased or decreased over time? Has the conviction rate changed over time? Has the probability that an offender will be convicted increased or decreased over time? Has the probability that a convicted offender will be sentenced to custody increased or decreased over time? Has the average sentence length changed over time? Has the average time served changed over time? Has the average time served per offender increased or decreased over time?

C. Issues of Comparability

The writers made Herculean efforts to comply with the template (see the appendix) and to achieve comparability over time. However, as the essays on individual countries explain, there are still problems of comparability. The most important concern crime definitions, victim surveys, and time served. There were fewer problems of comparability in regard to police-recorded crimes, persons convicted, persons sentenced to custody, and sentence lengths.

In regard to crime definitions and legal codes, there was a major problem in distinguishing between serious and minor assaults, and serious assaults in one country may not be very comparable to serious assaults in another. Changes over time in rates of serious assaults within a country are more valid than comparisons between countries. Burglary and vehicle theft caused difficulties in continental European countries (the Netherlands, Sweden, Switzerland) because they are not distinguished explicitly from other types of theft in legal codes. However, the authors were able to estimate the numbers of these crimes through various adjustments.

Between 1981 and 1999, the laws on rape in several countries were changed to make definitions more comprehensive (e.g., including anal and oral sex, males as victims and females as offenders, and acts between husbands and wives). Writers made various adjustments to estimate the number of rapes with male offenders and female victims in an effort to make the numbers comparable over time and between countries. During the same period, the wordings of questions in the national victim surveys in several countries were changed in order to reveal more domestic violence, but writers again made adjustments to make the numbers comparable over time. Robbery and homicide were more consistently defined over time.

The United States was the only country in which a large-scale national victimization survey was conducted every year. Sweden had a large-scale omnibus survey every year containing some victimization questions, but it did not provide data on robbery. The Netherlands had three different national victim surveys that permitted annual estimates, but they differed in some significant respects and their results were not totally concordant. England had eight large-scale national victim surveys between 1981 and 1999, Scotland had five, Switzerland had five, Canada had three (plus a large-scale city survey which permitted national estimates), and Australia had three (but national estimates could also be estimated from annual surveys in New South Wales, which accounts for about two-thirds of Australia's crime). Conclusions about trends and correlations based on five or fewer years inevitably are fragile.

The average time served was estimated in different ways in different countries. In Switzerland, it was available in a sophisticated correctional database. In the Netherlands, offenders serve fixed proportions of their sentences. In England, the estimate of average time served was based on release cohorts of prisoners. In the United States, the fraction of time served (based on release cohorts) was applied to sentences given to estimate the time expected to be served. In Scotland and Sweden, the expected time to be served was estimated from laws and parole regulations. In Australia, the average time served was estimated from the expected time to be served by the population of prisoners (obtained in a prison census); unfortunately, the daily population contains relatively more long-serving prisoners than entering or release cohorts. In Canada, it was not possible to derive a satisfactory estimate of time served.

These difficulties in obtaining comparable data in eight countries highlight fundamental problems and inadequacies of existing crime and case processing data in most countries. In no country was there a satisfactory measure of the number of offenders per crime, which is essential for linking crime data to offender data.

II. Cross-National Comparisons of Crime

Few sources of data are available to support cross-national analyses of crime rates or to test hypotheses about possible crime-reductive effects of changes in policy or practice—such as increases in certainty of conviction or prison commitment, or in severity of punishment.[9] Simple comparisons of recorded data from several countries are inherently unreliable for reasons already discussed.

Several compilations of data from numerous countries are available, but mostly they are little more useful. There are three principal sources of official data from multiple countries: the International Criminal Police Organization (Interpol), the United Nations, and the *European Sourcebook of Crime and Criminal Justice Statistics*.[10]

The Interpol data consist of undigested police data on recorded crimes from reporting nations.[11] They are subject to all the standard noncomparability problems and the additional ones that no one knows

---

[9] Although there is no doubt that having penalties compared with not having them has general deterrent effects, the clear weight of the evidence in the American literature is that changes in the severity of sanctions have few or no demonstrable crime-preventive effects (e.g., Blumstein, Cohen, and Nagin 1978; Nagin 1998; Doob and Webster 2003).

[10] The World Health Organization, in addition, has since 1951 collected data on homicides from health records of countries willing to provide them. The data do not distinguish between intentional and unintentional homicide.

[11] See http://www.interpol.int.

how accurate and complete the national reports are, or how consistently data are reported and recorded over time.

Data collected by the United Nations (UN) suffer from the same problems. The UN has since the mid-1970s surveyed member nations on recorded crime rates and counts. Questionnaires for the eighth survey covering 2001 and 2002 were distributed to 191 countries in 2003. Data from the seventh survey covering ninety-two countries for the three years 1998–2000 are available on the Web.[12]

The second edition of the *European Sourcebook of Crime and Criminal Justice Statistics* (Council of Europe, Committee of Experts 2003) provides official data on crime from thirty-nine countries for 1995–2000. National correspondents collect and submit national data on crime and other subjects.[13] A committee of experts reviews the data and undertakes a number of consistency checks (referring questions and problems back to the national correspondents). The report contains detailed discussions of definitional differences. At day's end, the data, though presented as cleanly and accurately as they can be, have not been adjusted to take account of definitional differences and, thus, cannot be used for cross-national and comparative analyses. Offense rates per 100,000 population are given for each year between 1995 and 2000 for intentional homicide, rape, robbery, assault, theft, motor vehicle theft, burglary, traffic offenses, and drug offenses, thus permitting at least trend analyses within countries (assuming consistent reporting and record keeping within a country and accurate reporting of that data to the sourcebook compilers).

The sourcebook introduction notes comparability problems that make comparative conclusions about absolute levels of crime suspect but argues that trend comparisons within and between countries are more credible so long as statistical and definitional circumstances are controlled (Council of Europe, Committee of Experts 2003, p. 20). Assuming that argument is plausible, one would conclude from the official data for 1995–2000 that homicide rates increased in only three of thirteen Western European countries for which results were available, burglary in only one of twelve, and motor vehicle theft in six of thirteen.

---

[12] See http://www.unodc.org/unodc/en/crime_cicp_surveys.html.

[13] Data are also compiled on prosecutions, convictions, sentences, and correctional populations. Victimization data are taken from the International Crime Victimization Survey. The introduction to the second edition (Council of Europe 2003, pp. 1–20) and European Sourcebook Group (2004) describe the collection and quality control system in detail.

Rape and robbery rates, however, increased in eleven of fourteen countries, and assault in all fourteen (2003, chap. 1).

The decreases are for offenses that are not especially susceptible to cultural changes affecting reporting and recording, and accordingly it would be reasonable to conclude that homicide, burglary, and motor vehicle theft declined in most countries. The increases are for assault and rape, for which both reporting and recording increased in many countries, and for robbery, for which reporting and recording may also have been affected by declining tolerance of violence (Blumstein and Beck 1999). Because the most reliable crime counts are for homicide, and assault and robbery rates should be probabilistically related to homicide rates, there is reason to be skeptical that the official data reported in the sourcebook reflect reality.[14] Accordingly, we believe that no conclusions about true crime trends can be drawn from sourcebook data about recorded rates of rape, robbery, and assault.

There are two potential sources of cross-national victimization data: national victimization surveys and the International Crime Victimization Survey. The former, not conducted annually in most countries, suffer from definitional differences similar to those that affect comparisons of official records. They also suffer from major methodological differences.[15] It would be difficult credibly to draw cross-national conclusions from a set of national surveys characterized by different definitions and instruments, administered by different methods, covering different time periods at differing intervals, and taking different approaches to telescoping.

The ICVS, conducted in many countries in 1989, 1992, 1996, and 2000, attempts to address those comparability problems by describing crimes in standardized plain-language terms rather than in terms of local criminal law definitions, using the same survey instrument in every country, and in most countries administering the survey to representative samples the same way (computer-assisted telephone interviews).

[14] If, for example, homicide rates are declining, accurate counts of assault and robbery also should show decline. Homicide is probably the most reliably counted crime, and health mortality statistics provide a validating check. Assuming no major changes in the lethality of weapons or the circumstances of assaults and robberies, their occurrence should be probabilistically correlated with the occurrence of homicides. If recorded serious assaults increase much more rapidly than recorded homicides, changes in reporting or recording are likely to be a major part of the explanation.

[15] One of the most significant is that only the United States survey uses bounding interviews to minimize telescoping and uses a panel model in which the same household remains in the survey for multiple (seven) waves of data collection (data from the first, bounding, wave are not reported).

Two major problems are low response rates, ranging in 2000 from 45 to 81 percent (with most in the high 50s and low 60s), and samples too small for adequate coverage of serious crimes (particularly rape and robbery; Kesteren, Mayhew, and Nieuwbeerta 2000, app. 1, table 1).[16]

The ICVS does provide some fairly robust findings, however: first, that overall crime rates as measured by victimization rose after 1988 in seven countries (Canada, England and Wales, Finland, France, the Netherlands, Scotland, and Switzerland), peaked in the early or mid-1990s, and fell through 2000 (in the United States, victimization fell continuously from 1988); second, that victimization rate rankings among the eight countries remained the same through all four waves except for the United States and Canada, which were high-rate countries in 1988 and low-rate ones in 2000. England and the Netherlands had high rates throughout, and Finland and Switzerland had low rates (Kesteren, Mayhew, and Nieuwbeerta 2000, pp. 91–92, figs. 15 and 16).

The data assembled for the project reported in this volume allow analyses not possible with data from any of the other sources described. Many cross-national comparisons can be carried out; the U.S. Bureau of Justice Statistics' versions of the essays in Farrington, Langan, and Tonry (2004) contain spreadsheets that provide the data on which tables and figures are based, and these, of course, can be used by others for original analyses.[17]

To provide illustrations, we focus in this introduction on one property crime, burglary, and one violent crime, robbery. We focus on these offenses because survey crime data are not available for rape and homicide, comparability problems between countries are greatest for serious assault, and motor vehicle theft is less interesting and less serious than burglary. In this section we focus on crime trends and in the next on punishment trends. We use both victimization and recorded crime rates.

A. Burglary

Figure 1 shows changes in the survey burglary rate for all eight countries over the twenty-year period. The rate was consistently highest

---

[16] One additional possibly important problem is that there may be significant national and cultural thresholds below which behaviors (e.g., forms of domestic and acquaintance violence, or household theft) are not seen as warranting mention, thereby creating selection effects that distort cross-national comparisons; in addition, because the ICVS is a household survey that relies heavily on computer-aided telephone interviews, it undercounts households lacking telephones and undercounts young, mobile, disadvantaged groups with high offending and victimization rates.

[17] These data may be obtained electronically from http://www.ojp.usdoj.gov/bjs.

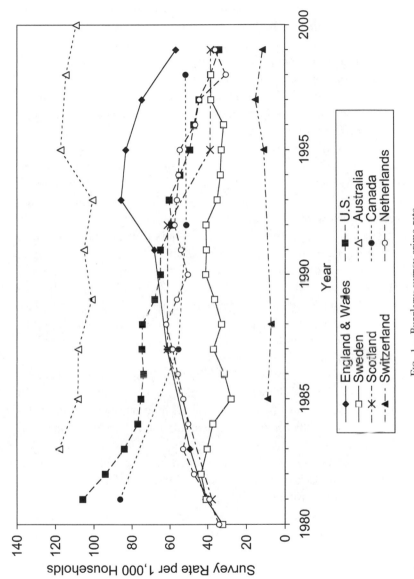

FIG. 1.—Burglary: survey crime rate

in Australia and lowest in Switzerland (followed by Sweden). It increased in England through 1993 and then decreased, while it decreased steadily in the United States.

Table 1 shows correlations between the survey burglary rate and the year. The correlations in table 1 were calculated in order to get a rough idea of whether survey crime rates were increasing or decreasing. We assume that a positive correlation higher than 0.4 indicates a general increase, a negative correlation less than −0.4 indicates a general decrease, and a correlation between 0.4 and −0.4 indicates no clear trend. These numbers are somewhat arbitrary but differences in correlations do reflect differences in trends.

The correlations indicate how close the relationship was to a linear trend; for example, the 0.76 correlation between survey burglary rate and year in Switzerland shows a general increase over the time period. The large negative correlations for the United States and Canada, by contrast, show the continuous and considerable declines in those countries. The correlations, however, are but crude indicators because they do not account well for long-term shifts in direction. For example, the 0.67 correlation between survey burglary rate and year in England and Wales shows that survey crimes generally increased over this period (there was a large increase from 1981–93 and a smaller decrease from 1993–99), but looking at the positive correlation alone might obscure the important finding of significant declines in the most recent years.

Correlations were positive in England (0.67) and Switzerland (0.76), negative in the United States (−0.97) and Canada (−0.83), and low in the other four countries. It should be borne in mind that these correlations are based on only four years for Canada and five years for Scotland and Switzerland.

Figure 2 shows changes in the recorded burglary rate for all eight countries. For at least some period after 1995, recorded burglary rates declined in most countries.

Absolute rates were highest over the entire period in Scotland and Australia and lowest in Switzerland and Sweden. Over two decades, rates increased steadily in Australia, decreased steadily in the United States, and trended gently downward in Canada. Correlations shown in table 1 between the recorded burglary rate and the year were positive for Australia (0.97), Switzerland (0.87), the Netherlands (0.78), and England (0.48) and negative for the United States (−0.95), Scotland (−0.64), Canada (−0.56), and Sweden (−0.44).

TABLE 1

Correlations with Year

	England and Wales	United States	Sweden	Scotland	Netherlands	Australia	Canada	Switzerland
Burglary								
Survey rate	.67	-.97	-.10	-.15	-.10	.02	-.83	.76
Recorded rate	.48	-.95	-.4	-.64	.78	.97	-.56	.87
Convictions/1,000 offenders	-.89	.82	-.84	-.83	-.87	-.84		-.86
Probability custody/conviction	.6	.41	-.63	.93		.53		.40
Average time served	.74	-.12	.53	.43		.82		.62
Robbery								
Survey rate	.91	-.69		.74	-.17	.31	-.20	.29
Recorded rate	.96	-.43	.91	.49	.93	.97	.07	.80
Convictions/1,000 offenders	-.88	.74		-.33	.77	.45		-.62
Probability custody/conviction	-.6	-.2	-.73	.81	-.10	-.90		-.92
Average time served	.92	-.13	.0	.11	.79	.23		.99

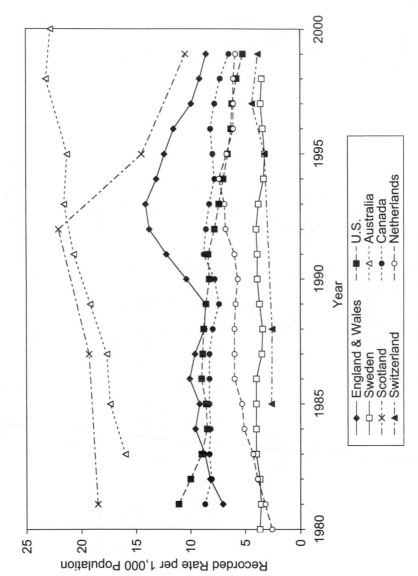

Fig. 2.—Burglary: recorded crime rate

B.   Robbery

Figure 3 shows the survey robbery rate. The pattern is less consistent than for burglary. The trend lines of many countries are erratic, at least partly resulting from the limited number of victim survey data points.

On average throughout the two decades, the survey robbery rate was highest in Canada and the Netherlands, and lowest in Scotland. In 1999, the survey robbery rate was lowest in the United States. It was not available for Sweden. The correlations in table 1 show that the survey robbery rate increased over time in England (0.91) and Scotland (0.74) but decreased over time in the United States (−0.69). Correlations in the other four countries were low.

Figure 4 shows the recorded robbery rate. Reported robbery rates fell during the 1990s in the United States, Canada, and Scotland, increased in England and Australia, and showed no clear trend in the other countries. On average throughout the two decades, the rate was highest in the United States (until 1998) and lowest in Switzerland. The correlations in table 1 show that over the full two decades, the rate increased in Australia (0.97), England (0.96), the Netherlands (0.93), Sweden (0.91), Switzerland (0.80), and Scotland (0.49), decreased in the United States (−0.43), and did not change in Canada (0.07).

The data summarized in this section could support a number of conclusions, some substantive and some methodological. Both survey and recorded data indicate that burglary rates fell in most countries in the latter half of the 1990s. In most countries, the trends shown by the two data sources are highly concordant, and there is little reason to doubt that burglaries became less common in most countries.

Trends are less concordant for robbery. Only in the United States and England were the survey and recorded crime rates highly correlated. According to both data sources, the robbery rate decreased in the United States and increased in England in the 1990s. The correlations in table 1 show that recorded robbery rates generally increased in most other countries (all except Canada), but, with the exception of Scotland, the survey robbery rates did not show similar increases. There was no clear trend in survey robbery rates in Australia, the Netherlands, Canada, or Switzerland.

III.   Cross-National Comparisons of Punishment
We are doubtful that available data are as yet sufficiently comparable to permit cross-national conclusions about the crime-preventive

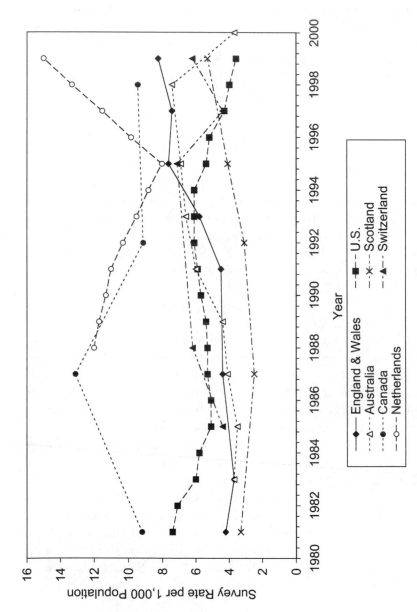

FIG. 3.—Robbery: survey crime rate

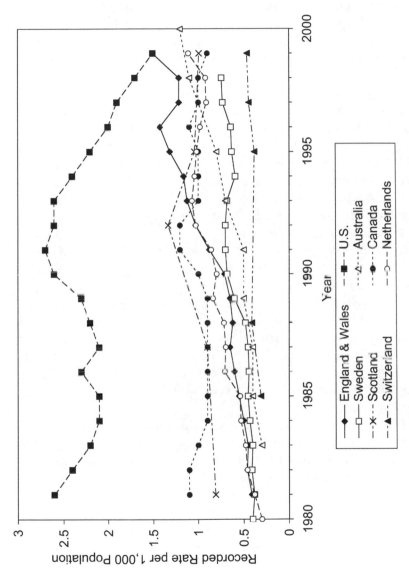

Fig. 4.—Robbery: recorded crime rate

Legend:
England & Wales — U.S.
Sweden — Australia
Scotland — Canada
Switzerland — Netherlands

effectiveness of penal policies to be drawn. Available data do, however, permit confident conclusions to be dawn about cross-national differences in the use and severity of punishment. We concentrate on three measures of punishment (the number of convictions per 1,000 offenders, the probability of custody following a conviction, and the average time served in custody). Crime rates may be differentially related to these different indices of risk and certainty.

A. Burglary

Figure 5 shows changes in the number of convictions per 1,000 burglary offenders as calculated from victim survey burglary rates. This is a measure of the certainty of punishment. Only in the United States did certainty in this sense increase. Canada is excluded from this figure because conviction data were not available before 1994. The number of convictions per 1,000 offenders was highest for Australia and Scotland and lowest for Sweden and England. The correlations in table 1 show that the probability of conviction per burglary decreased over time in England (−0.89), Sweden (−0.84), Scotland (−0.83), the Netherlands (−0.87), Australia (−0.84), and Switzerland (−0.86), but increased in the United States (0.82).

Figure 6 shows changes in one measure of the severity of punishment, the probability of custody following a burglary conviction. This was highest in the United States and Sweden (at least until 1994) and lowest in Australia. The correlations in table 1 show that this probability increased over time in Scotland (0.93), England (0.60), Australia (0.53), the United States (0.41), and Switzerland (0.40) but decreased over time in Sweden (−0.63).

Figure 7 shows changes in average time served per burglary prison sentence, a measure of the severity of punishment. This was highest in the United States (until 1994) and lowest in Sweden and Scotland. The correlations in table 1 show that this increased over time in Australia (0.82), England (0.74), Switzerland (0.62), Sweden (0.53), and Scotland (0.43) but not in the United States (−0.12).

Table 2 shows correlations with the survey crime rate. For the burglary survey crime rate versus convictions per 1,000 offenders, the correlations were clearly negative for England and Wales (−0.89), the United States (−0.86), and Switzerland (−0.85) but less clearly so for the other four countries. However, all of these correlations are limited by small numbers and by lack of control of numerous other factors that might influence crime rates over time. All we can say is that results are

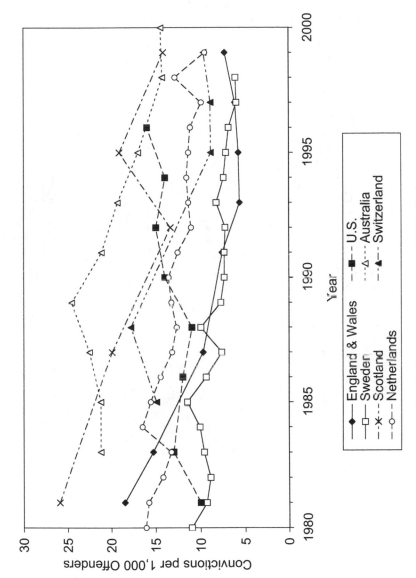

Fig. 5.—Burglary: convictions per 1,000 offenders

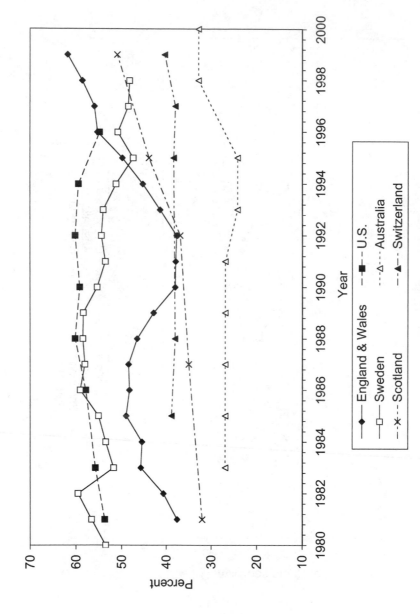

Fig. 6.—Burglary: probability of custody per conviction

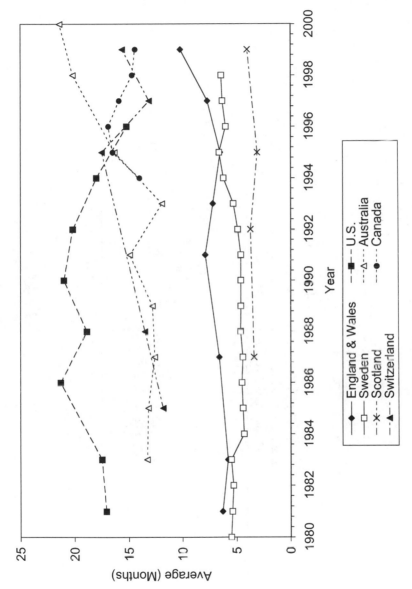

Fig. 7.—Burglary: average time served

Legend:
♦——England & Wales
□——Sweden
✳——Scotland
▲——Switzerland
■——U.S.
△——Australia
●——Canada

TABLE 2
Correlations with Survey Crime Rate

	England and Wales	United States	Sweden	Scotland	Netherlands	Australia	Canada	Switzerland
Burglary								
Recorded rate	.91	.98	.26	.74	.49	-.10	.76	.96
Convictions/1,000 offenders	-.89	-.86	-.37	-.35	-.10	-.45		-.85
Probability custody/conviction	.12	-.48	.10	-.43		.20		.03
Average time served	.10	-.01	-.01	.0		.40		.13
Robbery								
Recorded rate	.94	.81		-.01	-.34	.27	-.81	.20
Convictions/1,000 offenders	-.10	-.66		-.83	-.71	-.17		-.93
Probability custody/conviction	-.56	.17		.55	.22	-.23		-.39
Average time served	.79	-.18		-.12	-.63	.15		.34

or are not in agreement with particular hypotheses; hypotheses cannot be proved or disproved with these data. However, we can conclude that the data provide no support for some hypotheses, for example that survey burglary rates are negatively correlated with the severity of punishment; table 2 shows that correlations in five countries are close to zero and in the other country (Australia) the correlation was positive (0.40).

The survey and recorded crime rates for burglary were correlated over time in the United States (0.98), Switzerland (0.96), England (0.91), Canada (0.76), Scotland (0.74), and the Netherlands (0.49), but less so in Sweden (0.26) and not at all in Australia (−0.10). Correlations between the probability of custody following a conviction and the survey crime rate were substantial and negative only for the United States (−0.48) and Scotland (−0.43).

B. Robbery

Figure 8 shows the number of convictions per 1,000 robbery offenders. This was generally high in Scotland and the United States and generally low in Switzerland and England. The correlations in table 1 show that it increased over time in the Netherlands (0.77), the United States (0.74), and Australia (0.45) and decreased over time in England (−0.88), Switzerland (−0.62), and Scotland (−0.33).

Figure 9 shows the probability of custody following a conviction for robbery. This was lowest in Switzerland and usually highest in Sweden and the United States. The correlations in table 1 show that it decreased over time in Switzerland (−0.92), Australia (−0.90), Sweden (−0.73), and England (−0.60) and increased in Scotland (0.81).

Figure 10 shows the average time served for robbery. This was highest in the United States and Australia and lowest in the Netherlands and Sweden. According to the correlations in table 1, it increased over time in Switzerland (0.99), England (0.92), and the Netherlands (0.79) but did not change markedly in the other four countries.

Table 2 shows correlations with the survey crime rate. The survey and recorded robbery rates were highly correlated in England (0.94) and the United States (0.81) but not in any other country. The negative correlation in Canada (−0.81) was based on only four years. The number of convictions per 1,000 offenders was negatively correlated with the survey robbery rate in Switzerland (−0.93), Scotland (−0.83), the Netherlands (−0.71), and the United States (−0.66), but the correlations were low in England (−0.10) and Australia (−0.17). The

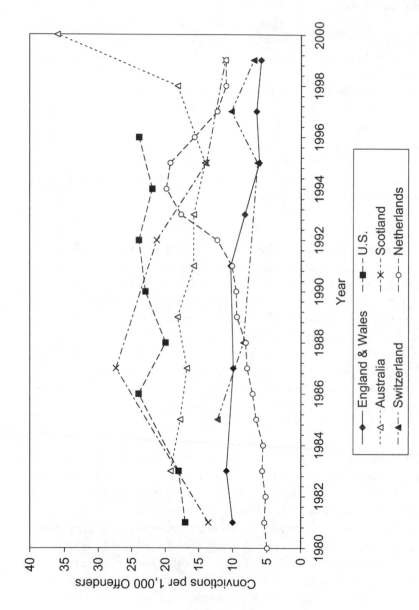

Convictions per 1,000 Offenders

Year

England & Wales — U.S. — Scotland
Australia — Switzerland — Netherlands

Fig. 8.—Robbery: convictions per 1,000 offenders

28

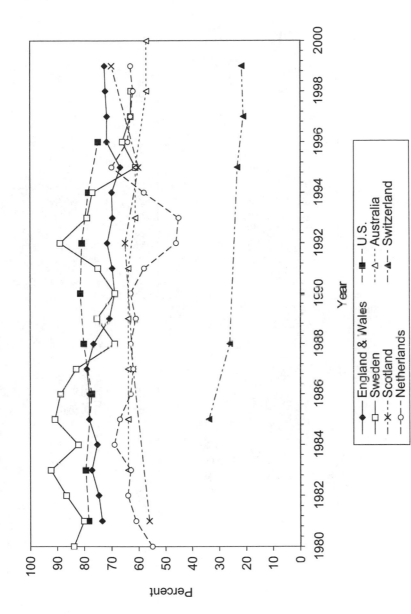

Fig. 9.—Robbery: probability of custody per conviction

Legend:
- England & Wales
- Sweden
- Scotland
- Netherlands
- U.S.
- Australia
- Switzerland

29

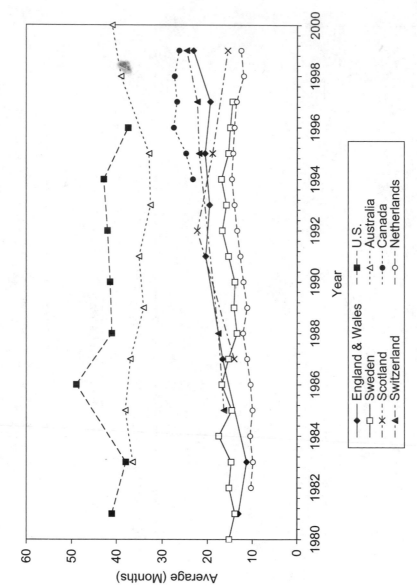

FIG. 10.—Robbery: average time served

probability of custody following a conviction for robbery was negatively correlated with the survey robbery rate only in England (−0.56); the correlation was positive in Scotland (0.55). The average time served for robbery was negatively correlated with the survey robbery rate only in the Netherlands (−0.63); the correlation was positive in England (0.79). Hence, there is no evidence that robbery rates are correlated with the severity of punishment, although in the majority of cases they were correlated with the risk of punishment.

IV. Advancing Cross-National Research on Crime and
Punishment

A number of conclusions emerge concerning crime, punishment, and cross-national studies.

A. Crime

The data and calculations reported here generally confirm inferences that can be drawn from ICVS and sourcebook data. First, burglary rates rose considerably in the 1980s and decreased in most countries from the early 1990s on; this is shown by both victim survey and official data. Second, robbery rates in most countries showed no clear trend, but they increased in England and Scotland and decreased in the United States. Third, in each of the eight countries, homicide rates either fell substantially toward the end of the twentieth century (Australia, Canada, Switzerland, and the United States) or were essentially flat at low levels between one and two per 100,000 population. Fourth, except for Canada, where both survey and recorded rates rose, and Sweden, where there was no clear pattern, motor vehicle theft rates fell in every country during the 1990s and in several during the 1980s.

B. Punishment

Some of the conclusions that emerge relate to cross-national comparisons of "punitiveness" generally and some solely to the eight countries. First, there can be no question that the United States has the most punitive crime control practices of the countries included in this volume (and probably generally). Throughout the twenty years covered, the United States had much the highest imprisonment rate per 100,000 people. Arguments can be made that the imprisonment rate is neither the only nor the best basis for comparing punitiveness. By all the other most plausible measures—probability of commitment given a conviction, average time served of those imprisoned, or years imprisonment per recorded crime or conviction—the United States ranks first.[18]

Second, during most of the period 1980–99, the probability that a burglary or a robbery would result in a court conviction fell in all the eight countries except in the United States. Those probabilities increased in the United States, which means that the increase in the U.S. imprisonment rate reflects, in addition to the factors discussed in the preceding paragraph, increased efficiency in turning crimes into convictions during a period when most of the other countries were becoming less efficient.

Third, countries vary significantly in the probability that prison sentences will be imposed. For burglary, broadly consistently throughout the twenty years, the United States, Sweden, and England imprisoned about half of convicted offenders, the Swiss and Scots about 40 percent, and the Australians about 30 percent. For robbery, also broadly consistently, the probability of imprisonment given a conviction was highest in the United States, Sweden, and England (70–80 percent) and lowest in Switzerland (around 30 percent).

Fourth, there appear to be stark differences in countries' tastes for sentence severity; average times served for burglary were two to three times longer in the United States, Australia, Switzerland, and Canada than in England, Sweden, and Scotland (see Blumstein, Tonry, and Van Ness, in this volume). Average time served for robbery was two to three times longer in the United States and Australia than in the other six countries; Canada and Switzerland, though not as severe for this offense as the United States and Australia, are at the top of the remaining six.

Fifth, countries' penal practices and punitiveness vary in ways that are misleadingly depicted by rankings in terms of the imprisonment rate per 100,000. The U.S. rate exceeding 700 per 100,000 is much the highest and results from a combination of high (and in 1980–99, increasing) chances that an offense resulted in a conviction, the highest probability of imprisonment given a conviction, and the highest average times served given a sentence of imprisonment. Sweden also had a high probability of imprisonment given a conviction but low chances an offense would result in a conviction and short average times served, resulting altogether in one of the lowest imprisonment rates among Western countries. Switzerland, by contrast, also has relatively low

---

[18] These observations are based on discussion in this essay and on the analyses and conclusions drawn in Blumstein, Tonry, and Van Ness (in this volume).

imprisonment rates per 100,000 but achieves this through a combination of moderately long average times served coupled with relatively low probabilities of imprisonment given a conviction.

C. Cross-National Studies

Laborious work by many people underlies this volume. Much can be learned from such efforts, however, and the essays in this volume demonstrate that it is possible to convert information from different data systems into more or less comparable form. Possibly some of the apparent findings are artifacts of offense definitions and recording conventions, but, if so, others will discover that.[19]

Efforts to analyze crime and punishment patterns cross-nationally would be made easier if countries improved their data systems. To be sure, no country is going to undertake a major overhaul of its information systems in order to make researchers' lives easier, but a number of improvements that would benefit policy makers and practitioners would also benefit researchers. These include the creation of vertically integrated data systems that permit tracking of individual offenders through the criminal justice process. In federal countries, they include development of improved integration or at least comparability of information systems across state or provincial lines. For all countries they include continued professionalization to improve the accuracy, completeness, and timeliness of data reporting.

Three major next steps are within the power of researchers. First, adjustments and appropriate estimation techniques should be developed for processing national data submitted for inclusion in bureaucratic compilations of national data such as those at Interpol, the UN, and the World Health Organization. This project and the sourcebook are showing the way forward. If international compilations were based on standard definitions or reflected application of standard estimation techniques, analyses such as those in this volume would be much easier to do. Second, sample sizes in the ICVS should be increased substantially, and investments made to enable achievement of higher

---

[19] It would be odd, for example, if it is true per figs. 6 and 9, that Switzerland most years imprisons 40 percent of convicted burglars and 20 percent of convicted robbers. Selection effects are the likeliest explanation, that definitions or case-processing methods produce convicted "burglars" whose offenses are on average more serious than those elsewhere, or produce "robbers" whose offenses are on average less serious than those elsewhere, or both. In other words, counting rules in Switzerland may produce "burglars" in Switzerland who are not comparable to burglars elsewhere.

participation rates. A great strength of the ICVS is that it uses a single (though translated) instrument in all participating countries, thereby reducing inconsistencies in definitions and reporting and recording practices. Third, the present effort should be replicated and extended by others in order to improve the adjustments and estimations required to make data cross-nationally comparable, and to advance our understanding both of how countries differ in their crime patterns and penal practices and of what differences different penal practices make.

APPENDIX

The Template for each Country Analysis

In the versions of the country analyses published in the companion BJS publication (Farrington, Langan, and Tonry 2004), each author was asked to follow the same organization and address the same topics:

Provide a brief description of the country and its criminal justice system, including an impressionistic account of developments in criminal and penal policy and other relevant changes in the society between 1981 and 1999.

Provide brief definitions of the six crimes. Residential burglary includes attempts. Vehicle theft (including taking and driving away) includes thefts of mopeds and motorcycles; generally, attempts are excluded from victim surveys but included in police figures. Robbery includes attempts. Only serious assault is counted; generally, attempts are excluded from victim surveys but included in police figures. Rape (of females by males) is measured only in police data; attempts are included. Where figures are given only for serious sex assault, an estimate is made for rape. Homicide includes murder, manslaughter and infanticide; attempts are excluded. As far as possible, one victim equals one crime; where figures are given for incidents rather than victims (e.g., of robbery), the number of victims is estimated. Authors were asked to discuss changes since 1980 in laws that affected the six offenses, and to specify adjustments made to maximize comparability over time. Also, they were asked to specify changes in the quality of crimes over time (e.g., the percentage of robberies involving firearms) where possible.

Specify sources of data. Authors were asked to specify the sources of all numbers so that the data could (in principle) be replicated in the future.

Describe victim survey data. Authors were asked to describe the victim surveys briefly, including design, sample sizes, response rates, sampling frame and coverage, method (e.g., face to face vs. telephone), and measures to combat telescoping. Specialized victim surveys were distinguished from omnibus social surveys including victimization questions. Authors were asked to provide raw data (numbers) plus confidence intervals where possible. Residential burglary and vehicle theft rates were specified per household, and robbery and serious assault rates were specified per population covered in the survey (e.g., all those ages sixteen and over). Victim survey data on rape (and, of course, homicide) were not presented. Differences since 1980 in data collection procedures that affect the four victim survey crimes were specified, as well as adjustments that were made to maximize comparability over time.

Describe police data. Authors were asked to define police-recorded crimes and to specify the precise step in processing that the crime was classified (e.g., when it is first reported). Changes since 1980 in police recording procedures that affected the six crimes were specified, as well as adjustments that were made to maximize comparability over time. Authors were asked to provide raw data (numbers) for each year and rates per population at risk.

Estimate the probability of police recording a reported offense. In order to estimate this, it was necessary to estimate the number of police-recorded crimes that were comparable to victim survey crimes. For burglary, comparable police-recorded crimes are residential burglaries. For vehicle theft, comparable police-recorded crimes are completed (not attempted) thefts of noncommercial vehicles. For robbery, comparable police-recorded crimes are noncommercial robberies of victims over the minimum age for the victim survey. For serious assault, comparable police-recorded crimes exclude victims under the minimum age for the victim survey. Then (formula 1):

$$B = \frac{R}{D},$$

where:

B = probability of the police recording a reported crime,
R = number of comparable crimes recorded by the police, and
D = number of crimes reported to the police according to the victim survey.

Estimate the average number of offenders per crime. Authors were asked to obtain the best possible estimate of this quantity from victim surveys, police records, or self-reported offending data. If necessary, subnational data or special surveys were used. Where the estimate was robust (e.g., from police records), the raw data for each year were used. Where the estimate was less robust (e.g., victim survey reports from burglary victims, where known offenders may be a small unrepresentative fraction of all cases), this quantity was averaged over all years.

Specify the number of convictions (i.e., persons convicted). Authors were asked to define the meaning of a "conviction," together with the minimum ages for juvenile and adult court. Changes over time (since 1980) that affected the six crimes were specified, as well as the adjustments that were made to maximize comparability over time. Raw data (numbers) were presented for each year and rates per population at risk (e.g., those over the minimum age for conviction). Problems created by foreigners who may be in the conviction numerator but not in the population denominator were discussed.

Estimate the number of convictions per 1,000 offenders. This was calculated using the following equation (formula 2):

$$N = V \times O,$$

where:

N = number of offenders who could in principle have been convicted (based on victim survey crimes),
V = number of victim survey crimes, and
O = average offenders per crime.

Where victim survey and police-recorded crimes are not comparable, it is necessary to scale up from victim survey crimes to police-recorded crimes (formula 3):

$$M = \frac{N \times P}{R},$$

where:

M = number of offenders who could in principle have been convicted (based on police-recorded crimes),
P = number of police-recorded crimes, and
R = number of police-recorded crimes that are comparable to victim survey crimes.

The number of convictions per 1,000 offenders is estimated as follows (formula 4):

$$X = \frac{C \times 1,000}{M},$$

where:

X = number of convictions per 1,000 offenders, and
C = number of persons convicted.

Of course, X is not the number of convictions per 1,000 different offenders, but is the number of convictions (occasions that a person is convicted) per 1,000 times that an offender commits a crime.

Specify the number of custodial sentences. Authors were asked to describe definitions of custody and different types of custodial sentences available for juveniles and adults. Secure hospital orders were included as custodial sentences but suspended sentences were not. Changes since 1980 that affected the six crimes were specified, as well as adjustments that were made to maximize comparability over time. The raw number of custodial sentences each year, and rates per population at risk, were given. The probability of custody following a conviction was calculated each year. The probability of custody per offender was calculated as follows (formula 5):

$$Y = X \times S,$$

where:

Y = number of custodial sentences per 1,000 offenders, and
S = probability of custody following a conviction.

Specify average sentence length and average time served. Authors were asked to calculate the average sentence length and average time served per custodial sentence, for each category of crime in each year. The bases of the estimates were described. Changes since 1980 that affected the six crimes were specified, as well as adjustments that were made to maximize comparability over time.

For life sentences for homicide, the effective sentence length was estimated using the following equation (formula 6):

$$L = \frac{T}{F},$$

where:

L = effective sentence length,
T = average time served for homicide on a life sentence, and
F = fraction of non–life sentences for homicide that are served in custody.

The average time served per offender was calculated using the following equation (formula 7):

$$Z = \frac{Y \times D}{1,000},$$

where:

Z = average time served per offender, and
D = average time served per custodial sentence.

Months were converted into days by multiplying by 30.44 (365.25/12).

Authors were asked to produce spreadsheets and graphs. Even if national victim survey data were available only for a limited number of years, authors were asked to present national police, conviction, and custody data for all available years. Linking probabilities (e.g., the number of convictions per 1,000 offenders) could be calculated only for years for which victim survey data were available, and so only these years were shown in spreadsheets. These are reprinted in the BJS volume by Farrington, Langan, and Tonry (2004) and are available at http://www.ojp.usdoj.gov/bjs.

Summarize time trends. Authors were asked to summarize trends over time in the following key measures:

a)   crime rates (according to victim surveys and police records);
b)   probability of reporting given a crime, probability of recording given a reported crime;

    c)   conviction rates per population, and convictions per 1,000 offenders;
    d)   number of custodial sentences per population, and number of custodial sentences per 1,000 offenders;
    e)   average sentence length, average time served, fraction of sentence served in custody; and
    f)   time served per 1,000 offenders.

Where time trends were reasonably linear, authors were asked to calculate correlations between key indicators (e.g., crime rates) and the year. It was considered that correlations would provide some indication of the magnitude of time trends. Also, authors were asked to present correlations among all survey and recorded crimes.

Possible explanations of time trends. Authors were asked to calculate correlations between crime rates (survey and recorded) and key national indicators such as demographic factors, unemployment rates, measures of prosperity and income disparity, and criminal justice measures such as the probability and severity of punishment, the number of police officers and the financial costs of police, courts, and prisons (in constant currency units). Of course, it was realized that it would not be possible to infer causal relationships from these correlations and that multivariate analyses were needed.

REFERENCES

Blumstein, Alfred, and Allen J. Beck. 1999. "Population Growth in U.S. Prisons, 1980–96." In *Prisons*, edited by Michael Tonry and Joan Petersilia. Vol. 26 of *Crime and Justice: A Review of Research*, edited by Michael Tonry. Chicago: University of Chicago Press.

Blumstein, Alfred, and Jacqueline Cohen. 1973. "A Theory of the Stability of Punishment." *Journal of Criminal Law and Criminology* 64:198–207.

Blumstein, Alfred, Jacqueline Cohen, and Daniel Nagin, eds. 1978. *Deterrence and Incapacitation: Estimating the Effects of Criminal Sanctions on Crime Rates.* Washington, D.C.: National Academy of Sciences.

Blumstein, Alfred, Michael Tonry, and Asheley Van Ness. In this volume. "Cross-National Measures of Punitiveness."

Cook, Philip J., and Nataliya Khmilevska. In this volume. "Cross-National Patterns in Crime Rates."

Council of Europe, Committee of Experts. 2003. *European Sourcebook of Crime and Criminal Justice Statistics, 2003.* 2d ed. Meppel, Netherlands: Boom Juridische Uitgevers. Also available at http://www.ministerievanjustitie.nl:8080/b_organ/wodc/reports/ob212i.htm.

Doob, Anthony N., and Cheryl Marie Webster. 2003. "Sentence Severity and Crime: Accepting the Null Hypothesis." In *Crime and Justice: A Review of Research*, vol. 30, edited by Michael Tonry. Chicago: University of Chicago Press.

European Sourcebook Group. 2004. "Second European Sourcebook of Crime and Criminal Justice Statistics." *Criminology in Europe* 3(3):3, 15–17.

Farrington, David P., and Darrick Jolliffe. In this volume. "Crime and Punishment in England and Wales, 1981–1999."

Farrington, David P., and Patrick A. Langan. 1992. "Changes in Crime and Punishment in England and America in the 1980s." *Justice Quarterly* 9:5–46.

Farrington, David P., Patrick A. Langan, and Michael Tonry, eds. 2004. *Cross-National Studies in Crime and Justice.* Washington, D.C.: U.S. Bureau of Justice Statistics.

Farrington, David P., Patrick A. Langan, and Per-Olof H. Wikström. 1994. "Changes in Crime and Punishment in America, England, and Sweden in the 1980s and 1990s." *Studies on Crime and Crime Prevention* 3:104–31.

Farrington, David P., and Per-Olof H. Wikström. 1993. "Changes in Crime and Punishment in England and Sweden in the 1980s." *Studies on Crime and Crime Prevention* 2:142–70.

Junger-Tas, Josine. 2001. "Dutch Penal Policies Changing Direction." In *Penal Reform in Overcrowded Times,* edited by Michael Tonry. New York: Oxford University Press.

Kesteren, John van, Pat Mayhew, and Paul Nieuwbeerta. 2000. *Criminal Victimisation in Seventeen Industrialized Countries.* The Hague: Ministry of Justice.

Langan, Patrick A., and David P. Farrington. 1998. *Crime and Justice in the United States and in England and Wales, 1981–96.* Washington, D.C.: U.S. Bureau of Justice Statistics (also available at http://www.ojp.usdoj.cgov/bjs).

Lappi-Seppälä, Tapio. 2001. "Sentencing and Punishment in Finland: The Decline of the Retributive Ideal." In *Sentencing and Sanctions in Western Countries,* edited by Michael Tonry and Richard Frase. New York: Oxford University Press.

———. 2004. "Imprisonment and Penal Policy in Finland." *Criminology in Europe* 4(1):3, 13–15.

Nagin, Daniel S. 1998. "Criminal Deterrence Research at the Outset of the Twenty-First Century." In *Crime and Justice: A Review of Research,* vol. 23, edited by Michael Tonry. Chicago: University of Chicago Press.

Smith, David J. 1999. "Less Crime without More Punishment." *Edinburgh Law* 3:294–316.

Tonry, Michael H. 2004. *Thinking about Crime: Sense and Sensibility in American Penal Culture.* New York: Oxford University Press.

Van Rullers, S., and W. M. E. H. Beijers. 1995. "Trends in Detentie—Twee eeuwen gevangenisstatistiek." *Justititiele Verkenningen* 21(6):25–53.

Wilson, James Q. 2002. "Crime and Public Policy." In *Crime: Public Policies for Crime Control,* edited by James Q. Wilson and Joan Petersilia. Oakland, Calif.: ICS Press.

Young, Warren, and Mark Brown. 1993. "Cross-National Comparisons of Imprisonment." In *Crime and Justice: A Review of Research,* vol. 17, edited by Michael Tonry. Chicago: University of Chicago Press.

Zimring, Franklin E., and Gordon Hawkins. 1991. *The Scale of Imprisonment.* Chicago: University of Chicago Press.

David P. Farrington and Darrick Jolliffe

Crime and Justice in England and Wales, 1981–1999

ABSTRACT

Serious property crimes in England and Wales increased from 1981 to 1993 and then decreased, while serious nonlethal violence increased during the entire period 1981–99. Increases in unemployment may have caused increases in property crime rates, and increases in prosperity may have caused increases in nonlethal violence. Increases in the risk of punishment may have caused decreases in crime rates, but increases in the severity of punishment probably did not. Conclusions are tentative because many factors that might possibly influence national crime rates over time could not be measured and controlled for.

This essay summarizes important trends in crime and justice in England and Wales between 1981 and 1999 and investigates possible explanations. Six serious offenses were studied: residential burglary, motor vehicle theft, robbery, serious assault, rape, and homicide (murder or manslaughter).

A criminal justice system involves a successive funneling process, shown in a simplified form: Crime Committed → Reported to Police → Recorded by Police → Offender Convicted → Sentenced to Custody → Sentence Length → Time Served → Prison Population. Of all crimes committed, only some are reported to the police. Of all crimes reported,

David P. Farrington is professor of psychological criminology, Institute of Criminology, Cambridge University, where Darrick Jolliffe is a Ph.D. student. The authors are grateful to Maureen Brown for efficient word processing and thank Margaret Ayres, Gordon Barclay, Tracey Budd, Billy Burns, Patrick Collier, LizAnne Dowds, Graham Kinshott, Duncan Lavin, Joanna Mattinson, Pat Mayhew, Catriona Mirrlees-Black, Chris Nuttall, Andrew Percy, Roger Stevens, and David Thomas and others from the Home Office for providing helpful information.

only some are recorded by the police. Of all crimes recorded, only some lead to the detection of an offender and to a conviction in court. Of all offenders found guilty in court, only some are sentenced to custody. These offenders receive sentences of different lengths, but they serve only a portion of their sentence in custody. Of course, there are many other possible stages that could have been shown, and many disposals other than imprisonment, but these are some of the most important stages. We could not study arrests for England and Wales because national arrest data were not collected before 1999 (Ayres, Murray, and Fiti 2003).

We focus on changes in crime rates and in legal punishment between 1981 and 1999. Two measures of crime are studied, based on victim surveys and police records. One measure of the risk of punishment is studied, namely, the probability of an offender being convicted. Two measures of the severity of punishment are studied, namely, the probability of being sentenced to custody after a conviction and the average time served in custody. Many other measures are presented in an earlier version of this essay published by the Bureau of Justice Statistics (Farrington and Jolliffe 2004), including the probability of a crime being reported to the police, the probability of a reported crime being recorded by the police, average sentence length, and the percentage of a sentence that is served in custody.

Here is how this essay is organized. Section I presents key information about England and Wales in 1981–99 and describes the criminal justice system. Section II reviews changes in crime rates over time. Section III discusses changes in the risk and severity of punishment over time and explanations based on criminal justice system changes. Section IV reviews explanations of changes in crime rates based mainly on demographic and economic factors and investigates whether there is any evidence for or against the hypothesis that changes in punishment influence changes in crime rates. Technical details about data sources are presented in the appendix and in Farrington and Jolliffe (2004).

Serious property crimes (burglary and vehicle theft) increased between 1981 and 1993 and then decreased up to 1999, whereas serious nonlethal violence (assault, robbery, and rape) increased steadily during this time period. Homicide fluctuated and increased slightly. The risk of conviction for a serious property crime decreased from 1981 to 1993 and then increased, whereas the risk of conviction for a nonlethal violent crime decreased from 1981 to 1999. The severity of legal punishment stayed constant or decreased between 1981 and the early 1990s for serious property crimes and then increased up to 1999. The severity of punishment for serious violent crimes increased steadily from 1981 to 1999.

We investigate the plausibility of a number of explanations of these crime trends using national data on economic indicators. It is plausible to suggest that increases in unemployment caused increases in property crime rates and that increases in economic prosperity caused increases in violent crime rates. We also conclude that increases in the risk of punishment may have caused decreases in crime rates but that increases in the severity of punishment did not. Our conclusions are tentative because we could measure only a few of the many factors that might influence national crime rates over time.

I. England and Wales

Great Britain (G.B.) is the island containing England, Wales, and Scotland, while the United Kingdom (U.K.) consists of Great Britain and Northern Ireland. Many statistics are collected for Great Britain or the United Kingdom rather than for England and Wales (see Office for National Statistics 2000a, 2001). In 1999, the resident population of England was 49.8 million, compared with 2.9 million in Wales. The population density of England is high (147 people per square mile, compared with fifty-four in Wales). Between 1981 and 1999, the population increased by only 6.3 percent in England and by only 4.4 percent in Wales.

The United Kingdom is a Western industrialized democracy and a constitutional monarchy. The U.K. parliament contains MPs from England (529), Wales (40), Scotland (73), and Northern Ireland (18). Unlike England, the other three countries have separate national bodies responsible for their central administration. The United Kingdom has an aging population, and projections are that the median age will continue to rise from its 1999 value of thirty-seven. In that year, life expectancy was seventy-five years for males and eighty for females. There are over 300,000 marriages and over 150,000 divorces each year in the United Kingdom, and there has been a big increase in single-person and single-parent households in recent years. In 1999, the G.B. resident population included 6.7 percent from nonwhite ethnic minority groups, of which the most prevalent were South Asians (Indians, Pakistanis, Bangladeshis—3.4 percent) and blacks (Africans, Caribbeans—2.1 percent).

The U.K. National Health Service provides a full range of medical services available to all residents regardless of income. All children aged five to sixteen are required by law to receive full-time education, and about two-thirds of children ages three to four were attending preschool education in 1999. About one-third of people continued in higher education after age eighteen, and this has increased considerably in recent years.

The United Kingdom is a relatively prosperous country. The value of all goods and services produced in the U.K. economy for final consumption is measured by the gross domestic product (GDP). In 1999, the GDP at current market prices totaled £891 billion, or about £15,000 per person. The average annual growth in GDP at constant market prices between 1995 and 1999 was 2.9 percent. Inflation is currently low, at about 2 percent. About 85 percent of males and 73 percent of females of working age are economically active, and the unemployment rate is historically low at 5.2 percent for England and 6.1 percent for Wales. In the United Kingdom, over 70 percent of households have at least one car, and over 25 percent have at least two cars.

A.   The Criminal Justice System

England and Wales have a common criminal justice system, while Scotland and Northern Ireland have different systems. In England and Wales, the Home Office is responsible for the criminal law and the police, prison, and probation services, and it publishes most criminal justice statistics (Chapman and Niven 2000). In 1999, the Lord Chancellor's Department was responsible for the courts, and the attorney general was responsible for the Crown Prosecution Service (CPS). In 2003, the Lord Chancellor's Department was replaced by the Department for Constitutional Affairs. There is an adversarial system of justice, and most cases are sentenced by a panel of three unpaid lay people in magistrates' courts. The more serious (indictable) offenses are processed by judges and juries in the crown courts. We focus particularly on features of the criminal justice system that are relevant to our measures.

There are forty-three police forces in England and Wales and a total of about 125,000 police officers, or approximately one officer per 420 persons in 1999. After the police arrest a suspect, they have to decide whether to charge the person, issue a formally recorded caution or an informal warning, or take no further action. (A new system of reprimands and final warnings for young offenders was introduced on April 1, 2000.) If the police decide to charge the person, the Crown

Prosecution Service reviews the case. If the CPS considers that there is insufficient evidence for a realistic prospect of conviction or that prosecution is not in the public interest, it may discontinue the proceedings (Chapman and Niven 2000). If not, the CPS will prosecute the case in the crown court or magistrates' court.

The minimum age of criminal responsibility in England and Wales is ten. Persons aged ten to seventeen are tried separately from adults in special youth courts, although they may be tried in adult magistrates' courts or crown courts, depending on the seriousness of their offenses. In 1999, the main custodial sentence for those aged fifteen to twenty was detention in a young offender institution, while persons aged twelve to fourteen could be given secure training orders. From April 1, 2000, the main custodial sentence for those aged twelve to seventeen became the detention and training order. Persons aged twenty-one or over can be sent to prison. Those receiving fixed sentences of less than four years are released after serving half the sentence, while those serving sentences of four years or more can be released by the parole board after serving half their sentence and must be released after serving two-thirds of their sentence (unless they misbehave in prison). In 2004, the prison and probation services were amalgamated into the National Offender Management Service.

Since the Labour government came to power in 1997, it has pursued a two-pronged approach of increasing both prevention and punishment. The Crime and Disorder Act 1998 especially focused on prevention, setting up "crime and disorder partnerships" in local areas to take charge of local crime-reduction initiatives and establishing youth offending teams to oversee rehabilitative and restorative justice programs for young offenders. Regarding punishment, the Crime (Sentences) Act 1997 specified that an offender aged eighteen or over on a second conviction for a serious violent or sexual offense should receive an automatic life sentence unless there are exceptional circumstances. It also specified that an offender aged eighteen or over on a third conviction for residential burglary should receive a minimum sentence of three years imprisonment, but this did not take effect until 2000.

B. *Putting Numbers into the Flow Diagram*

From here on in this essay, we mean "England" to include Wales (in order to simplify the exposition). The English criminal justice system can easily be described using a simplified flow diagram such as that presented above. It is much more difficult to quantify the system in practice by specifying the exact number of offenders flowing through at each stage. Such a specification would have great theoretical and practical relevance. For example, it would help to determine whether changes in prison populations were caused by changes in crime rates, reporting, recording, conviction rates, the probability of custody, sentences given, or time served.

One of the main aims of this essay is to estimate the number of offenders at each stage of the system for different offenses in different years. However, a key problem is that national longitudinal data are not available in England for tracking individual offenders across the different stages of the criminal justice system. However, aggregate national data are available for each of the stages separately (e.g., crimes committed, persons convicted, persons sentenced to custody). These separate counts do not arise from tracking the same individuals across stages, but they permit reasonably accurate estimates of the flow of offenders from one stage to the next.

There are major problems in obtaining comparable data over time because there are important changes in definitions of offenses, survey questions, laws, police-recording practices, types of custodial sentences, and parole policies—to mention only a few factors that influence the five measures of crime and punishment that are the main focus of this essay. The appendix details numerous adjustments that were made to official figures in the interest of obtaining comparable data between 1981 and 1999. Merely reporting official figures without these adjustments would have produced misleading conclusions about changes over time.

II.   Changes in Crime Rates

Data on crime rates are available from official records and on victimization rates from the British Crime Survey (BCS). Burglary and motor vehicle theft rose from 1981 to 1993 and then declined. Violent crime patterns are harder to summarize but generally increased and did not decline after 1993.

A.   Victimization Rates

The first national victimization survey (the British Crime Survey) was conducted in 1982 and measured crime committed in calendar year 1981. Subsequent national victimization surveys were carried out at two-year or four-year intervals up to 1999 (see the appendix). Beginning in 2001 (measuring crimes committed in 2000), the BCS has been conducted annually.

Figure 1 shows changes in the residential burglary victimization rate (per 1,000 households) between 1981 and 1999; the scale is shown on the left-hand axis. The burglary rate more than doubled between 1981 and 1993 (from forty-one to eighty-six per 1,000 households) but then decreased by one-third up to 1999 (to fifty-seven per 1,000 households).

To determine whether the survey crime rate tended to increase over time, the crime rate was correlated with the year. This correlation had the limitation that it was based on only eight years (for survey crimes). Since the correlation coefficient can vary from zero (no relationship) to one (a perfect relationship), a correlation of .5 or greater was considered to show that crime rates were increasing over time. Table 1 shows that the correlation for burglary was .67, indicating an increase over time, and that the magnitude of this increase between 1981 and 1999 was 38 percent (from 40.9 to 56.6 burglaries per 1,000 households).

For burglary, the correlation is rather misleading, because the trend over time was not linear: burglaries increased up to 1993 and then decreased up to 1999. Consequently, table 2 divides the time period into 1981–93 and 1993–99. Between 1981 and 1993, the burglary rate increased steadily over time (a correlation of .97), and the total increase was 109 percent, showing that the rate more than doubled. Between 1993 and 1999, the burglary rate decreased steadily over time (a correlation of −.94), and the total decrease was 34 percent.

Similar trends were found for vehicle theft; figure 1 shows that the survey crime rate increased by two-thirds between 1981 and 1993 (from sixteen to twenty-six crimes per 1,000 households) but then decreased back to below the 1981 figure by 1999 (to fifteen crimes per 1,000 households). This is remarkable in light of the 47 percent increase in the number of motor vehicles registered (from 19,347,000 in 1981 to 28,368,000 in 1999; G.B. figures from Office of National Statistics 2001).

Table 1 shows that the correlation between the crime rate and the year was low (.22), because of the nonlinear trend over time, and that there was a very small decrease in the crime rate of 4 percent between 1981 and 1999. We do not focus on statistical significance in this essay (because of estimation problems with the survey data and the non-applicability of ideas of significance to the official population-based

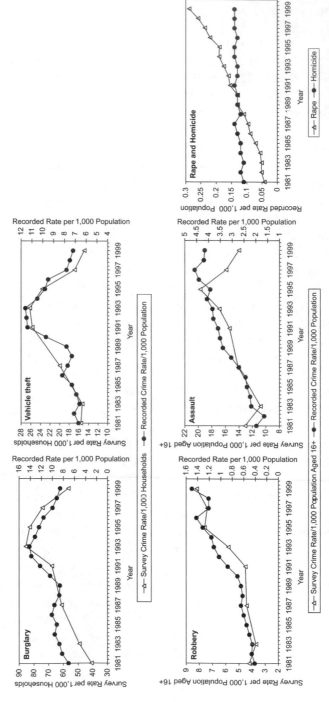

Fig. 1.—Survey and recorded crime rate for burglary, vehicle theft, robbery, and assault; for rape and homicide, recorded crime rate per 1,000 population. Note: Rape rate is per 1,000 female population; homicide figures have been multiplied by ten.

TABLE 1

Correlations with Year and Percentage Changes, 1981–99

	Burglary	MVT	Robbery	Assault	Rape	Homicide
Survey crime rate	.67	.22	.91	.62	N.A.	N.A.
	(+38)	(−4)	(+96)	(+6)		
Recorded crime rate	.48	.44	.96	.97	.99	.81
	(+22)	(+8)	(+266)	(+110)	(+588)	(+26)
Probability (conviction/offender)	−.89	−.90	−.88	−.87	−.95	−.30
	(−60)	(−68)	(−42)	(−40)	(−74)	(0)
Probability (custody/conviction)	.60	.42	−.60	.80	.65	.70
	(+64)	(+14)	(−1)	(+125)	(+10)	(+9)
Average time served	.74	−.57	.92	.50	.97	.91
	(+62)	(−12)	(+76)	(+22)	(+140)	(+52)

NOTE.—Percentage changes 1981–99 in parentheses. MVT = motor vehicle theft; N.A. = not applicable.

data), but we should note that such a small decrease would not be statistically significant.

Table 2 shows that the survey vehicle theft rate steadily increased between 1981 and 1993 (a correlation of .98 with year and a total 68 percent increase). However, it then steadily decreased between 1993 and 1999 (a correlation of −.98 with year and a total 43 percent decrease). The 43 percent decrease (from 26.2 to 14.9 vehicle thefts

TABLE 2

Correlations with Year and Percentage Changes (Different Time Periods)

	1981–93	1993–99
Burglary:		
Survey crime rate	.97 (+109)	−.94 (−34)
Recorded crime rate	.85 (+101)	−.99 (−39)
Probability (conviction/offender)	−.98 (−69)	.92 (+30)
Probability (custody/conviction)	−.12 (+10)	.98 (+49)
Average time served	.83 (+14)	.82 (+42)
Motor vehicle theft:		
Survey crime rate	.98 (+68)	−.98 (−43)
Recorded crime rate	.89 (+73)	−.98 (−38)
Probability (conviction/offender)	−.99 (−77)	.92 (+36)
Probability (custody/conviction)	−.69 (−22)	.70 (+26)
Average time served	−.96 (−35)	.97 (+35)

NOTE.—Percentage changes in parentheses.

per 1,000 households) is of the same magnitude as the 68 percent increase (from 15.6 to 26.2 vehicle thefts per 1,000 households). Detailed spreadsheets showing all the numbers can be found in Farrington and Jolliffe (2004).

Unlike burglary and vehicle theft, the survey robbery rate continued to increase between 1993 and 1999 (fig. 1). Table 1 shows a correlation with the year of .91 (indicating a steady increase) and a total increase of 96 percent. The robbery rate almost doubled between 1981 and 1999, from 4.2 to 8.2 robberies per 1,000 population aged sixteen or over.

The serious assault (wounding) rate increased by 50 percent between 1981 and 1995 (from 13.1 to 19.7 per 1,000 population aged sixteen or over) but then decreased by 30 percent between 1995 and 1999 (fig. 1). Table 1 shows a correlation with the year of .62 (indicating an increase) but a total increase of only 6 percent, which is negligible.

We do not show trends in different time periods for assault because, unlike burglary and vehicle theft, the police-recorded data for assault did not show the same trends as the survey data and because the survey questions for assault changed over time. As explained in the appendix, new methods of measuring domestic violence were introduced in 1993, which caused an increase in the number of survey-reported assaults. The Home Office kindly provided us with estimates of what the figures would have been using the old methods, but it is nevertheless true that the survey assault figures are less comparable over time than the figures for burglary, vehicle theft, or robbery (where the questions did not change).

B. Recorded Crime Rates

The methods used to obtain comparable numbers of police-recorded crimes over time are detailed in the appendix. Of the four BCS offenses, the greatest problem of comparability between the survey and police definitions arose for serious assault. In the figures, recorded crime rates are shown for all years 1981–99.

Figure 1 shows that, like the survey burglary rate, the police-recorded residential burglary rate doubled between 1981 and 1993 (from 7.1 to 14.1 per 1,000 population; see the right-hand axis) and then decreased up to 1999 (to 8.6 per 1,000 population). Table 1 shows that the recorded burglary rate correlated only .48 with the year, no doubt because of the nonlinear relationship. Table 2 shows that the recorded burglary rate changed in very similar ways to the survey burglary rate between 1981–93 and 1993–99.

Similar results were obtained for vehicle theft. The police-recorded rate increased by 73 percent between 1981 and 1993 (from 6.7 to 11.6 per 1,000 population) and then decreased back to 7.2 per 1,000 population in 1999 (fig. 1). Why were these serious property crimes increasing substantially between 1981 and 1993 and then decreasing substantially between 1993 and 1999? What happened around 1993 to change these trends so dramatically? We will return to these questions later.

Unlike burglary and vehicle theft, the police-recorded robbery rate continued to increase (irregularly) after 1993, as did the survey robbery rate. The recorded robbery rate almost quadrupled between 1981 and 1999 (from 0.4 to 1.5 per 1,000 population; fig. 1). Table 1 shows this as a 266 percent increase and a correlation of .96 between the robbery rate and the year (indicating a steady increase).

Unlike the survey assault rate, the police-recorded rate of serious assault (wounding) continued to increase (irregularly) after 1995 (fig. 1). Between 1981 and 1999, the recorded assault rate doubled (from 2.0 to 4.1 per 1,000 population). Table 1 shows this as a 110 percent increase and a correlation of .97 between the assault rate and the year.

English trends in rape and homicide can be studied only in police-recorded data. As explained in the appendix, although the legal definition of rape was widened in 1994, we were able to obtain comparable numbers of offenses involving male offenders and female victims after this date (as well as before). Figure 1 shows that the recorded rape rate increased sevenfold between 1981 and 1999 (from .04 to .29 per 1,000 females). Table 1 shows this as a 588 percent increase and a correlation of .99 between the rape rate and the year. The recorded homicide (murder and manslaughter) rate fluctuated from year to year (between .011 and .014 per 1,000 population) but showed an increasing trend (as indicated by the correlation with the year of .81). In order to show rape and homicide rates in the same figure, the homicide rate has been multiplied by ten.

In most cases, changes in survey crime rates were highly correlated with changes in police-recorded crime rates (Farrington and Jolliffe 2004). Survey and recorded crime rates correlated .91 for burglary, .97 for vehicle theft, and .94 for robbery, but only .67 for assault. The correlation was lower for assault because the survey rate showed a greater decrease after 1995; between 1981 and 1995, the correlation for assault was .88 (Langan and Farrington 1998, p. 13).

Between 1981 and 1999, the probability of a crime being reported to the police (according to victims in the BCS) did not change markedly.

The correlation between this probability and the year was $-.20$ for burglary, $.22$ for vehicle theft, $.09$ for robbery, and $.18$ for assault (Farrington and Jolliffe 2004).

The probability of a reported crime being recorded by the police was calculated by comparing the number of survey crimes reported to the police (according to victims) with the number of comparable crimes recorded by the police (see the appendix). This probability decreased over time for burglary and vehicle theft (correlations with the year $-.90$ and $-.72$, respectively) and increased over time for robbery ($r = .55$) and assault ($r = .79$).

C. Conclusions about Changes in Crime

Survey and police-recorded figures show that the rate of burglary and vehicle theft increased steadily (with perhaps a small dip between 1986 and 1989) up to 1993 and then decreased steadily. Changes after 1999 are outside the scope of this essay, and we cannot reach definite conclusions about them without making numerous adjustments to the official figures to achieve comparability over time and without obtaining special data from the Home Office. However, the indications are that survey burglary and vehicle theft continued to decrease up to 2002–3, that recorded vehicle theft continued to decrease up to 2002–3, and that recorded residential burglary decreased up to 2000–2001 but then increased by about 9 percent up to 2002–3 (Simmons and Dodd 2003, pp. 37–44). We therefore conclude that serious property crimes (burglary and vehicle theft) increased up to 1993 and then decreased.

Survey and police-recorded figures show that the robbery rate increased steadily from 1981 to 1999. Police-recorded figures show that the rape rate increased steadily from 1981 to 1999 and that the homicide rate fluctuated and increased slightly. However, for serious assault, the recorded figures show a steady increase, but the survey figures show an increase up to 1995 and then a decrease. What should we conclude about trends in serious assault?

After 1999, serious assault according to the BCS increased up to 2002–3 by about 9 percent, but robbery decreased by 26 percent. Police-recorded serious assault increased by about 6 percent up to 2001–2, but after this the figures were enormously (and artifactually) increased by April 2002 changes in recording practices. Police-recorded robbery increased dramatically between 1998–99 and 2001–2 (by about 92 percent for robbery of personal property, which began to be identified as a separate category; see Simmons and Dodd 2003, pp. 37–44). Hence, there was a great divergence in robbery trends after 1999 according to survey versus recorded figures.

Returning to serious assault, the decrease in the survey assault rate after 1995 might have been affected by changes in the questions on domestic violence (despite our adjusted figures); the police-recorded figures showed an increase up to 1999; after 1999, there was an increase in both survey and recorded figures, and there was an increase in other types of serious violence between 1981 and 1999. We therefore consider that the most plausible conclusion is that serious assault generally increased between 1981 and 1999, and hence we conclude that, in general, serious nonlethal violence increased steadily during this time period.

III.   Changes in Punishment

For most offenses studied, the severity of punishment of convicted offenders, whether measured by the probability of custody, average length of prison sentence, or average time served, increased between 1981 and 1999. Probabilities of conviction, relative to estimated offender numbers based on victimization data, decreased markedly over time for all offenses except homicide.

A.   Probability of an Offender Being Convicted

Estimating the probability that an offender will be convicted is not straightforward. When comparing the number of survey offenses with the number of persons convicted, it is necessary to take into account the average number of co-offenders and any noncomparability between survey offenses and police-recorded offenses.

To relate offenses to offenders, the average number of offenders committing each offense must be considered. This is because one offense committed by two offenders can lead to two convictions (if both offenders are convicted). Thus, the number of offenders at risk of conviction is the number of offenses multiplied by the average number of offenders per offense. Merely comparing the number of offenses with the number of offenders convicted is like comparing apples with oranges. Unfortunately, the importance of co-offending (Reiss and Farrington 1991) has not always been appreciated. It is also necessary to compare the number of survey offenses with the number of persons convicted for offenses that would have been included in the survey (e.g., excluding nonresidential burglaries, thefts of commercial vehicles, and robbery and assault victims under age sixteen; see the appendix).

As an example of the calculation, there were about 1,242,000 residential burglaries in 1999, according to the BCS, and an estimate of 1.8 offenders per offense. Therefore, there could in principle have been about 2,235,000 convictions (1,242,000 × 1.8). In fact, there were about 16,400 convictions for residential burglary in 1999, yielding an estimate that the probability of an offense (or, rather, of one offender committing one offense) leading to a conviction was one in 136. In figure 2, this is shown as 7.3 convictions per 1,000 residential burglary offenders (rather than a probability of .0073). More details of the calculation are given in the appendix.

Unfortunately, national estimates of the average number of offenders per offense are not published in the Home Office Criminal Statistics. Our estimate for burglary was kindly provided by BCS researchers (see the appendix), but victims knew how many co-offenders were involved in only a small fraction of burglaries. The average number of co-offenders has a direct effect on the estimate of the probability of an offender being convicted. For example, if this average were 2.0 rather than 1.8 (11 percent greater), there would be 6.6 rather than 7.3 convictions per 1,000 offenders (10 percent less). Because we did not want year-to-year fluctuations in our estimates of this average (which was often based on small numbers) to influence year-to-year fluctuations in the probability of conviction, we used the average number of co-offenders over all years (i.e., 1.8 for burglary) in estimating the probability of conviction in each year.

Of course, the probability of a burglary offender being convicted for burglary sooner or later is much greater than one in 136, because the average burglar commits several burglaries. In the Cambridge Study in Delinquent Development, which is a long-term follow-up study of 411 South London males, forty-two burglars committed 346 burglaries between ages fifteen and eighteen according to their self-reports (an average of eight each; see West and Farrington 1977, pp. 27–28). In the same study, 58 percent of males who committed burglary between ages ten and thirty-two (according to their self-reports) were convicted of burglary sooner or later (Farrington 1989). Since burglars and other offenders tend to be versatile in committing several different types of offenses, the probability of a burglar being convicted of any offense sooner or later is thus higher than 58 percent.

A probability of one in 136 burglaries leading to a conviction for burglary greatly underestimates the probability of a burglary (i.e., one offender committing one offense) being detected. Some apprehended

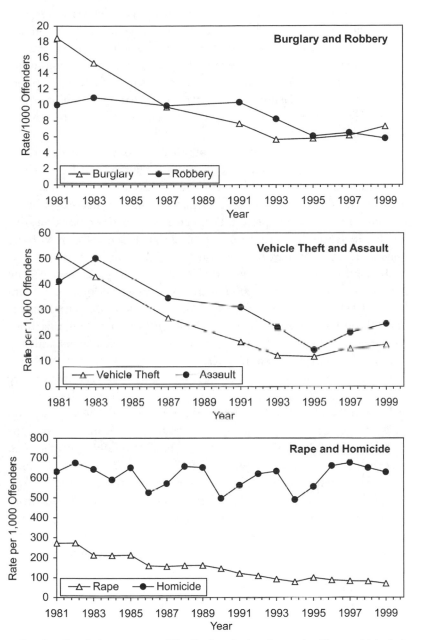

Fig. 2.—Conviction rate per 1,000 offenders for burglary and robbery, vehicle theft and assault, and rape and homicide. Note: Rape rate is per 1,000 male offenders.

burglars are dealt with by informal or formally recorded warnings, and several burglaries may be dealt with or taken into consideration on one occasion of conviction. However, we believe that it is not unrealistic to estimate that the average burglar in 1999 could commit 136 burglaries for every occasion of conviction for burglary (i.e., for every opportunity for a legal punishment in court), and that this probability of an offense leading to a conviction is an important measure of the risk of legal punishment.

Figure 2 (top) shows that the number of convictions per 1,000 residential burglary offenders decreased steadily from 1981 to 1993, from 18.5 to 5.6. Table 2 shows that the correlation between this number and the year was −.98, and that the number decreased by 69 percent during this time period. Between 1993 and 1999, however, this number increased from 5.6 to 7.3. Table 2 shows a correlation with the year of .92 and a 30 percent increase during this time period.

Similar results were obtained for vehicle theft (fig. 2, center). The number of convictions per 1,000 offenders decreased dramatically from 51.6 in 1981 to 12.1 in 1993. Table 2 shows a correlation with the year of −.99 and a decrease of 77 percent. Between 1993 and 1999, this number increased from 12.1 to 16.5. Table 2 shows a correlation with the year of .92 and a 36 percent increase.

The number of convictions per 1,000 robbers stayed reasonably constant from 1981 to 1991 (at about ten) but then decreased to 5.8 in 1999 (fig. 2, top). Table 1 shows a correlation with the year of −.88 and a 42 percent decrease from 1981 to 1999. The number of convictions per 1,000 assaulters decreased from 1981 to 1995 (from 41.2 to 14.4) but then increased to 24.6 in 1999 (fig. 2, center). Table 1 shows a correlation with the year of −.87 and a 40 percent decrease.

The number of rape and homicide offenders was estimated from police-recorded crimes, not from victim survey crimes. The number of convictions per 1,000 rapists decreased from 272 in 1981 to seventy-one in 1999 (fig. 2, bottom). Table 1 shows a correlation with the year of −.95 and a 74 percent decrease. The number of convictions per 1,000 homicide offenders showed no clear trend, fluctuating around 600 (fig. 2, bottom). Table 1 shows a small correlation with the year ($r = -.30$) and a zero change.

The number of convictions for burglary, vehicle theft, and assault decreased steadily from 1981 to 1999 (Farrington and Jolliffe 2004). Therefore, the decrease up to 1993 in the probability of an offender being convicted reflected both a decrease in the number of convictions and an increase in the number of offenses. Later in the 1990s, the increase in the probability of an offender being convicted for these offenses was largely attributable to the decrease in the number of survey offenses, although there was an increase in the population conviction rate for assault between 1995 and 1999 (of 21 percent, compared with a 29 percent decrease in the survey crime rate; see Farrington and Jolliffe 2004).

The number of convictions for robbery, rape, and homicide, however, increased steadily from 1981 to 1999. The probability of a robbery offender being convicted stayed constant between 1981 and 1991 because offenses and convictions were both increasing slowly at the same rate. After 1991, the increase in the number of robbery offenses outstripped the increase in the number of robbery convictions, causing the decrease in the probability of an offender being convicted. For rape, the increase in the number of offenses outstripped the increase in the number of convictions for the whole time period, causing the steady decrease in the probability of an offender being convicted. For homicide, the increase in the number of convictions was comparable to the increase in the number of offenses, which meant that the probability of an offender being convicted stayed tolerably constant.

Decreases in the probability of conviction in the 1980s could have been caused by the increasing use of recorded cautions and unrecorded warnings for detected offenders (Home Office 1985, 1990b; Farrington 1992); the Police and Criminal Evidence Act 1984, implemented in January 1986, which increased procedural safeguards for accused persons (Irving and MacKenzie 1989); the introduction of the Crown Prosecution Service in 1986, with lawyers replacing police officers as prosecutors, leading to an increasing tendency to discontinue cases rather than prosecute them (Home Office 1993, table 6.2); and the requirement for advance disclosure of the prosecution case in May 1985. Other changes affected specific offenses. For example, new charging standards for assault were introduced on August 31, 1994, which downgraded some convictions from indictable wounding (which we counted) to nonindictable common assault (which we did not count).

B. Probability of Custody Following a Conviction

Types of custodial sentences are explained in the appendix. The probability of receiving a custodial sentence after a conviction for residential burglary increased somewhat in the early 1980s and decreased somewhat in the late 1980s but overall did not change

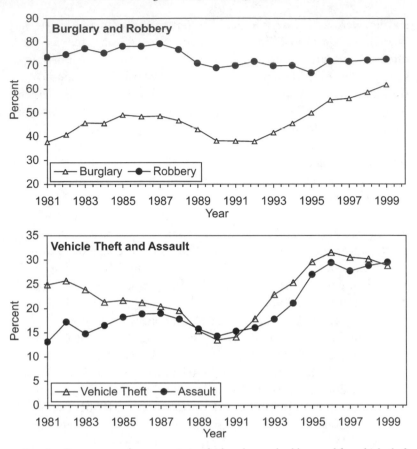

FIG. 3.—Percent custody per conviction for burglary and robbery and for vehicle theft and assault.

markedly between 1981 and 1993 (at about 42 percent). However, it then increased to 62 percent in 1999 (fig. 3, top). The probability of custody following a conviction for vehicle theft decreased from 25 percent in 1981 to 14 percent in 1991 but then increased to about 30 percent in 1995–99 (fig. 3, bottom). The probability of custody after a conviction for robbery decreased between 1987 (79 percent) and 1995 (67 percent) but generally stayed around the 70 percent level (fig. 3, top). Like burglary, the probability of custody after a conviction for assault increased somewhat in the early 1980s and decreased somewhat in the late 1980s but overall stayed tolerably constant from 1981 to 1993. However, it then increased from 18 percent in 1993 to 29 percent in 1999 (fig. 3, bottom). The probability of custody after a conviction for rape or homicide was always very high (around 90–95 percent; not shown in a figure).

Table 1 shows that the probability of custody after a conviction increased over time for burglary ($r = .60$), assault ($r = .80$), rape ($r = .65$), and homicide ($r = .70$) and decreased over time for robbery ($r = -.60$). Table 2 shows that, for vehicle theft, this probability decreased in 1981–93 ($r = -.69$) but increased in 1993–99 ($r = .70$). For burglary, this probability did not change in 1981–93 ($r = -.12$) but increased in 1993–99 ($r = .98$).

The decreases in the probability of custody in 1987–91 could have been caused by Home Office pronouncements encouraging judges and magistrates to avoid sending offenders to prison as far as possible, especially for nonviolent offenses such as burglary and vehicle theft (Home Office 1988a, 1990a). Also, the downgrading of the offense of unauthorized taking of a motor vehicle to a nonindictable offense (in the Criminal Justice Act 1988) encouraged sentencers to treat it as a relatively trivial offense and to use noncustodial penalties. The Criminal Justice Act 1991, implemented on October 1, 1992, discouraged the use of custody for nonviolent offenses, generally prevented sentencers from taking account of previous convictions or of more than two current offenses, required that persons aged seventeen should be dealt with as juveniles rather than as adults, and reduced maximum prison sentences for nonresidential burglary and theft.

Wilson (1997) argued that, up to and including the 1991 act (which greatly reduced the ability of sentencers to pass custodial sentences), Home Office policy makers were primarily concerned with minimizing or (preferably) reducing the prison population. However, the 1991 act also greatly reduced the use of suspended prison sentences (requiring that they could only be given in exceptional circumstances), and this arguably might have led to an increase in (unsuspended) prison sentences.

Home Office policy changed in May 1993 when Michael Howard became Home Secretary. Insisting that "prison works," he encouraged judges and magistrates to make more use of custodial sentences and introduced new laws to facilitate this. For example, the Criminal Justice Act 1993 repealed the provisions in the Criminal Justice Act 1991 that prevented sentencers from taking account of previous convictions or of more than two current offenses (with effect from August 16, 1993) and doubled the maximum custodial sentence for persons aged fifteen to seventeen from one year to two years (from February 3, 1995).

The Crime (Sentences) Act 1997, implemented on October 1, 1997, required an automatic life sentence (unless there were exceptional circumstances) for a person aged eighteen or over convicted for the second time for a serious violent or sexual offense (including homicide, rape, assault causing grievous bodily harm, and robbery involving the use of real or imitation firearms). In addition, it required a minimum sentence of three years imprisonment (unless there were exceptional circumstances) for a third conviction for residential burglary; however, as all three of these convictions had to occur after December 1, 1999, no offenders were affected by this in 1999.

C.   Average Time Served

Offense-specific data on average time served are not routinely published but were kindly supplied (for released prisoners and young offenders) by the Home Office. The average time served in custody after sentence for burglary stayed reasonably constant between 1981 and 1995 (at six to seven months) but then increased to 10.2 months in 1999 (fig. 4, top). The average time served for vehicle theft decreased from 4.8 months in 1981 to 2.8 months in 1991 but then increased to 4.2 months in 1999 (fig. 4, center). The average time served for robbery increased irregularly from thirteen months in 1981 to twenty-three months in 1999 (fig. 4, top). The average time served for assault peaked in 1991 at 8.2 months but otherwise showed no clear trend (fig. 4, center). The average time served for rape more than doubled, from twenty months in 1981 to forty-nine months in 1999 (fig. 4, bottom). The average time served for homicide increased from sixty-nine months (5.8 years) in 1981 to 105 months (8.8 years) in 1993 but then stayed tolerably constant (fig. 4, bottom).

Table 1 shows that the average time served increased over time for all offenses except vehicle theft. The average time served decreased over time for vehicle theft ($r = -.57$). Table 2 shows that the average time served for vehicle theft decreased in 1981–93 ($r = -.96$) but increased in 1993–99 ($r = .97$).

The average time served depends partly on the average sentence length and partly on the fraction of the sentence that is served in custody. The average sentence length increased for all offenses except vehicle theft ($r = .07$). In general, trends in sentence length were similar to trends in time served. The percentage of time served decreased in the 1980s for burglary, vehicle theft, and assault but then remained tolerably constant until increasing between 1997 and 1999.

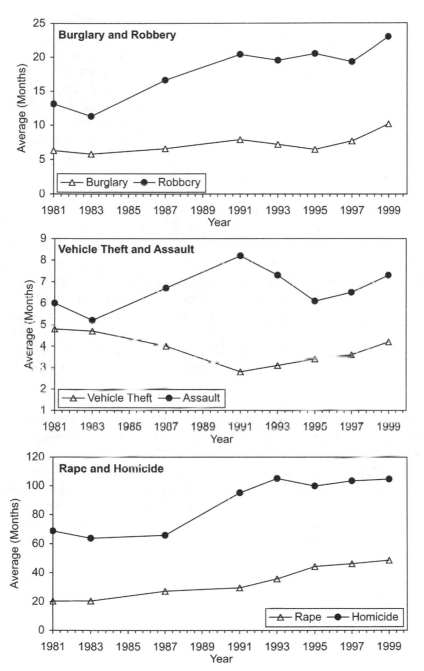

Fig. 4.—Average time served for burglary and robbery, vehicle theft and assault, and rape and homicide.

For robbery, rape, and homicide, the percentage of time served was tolerably constant from 1981 until the increase between 1997 and 1999.

The decreases in the early 1980s in the average time served in custody might be attributed to two changes designed to limit the prison population. In 1981, a prisoner became eligible for parole after serving one-third of the sentence and generally had to be released after serving two-thirds (unless the person behaved badly in prison). The minimum time that had to be served before a prisoner became eligible for parole was twelve months, and prisoners were typically paroled for the last eight months or so of their sentences. In July 1984, the minimum time that had to be served before parole eligibility was decreased from twelve to six months, and a near-automatic parole system was introduced for short-sentence inmates (Home Office 1988*b*, p. 4).

In August 1987, the amount of remission for sentences of twelve months or less was increased from one-third to one-half, causing an immediate mass release of about 3,500 prisoners (Home Office 1989, p. 19). The Criminal Justice Act 1991 introduced the present system on October 1, 1992. All prisoners serving under four years are automatically released after serving half their sentences, while prisoners serving four years or more become eligible for release on parole after serving half their sentences and must be released after serving two-thirds (unless they misbehave in prison).

There were two main reasons why the average time served for homicide increased. First, the number of murder convictions (carrying a mandatory life sentence) increased, whereas the number of manslaughter (including infanticide) convictions stayed constant. For example, in 1981, 126 offenders were convicted for murder and 262 for manslaughter, whereas in 1999, 252 offenders were convicted for murder and 264 for manslaughter. Second, the average time served by life-sentence prisoners increased from 126 months in 1981 to 160 months in 1999.

D. *Conclusions about Changes in Punishment*

For burglary and vehicle theft, the probability of an offender being convicted decreased dramatically between 1981 and 1993 and then increased somewhat between 1993 and 1999. For serious assault, this probability decreased dramatically up to 1995 but then increased somewhat up to 1999. For rape, this probability decreased dramatically from 1981 to 1999. For robbery, this probability stayed reasonably constant up to 1991 but then decreased up to 1999. For homicide, this probability showed no clear trend over time.

The most questionable of these findings concerns the increase in the probability of conviction for serious assault between 1995 and 1999. This increase was largely driven by the decrease in the survey assault rate, which we have previously indicated we consider dubious. If we disregard this increase, the probability of conviction for a serious property crime decreased from 1981 to 1993 and then increased, whereas the probability of conviction for a nonlethal violent crime decreased from 1981 to 1999.

The probability of receiving a custodial sentence after conviction for burglary or assault increased somewhat in the early 1980s, decreased somewhat in the late 1980s, and then increased more markedly in the 1990s. For vehicle theft, this probability decreased between 1981 and 1991 and then increased. For robbery, rape, and homicide, this probability was always high and did not change markedly.

The average time served for burglary showed no clear trend up to 1995 but then increased. The average time served for vehicle theft decreased between 1981 and 1991 and then increased up to 1999. The average time served for assault showed no consistent trend but was greatest in 1991. The average time served for robbery, rape, and homicide increased steadily.

If we combine the probability of custody and the average time served to produce a summary measure of the severity of punishment (average time served per conviction), we find that, for burglary, severity increased somewhat between 1981 and 1987, stayed constant up to 1995, and then increased dramatically up to 1999; for vehicle theft, severity decreased dramatically from 1981 to 1991 and then increased dramatically up to 1999; for robbery, assault, rape, and homicide, severity increased steadily from 1981 to 1999 (Farrington and Jolliffe 2004). We therefore conclude that for serious property offenses, the severity of punishment stayed constant or decreased between 1981 and the early 1990s and then increased dramatically. For serious violent offenses, the severity of punishment increased steadily from 1981 to 1999.

IV. Explaining Changes in Crime Rates
Serious property crimes increased between 1981 and 1993 and then decreased up to 1999, whereas serious nonlethal violence increased steadily during the whole time period. What hypotheses might be proposed and tested to explain these crime trends?

It is difficult to test explanations of changes in national crime rates over time. This is because of the difficulty of controlling statistically for all possible influences on crime rates. A great deal is known about risk factors for offending by individuals. These include individual factors such as impulsivity and low intelligence; family factors such as antisocial parents, poor parental supervision, large family size, and disrupted families; and socioeconomic factors such as low family income and unemployment, delinquent peers, high-delinquency-rate schools, criminal areas, and criminal opportunities (e.g., Farrington 1998, 2004). Little is known about differential effects of these factors on different types of crimes because of the prevailing belief that offending is primarily versatile. Nevertheless, it is possible in studies based on individuals to control for numerous explanatory variables and to determine the time ordering of different explanatory variables and offending.

In studies based on countries, many risk factors (e.g., impulsivity, parental supervision) are not measured repeatedly at the national level. Even where there are repeated national data on a risk factor (e.g., unemployment), the method of measurement may change over time, and the national variable (e.g., the claimant count) may not accurately reflect the theoretical construct of unemployment. There are also great problems of causal lag and causal order caused by the (usually) annual data. After what time lag, for example, is an increase in the unemployment rate likely to cause an increase in the crime rate? If the time lag were short (e.g., one month), then it would not be reasonable to investigate how far the unemployment rate in one year predicted the crime rate in the next year. However, if the unemployment rate in one year is used to predict the crime rate in the same year, this raises problems of causal order.

It is a great challenge to explain increases in property crime up to 1993 and decreases after 1993. Most possible causal factors did not change dramatically around 1993. Of course, it is possible that one causal factor influenced the increase in crime up to 1993 and that a different causal factor influenced the decrease after 1993. It is also possible that numerous causal factors influence crime rates to different degrees in different time periods.

If anything, it is even more difficult to explain the steady increase in nonlethal violent crime from 1981 to 1999. This is because many national indicators change linearly and hence are correlated with a linear trend in crime. For example, it is likely that the consumption of ice cream would be highly correlated with the number of violent crimes over time (Tarling 1982), but few researchers would suggest that consuming ice cream makes people more violent.

Our modest aim in this essay is to rate explanations of changes in crime rates as plausible or implausible. We cannot draw any more definite conclusions. As an example, consider the hypothesis that improved security of houses and vehicles caused the decreases in residential burglary and vehicle theft after 1993. The problem is that (although it would be difficult to obtain a national indicator) security was improving throughout the whole time period 1981–99. Why should there have been a dramatic change in 1993? We therefore consider that improved security is an implausible explanation of trends in serious property crimes.

A variant of the security hypothesis focuses on the deterrent effect of the use of closed-circuit television (CCTV) on crime. According to Armitage (2002), the number of surveillance cameras in England and Wales increased from 100 in 1990 to 400 in 1994, 5,200 in 1997, and 40,000 in 2002. Could the massive expansion of CCTV surveillance after 1993 explain the decreases in burglary and vehicle theft after 1993? The best existing evaluations of CCTV suggest that it has no effect on violence but causes a decrease in vehicle crime (Welsh and Farrington 2004).

Changes in some risk factors would predict a decrease in crime over time. For example, average family size has decreased, poor housing has decreased, and poverty has decreased (at least in absolute terms, if not relatively). Consequently, changes in these risk factors are implausible explanations of the observed time trends in property and violent crimes. The same is true for some opportunity risk factors. Because of increasing prosperity, there are steadily increasing numbers of vehicles and steadily increasing amounts of property that could be stolen. However, if crime increased according to criminal opportunities, property crime should have increased steadily from 1981 to 1999, but it did not. Therefore, opportunity-based explanations of the observed crime trends seem implausible.

A. Previous English Studies of Economic Factors

In recent years, the most important attempts to explain and predict changes in (recorded) crime rates in England have been carried out by economists interested in the relationship between crime and economic prosperity. For the period 1950–87, Field (1990) found that year-to-year changes in burglary, robbery, and theft of vehicles were negatively correlated with year-to-year changes in personal consumption (the average personal expenditure per capita, adjusted for inflation). However, year-to-year changes in violence and sex crime rates were positively correlated with year-to-year changes in personal consumption.

In attempting to explain these results, Field (1990) suggested that increases in prosperity meant that people in marginal economic groups were better able to obtain income legitimately and hence had less need to commit property crimes in order to obtain income. However, increases in prosperity also meant that people in marginal economic groups went out more and drank more alcohol, both of which led to increases in violence and sex crimes. Indeed, he showed that year-to-year increases in the amount of beer consumed were significantly positively related to year-to-year increases in the rate of violent crime.

Field (1990) also found that year-to-year increases in the number of young males (ages ten to twenty-nine) were positively related to year-to-year increases in all crimes except robbery. Increases in police strength were negatively related to increases in theft of vehicles and sex offenses, and positively related to increases in violence. Increases in the police clearance rate in one year predicted decreases in violence and theft of vehicles in the next year. Increases in car ownership correlated with increases in theft of vehicles, and increased unemployment in one year predicted increased violence in the next year.

Pyle and Deadman (1994) attempted to replicate Field's conclusions on property crime (including burglary and robbery) using data that they collected from 1946 to 1991. They concluded that personal consumption and GDP (negatively related to changes in crime) and unemployment (positively related to changes in crime) were essentially interchangeable. They also found that decreases in the conviction rate per recorded offense were correlated with increasing crime rates.

Using Pyle and Deadman's (1994) data set, Hale (1998) aimed to predict both year-to-year changes in crime rates and long-term levels of crime. In agreement with Field (1990), Hale found that year-to-year changes in burglary were negatively related to changes in personal consumption, as well as to police numbers and conviction rates per recorded offense. However, year-to-year changes in robbery were positively related to changes in personal consumption in the previous year, and to changes in the unemployment rate, and negatively related to changes in police numbers. Long-term burglary and robbery levels were positively related to personal consumption; all were increasing over this time period.

TABLE 3

Correlations with Crime Rates

	Burglary	MVT	Robbery	Assault	Rape	Homicide
Percent males unemployed	.48	.73	−.41	.28	−.29	−.12
Personal consumption/population	.57	.12	.88	.51	.93	.78
GDP/population	.67	.25	.90	.64	.99	.80
GDP change	.26	.50	−.23	.05	.10	.35
Beer consumption/population	−.69	−.27	−.93	−.69	−.90	−.68
Percent population age fifteen to twenty-four	−.65	−.20	−.94	−.67	−.96	−.71
Percent population male age fifteen to twenty	−.83	−.47	−.84	−.80	−.92	−.77
Number of vehicles/population	.62	.21	.87	.55	.97	.80
Police strength/population	.56	.86	−.41	.35	−.06	.17
Conviction rate/offender	−.75	−.67	−.91	−.88	−.92	−.43
Probability (custody/conviction)	.12	−.50	−.56	.49	.62	.56
Average time served	.10	−.88	.79	.33	.96	.58
Conviction rate/offender A	−.86	−.74	−.96	.82	.91	.13
Conviction rate/offender B	−.42	−.40	−.76	.90	−.93	−.01

NOTE.—Survey crime rates for burglary, MVT, robbery, and assault (except conviction rate/offender: recorded crime rates); recorded crime rates for rape and homicide. GDP = gross domestic product, MVT = motor vehicle theft; A = crime rate first; B = conviction rate first.

There have been several other studies of crime and the business cycle in England. For 1988–96, Witt, Clarke, and Fielding (1999) found that year-to-year changes in burglary and vehicle crime were positively correlated with year-to-year changes in the unemployment rate and in the number of cars per capita, and negatively related to the number of police per capita in the previous year. Dhiri and his colleagues (1999) found that long-term trends in burglary were positively correlated with personal consumption and with the number of young males in the population.

B. Correlations with Demographic and Economic Factors

In light of all this previous research, table 3 shows correlations between crime rates and previously identified key indicators (per capita): number of males unemployed, personal consumption (consumer expenditure), GDP, beer consumption, number of young persons or young males in the population, number of vehicles, and police strength. Personal consumption and GDP were adjusted for inflation. In addition, correlations between crime rates and the year-to-year change in GDP are shown. All the previous economic studies were based on recorded crime rates, but survey crime rates are arguably more accurate. Survey crime rates could be used for burglary, vehicle theft, robbery, and assault, but police-recorded crime rates had to be used for rape and homicide. We did not attempt to do any complex econometric analyses. The data were obtained from the Office of National Statistics (2000b, 2001).

Table 3 shows that the male unemployment rate was positively correlated with burglary ($r = .48$) and vehicle theft ($r = .73$) from 1981 to 1999, but not with violent crimes. Figure 5 (top) shows that the male unemployment rate increased in the early 1980s, decreased in the late 1980s, increased to a peak in 1993, and then decreased up to 1999. Hence, the male unemployment curve is similar to the curves for recorded burglary and vehicle theft (fig. 1). Changes in unemployment, therefore, are a plausible explanation of changes in property crime. In the Cambridge Study in Delinquent Development, males committed more crimes during periods of unemployment than periods of employment, and this effect was found only for crimes involving material gain (not for violence, vandalism, or drug use; Farrington et al. 1986). Therefore, it is plausible that unemployment causes a lack of money, which in turn causes property offending to get money.

Inflation-adjusted personal consumption (consumer expenditure) per capita was positively correlated with all types of crimes except vehicle theft, and the same was true of inflation-adjusted GDP per capita. In general, personal consumption and GDP per capita tended to increase over time, whereas vehicle theft increased a great deal and then decreased a great deal. Hence, increases in prosperity are a plausible explanation of increases in violent crime rates, possibly because they enable economically marginal people to go out more and drink more (Field 1990). However, there is the "ice cream" problem in interpreting this correlation.

The year-to-year percentage change in GDP was generally weakly related to crime rates but was most strongly related to vehicle theft ($r = .50$). Figure 5 (top) shows that the year-to-year change in GDP had a somewhat similar distribution to the male unemployment rate. However, these two variables correlated only .18 between 1981 and 1999. We conclude that it is implausible that year-to-year changes in GDP could explain the observed crime trends.

Surprisingly, beer consumption per capita was negatively related to all types of crimes. This was because beer consumption decreased

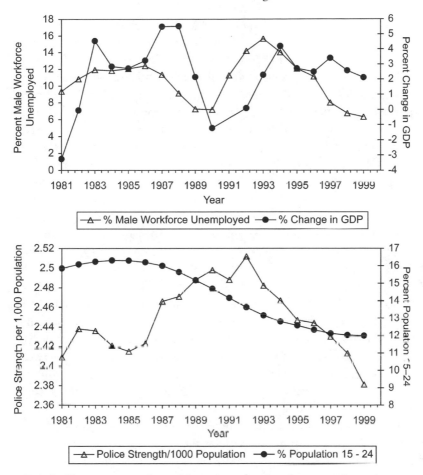

FIG. 5.—Top, percent male workforce unemployed and percent change in gross domestic product. Bottom, police strength per 1,000 population and percent population ages fifteen to twenty-four.

steadily between 1981 and 1999. Therefore, changes in beer consumption is an implausible explanation of the observed changes in crime rates. Similarly, the proportion of young people (or young males) in the population was negatively related to all types of crimes. Figure 5 (bottom) shows that this proportion peaked in the early 1980s and then decreased. Hence, this is an implausible explanation of changes in crime rates between 1981 and 1999.

The number of vehicles per capita increased steadily between 1981 and 1999, and hence was positively correlated with the number of violent crimes. However, it is implausible that an increase in the number of vehicles should cause an increase in the number of violent crimes. It should be noted that the number of vehicles was least strongly correlated ($r = .21$) with trends in vehicle theft.

Figure 5 (bottom) shows that police strength per capita increased to a peak in 1993 and then decreased. Not surprisingly, therefore, it was positively correlated with burglary ($r = .56$) and vehicle theft ($r = .86$) but only weakly related to violent crimes. It is implausible to suggest that increases in police strength might cause increases in property crimes. It is more plausible to suggest that increases in property crimes might cause increases in police strength.

C.   Could Changes in Punishment Influence the Crime Rate?

Previous publications (Farrington and Langan 1992; Farrington and Wikström 1993; Farrington, Langan, and Wikström 1994; Langan and Farrington 1998) investigated correlations between changes in crime rates and changes in the risk and severity of legal punishment. The latest in the series (Langan and Farrington 1998, p. 38) concluded that there were consistent negative correlations between risk measures and crime rates in England, but not in the United States, and that there were no consistent correlations between severity measures and crime rates in either country. Although they cautioned against drawing causal conclusions from correlations, some politicians apparently used this research to justify their argument that "prison works." In turn, this provoked some criminologists who were opposed to imprisonment to criticize the research. For example, Doob and Webster (2003, p. 161) said that "several of their results do not support their general conclusion that punishment severity affects crime trends." Langan and Farrington (1998) did not make that claim. When Doob was challenged to specify the place in the 1998 publication where this statement was made, he failed to do so.

Table 3 shows correlations between the crime rate and the three measures of the risk and severity of legal punishment. Of course, it must be realized that these correlations are based only on a few years of data (eight for survey crimes and nineteen for recorded crimes in this essay). We believe that our measure of the risk of punishment (the number of convictions per 1,000 offenders) is more accurate than those used by other researchers (e.g., the ratio of the number of convictions to the number of recorded crimes).

The measure of risk—the number of convictions per 1,000 offenders—was strongly and negatively related to all types of survey and recorded crimes. It might be expected that property crimes might be more influenced by the risk of punishment than violent crimes (on the grounds that property crimes are more likely to involve a rational calculation), but robbery, assault, and rape had the highest correlations with risk. The lowest correlation was for homicide ($r = -.43$). However, the measures of severity—the probability of custody following a conviction and the average time served—were not consistently negatively related to survey or recorded crime rates. The strongest negative relationship between the crime rate and the severity of punishment was for vehicle theft, which correlated $-.50$ with the probability of custody following a conviction and $-.88$ with the average time served. However, the burglary rate was not correlated with either measure of severity.

Correlations between survey crime rates and the number of convictions per 1,000 offenders might be considered problematic because the number of convictions per 1,000 offenders is not logically independent of the number of survey crimes. Nevertheless, it is not necessarily true that these two measures must be negatively correlated. If the number of survey crimes increased by 10 percent, for example, the number of convictions per 1,000 offenders could decrease by 10 percent (if the number of convictions stayed constant), stay constant (if the number of convictions increased by 10 percent), or increase by 10 percent (if the number of convictions increased by 20 percent). Since the recorded crime rate is logically independent of the number of convictions per 1,000 offenders, this rate is shown in table 3.

If the probability of being convicted influences the behavior of potential offenders, it might be expected that the number of convictions per 1,000 offenders might predict the crime rate rather than the reverse. At the bottom of table 3, "conviction rate/offender A" indicates predictive (lagged) correlations with the crime rate in one year predicting the number of convictions per 1,000 offenders in the next year ("crime rate first"). "Conviction rate/offender B" indicates predictive correlations with the number of convictions per 1,000 offenders in one year predicting the crime rate in the next year ("conviction rate first").

For three crimes (burglary, vehicle theft, and robbery), the negative correlations between conviction rates and crime rates were substantially greater for crimes predicting convictions rather than for the reverse. The "crime rate first" and "conviction rate first" correlations were similar for assault and rape and negligible for homicide. These results suggest that increasing crime causes decreasing risk, or that changes in the probability of punishment have a quick effect (in less than one year) on the crime rate, or that they do not have a deterrent effect on crime.

In light of this last result, should we conclude that it is plausible or implausible that changes in the risk of punishment influence changes in the crime rate? Bearing in mind the consistent correlations in table 3, our conclusion is that this hypothesis is plausible and that changes in the risk of punishment might influence the crime rate in less than one year. However, it is implausible that changes in the severity of punishment influence the crime rate. On the contrary, it seems more likely that increases in crime cause increases in the severity of punishment.

D. Conclusions about Explanations of Crime Rates

It is plausible to suggest that changes in property crime rates between 1981 and 1999 might have been influenced by changes in unemployment and (after 1993) by increases in the prevalence of CCTV. It is also plausible to suggest that increases in violent crime rates might have been influenced by increases in economic prosperity. Both types of crimes might have been influenced by changes in the risk of punishment but not by changes in the severity of punishment. Other explanations that we considered (demographic changes, beer consumption, opportunity, security, police strength) were deemed to be implausible.

It is unlikely that any single factor will explain changes in crime rates over time. Different factors may influence different types of crimes in different time periods, possibly depending on the magnitude of change in the explanatory factor. Large changes in short time periods might be expected to have greater effects. For example, the dramatic decrease in the probability of conviction for vehicle theft (from fifty-two convictions per 1,000 offenders in 1981 to only twelve in 1993) might be expected to have a detectable effect on vehicle theft. However, we have to admit that the correlations reported are thought provoking but do not provide a convincing explanation of the crime trends because of our inability to measure and control for numerous causal factors.

V.   Conclusions

This essay presents basic data on changes in crime and punishment over time that need to be explained by criminological theories. More research is needed, especially to explain why residential burglary and vehicle theft increased so much in 1981–93 and then decreased so much in 1993–99, using more national indicators. More attempts should be made to obtain national estimates of possible causal factors. It is particularly important that the Home Office annually publish the best available data on the average number of offenders committing each type of offense.

Perhaps the major problem in doing these analyses is to achieve comparable data over time. Unfortunately for researchers, the definitions of crime, laws, and the operation of the criminal justice system—not to mention the methods of victimization surveys—keep changing. We recommend that, whenever changes are made, the Home Office routinely carry out research to estimate their effects and, if possible, attempt to continue previous data series. Also, more attempts should be made to achieve comparability between victim survey, police, court, and prison data. It would be helpful, for example, if measures of the quality of offenses (e.g., using injury severity scales for assaults) were routinely collected.

There is a pressing need for more longitudinal studies tracking offenders through the criminal justice system to estimate quantities such as the probability of an offender being convicted. This would be greatly facilitated if each person had an identification number that stayed with him or her at each stage of the system. Ideally, these analyses should be expanded to more stages of the criminal justice system, such as arrest and prosecution, and to more types of offenses.

More research is needed on the explanations that we find most plausible, namely, that changes in crime rates over time are influenced by changes in unemployment and in the risk of punishment. These hypotheses should be tested using a variety of methods including surveys and experiments. We hope that this volume will help to establish how much they might be applicable in different countries. We also hope that this essay and the others in this volume might inspire future efforts to collect comparable data on crime and punishment in different countries.

APPENDIX

Sources of Data

The same methods are used in this essay as in Langan and Farrington (1998). For more technical details and all numbers, Farrington and Jolliffe (2004) should be consulted. We focus especially on the eight years with British Crime Survey data on numbers of crimes (1981, 1983, 1987, 1991, 1993, 1995, 1997, 1999). Where information is available for all nineteen years (e.g., on police-recorded crimes), these are presented. In general, sources of data are given in this appendix only for the most recent years (1997 and 1999); for sources of data in earlier years, earlier publications (Farrington and Langan 1992; Farrington, Langan, and Wikström 1994) should be consulted.

I. Comparability

There are two main problems of comparability: over time, and between victim survey and criminal justice data. Legal definitions of burglary (entering as a trespasser to commit theft or damage), robbery (theft involving force or threat), motor vehicle theft (theft or unauthorized taking of motor vehicles), and homicide (murder, manslaughter, or infanticide) are relatively clear and constant over time. Attempts are included with completed crimes, except for vehicle theft in survey data and homicide in criminal justice data. Attempted vehicle theft was not included with vehicle theft in the BCS because of the difficulty of distinguishing between attempted theft of vehicles and attempted theft from vehicles. Attempted murder is a separate legal category in England.

Between 1981 and 1999, the legal definitions of burglary, robbery, and homicide did not change in England. Unauthorized taking of a motor vehicle was downgraded from an indictable (more serious) to a summary (less serious) offense in the Criminal Justice Act 1988 (with effect from October 12, 1988). Subsequently, a new offense of aggravated vehicle taking was created by the Aggravated Vehicle Taking Act 1991 (with effect from April 1, 1992). Hence, for comparability with earlier years, English motor vehicle theft in 1999 comprised four legal categories: theft of a motor vehicle (indictable), unauthorized taking of a motor vehicle (summary), and aggravated vehicle taking (indictable and summary).

Rape (including attempted rape) is a more problematic offense. In England in 1981, rape had to involve a male offender and a female victim, and required penetration of the vagina by the penis. Husbands could not be convicted of raping their wives. No male under age fourteen could be convicted of rape, but female offenders were included in the rape statistics if they aided or abetted rape. The minimum age for a rape conviction was decreased from fourteen to ten—the minimum age of conviction for other offenses—in the Sexual Offenses (Amendment) Act 1993 (with effect from September 20, 1993). The definition of rape was changed in the Criminal Justice and Public Order Act 1994 (with effect from November 1, 1994) to include male victims, spouse victims, and anal intercourse. However, the majority of rape offenses continue to involve male offenders, female victims, and vaginal intercourse. Consensual sex with girls under sixteen is placed in a different legal category. It is possible to identify the numbers of male offenders and female victims in the official criminal statistics. The sample size in the BCS is too small to yield a survey estimate of rape.

Serious assault poses the greatest problem. In England up to 1997, the BCS (and the police-recorded figures) distinguished between the indictable offense of wounding (causing actual or grievous bodily harm) and the summary offense of common assault. Serious assault is defined as wounding in this essay. Wounding occurs if the victim receives some kind of cut or wound, where the skin or a bone is broken, or if medical attention is needed, whereas common assault occurs if the victim is punched, kicked, or jostled, with negligible or no injury. Minor bruising or a black eye counts as negligible injury. Attempted assaults are not counted as wounding in the BCS. Because of legal problems, such as establishing intention, most attempted assaults would also not be counted as wounding by the police. The legal definition of wounding did not change between 1981 and 1997. Ideally, it would be desirable to use an injury severity scale to classify the seriousness of assaults.

The Home Office rules specifying how crimes are counted by the police did not change between January 1980 and March 1998. From April 1998, new counting rules were introduced (see Povey and Prime 1999). At the same time, police-recorded crimes began to be presented in the annual criminal statistics on a financial year basis (e.g., April 1998–March 1999) rather than on a calendar-year basis, although data on convictions and sentencing continued to be presented for each calendar year.

The new counting rules particularly affected the number of police-recorded criminal damage and fraud offenses. They had a negligible impact on five of our six offenses (all except serious assault). The main effect was on the "other wounding" category (8), which was extended to include possession of weapons (8B), harassment (8C), and (from April 1999) racially aggravated wounding (8D). However, the number of other woundings in the original category (8A) was still presented, and Povey and Prime (1999, table 6) estimated that this number was only 3.2 percent less than the total number of other woundings under the old rules. Therefore, the number of police-recorded woundings in 1999 (categories 8A and 8D) may be about 3 percent less than in 1997 because of the change in the counting rules.

Great efforts have been made to ensure that crime definitions in the BCS are comparable to those in official (police) statistics, but some differences are inevitable. For example, the BCS does not include thefts of commercial vehicles or crimes against organizations or against persons under sixteen. However, the police statistics can be adjusted to obtain figures, which are comparable to victim survey estimates (see Kershaw et al. 2000, app. C).

II. Survey Offenses

The number of victim-survey offenses, comparable population figures (number of households and number of persons ages sixteen or over), and the probability of reporting to the police were obtained from the BCS (Mirrlees-Black et al. 1998; Mattinson 1999, 2000; Kershaw et al. 2000; Budd 2001). For example, the BCS estimated that there were 345,994 robberies in 1999 and that 30 percent of them were reported to the police. Since there were an estimated 41,996,000 persons aged sixteen or over in 1999, the survey robbery rate was 8.24 per 1,000 population at risk; disregarding repeat victims, about one in every 121 persons was robbed in 1999. The sample size of the BCS was initially just over 10,000, and then it gradually increased to 19,400 in 1999. All BCS figures, of course, have confidence intervals about them. For example, the 95 percent confidence interval for the robbery rate in 1999 was from 5.06 to 11.42 per 1,000 population. Confidence intervals are narrower for the other three offenses, which are more prevalent.

The BCS survey crime rates for residential burglary and vehicle theft are per 1,000 households, while rates for robbery and serious assault (wounding) are per 1,000 population ages sixteen or over. Vehicle theft figures refer to completed thefts only. Other population estimates came from the Office for National Statistics (e.g., 2000b).

The main change in the BCS over the years was the addition of a new screening question for domestic violence ("Has any member of your household deliberately hit you with their fists or with a weapon of any sort or kicked you or used force or violence in any other way?") and a new victim form in 1993. This caused an increase in the number of victim-survey offenses of serious assault. Mayhew (1997) and Mattinson (1999, 2000) provided serious assault estimates with and without the new domestic violence screening question; for example, the figures were 810,994 (without) and 860,395 (with) in 1995. For comparability with the 1981–91 figures, the "without" figures are used in these analyses.

For burglary, vehicle theft, robbery, and serious assault, the average number of offenders per offense was provided from the BCS by Mirrlees-Black (1996) and Mattinson (1999, 2000). For homicide, this was obtained from the annual criminal statistics (e.g., Home Office 1998a, p. 71; 2000a, p. 75). The average over all years was used in estimating probabilities. This was 1.8 for burglary, 2.1 for vehicle theft, 2.3 for robbery, 2 for serious assault, and 1.1 for homicide. For rape, the only national data on the number of offenders per offense seem to be that published by Grace, Lloyd, and Smith (1992) for offenses committed in 1985. They reported that, for police-recorded offenses, there were 1.1 offenders per rape offense. This figure was used in all calculations.

III. Police-Recorded Offenses

The number of police-recorded offenses was obtained from the annual criminal statistics (e.g., Home Office 1998a, tables 2.15–2.18; 2000a, tables 2.15–2.18). The number of recorded offenses in the calendar year 1999 was provided by Lavin (2001). The number of police-recorded offenses refers to the number initially recorded by the police in each offense category in each year, irrespective of later court proceedings. Assault comprised section 5 wounding (mainly causing grievous bodily harm) and sections 8A and 8D wounding (mainly causing actual bodily harm). Vehicle theft comprised theft or unauthorized taking of motor vehicles and aggravated vehicle taking. Only rape of a female was counted. For example, there were 78,884 recorded robberies in 1999. Since the resident population was estimated to be 52,690,000 in 1999, the police-recorded robbery rate was 1.5 robberies per 1,000 population (one robbery per 668 citizens).

The numbers of police-recorded offenses that were comparable to survey offenses were estimated by Mayhew (1996), Mattinson (1999, 2000), and Budd (2001). The estimation procedures were explained by Mirrlees-Black et al. (1998, pp. 75–83) and Kershaw et al. (2000, pp. 115–21). For example, in 1997 the total number of recorded robberies was 64,878 (63,072 recorded by the police and 1,806 recorded by the British Transport Police). Excluding an estimated 20 percent of cases where the victim was ages under sixteen, 51,902 of these recorded robberies were considered to be comparable to the 345,994 BCS robberies. The main adjustments to recorded crimes were to exclude thefts of commercial vehicles, attempted vehicle thefts, and victims under sixteen. However, robberies of business property were counted in the BCS.

IV. Convictions

The number of persons convicted for each offense was obtained from the annual supplementary criminal statistics (e.g., Home Office 1998b, annex A; 2000b, annex A). In earlier years, it was necessary to add convictions in crown courts and magistrates' courts. It was also necessary to add different offense categories (murder, manslaughter, infanticide, and manslaughter due to diminished responsibility for homicide; sections 5 and 8 woundings for assault; theft of a motor vehicle, unauthorized taking, and indictable and summary aggravated vehicle taking for vehicle theft). As already explained, rape convictions since 1994 can include male and female victims and male and female offenders. The supplementary criminal statistics showed that there were 601 male offenders with female victims in 1999.

As an example, 5,626 persons were convicted for robbery in 1999. Since there were an estimated 46,029,000 persons ages ten or over in 1999 (Office for National Statistics 2000b), the conviction rate for robbery was 0.122 per 1,000 population at risk. Since there were an estimated 345,994 robberies in 1999 and an estimated 2.3 offenders per offense, there were an estimated 795,786 offenders (not necessarily different persons) who could in theory have been convicted for BCS-comparable robberies if the criminal justice system had been 100 percent efficient. Since BCS-comparable robberies comprised 82 percent of all recorded robberies in 1999 (64,472/78,884), it could be estimated that there were 973,675 offenders at risk of conviction for all types of robberies.

Dividing this number by the number of persons convicted (5,626) yields the estimate that there were 173 offenders per conviction, or that the probability of conviction for each robbery offender was .0058 in 1999 (5.8 convictions per 1,000 offenders). Alternatively, it might be said that the average robber could commit 173 robberies for every one court appearance leading to conviction. This neglects cautions (576 for robbery in 1999) and multiple offenses dealt with on one court appearance, on the assumption that one conviction provides one opportunity for legal punishment as far as the offender is concerned. The calculations for rape and homicide were based only on police-recorded offenses.

V. Probability of Custody

The number of persons sentenced to custody for each offense was obtained from the supplementary criminal statistics (e.g., Home Office 1998b, annex A; 2000b, annex A). As before, it was necessary to add crown courts and magistrates' courts and different offense categories. It was also necessary to add different types of custodial sentences (in 1999: imprisonment, detention in a young offender institution, secure hospital order, secure training order, detention under section 53 of the Children and Young Persons Act 1933; in 1981: imprisonment, Borstal (an institution for offenders ages fifteen to twenty), detention center, secure hospital order, detention under section 53 of the Children and Young Persons Act 1933). As an example, 4,085 offenders were given custodial sentences for robbery in 1999, or 73 percent of all convicted robbery offenders.

VI. Average Time Served

Offense-specific data on average sentence length and average time served in prison by released prisoners (including juveniles) in 1997 and 1999 were supplied by Stevens (1999, 2000). The figures were provided for burglary in general, not for residential burglary specifically. The results shown in figure 4 are based on offenders released in 1982, 1984, 1988, 1991, 1993, 1995, 1997, and 1999. Initially, it was thought that the following year was the most relevant (e.g., because most robbers sentenced to custody in 1981 were released in 1982). However, 1992 data were not available at the time of the analysis by Farrington, Langan, and Wikström (1994), so 1991 data were used, and for consistency 1993, 1995, 1997, and 1999 data were used subsequently.

The offense categories of prisoners are slightly different from those used in the criminal statistics, but "assault" and "wounding" in the prison data are approximately equivalent to the two "wounding" categories (5 and 8) in the criminal statistics, and "taking and driving away" in the prison data covers at least 95 percent of those sentenced to custody for vehicle theft in the criminal statistics (Barclay 1993). The average sentence length and average time served for assault were weighted combinations of the assault and wounding categories (weighted by the number of released offenders). As an example, the average sentence length for robbery releasees in 1999 was forty months, and the average time served was twenty-three months, or 58 percent of the sentence.

There are no English national data routinely published on time served in custody before conviction. However, the report of the Carlisle Committee (1988, p. 147), based on 1987 releasees, estimated that about 10 percent of a prisoner's sentence was spent on remand before sentencing. The figures on average time served after conviction in the tables have not been adjusted to take this time into account.

REFERENCES

Armitage, Rachel. 2002. *To CCTV or Not? A Review of Current Research into the Effectiveness of CCTV Systems in Reducing Crime.* London: National Association for the Care and Resettlement of Offenders.
Ayres, Margaret, Liza Murray, and Ransford Fiti. 2003. *Arrests for Notifiable Offences and the Operation of Certain Police Powers under PACE, England and Wales, 2002/03.* Statistical Bulletin 17/03. London: Home Office.
Barclay, Gordon C. 1993. Personal communication with David P. Farrington. London: Home Office.

Budd, Tracey. 2001. Personal communication with David P. Farrington. London: Home Office.

Carlisle Committee. 1988. *The Parole System in England and Wales.* London: H.M. Stationery Office.

Chapman, Becca, and Stephen Niven. 2000. *A Guide to the Criminal Justice System in England and Wales.* London: Home Office.

Dhiri, Sanjay, Sam Brand, Richard Harries, and Richard Price. 1999. *Modelling and Predicting Property Crime Trends in England and Wales.* London: Home Office.

Doob, Anthony N., and Cheryl M. Webster. 2003. "Sentence Severity and Crime: Accepting the Null Hypothesis." In *Crime and Justice: A Review of Research*, vol. 30, edited by Michael Tonry. Chicago: University of Chicago Press.

Farrington, David P. 1989. "Self-Reported and Official Offending from Adolescence to Adulthood." In *Cross-National Research in Self-Reported Crime and Delinquency*, edited by Malcolm W. Klein. Dordrecht, Netherlands: Kluwer.

———. 1992. "Trends in English Juvenile Delinquency and Their Explanation." *International Journal of Comparative and Applied Criminal Justice* 16:151–63.

———. 1998. "Predictors, Causes and Correlates of Male Youth Violence." In *Youth Violence*, edited by Michael Tonry and Mark H. Moore. Vol. 24 of *Crime and Justice: A Review of Research*, edited by Michael Tonry. Chicago: University of Chicago Press.

———. 2004. "Conduct Disorder, Aggression and Delinquency." In *Handbook of Adolescent Psychology*, 2d ed., edited by Richard M. Lerner and Laurence Steinberg. New York: Wiley.

Farrington, David P., Bernard Gallagher, Lynda Morley, Raymond J. St. Ledger, and Donald J. West. 1986. "Unemployment, School Leaving, and Crime." *British Journal of Criminology* 26:335–56.

Farrington, David P., and Darrick Jolliffe. 2004. "Crime and Punishment in England and Wales." In *Cross-National Studies in Crime and Justice*, edited by David P. Farrington, Patrick A. Langan, and Michael H. Tonry. Washington, D.C.: Bureau of Justice Statistics.

Farrington, David P., and Patrick A. Langan. 1992. "Changes in Crime and Punishment in England and America in the 1980s." *Justice Quarterly* 9:5–46.

Farrington, David P., Patrick A. Langan, and Per-Olof H. Wikström. 1994. "Changes in Crime and Punishment in America, England and Sweden between the 1980s and the 1990s." *Studies on Crime and Crime Prevention* 3:104–31.

Farrington, David P., and Per-Olof H. Wikström. 1993. "Changes in Crime and Punishment in England and Sweden in the 1980s." *Studies on Crime and Crime Prevention* 2:142–70.

Field, Simon. 1990. *Trends in Crime and Their Interpretation.* London: H.M. Stationery Office.

Grace, Sharon, Charles Lloyd, and Lorna J. F. Smith. 1992. *Rape: From Recording to Conviction.* London: Home Office.

Hale, Chris. 1998. "Crime and the Business Cycle in Post-war Britain Revisited." *British Journal of Criminology* 38:681–98.

Home Office. 1985. *The Cautioning of Offenders*. Circular no. 14/1985. London: Home Office.

———. 1988*a*. *Punishment, Custody and the Community*. London: H.M. Stationery Office.

———. 1988*b*. *Report of the Parole Board, 1987*. London: H.M. Stationery Office.

———. 1989. *Prison Statistics, England and Wales, 1988*. London: H.M. Stationery Office.

———. 1990*a*. *Crime, Justice and Protecting the Public*. London: H.M. Stationery Office.

———. 1990*b*. *The Cautioning of Offenders*. Circular no. 59/1990. London: Home Office.

———. 1993. *Criminal Statistics, England and Wales, 1991*. London: H.M. Stationery Office.

———. 1998*a*. *Criminal Statistics, England and Wales, 1997*. London: The Stationery Office.

———. 1998*b*. *Criminal Statistics, England and Wales, Supplementary Tables, 1997*. London: Government Statistical Service.

———. 2000*a*. *Criminal Statistics, England and Wales, 1999*. London: The Stationery Office.

———. 2000*b*. *Criminal Statistics, England and Wales, Supplementary Tables, 1999*. London: Government Statistical Service.

Irving, Barrie L., and Ian K. MacKenzie. 1989. *Police Interrogation*. London: Police Foundation.

Kershaw, Chris, Tracey Budd, Graham Kinshott, Joanna Mattinson, Pat Mayhew, and Andy Myhill. 2000. *The 2000 British Crime Survey, England and Wales*. Statistical Bulletin 18/00. London: Home Office.

Langan, Patrick A., and David P. Farrington. 1998. *Crime and Justice in the United States and in England and Wales, 1981–96*. Washington, D.C.: Bureau of Justice Statistics.

Lavin, Duncan. 2001. Personal communication with David P. Farrington. London: Home Office.

Mattinson, Joanna. 1999. Personal communication with David P. Farrington. London: Home Office.

———. 2000. Personal communication with David P. Farrington. London: Home Office.

Mayhew, Pat. 1996. Personal communication with David P. Farrington. London: Home Office.

———. 1997. Personal communication with David P. Farrington. London: Home Office.

Mirrlees-Black, Catriona. 1996. Personal communication with David P. Farrington. London: Home Office.

Mirrlees-Black, Catriona, Tracey Budd, Sarah Partridge, and Pat Mayhew. 1998. *The 1998 British Crime Survey*. Statistical Bulletin 21/98. London: Home Office.

Office for National Statistics. 2000*a*. *Britain 2001: The Official Yearbook of the United Kingdom*. London: The Stationery Office.

————. 2000*b*. *Estimated Resident Population at Mid-1999 by Single Year of Age and Sex, England and Wales*. Titchfield, Hampshire: Office for National Statistics.

————. 2001. *Annual Abstract of Statistics, United Kingdom*. London: The Stationery Office.

Povey, David, and Julian Prime. 1999. *Recorded Crime Statistics, England and Wales, April 1998 to March 1999*. Statistical Bulletin 18/99. London: Home Office.

Pyle, David J., and Derek F. Deadman. 1994. "Crime and the Business Cycle in Post-war Britain." *British Journal of Criminology* 34:339–57.

Reiss, Albert J., and David P. Farrington. 1991. "Advancing Knowledge about Co-offending: Results from a Prospective Longitudinal Survey of London Males." *Journal of Criminal Law and Criminology* 82:360–95.

Simmons, Jon, and Tricia Dodd, eds. 2003. *Crime in England and Wales, 2002/ 2003*. Statistical Bulletin 07/03. London: Home Office.

Stevens, Roger. 1999. Personal communication with David P. Farrington. London: Home Office.

————. 2000. Personal communication with David P. Farrington. London: Home Office.

Tarling, Roger. 1982. "Unemployment and Crime." *Home Office Research Bulletin* 14:28 33.

Welsh, Brandon C., and David P. Farrington. 2004. "Evidence-Based Crime Prevention: The Effectiveness of CCTV." *Crime Prevention and Community Safety* 6(2):21–33.

West, Donald J., and David P. Farrington. 1977. *The Delinquent Way of Life*. London: Heinemann.

Wilson, James Q. 1997. "Criminal Justice in England and America." *Public Interest* 126:3–14.

Witt, Robert, Alan Clarke, and Nigel Fielding. 1999. "Crime and Economic Activity: A Panel Data Approach." *British Journal of Criminology* 39:391–400.

David J. Smith

Crime and Punishment in Scotland, 1980–1999

ABSTRACT

The substantial rises in crime in Scotland during the golden era between 1950 and 1973 tended to level off after 1980, although this did not apply to the most serious crimes of rape and homicide. There was no sustained or substantial rise in the production of convictions for homicide, rape, robbery, serious assault, burglary, or motor vehicle theft. The chance that an offender would be caught and punished tended to decline over the period 1981–99, with only minor and short-term exceptions. In broad terms, rising crime leveled off in Scotland even though the system was becoming less effective at catching and punishing offenders. The Scottish case suggests that the effectiveness of criminal justice in catching and punishing offenders is not a major factor influencing changes in the level of crime.

Trends in crime and punishment in Scotland have been substantially different from those in England and Wales in the period since 1950. Comparisons between Scotland and England are particularly useful because the two countries, being closely related although distinct, are politically, culturally, and economically similar in many ways. If there is a contrast in trends between the two countries, then possible explanations can be narrowed down to a reasonably small number. By contrast, possible explanations for a difference in trends between England and, say, the United States or Japan, are far more numerous. The comparison between Scotland and England and Wales strongly suggests

David J. Smith is honorary professor, University of Edinburgh, and visiting professor, London School of Economics. The author thanks Elizabeth Levy and Alison Brown for help in gathering and computing statistics and Lesley Fordyce, Katy Barrett, and Sandy Taylor at the Scottish Executive for supplying statistics. This work was funded by the Scottish Executive in Edinburgh and the Home Office in London.

that changes in the amount or likelihood of punishment are not the main driver of changes in the level of crime.

The rise in recorded crime in Scotland since 1950 was considerably less than in England and Wales.[1] For example, between 1950 and 1995, recorded robberies increased by fifteen times in Scotland, compared with sixty-seven times in England; housebreaking increased by less than three times in Scotland, whereas burglaries increased by over thirteen times in England. In Scotland, the increases were considerably greater over the first twenty-one years, from 1950 to 1971, than over the following period from 1972, whereas in England, the increases were greater over the later period.[2] Crime survey results for Scotland show a flat trend from 1981 to 1992 and a falling trend from 1992 to 1999 in all survey crimes. These trends in Scotland contrast sharply with the continued rise in recorded and survey crime in England up to the mid-1990s. From the available evidence, it is not possible to establish a clear explanation for this contrast between similar countries with distinct but similar criminal justice systems. One explanation that seems to be ruled out by the evidence presented in this essay is that the slower rise and earlier leveling off of crime in Scotland was caused by an increase in the probability or severity of punishment. There was no marked increase over the period of the crime surveys (1981–99) in the number of convictions, the probability of conviction, or the severity of sentences for the offenses considered here, although there were some substantial short-lived changes in some instances.

This essay summarizes information on trends in crime and punishment that was set out in more detail, and with fuller documentation of methods, in Smith (2004). The evidence is used to support a general argument of a negative kind: that changes in effective deterrence by the criminal justice system are not the main driver of changes in levels of crime. I do not argue that the criminal justice system has no deterrent effect: on the contrary, I assume that it does and that, if there were no effective enforcement of the criminal law, the level of crime would rise. Instead, I argue that marginal changes in the amount or likelihood of punishment within the range of variation observed in modern liberal

---

[1] Hereafter, for convenience and with apologies to the Welsh, references to England should be understood to refer also to Wales, which is, with England, part of a single fully integrated legal system.

[2] These statistics are fully documented, with their sources, in Smith and Young (1999).

democracies have a minor influence on levels of crime, as compared with other factors.

It has been extraordinarily difficult to produce statistics on crime and punishment to a common pattern, even for the seven countries included in this comparative study, all of which have a run of results from crime surveys, as well as recorded crime statistics, for a stretch of nearly two decades beginning in 1981. This has cleared the ground for comparative research, yet enormous limitations and problems remain. A large number of factors—structural, economic, cultural, political—can influence the level of crime, yet very few of these could be examined in the present volume. Where there is a multitude of possible influences, it is difficult or impossible to isolate the influence of one particular factor, such as the amount or likelihood of punishment. It is difficult to achieve the statistical power needed to control for a range of factors with a sample of only seven countries. A still more recalcitrant problem is that most available types of analysis demonstrate only an association between events such as changes in the likelihood of punishment, given an offense, and changes in the level of crime. The causal arrow could run from levels of punishment to levels of crime (as assumed by Langan [in this volume]) or else in the opposite direction (as the criminal justice system struggles to cope with rising crime). More likely, the causal arrows could simultaneously run in both directions, and, if so, specification of suitable mathematical models becomes extremely difficult.

Bearing in mind these limitations and difficulties, this essay does not attempt to substantiate any explanation for trends in crime and punishment in Scotland. Instead, it has four more limited aims: the first is to use the England/Scotland comparison as a natural experiment with which to test the Farrington and Langan (1992) hypothesis that changes in the likelihood of sanctions drive crime trends and, more specifically, account for the contrast in the 1980s between rising crime in England and falling crime in the United States. The second aim is to analyze the problems that arise in using comparative research to evaluate the effects of the criminal justice system on the level of crime. The third is to develop hypotheses that might help to explain divergent crime trends in Scotland, as compared with those in England. The final one is to comment on future research strategies that, building on the statistical series begun in this volume, might better address the leading research problems, especially the effects of marginal changes in levels of punishment. The answers to the questions addressed by comparative research in this field are of the highest importance for policy. If Langan (in this volume) is right, then the exceptionally high imprisonment rates in the United States and Russia are effective in reducing crime (although the example of the United States makes this seem more plausible than does the example of Russia). If Langan is wrong, then exceptionally large numbers of people are imprisoned in the United States without any benefit to the public. Because the questions are so important, high levels of rigor should be applied when assessing the results of research.

Section I of the essay briefly reviews the context provided by the Scottish political, legal, and criminal justice systems. Section II sets out the methods used to analyze statistics on crime and punishment in Scotland, in parallel with the analyses conducted for the other six countries. Section III presents the findings on trends in crime and punishment in Scotland, with brief commentary and with comparisons especially with England and Wales. Section IV discusses the findings in relation to the four aims set out above and crystallizes conclusions and recommendations for further research, continuing the tradition started by Farrington and Langan (1992) and developed in this volume.

I. Context

Since 1603, Scotland has been part of a multinational British state, although the threads of integration have been drawn more tightly or loosely at different periods and the form of the political institutions that link Scotland with the other British nations has changed at various times. Throughout the long history of the shifting relationships among the nations within the British Isles, the legal system of Scotland has always remained distinct, as have its educational system and established church. In Scots law, common-law principles have even more influence than in English law; yet, at the same time, Scots law has also been more strongly influenced by a civil and Roman law tradition received from a range of other European countries. Nevertheless, the similarities between Scots and English law are close, and the police and criminal justice systems in the two countries are also organized along broadly similar lines. Scotland is a small country of around 5 million people with its own separate law and criminal justice system, but it maintains a close relationship with England, a large nation that has ten times Scotland's population and economic output.

Scotland has a predominantly adversarial system of criminal justice, although the public prosecutor in Scotland (unlike in England) is a long-established institution, and, partly for that reason, there are considerable inquisitorial elements in pretrial procedure. Although the flow of criminal process can be extremely complex in detail, there are a few leading points that are worth noting in the context of this essay. First, the procurator fiscal, the central element of the public prosecution system, takes most of the key decisions that determine whether complaints will result in criminal proceedings. Overall responsibility for public prosecutions rests with the lord advocate, who is the principal law officer of the Crown in Scotland and a member of the government in power at the time. But the lord advocate deals with prosecution through the procurator fiscal service, which processes all criminal cases and prosecutes criminal cases in the lower courts (sheriff and district).[3] The police and other bodies submit reports of crimes and offenses committed to the procurator fiscal, who then decides whether to dispose of them by prosecution or some other method.

Second, the Scottish system avowedly incorporates a large element of discretion in decision making about prosecution or other disposal of cases. Following Young (1997, p. 69), the Scottish system works on the "principle of opportunity and expediency," in contrast to systems in which the prosecutor must, in theory, proceed in every case if there is sufficient evidence: these are said to work on the "principle of legality." "Generally, there are said to be two grounds on which prosecution decisions are made: whether there is enough evidence to justify a prosecution and whether it is in the public interest to do so" (Young 1997, p. 65).

Third, there has been continuing pressure, over a period of many years, to divert cases from the courts. This development was given particular impetus by the reports of the Thomson Committee (1975) and the Stewart Committee (1983), which advocated that prosecution should be reserved for more serious crimes. It has led, for example, to the introduction of fiscal fines, under which the procurator fiscal makes the offer of a fixed penalty as an alternative to prosecution in court. Diversion to psychiatric, reparation, or mediation schemes and to social work services is also possible, although less widely used.

Fourth, since 1971, Scotland has had a unique system of children's hearings that deals with most complaints against children up to the age of sixteen and may continue to deal with them until they reach the age of eighteen. The main features of this system are that the hearings deal

---

[3] Prosecution in the High Court of Justiciary is conducted for the lord advocate by advocates depute, of which there are twelve.

with a wide range of matters affecting children, whether as victims, accused, or both; they are tribunals of lay members and not courts; they do not decide on questions of guilt, so if the child denies an offense, the matter may have to be referred to a court for such a decision; the central criterion of their decision making is the welfare of the child, so their disposals are never explicitly punitive.[4]

Fifth, Scotland has no national police force; instead, it has eight regional forces (after a series of amalgamations of much larger numbers in the past). Like the prosecution, the police are expected to exercise wide discretion. It has been shown that the police do not record many crimes and offenses that are reported to them and that they exercise considerable discretion in deciding whether to refer cases to the procurator fiscal or take some other course.

These broad points are illustrated in more detail by figure 1, a general flowchart showing numbers passing through each stage of the process in a recent year (1999). It shows, for example, that the police recorded 435,703 crimes (more serious) and 504,450 offenses (less serious) but cleared up 43 percent of the crimes and 96 percent of the offenses.[5] Of the 672,502 crimes and offenses cleared up, only 281,708 (42 percent) were reported to the procurator fiscal, so the police decided to deal with a very large number in other ways. The number of persons proceeded against in court was 52 percent of the number of reports received by the procurator fiscal, and this proportion has been falling in recent years as various avenues of diversion have opened up.[6] For example, the proportion of reports leading to proceedings dropped from 58 percent in 1994 to 52 percent in 1999. The flowchart also shows the many disposals by procurator fiscals that bypass prosecution. For example, the procurator fiscal referred 2,222 cases to the reporter, who is the gatekeeper to the children's hearings, issued 18,709 fiscal warnings, and

---

[4] Bottoms and Dignan (2004) provide a detailed discussion of the children's hearings and contrast their operations and ideology with those of the English youth justice system.

[5] Broadly, they satisfied themselves that they had evidence pointing to the offender. Although there are official criteria for defining a clear-up, there is evidence in England that these have been applied in widely different ways by different police forces. The clear-up rate is high for offenses, as distinct from crimes, because many offenses, e.g., public disorder, only become known to police if the offender is identified.

[6] There may be some problems with counting rules here, since "reports received by the procurator fiscal" are cases, whereas "persons proceeded against" refers to occasions on which a person is proceeded against. Both "cases" and "persons proceeded against" may involve more than one offense, but they may not always correspond, i.e., one case may give rise to more than one set of proceedings.

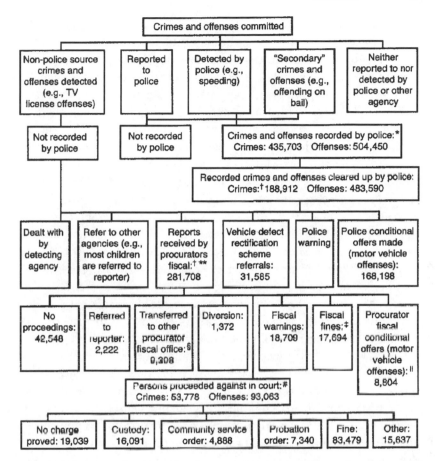

FIG. 1.—Overview of action within the criminal justice system, 1999. Source: Scottish Executive 2000. A number of outcomes may result in subsequent prosecutions or referrals to other agencies, for example, if a condition such as the payment of a fixed penalty is not complied with. For simplicity, these pathways are not shown in the diagram. *Crimes recorded in 1999 may not be cleared up or dealt with until 2000 or later. †A report to the procurator fiscal may involve more than one crime or offense and more than one alleged offender. ‡The total number of reports to the procurator fiscal includes reports on noncriminal matters such as sudden deaths. § Includes cases associated with other cases within the same procurator fiscal's office. ‖Figures relate to offers accepted. #Figures for persons proceeded against count the number of occasions on which a person is proceeded against. **Estimated date.

imposed 17,694 fiscal fines. Among the 146,841 persons who came to court, 87 percent were found guilty on some charge, and 16,091 (11 percent) received a custodial sentence.

There are two forms of trial: solemn procedure and summary procedure. The more serious cases are normally heard by solemn procedure, but the vast majority are heard by summary procedure. The essential difference is that, in summary procedure, the case is heard by a judge sitting alone, whereas in solemn procedure, the verdict is decided by a jury of fifteen citizens while the sentence is determined by the judge. In addition to deciding whether a person should be prosecuted, the procurator fiscal decides which procedure will be used (although there is little or no room for discretion in the case of certain crimes and offenses).

There are three levels of criminal court in Scotland: the District Court, the Sheriff Court, and the High Court of Justiciary. The judges in the district courts are called justices and are lay individuals, except that in Glasgow there are also stipendiary magistrates who are professional lawyers. District courts only hear cases under summary procedure. The sheriff courts have jurisdiction in both summary and solemn criminal cases. The sheriff who presides is an experienced professional lawyer. The High Court of Justiciary deals only with serious cases and ones that raise important points of law that need to be decided.

In the Scottish system, the accused must plead guilty or not guilty before the trial. If the plea is guilty, the court proceeds directly to sentencing and there is no trial. The great majority of cases (98 percent) are heard by summary procedure, and in most of these cases the plea is guilty. Only 1 percent of cases involves a trial in which evidence is led. There is an elaborate procedure, in both summary and solemn cases, through which the court examines the evidence before a trial, and the accused normally decides on a plea at some point during this procedure. It is this pretrial investigatory procedure that is largely inquisitorial in character.

By far the most common sanction is the fine, which was the main penalty imposed on 66 percent of offenders found guilty in 1999 (the latest year for which statistics are presented in this study). As might be expected, the proportion of offenders given fines was lower (43 percent) for those found guilty of "crimes" as distinct from the less serious "offenses" and was lower again (25 percent) for nonsexual crimes of violence. In the same year, 13 percent of all found guilty of crimes or offenses and 24 percent of those found guilty of crimes only were sentenced to custody. Ten percent of all found guilty of crimes or offenses and 13 percent of those found guilty of crimes only were given a caution or admonition, the difference being that a caution may include lodging a sum of money for a period to guarantee good behavior.

Probation is a noncustodial sentence in which the offender is placed under the supervision of a social worker for a period of between six months and three years; before imposing it, the court must obtain a social inquiry report and the judge must explain the conditions attaching to the order to the offender and obtain his or her agreement to them. In 1999, probation was imposed on 6 percent of all found guilty of crimes or offenses and on 11 percent of those found guilty of crimes only.

A community service order is a requirement that the offender will undertake unpaid work in the community under the supervision of a social worker (between forty and 300 hours in total). The offender must consent, and suitable work must be locally available. These orders were imposed as the main penalty on 4 percent of all guilty offenders and on 6 percent of those guilty of crimes in 1999.

Other disposals accounted for the remaining 2 percent of offenders found guilty. These include supervised attendance orders, primarily a mechanism for dealing with fine defaulters by having them undertake activities under the direction of the supervising officer, and compensation orders, which require the offender to pay money to the victim in compensation for the offense. Compensation orders are more commonly used as a secondary punishment, although the number of orders halved over the ten years up to 1999. Nevertheless, compensation orders, including those imposed as a secondary punishment, were 4.2 percent of all convictions and 9.2 percent of convictions for crimes in 1999.

Before 1993, all prisoners sentenced to under eighteen months were released automatically on remission when they had served two-thirds of their sentence. Those sentenced to eighteen months and over became eligible for parole when they had served one-third of their sentence. The decision on whether and when to release them rested with the parole board, an independent body including members having various kinds of background and experience. If refused parole, those sentenced to eighteen months and over would normally be released after serving two-thirds of their sentence. From 1993, all prisoners sentenced to under four years were released automatically on remission at half sentence. Prisoners sentenced to four years or over were eligible for release on parole at half sentence, but if refused parole, they were released at the two-thirds stage.

II. Methods

This analysis aims to marshal the best available evidence on crime trends for selected crimes in Scotland from 1981 onward, using crime surveys and recorded crime statistics. Following the methods agreed upon for this comparative study, an important objective is to make close comparisons among the estimates from crime surveys and police records. This involves adjusting the recorded crime statistics to bring them in line with the coverage of crime surveys: for example, thefts of commercial vehicles and offenses against children are not covered by the Scottish Crime Survey. However, a further aim is to show the unadjusted recorded crime statistics, as these provide an alternative measure and, hence, an alternative trend line.

The analysis aims to estimate the numbers at key stages of the criminal process (convictions, sentences of custody) and the average lengths of custodial sentences. The purpose is to make these estimates closely comparable with the statistics on levels of crime, so that, for example, the number of convictions can be related to the number of offenders. As discussed further below, there are considerable difficulties involved in achieving this, and estimates are inevitably based partly on guesswork. However, these guesses do not have a critical influence (or often any influence) on trends over time, and it will be largely by focusing on time trends that methodological difficulties can be overcome.

It should be clear, even from the summary account of the Scottish criminal justice process, that the path from offense to successful prosecution or some alternative outcome can have many twists, loops, and bends—and usually does. The key stages selected for consideration in this comparative project leave out much of the process, so it cannot be an aim to describe any significant part of the richness and complexity of the system. Rather, the aim is to provide a few key indicators that can be the focus of comparison among countries. Because the main indicators chosen are crime, convictions, and custodial sentences, the results will be relevant mainly to debate about the deterrent effect of criminal process and sanctions. I argue that Scotland is a crucial example in this debate.

A. Definitions of the Six Crimes

Although there have been major changes in the definition of some offenses, these fortunately fall outside the period covered by the present analysis. The most serious remaining problems relate to assault; these make it impossible to provide consistent and reliable statistics for serious as distinct from petty assault. Definitions of each of the six offenses covered are set out below.

1. *Burglary*.   A substantial proportion of all housebreaking (as burglary is known in Scotland) involves commercial premises and cannot therefore be covered by the Scottish Crime Survey. In this essay,

recorded crime statistics are provided for all housebreaking, but an estimate is also given for domestic housebreaking. There was a major definitional revision in 1972, a matter outside the scope of the present analysis; this would need to be considered when looking at longer-term trends in the recorded crime figures on housebreaking.

The crime survey definition: break-in and attempted break-ins to residential property whether or not anything was taken. The recorded crime definition: theft by housebreaking, housebreaking with intent to steal, and attempted housebreaking with intent to steal.

2. *Motor Vehicle Theft.*   These offenses do not include theft from a motor vehicle if there was no attempt to take or drive away the vehicle itself. The Scottish Crime Survey does not cover theft of commercial vehicles, which are a considerable proportion of those shown in the recorded crime statistics.

Crime survey definition: theft of privately owned car, van, motorbike, motor scooter, or moped. Recorded crime definition: theft of motor vehicle and contents including taking and driving away; including attempts.

3. *Robbery.*   This offense is defined essentially similarly in police and victimization survey data. Police data include commercial robberies, but, as robberies necessarily involve individual victims (whether or not acting as employees), most should be reflected in victimization data. However, police data include robberies in which the victim was under sixteen, and victim survey data do not (adjustments made in this analysis take this last difference into account).

Crime survey definition: robbery and attempted robbery. Recorded crime definition: robbery and assaults with intent to rob.

4. *Assault.*   Assault is a common-law offense in Scotland, and there is no significant distinction in law between serious and petty assault. However, recorded crime statistics for many years have shown a separate count for serious assault. An assault is now defined as serious if the victim sustained an injury resulting in detention in hospital as an inpatient or any of the following injuries, whether or not detained in hospital: fractures, concussion, internal injuries, crushing, severe cuts or lacerations, or severe general shock requiring medical treatment. There was a change in this definition in 1990, which, when applied to the 1989 data, reduced the count for serious assaults to 84 percent of the count based on the old definition. Scottish Crime Survey reports have never shown serious assault separately, because the margins of error would be wide (as the crime is relatively uncommon). The main series

of statistics in this essay is for serious and petty assault combined: this overcomes definitional problems in recorded crime statistics and supports comparison with crime survey estimates. A series of recorded crime statistics for serious assault alone for 1980–99 is also shown. For 1980–88, the statistics have been adjusted to deal with the definitional problem.

Crime survey definition (all assault): serious wounding, other wounding, assault with injury, and attempted assault. Recorded crime definitions: serious assault: attempted murder, assault where the victim sustained an injury resulting in detention in hospital as an in-patient or sustained injuries involving fractures, concussion, internal injuries, crushing, severe cuts or lacerations, or severe general shock requiring medical treatment. Petty assault: other assaults.

5. *Rape.*   Because numbers would be too small, crime survey results are not available. The recorded crime definition is rape and assault with intent to rape. It does not include indecent assault.

6. *Homicide.*   The definition (recorded crime statistics only) includes murder, common-law culpable homicide, and statutory culpable homicide. It does not include causing death by dangerous driving, which is known in Scotland as statutory homicide under Sections 1 and 3A of the Road Traffic Act of 1988.

B. Scottish Crime Survey Data

The first crime survey was carried out in Scotland in 1982 as part of the first British Crime Survey. Further surveys have been carried out in 1988, 1993, 1996, and 2000. In each case, the victimization estimates refer to the calendar year prior to the survey. After the first survey in 1982, the Scottish Crime Survey has been carried out independently from the "British" Crime Survey, which, despite the name, covers only England and Wales. Because close comparisons are made between survey and recorded crime statistics, offense definitions must inevitably be different in detail in Scotland. Some other technical differences between the British and Scottish surveys developed in the 1980s, but in the 1990s the surveys have been closely harmonized, although separately managed.

The sample size for each Scottish survey was around 5,000 during the period under review (the survey was radically redesigned with effect from 2004). Because victimization is not common, estimates based on a sample of this size are subject to substantial margins of error, wide enough to make it difficult to discern trends for some offenses. Confidence intervals allowing for the stratified probability design of the sample are shown in Smith (2004) but are not reproduced here.

The 1982 and 1988 crime surveys were conducted only in central and southern Scotland, which currently includes about 86 percent of the total population of Scotland. From 1993 onward, the surveys were extended to the whole of Scotland (with the exception of small islands). The statistics in the present study "inflate" the results of the 1982 and 1988 surveys to produce estimates of crime rates for the whole of Scotland. The method used to inflate these results differs from that used in the original survey reports and is explained in detail in Smith (2004). Survey-based crime rates were calculated by relating the new inflated survey-based estimates of the volume of crime to estimates of the number of households (household crime) or the number of persons aged fifteen and older (personal crime) in the relevant year. The proportion of crimes identified by the survey that were reported to the police is estimated from the published results of the surveys.

C. Police-Recorded Crime

In Scotland, crimes are recorded by the police when they are reported to them. The police may or may not take action with respect to a recorded crime, so the fact that it has been recorded does not imply that any investigation has been launched. Nevertheless, one traditional method of assessing police performance is in terms of the proportion of recorded crimes that are "cleared up," that is, crimes for which the police believe they have identified an offender. This means that the structure of the system imposes pressure on the police to maintain the clear-up rate, and one way of achieving that is to avoid recording crimes that are unlikely to be cleared up. The present findings suggest that a considerable proportion of crimes reported to the police are not recorded by them. This may often be for legitimate reasons (e.g., the police believe there was no offense). Over the period covered by this analysis (1981–99), there was increasing emphasis on assessing police performance, accompanied by the development of much more elaborate measures of performance. Thus, while pressure to improve performance certainly increased, the range of measures available also became more diverse, so that relatively less weight was placed on clear-up rates.

This was the changing background to police-recording practices. At the same time, there was an increase in the technical resources of the police and probably an improvement in crime-recording systems. In the official report on recorded crime in Scotland, it is stated that "both

Fife Constabulary and Lothian and Borders police introduced improved crime recording systems which led to substantial increases in the numbers of crimes they recorded. It is likely that, had the recorded crime figures not been affected by the changes in recording systems, the increases in these two areas would have been more than offset by the substantial decrease in crime recorded in Strathclyde, and the overall crime figures for Scotland would have fallen" (Scottish Executive 2000, sec. 2). There were no important changes in the formal rules governing the recording of crime by the police, except for specific new provisions for recording racially motivated incidents.

It was necessary for the analysis reported here to produce estimates of the volume of recorded crime in each offense category that was comparable to crime covered by the survey. Statistics on the number of crimes recorded by the police in the relevant offense categories (see definitions above) were provided by the Home Department.[7] However, recorded crime statistics include a substantial number of incidents that could not be counted in the crime survey for a variety of reasons. Over the years, the Home Department has collected information from police forces and from other sources, from which reasonable estimates can be made of the proportion of police-recorded offenses that could not be picked up by the crime survey. These were used to "deflate" the police-recorded counts, so as to produce estimates of the number of recorded incidents that are comparable with incidents covered by the survey. For example, the recorded count of housebreaking that is comparable with the survey count does not include break-ins into commercial premises, the comparable count of motor vehicle thefts does not include thefts of commercial vehicles, and the comparable counts of robberies and of assaults do not include incidents where the victim was aged under sixteen. Details of the method of estimation are given in Smith (2004).

D. Average Number of Offenders per Offense

A single offense often involves more than one offender. In order to link statistics on crime incidents with those on convictions, it is necessary to estimate the average number of offenders per offense. This makes it possible, for example, to estimate the probability that a crime survey offense will lead to a conviction. For the four offenses covered by

[7] Statistics provided by the Home Department correspond with the published statistics (Scottish Executive, annual) but make some use of unpublished analyses.

the crime survey (housebreaking, motor vehicle theft, robbery, and assault), the results from three crime surveys (1992, 1995, and 1999) were used to calculate the mean number of offenders per offense from victims' reports. In the case of homicide, counts are published of the numbers of victims and accused, and these have been used to calculate the number of offenders per offense. In the case of rape, no relevant data are published in Scotland, and the estimates used by Farrington and Jolliffe (in this volume) for the number of offenders per offense in England have been arbitrarily applied to Scotland. It is because these estimates are fragile (with the exception of the one for homicide) that they have been held constant over the five years covered. This means that they do not influence trends over time within Scotland. They do, of course, influence the absolute probabilities for Scotland, notably the probability that an offender will be convicted. Not much credence can be given to these probabilities as absolute figures.

E. Convictions and Sentences of Custody

The published statistics in Scotland count the number of persons convicted ("with a charge proved") on a specific court appearance according to the main offense for which they were convicted (Scottish Executive, annual). There are no formal cautions in Scotland (unlike England), so that only convictions stand to be considered. Statistics on the main penalty are included in the same publication.

This highlights another major problem with calculating a conviction probability. The problem is that several crimes or offenses are often dealt with at the same court appearance; whether different crimes or offenses are dealt with at a single appearance or at several appearances may be arbitrary or haphazard. When someone is given several concurrent sentences, is he being convicted once or several times? The answers given to that and other related questions, which appear to be fanciful questions in themselves, nevertheless would have drastic consequences for the calculation of probabilities of conviction. By simply adopting the counting rules used by officialdom, I have swept these questions under the carpet.

F. Length of Sentence

The mean length of custodial sentence for each crime category was provided by the Justice Department. These averages were for persons sentenced during the year in question. For 1981, 1987, 1992, and 1995, the mean sentence length for all housebreaking (not domestic housebreaking) was used. For 1999, the mean sentence length for domestic housebreaking was provided.

Prison sentences for murder may be determinate (a specific number of years) or indeterminate (a life sentence). A very small number of life sentences are handed out for rape. There is a problem in deciding what to count as the length of sentence (as opposed to the time actually served) in the case of an indeterminate life sentence. The general approach adopted was to assume that life sentence prisoners serve the same proportion of their sentence as those given determinate sentences for homicide. Further details of the estimation procedure are given in Smith (2004, app. 1).

G. Average Time Served

The Justice Department does not collect or report data on the time served by prisoners convicted of different offenses. This analysis therefore established as far as possible what proportion of the sentence each category of prisoner was legally expected to serve. The relevant legal rules changed over the period of the study, and these changes are reflected in the estimates. Not all of the data required were available, so at several points the calculations are rough approximations.

In the case of homicide, this same method was used to calculate the average time served by those given determinate sentences. For those serving life sentences, statistics on time served by those released in each relevant year were collected from the annual reports of the Parole Board for Scotland. These were used as an estimate of the time to be served by those starting life sentences in the same year. Fuller details of the calculations are given in Smith (2004, app. 1).

The method used to estimate sentence length and time served for homicide is open to many possible objections. For those sentenced to life imprisonment, the concept of length of sentence is inherently paradoxical, and the only information on time served is historic: it relates to prisoners currently released, and it may not eventually apply to those currently entering prison. It is so difficult to follow the logic of these calculations that it is impossible to imagine that they reflect the real expectations of individuals sentenced by the courts.

III. Findings

As in other developed countries (with the exception of Japan), there was a substantial rise in recorded crime in Scotland during the "golden era" of economic growth and prosperity following the Second World War

(Smith and Young 1999). Between 1950 and 1980, violent crime rose by a factor of 8.7, housebreaking by a factor of 2.9, and theft by a factor of 5.3. These rises were, however, considerably smaller than in neighboring England. In broad terms, these rising trends tended to level off after 1980, whereas in England the rise continued strongly up to 1995 and beyond in the case of violent crime (see Farrington and Jolliffe, in this volume).

For housebreaking and robbery, there was little or no rise in the rate of recorded crime over the period 1981–99 (fig. 2). This was in contrast with the trends in the previous thirty years.

For theft of motor vehicles, there was little net change in recorded crimes over the period from 1981 to 1999, but there was a local rise in 1992, followed by a fall back toward the 1981 level. There were, however, continued rises in the rates of recorded assault, rape, and homicide.[8]

In the case of assault, most of the statistics shown in this report are for all assaults, since crime survey estimates for serious assaults would be based on very low sample sizes and would therefore be unreliable. However, two panels in figure 2 show the trends in recorded serious and petty assaults.[9] Serious assaults accounted for about 12 percent of all assaults both at the beginning and at the end of the period from 1972 to 1999, although this share rose to about 14 percent in the late 1980s and early 1990s. Over the period 1981–99 (on which I focus in this analysis), the rate of increase in serious assaults and all assaults was almost exactly the same, but the upward trend in total assaults was more consistent, whereas the trend in serious assaults was subject to more annual variations. The two trends parted company in the 1980s and 1990s, as serious assault rose more quickly than total assaults, but they came together again in the late 1990s as the upward trend in serious assaults leveled off.

Confidence limits for the survey-based crime rates are fairly wide, so that nearly all changes between one survey and the next are probably nonsignificant (see Smith 2004, tables 1–4). The survey-based rate of housebreaking showed a rise between 1981 and 1987, remained level to

[8] There are around 100 homicides a year recorded in Scotland. Because this number is fairly small, there are considerable random fluctuations from year to year. Only the rates for the selected years are shown in this report, but from a closer study of the annual rates, it is clear that there was in fact a gentle upward trend over the period 1981–99.
[9] The detailed statistics are given in Smith (2004, table 1). Figures for the period 1972–88 have been adjusted to allow for a change in the definition of serious assault from 1989.

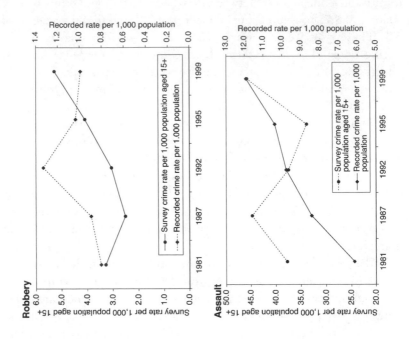

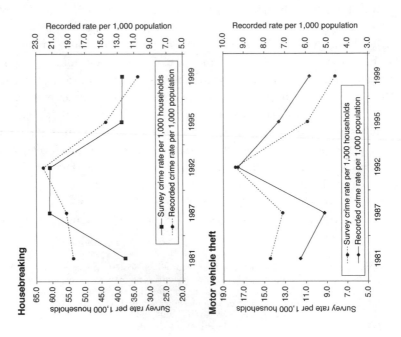

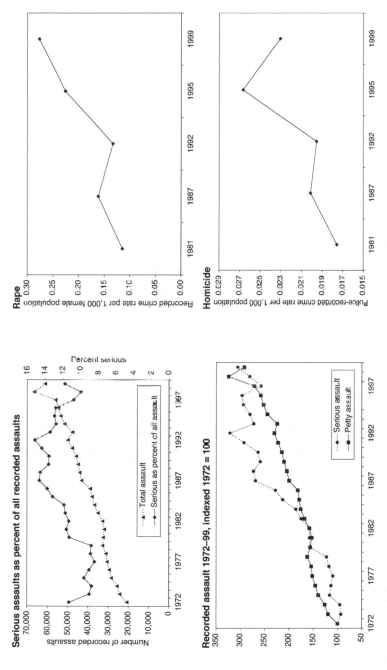

Fig. 2.—Survey and recorded crime rates. Sources: Chambers and Tombs 1984; Kinsey and Anderson 1992; Anderson and Leitch 1996; MVA 1998, 2000, and personal communication (unpublished tabulations from three Scottish crime surveys on the number of offenders as reported by victims); General Register Office for Scotland 2002; Scottish Executive Justice Department, personal communications (statistics on sentence lengths and on recorded crime and convictions in more detail than shown in the *Statistical Bulletin*); Scottish Office, annual statistical bulletins on recorded crime.

1992, then fell back to its 1981 level in 1995 and 1999. This was similar to the trend for recorded housebreaking, except that there was no rise in the recorded count between 1981 and 1987. There was a broad pattern of decline over the five surveys in the rate of motor vehicle theft, although this was interrupted by a rise in 1992. The drop over the whole period between 1981 and 1999 is only on the borderline of statistical significance. There was no significant change in the survey-based rates of robbery or assault. This broadly level trend for survey-based estimates of the four offenses in Scotland contrasts with strong rises in the survey-based estimates for England up to 1995 (see Farrington and Jolliffe, in this volume).

A. Reporting to the Police and Recording by the Police

The proportion of incidents that are reported to the police is estimated from crime survey data, but unfortunately these percentages are based on fairly small numbers. For example, the prevalence of all violent victimization in the 1996 survey was about 5 percent, which means that about 250 survey respondents were victims of violent incidents. Consequently, the number of those who were victims of specific attacks, such as robbery or assault, was still smaller. Although there appear to have been some changes in the rate of reporting for the four crime categories covered, these were not statistically significant. The calculations of the proportions of reported incidents recorded by the police depend on the survey-based estimates of the numbers reported. Although, as figure 3 shows, there appear to have been some sharp changes, it is unsafe to conclude that these really occurred. A particular problem with the findings on theft of motor vehicles is that, in 1992, 1995, and 1999, the police recorded more comparable offenses than are estimated from the survey to have occurred. If we think of these results as probabilities (the probability of reporting a victim survey offense, the probability of police recording a reported offense), then the product of the two probabilities is the probability that a victim survey offense will be recorded by the police. Changes in this overall probability of incidents being recorded were also inconsistent over the period from 1981 to 1999, so that no broad generalization can reasonably be made (see Smith 2004, tables 1–4).

B. Conviction and Custody Rates

Figure 4 reflects the rate at which the criminal justice system produces convictions and puts people behind bars. The numbers of

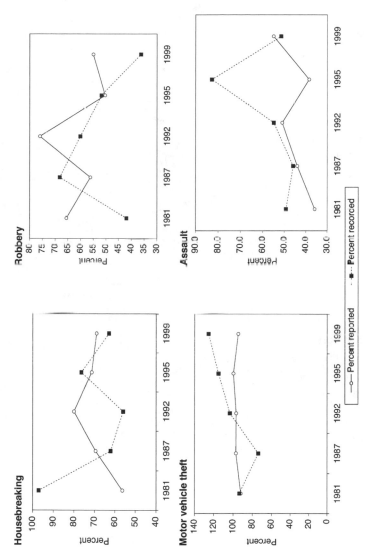

FIG. 3.—Percent reported to police and percent recorded of reported: housebreaking, motor vehicle theft, robbery, and assault. Sources: Chambers and Tombs 1984; Kinsey and Anderson 1992; Anderson and Leitch 1996; MVA 1998, 2000, and personal communication (unpublished tabulations from three Scottish crime surveys on the number of offenders as reported by victims; General Register Office for Scotland 2002; Scottish Executive Justice Department, personal communications (statistics on sentence lengths and on recorded crime and convictions in more detail than shown in the *Statistical Bulletin*); Scottish Office, annual statistical bulletins on recorded crime.

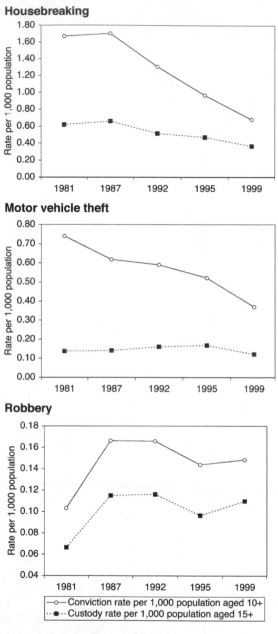

Housebreaking

Motor vehicle theft

Robbery

—o— Conviction rate per 1,000 population aged 10+
··■·· Custody rate per 1,000 population aged 15+

Fɪɢ. 4.—Conviction and custody rates per 1,000 population: housebreaking, motor vehicle theft, robbery, assault, rape, and homicide. Sources: General Register Office for Scotland 2002; Scottish Executive Justice Department (personal communication, statistics of convictions in more detail than shown in the *Statistical Bulletin* and on sentence length); Scottish Office, annual. *Rates for rape only are per 1,000 male population.

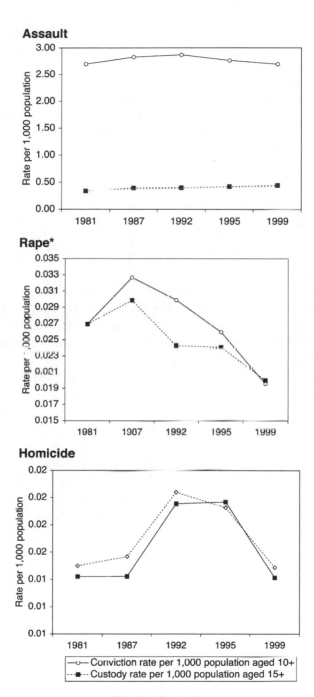

FIG. 4.—*Continued*

convictions and custodial sentences are shown as rates in relation to the population (which in Scotland has almost remained constant), so the statistics are not dependent on crime survey estimates. There was no sustained or substantial rise in convictions for any of the six offenses. For housebreaking and motor vehicle theft, there was a substantial drop in the conviction rate over the period 1981–99, and for rape there was a decline from 1987 after an earlier rise, so that by 1999 the conviction rate was considerably lower than in 1981. The conviction rate for assault remained level, whereas for homicide it rose in 1992, but then fell back by 1999 to its 1981 level. Robbery was something of an exception, as the conviction rate rose sharply between 1981 and 1987 but then leveled off and later fell back. Rates of custody mirrored conviction rates fairly closely, except that the decline in convictions for motor vehicle theft was not accompanied by a decline in custodial sentences.

Figure 5 expresses convictions and custodial sentences as rates in relation to an estimate of the number of offenders. These estimates of the numbers of offenders are fragile, for reasons discussed in Section II, which covers methods. The findings give an indication of the risk that a person committing an offense on a particular occasion would be convicted and given a custodial sentence. For four of the offenses (housebreaking, vehicle theft, robbery, and assault), the risks of conviction were low in absolute terms. They ranged between 2 and 4 percent, which implies that a person would, on average, commit between twenty-five and fifty offenses for each conviction. For homicide, the risks of conviction were high (more than 50 percent at the beginning of the period), and for rape they were middling (17 percent at the beginning of the period). For rape and homicide, most convicted offenders received custody, so that custody and conviction rates were quite similar. For the other offenses, the risks of custody were very low.

The most important finding here is that risks of conviction tended, if anything, to decline between 1981 and 1999. Some pattern of decline is evident for housebreaking, theft of motor vehicle, rape, and homicide, although the declines were not consistent from one survey to the next. In particular, the risk of conviction for rape and homicide increased in 1992 before declining again in 1995 and 1999. For robbery, there was an increase in 1987 in the probability of conviction, followed by a decline and leveling out, so that from 1995 the level was the same as in 1981. For assault, the level of risk remained more or less level over the period (the blip in 1995 is well within the range of sampling error).

For housebreaking, theft of motor vehicle, and assault, changes in the risk of custody were slight. For robbery, there was a short-lived increase in the risk of custody in 1987, which mirrors the increase in risk of conviction at that time. For homicide, the risk of custody declined slightly, mirroring the risk of conviction, with a short-lived increase in 1992. For rape, the risk of custody declined substantially, mirroring the decline in the risk of conviction.

C. Custodial Sentences

Custodial sentences were given in around 80–90 percent of cases where there was a conviction for rape or homicide, and this proportion changed little over the period. Custodial sentences as a proportion of convictions rose substantially for housebreaking and motor vehicle theft over the period, and there were lesser rises for robbery and assault. The broad picture is a decline in the system's production of convictions but a rise in its proportionate use of custody. This rise in the proportionate use of custody (as opposed to fines, community service, etc.) was accompanied by some decline in the proportion of the custodial sentence actually served (fig. 6)

The average length of custodial sentences tended to increase between 1987 and 1999 (fig. 7; these statistics are not available for 1981). These increases were particularly marked for housebreaking and assault as well as for robbery over the period 1987–92. The increased sentences were offset by the decline in proportion of sentence served (fig. 6), so there was little or no increase in average time served, depending on the specific offense (fig. 7).

Average time served (fig. 7) is an average among those sentenced to custody, whereas days served per conviction (fig. 8) relates time served to all of those convicted of the offense, whether they were sentenced to custody or not. Because there was generally an increasing use of custody (fig. 6), days per conviction rose more than average time served. The other line shown in figure 8 is days served per offender, which makes use of the survey-based estimates of the number of persons committing an offense on a specific occasion. Days served per offender increased considerably for housebreaking, motor vehicle theft, and assault, whereas it declined considerably for robbery. It zigzagged for rape and homicide.

IV. Implications

The statistics presented in this essay are fragile in a number of ways. First, police recording practices may have changed in unquantifiable

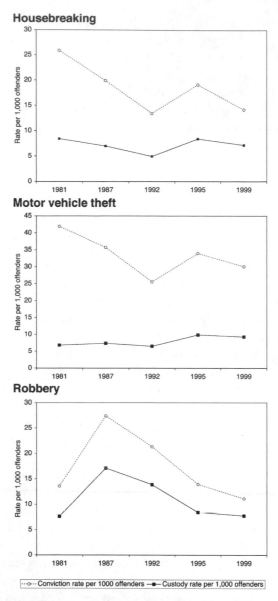

FIG. 5.—Conviction and custody rates per 1,000 offenders: housebreaking, motor vehicle theft, robbery, assault, rape, and homicide. Sources: Chambers and Tombs 1984; Kinsey and Anderson 1992; Anderson and Leitch 1996; MVA 1998, 2000, personal communication; General Register Office for Scotland 2002; Parole Board for Scotland, annual reports; Scottish Executive Justice Department, personal communication (statistics on sentence lengths and on recorded crime and convictions in more detail than shown in the *Statistical Bulletin*); Scottish Office, annual statistical bulletins on recorded crime and court proceedings.

Assault

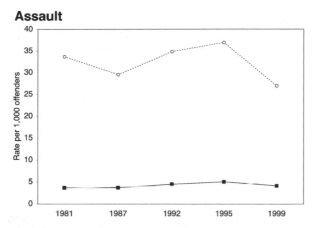

Rape

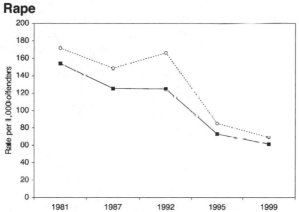

Homicide

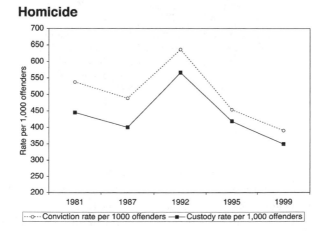

····o···· Conviction rate per 1000 offenders —■— Custody rate per 1,000 offenders

FIG. 5.—*Continued*

109

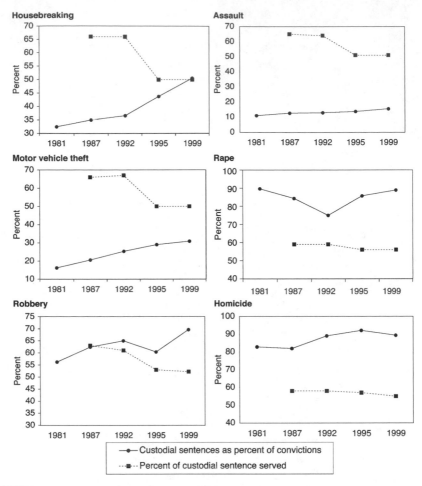

Fig. 6.—Custody as percent of convictions and percent of custodial sentence served: housebreaking, motor vehicle theft, robbery, assault, rape, and homicide. Sources: Parole Board for Scotland, annual reports; Scottish Executive Justice Department, personal communication (statistics of convictions in more detail than shown in the *Statistical Bulletin* and on sentence length); Scottish Office, annual *Statistical Bulletin: Criminal Justice Series: Recorded Crime in Scotland*.

ways, and there has probably been a tendency for the police to record an increasing proportion of crimes reported to them. Second, sampling errors associated with survey-based estimates of crime rates are large, and the error is increased by the need to adjust the estimates from the 1982 and 1988 surveys because they covered only central and southern Scotland. Third, estimates of the number of offenders per offense are unreliable, and there is no good information about any changes over

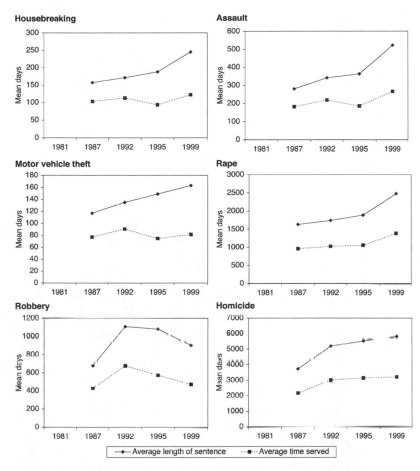

Fɪɢ. 7.—Average sentence length and average time served: housebreaking, motor vehicle theft, robbery, assault, rape, and homicide. Sources: Parole Board for Scotland, annual; Scottish Executive Justice Department, personal communication (statistics of convictions in more detail than shown in the *Statistical Bulletin* and on sentence length).

time in this statistic. Fourth, the calculations of time served for all offenses and for sentence length, in the case of homicide, involve a number of dubious assumptions and approximations. Finally, serious conceptual problems mean it is often not clear what is being counted. For example, statistics on convictions in Scotland count one offense per case even though several offenses may be adjudicated. In law, the offender may have been "caught" and "punished" with respect to other offenses decided at the same appearance, but these are not counted as "convictions" in the statistics. However, any punishment with respect

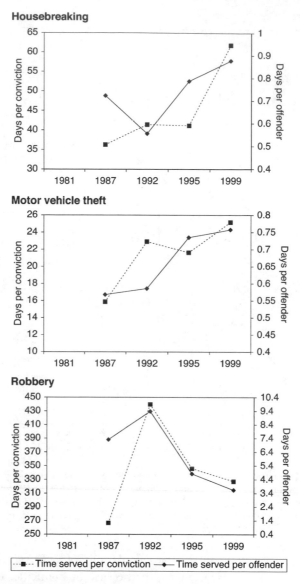

Fig. 8.—Time served per conviction and per offender: housebreaking, motor vehicle theft, robbery, assault, rape, and homicide. Sources: Chambers and Tombs 1984; Kinsey and Anderson 1992; Anderson and Leitch 1996; MVA 1998, 2000, and personal communication (unpublished tabulations from three Scottish crime surveys on the number of offenders as reported by victims); General Register Office for Scotland 2002; Parole Board for Scotland, annual reports; Scottish Executive Justice Department personal communication (statistics on sentence lengths and on recorded crime and convictions in more detail than shown in the *Statistical Bulletin*); Scottish Office, annual statistical bulletins on recorded crime and court proceedings.

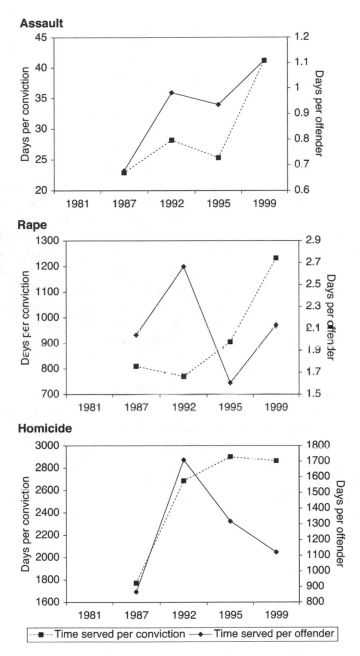

FIG. 8.—*Continued*

to these secondary offenses is likely to be concurrent and subsumed under the punishment for the main offense, so it is unclear whether the offender has been caught or punished with respect to these secondary offenses in any way that makes an impact, especially if he or she admitted to them voluntarily to avoid the possibility of future prosecution.

A. Testing the Farrington and Langan Hypothesis

Bearing in mind these difficulties, a few very simple conclusions can be drawn from the findings. First, the substantial rises in crime in Scotland during the golden era between 1950 and 1973 tended to level off after 1980, although this did not apply to the most serious crimes of rape and homicide. Second, there was no sustained or substantial rise in the production of convictions for any of the six offenses covered. Instead, the chance that an offender would be caught and punished tended to decline over the period 1981–99, with only minor and short-term exceptions. In broad terms, therefore, rising crime leveled off in Scotland, even though the system was becoming less effective at catching and punishing offenders. At the same time, Scottish judges tended to make increasing use of custodial sentences over the period, and there was some increase in the average lengths of custodial sentences, partly compensated for by a decline in the proportion of the sentence actually served.

From these findings, it could be argued that an increase in the severity of sentences, and not in the probability of conviction, caused crime to level off. This would be the exact opposite of the argument of Bentham and other early deterrence theorists. It would, however, be an implausible argument for those offenses (housebreaking, vehicle theft, robbery, and assault) for which only a minority of offenders are given custodial sentences in any case. Instead, the findings are wholly consistent with the theory that the leveling off of crime increases in Scotland had no connection with the effectiveness or punitiveness of the criminal justice system.

The hypothesis originally proposed by Farrington and Langan (1992) was that rising crime in England in the 1980s could be explained by the declining effectiveness of the system in catching and punishing offenders, whereas falling crime in the United States could be explained by increasing effectiveness of the criminal justice system and, hence, increased deterrence and incapacitation of offenders.

The comparison between England and Scotland constitutes a critical test of this hypothesis, since crime leveled off in Scotland some fifteen years earlier than in England. If changes in the likelihood of conviction, punishment, and imprisonment, given an offense, are a major factor driving changes in crime rates, then we should find that the earlier leveling off of crime in Scotland was accompanied by a rise in the probability of conviction and punishment, in contrast to an opposite trend in England. This prediction from the hypothesis is not confirmed.

Instead, crime leveled off in Scotland as the system became less effective at catching and punishing offenders. This comparison between trends in England and Scotland constitutes rather convincing evidence because the two countries are closely similar in many ways, forming two parts of a multinational state. If the hypothesis is that in modern societies, increases in the probability of punishment, or more generally in the effectiveness of the criminal justice system, are needed to reverse an upward trend in crime, then this can be disproved by a single example (although there may be other examples as well). The example of Scotland in the 1980s and 1990s shows that it is possible to have "less crime without more punishment" (Smith 1999).

B. Problems of Comparative Research

Although this single comparison can generate some insight, there remain huge problems in using comparative research to assess the deterrent effects of the criminal justice system. Generating the statistics needed to make valid comparisons between countries is very difficult and can only be done for the limited number of countries that have a time series of crime survey results. At present, it would therefore be difficult to extend the comparisons beyond the seven countries covered by this volume. Even within these countries, there are changes in legal definitions and counting rules that will make it difficult to extend the time series over the next ten years (e.g., in England). Although a strong form of the deterrence hypothesis, as stated above, can be tested by making suitable comparisons between pairs of countries, it would be much more useful to evaluate the effects of catching and punishing more offenders in comparison with the effects of other policies and social changes. This would allow us to assess the effects of increasing punitiveness compared with those of alternative policies. To do that we need a multivariate design, which would simultaneously evaluate the effects of a range of variables, including the probability of conviction and punishment, on the level of crime. It is difficult to find the statistical elbow room to carry out such an analysis, because comparable data can be generated for such a small number of countries. There are also formidable problems, of course, in generating comparable data on the other explanatory variables that need to be included.

A still more challenging problem is that of establishing the direction of causation. There may be reasons for thinking that if more offenders are caught and punished, crime will thereby be reduced, although as argued by Nagin (1998) and by von Hirsch et al. (1999), these are not self-evidently true. However, there are reasons for thinking that changes in the level of crime will lead to changes in the effectiveness of the system in catching and punishing offenders—and these can hardly be gainsaid. In Japan, recorded crime remained level or declined between 1950 and 2000 (Hamai 2001), and the number of police and court personnel also remained fairly steady, so that the resources that could be devoted to each recorded crime remained roughly constant.

In England, recorded crime increased tenfold over the same period, and some serious crimes such as robbery and burglary increased by much larger factors still, whereas the number of police and court personnel increased only slightly. Consequently, the resources available to deal with each recorded crime in England declined dramatically, whereas these remained constant in Japan.

Let us suppose that, from the early 1980s, increasing crime in England and declining crime in the United States were in both cases caused by societal changes unconnected with criminal justice. For example, the continuing increase in England might have been caused by changes in the family or increased opportunities for theft; the decline in the United States might have been caused by changes in drug markets and strengthened informal controls. In England, rising crime would inevitably lead to declining effectiveness of the criminal justice system in catching and punishing offenders because resources would be increasingly stretched as the volume of crime increased. In the United States, by contrast, as crime declined, the system would become more effective at catching and punishing criminals because increasing resources would be available to deal with each recorded crime. Thus the mechanisms that link changes in the level of crime with changes in the effectiveness of the criminal justice system are simple and powerful when we consider the causal arrow pointing from crime levels toward criminal justice.

By contrast, the mechanisms that may provide linkage in the opposite direction, running from changes in criminal justice to changes in crime levels, are far more obscure. As long as they remain in prison, convicted criminals are prevented from offending in society at large, but it is very hard to estimate how much crime is actually prevented through incapacitation in this way (because we do not know how much crime prisoners would have committed had they been at large or whether other offenders have stepped into their shoes). Increases in the effectiveness of the criminal justice system might have a deterrent effect, but this is so only if they are noticed and they are large enough to influence potential offenders. It is not obvious that changes within the range of what is possible in a modern liberal democracy are noticeable or influential.

It seems unlikely that comparison of the statistics compiled in this volume will provide, on its own, convincing evidence about the influences running in both directions between levels of crime and punishment. This is because many different statistical models could be proposed to account for the patterns of association, and it may not be possible to choose among them without further information of a different kind. Crucially, the nature of the model would vary depending on whether or not it is assumed that crime and punishment simultaneously influence each other. To put this in econometric terms, the "specification" of the model must depend on assumptions or decisions arising outside the pattern of associations that we are seeking to explain.

One way of dealing with this problem is to find a situation where it is certain that a change in either the amount of crime or the amount of punishment has been brought about by some independent cause. This was the approach adopted by Levitt (1996), who studied changes in levels of crime in states where the amount of punishment was suddenly reduced because of prison overcrowding legislation.

A different way forward is to go inside the "black box" that connects crime and punishment and to study the detailed mechanisms. As described by Nagin (1998), there is an increasing body of research that describes the influence of the likelihood and severity of punishment on offenders' perceptions of risks. However, there seems to be little or no research on the influence of the level of crime on the capacity of the system to respond. Once these linkages are better understood, there will be a firmer basis for specifying statistical models to explain the patterns of association between trends in crime and punishment.

C. Explaining Divergent Trends in Scotland

Because England and Scotland are similar in many ways and both belong to the same multinational state, it seems surprising that crime trends in the two countries diverged quite widely after 1980. At present, it is quite impossible to explain why crime rates leveled off in Scotland some fifteen years earlier than in England. Although detailed information is not presented here, it is likely that social and economic conditions and trends were quite similar in the two countries over this period, and any differences are ones that might be expected to lead to higher crime rates in Scotland. For example, absolute levels of unemployment, poverty, and income inequality were as high in Scotland as in England, and changes in these indices of deprivation were also similar in the two countries. Scotland is known to have high rates of alcohol and drug abuse, which are closely related to crime, and rates of use of illegal drugs probably rose as fast in Scotland as in England over the period from 1980. A possible cause of rising crime in the postwar period is changes in family functioning associated with rising rates of family breakup, single parenthood, and families with stepparents. However, these changes in family structures proceeded at about the same rate in Scotland as in England.

There is good evidence that crime trends are associated with the effectiveness of social controls (Smith 1995; Garland 2001). It is possible that informal social controls survived postwar social and economic transformations better in Scotland than in England. This could be associated with Scotland's distinctive political culture, which emphasizes civic pride and communal values more than in England. This, in turn, is associated with a stronger emphasis on social welfare policy in Scotland and with higher public spending—subsidized by the English taxpayer—on health, education, and social services. "In Scotland," according to McAra (1999, p. 378), "there has been a more democratic tradition within dominant institutions ... particularly with regard to education and the church. This has been accompanied by a strong socialist tradition, especially at local government level. ... These factors could be said to have contributed to the construction of a civic culture which valorizes community, public provision of welfare, and mutual support ... and which intermittently becomes linked to a broader sense of Scottish identity."

The communitarian and welfarist theme carries over into Scottish criminal justice policy. Although there are no simple or stark contrasts between Scottish and English policy and practice in the criminal justice arena, the predominant rationale of the Scottish system is rehabilitative and reintegrative. Since 1971, the system of youth justice in Scotland has been substantially different from that in England, although in recent years each system has adopted ideas and practices from the other. In its ideology, the Scottish system emphasizes the welfare of the child, avoids punishment and stigmatization, aims to divert young people from formal criminal process, and involves members of the public rather than professionals in decision making. However, there has always been a punitive strand in Scottish policy, and the need to protect the public has always been recognized. This strand has continued in the context of the children's hearing system, as shown by the fact that proportionately as many children are held in secure accommodation in Scotland as in England. Nevertheless, it is possible that the Scottish system, through avoiding stigmatizing young people for longer, has helped them to avoid long-term criminal careers, where the English system might not have done. However, this remains speculative and unproven, because we know too little about what the children's hearing system actually delivers to young offenders in Scotland in comparison to what is delivered in England.

At a broader level of analysis, various commentators have argued that penal systems have been undergoing a process of transformation over the past twenty to thirty years, although they do not agree as to the nature of these changes. Feeley and Simon (1994) have emphasized a move toward managing risks rather than changing offenders, Garland (1996) has proposed a bifurcation between punitive and preventive strategies, and Bottoms (1994) has argued that there is increasing focus on individual rights and just deserts in punishment. It can be argued that Scottish civic culture has tended to resist and postpone such changes. This might help to explain why the Scottish system did not become more effective in catching and punishing offenders over the period between 1981 and 1999. However, it seems extremely difficult to move from such broad and general accounts of the transformation of penal systems to an explanation for different trends in crime and punishment in Scotland and England.

D. Future Research Strategies

Progress can best be made by pursuing a combination of research strategies. The analyses presented in this volume can be used as the core of an expanding set of comparative studies based on rigorously comparable measures and using statistical models to track the relationships between crime and punishment. The problem of limited elbow room for analysis can be tackled by increasing the number of data points (years for which data are available) and the number of countries included. A wide range of variables describing social and economic change should gradually be included in the analyses. At the same time, an understanding of the mechanisms linking crime and punishment should be pursued through detailed and concrete studies of, for example, offenders' perceptions of risks and of the responses of the police and the courts to changing workloads. Statistical models specified to describe the comparative statistics should be based on plausible assumptions about these mechanisms.

A different but complementary approach, suggested by Farrington and Langan's (1992) comparison between England and the United States or the present comparison between Scotland and England, is to look for natural experiments that provide an opportunity for evaluating a theory. Perhaps this approach will become more valuable if a case study approach is used to study a small number of cases in much greater depth.

REFERENCES

Anderson, Simon, and Susan Leitch. 1996. *Main Findings from the 1993 Scottish Crime Survey*. Edinburgh: Scottish Office Central Research Unit.

Bottoms, Anthony E. 1994. "The Philosophy and Politics of Punishment and Sentencing." In *The Politics of Sentencing Reform*, edited by C. Clarkson and R. Morgan. Oxford: Oxford University Press.

Bottoms, Anthony E., and James Dignan. 2004. "Youth Justice in Great Britain." In *Youth Crime and Youth Justice: Comparative and Cross-National Perspectives*, edited by Michael Tonry and Anthony N. Doob. Vol. 31 of *Crime and Justice: A Review of Research*, edited by Michael Tonry. Chicago: University of Chicago Press.

Chambers, Gerald, and Jacqueline Tombs, eds. 1984. *The British Crime Survey Scotland*. Edinburgh: H.M. Stationery Office, Scottish Office Central Research Unit.

Farrington, David P., and Patrick. A. Langan. 1992. "Changes in Crime and Punishment in England and America in the 1980s." *Justice Quarterly* 9:5–46.

Feeley, Malcolm, and Jonathan Simon. 1994. "Actuarial Justice: The Emerging New Criminal Law." In *The Futures of Criminology*, edited by David Nelken. London: Sage.

Garland, David. 1996. "The Limits of the Sovereign State: Strategies of Crime Control in Contemporary Society." *British Journal of Criminology* 36:445–71.

———. 2001. *The Culture of Control: Crime and Social Order in Contemporary Society*. Oxford: Oxford University Press.

General Register Office for Scotland. 2002. Historic population estimates. Available at http://www.gro-scotland.gov.uk/grosweb.nsf/pages/popest.

Hamai, Koichi. 2001. "Prison Population in Japan Stable for 30 Years." In *Penal Reform in Overcrowded Times*, edited by Michael Tonry. Oxford: Oxford University Press.

Kinsey, Richard, and Simon Anderson. 1992. *Crime and the Quality of Life: Public Perceptions and Experiences of Crime in Scotland; Findings from the 1988 British Crime Survey.* Edinburgh: Scottish Office Central Research Unit.

Levitt, Stephen D. 1996. "The Effect of Prison Population Size on Crime Rates: Evidence from Prison Overcrowding Litigation." *Quarterly Journal of Economics* 111:319–51.

McAra, Lesley. 1999. "The Politics of Penality: An Overview of the Development of Penal Policy in Scotland." In *Criminal Justice in Scotland*, edited by Peter Duff and Neil Hutton. Aldershot: Dartmouth.

MVA. 1998. *Main Findings from the 1996 Scottish Crime Survey.* Edinburgh: Scottish Office Central Research Unit.

———. 2000. *The 2000 Scottish Crime Survey: First Results.* Edinburgh: Scottish Executive Central Research Unit.

Nagin, Daniel S. 1998. "Criminal Deterrence Research at the Outset of the Twenty-First Century." In *Crime and Justice: A Review of Research*, vol. 23, edited by Michael Tonry. Chicago: University of Chicago Press.

Parole Board for Scotland. Annual. "Report." Edinburgh: Stationery Office.

Scottish Executive. Annual. *Criminal Proceedings in Scottish Courts.* Edinburgh: Scottish Executive.

———. 2000. *Criminal Proceedings in Scottish Courts, 1999.* Edinburgh: Scottish Executive.

Scottish Office. Annual. *Statistical Bulletin: Criminal Justice Series: Recorded Crime in Scotland.* Edinburgh: Scottish Office (Scottish Executive from 1998).

Smith, David J. 1995. "Youth Crime and Conduct Disorders: Time Trends, Patterns, and Causal Explanations." In *Psychosocial Disorders in Young People: Time Trends and Their Causes*, edited by Michael Rutter and David J. Smith. Chichester: Wiley.

———. 1999. "Less Crime without More Punishment." *Edinburgh Law Review* 3:294–316.

———. 2004. "Trends in Crime and Punishment in Scotland." In *Cross-National Studies in Crime and Justice*, edited by David P. Farrington, Patrick A. Langan, and Michael H. Tonry. Washington, D.C.: U.S. Department of Justice, Bureau of Justice Statistics.

Smith, David. J., and Peter J. Young. 1999. "Crime Trends in Scotland since 1950." In *Criminal Justice in Scotland*, edited by Peter Duff and Neil Hutton. Aldershot: Dartmouth.

Stewart Committee. 1983. *Keeping Offenders out of Court: Further Alternatives to Prosecution.* Cmnd 8958. Edinburgh: H.M. Stationery Office.

Thomson Committee. 1975. *Criminal Procedure in Scotland: Second Report by the Committee Appointed by the Secretary of State for Scotland and the Lord Advocate.* Cmnd 6218. Edinburgh: H.M. Stationery Office.

Von Hirsch, Andrew, Anthony E. Bottoms, Elizabeth Burney, and Per-Olof Wikström. 1999. *Criminal Deterrence and Sentence Severity: An Analysis of Recent Research.* Oxford: Hart.

Young, Peter. J. 1997. *Crime and Criminal Justice in Scotland.* Edinburgh: Stationery Office.

Patrick A. Langan

Crime and Punishment in the United States, 1981–1999

ABSTRACT

Periods of variation in criminal punishment provide natural opportunities to investigate effects on crime. In general, punishment severity (sentence length and time served, for example) did not vary over the period investigated in this study, while punishment risk did: most notably, both arrest and conviction rates rose. As the risk of legal punishment rose, crime fell, which suggests, but by no means proves, a causal connection. It is impossible to identify from existing national data the specific policies and practices that produced rising arrest and conviction rates in the United States.

In 1999, police statistics recorded fewer than 16,000 homicides in the United States. Government statisticians had to go back to the 1960s to find a year with fewer homicides. Also in 1999, national crime victimization surveys registered record lows for robbery (800,000), serious assault (1.5 million), and home burglaries (3.7 million). Going all the way back to the survey's first year (1973), statisticians could find no safer time. What caused the remarkable drop in crime in America? No one really knows for sure, and no one predicted it, but experts are pointing to a variety of likely causes, including the criminal justice system itself.

A number of researchers attribute some of the drop to innovations in policing, such as increased directed patrols of street corners with high crime rates, proactive targeted arrests of career criminals, proactive drunk driving arrests, and problem-oriented policing (Eck and Maguire 2000; Sherman and Eck 2002).

Patrick A. Langan is senior statistician, Bureau of Justice Statistics, U.S. Department of Justice. I thank Matthew Durose and Erica Schmitt for their assistance.

Unprecedented prison population growth in America is widely credited with playing a role (Reiss and Roth 1993; Marvell and Moody 1997; Rosenfeld 2000). In theory, rising imprisonment rates reduce crime two ways: through prisons' deterrent effect, crimes are not committed because would-be offenders fear being caught and put in prison; through their incapacitative effect, growing numbers of convicted criminals are physically prevented from committing new crimes (outside of prison).

And what accounts for growing imprisonment in the United States since the early 1970s? Presumably reflecting the greater emphasis that government officials began placing on deterrence and incapacitation as goals in the administration of justice, numerous changes occurred throughout the justice system, all leading to rapid expansion of the prison population. Among them were increases in the arrest rate (Langan 1991), increases in the conviction rate for those arrested (Langan 1991), increases in the imprisonment rate for those convicted (Langan 1991; Cohen and Canela-Cacho 1994), and increases in prison-return rates for those released prisoners who violated parole (Messinger et al. 1988, p. 5). Unfortunately, policies that produced these increases are not well established in the research literature. Cohen and Canela-Cacho (1994) attribute some of the increase in the imprisonment rate (for those convicted) to sentencing guidelines and mandatory minimum prison terms. Numerous other possible contributors remain unexamined. Messinger et al. (1988, p. 6) attribute some of the increase in parole revocation rates to more frequent drug testing, a change that reflects the growing importance that officials assign to surveillance as a critical parole function. These researchers lack data on numerous other possible contributors they acknowledge may account for rising revocation rates: revised guidelines issued by the parole board regarding which parole violations it wants to be informed of, parole officers' reporting more violations to the board, and closer ties between parole officials and the police.

This essay further investigates the effect of the criminal justice system on the drop in crime. Undoubtedly factors outside the control of the justice system—unemployment, poverty, demographic characteristics of the population, and so forth—also affect crime, but they are beyond the scope of this analysis.

This analysis is largely an update of the 1998 study *Crime and Justice in the United States and in England and Wales, 1981–96* published by the Bureau of Justice Statistics (BJS) (Langan and Farrington 1998). The update includes U.S. crime rates beyond 1996, and adds an additional year of punishment data (for 1996). This analysis is also a condensed version of a fuller one by the author (Langan 2004) titled "United States," published by BJS in *Cross-National Studies in Crime and Justice* (Farrington, Langan, and Tonry 2004). This essay reports the key findings from the fuller version and, due to space limitations, leaves out numerous graphs, tables, and methodological details. It also leaves out many of the findings on rape because of data quality concerns.

Section I describes the United States and its criminal justice system. Section II documents the drop in U.S. crime over the study period 1981–99. Section III describes the flow of cases across America's criminal justice system over much of the period with two sets of measures: risk and severity of legal punishment. Findings indicate that punishment severity did not generally vary over the period, while punishment risk did. Connections between punishment trends and crime rates are investigated in Section IV. Results indicated that, as the risk of criminal punishment rose in the United States, crime fell. The effect on crime of changing punishment severity could not be investigated adequately because too few instances of rising or falling severity characterized the period. In those relatively few instances where severity rose, crime generally fell; in those where severity fell, crime generally rose. Section V discusses results. Section VI highlights obstacles to analyses of this kind and offers ideas for future research.

I. America's Criminal Justice System

Official governance in the United States is spread across three levels: a national (or federal) government, fifty state governments, and thousands of local governments. The 1787 Constitution of the United States limits the role of the federal government and grants to the states all powers it does not delegate to the national government.

America's form of representative democracy is unusual among Western countries in having large numbers of publicly elected officials in the executive and legislative branches at all three levels, and large numbers of popularly elected judges in the judicial branch at the state level. By contrast, in many of the world's representative democracies, the only popularly elected offices are those in the national legislature.

This feature of American democracy—vast numbers of popularly elected officials at all levels—makes the American criminal justice system unique. At the same time, in matters of structure, organization, and practice, the American system has much in common with many others around the world.

A. The System's Uniqueness

Owing to federalism—the division of authority between the national government and the state governments—no one level of government has overall responsibility for justice administration in the United States. Through the awarding of grants and other incentives, the federal government encourages states and localities to adopt particular policies and standards. But the federal government's authority is constitutionally limited. For example, it cannot stop states from releasing prisoners before they serve 85 percent of their sentence, but it can (and does) offer them money to keep prisoners in at least that long.

While the federal government has no overall responsibility for justice administration, through the U.S. Supreme Court it does have ultimate responsibility for safeguarding rights and liberties guaranteed under the U.S. Constitution. The Supreme Court's rulings in that regard—for example, that persons arrested by the police must be informed of certain rights—are binding across the country. Criminal justice agencies at all levels must abide by its decisions. Each state has its own constitution, and state court rulings establish additional procedural protections applicable to criminal cases in that state.

The types of crimes that are the subject of this analysis—called "felonies," widely defined as crimes punishable by confinement in a state or federal prison—are violations of the laws of the fifty states and the federal government. Each of these fifty-one jurisdictions has its own criminal justice system for handling felonies: its own laws and lawmakers, police, prosecutors and public defenders, courts and judges, prisons and jails, probation and parole officials, and coroners and medical examiners, among others.

Collectively, the fifty state criminal justice systems dwarf the federal system in workload, expenditures, and personnel. State courts account for about 95 percent of the nation's roughly 1 million felony convictions each year; federal courts, a mere 5 percent. Put another way, the state court in just one county in the United States—Los Angeles County, California—convicts about as many people of a felony each year as do all ninety-four of the nation's federal district courts combined. Moreover, of the nation's approximately 2 million justice system officials (criminal and civil), 59 percent are local, 32 percent are state, and only 9 percent are federal government employees (Gifford 2002, table 5).

While thousands of localities across the nation also have their own laws and justice officials, local government does not have original jurisdiction over felonies. That is, local government cannot pass laws declaring a crime to be a felony; only state and federal governments can do that. Accordingly, because the focus here is on serious crimes, the study talks about fifty-one criminal justice systems in the United States—the fifty state systems plus the federal one—rather than thousands of them. Yet crime control in the United States is often (accurately) described as mostly a state and local matter. That is because the hundreds of thousands of criminal justice officials at the local level—employees of such agencies as the city or county police department, the sheriff's office, the coroner's office, the prosecutor's office, the county court, and the local jail—are authorized to enforce state felony laws.

There is another important reason why crime control in America is overwhelmingly a state and local matter. To an extent perhaps unparalleled in the world, the people locally elect officials of America's criminal justice system. In forty-seven states, the felony prosecutor in the county where a person lives is someone the people of that county elected into office (DeFrances 2002, p. 11). In thirty-nine states, each felony court judge in the county where a person resides is also someone the voters of that county elected (Rottman et al. 2000). To varying degrees and with substantial variations among states, other county officials are locally elected as well: the coroner, sheriff, probate court judge, traffic court judge, justice of the peace, public defender, and even the clerk of the court, among others (U.S. Department of Commerce 1995). Appellate court judges in thirty-nine states and attorneys general in forty-three states are also voted into office, though in statewide and circuit-wide popular elections, not local ones (Rottman et al. 2000).

This feature of America's criminal justice system—thousands of popularly elected officials—sets it apart from perhaps any other in the world. To illustrate, with minor exceptions (prosecutors and judges in eighteen of Switzerland's thirty-four cantons), when Australians, Canadians, Scots, Swedes, Swiss, the English, and the Dutch go to vote, they do not find on their ballots any candidates for sheriff, prosecutor, judge, coroner, court clerk, or public defender.

America's justice system critics and defenders alike believe this feature makes a difference. Critics look at the American system and complain that it is overpoliticized, meaning run by too many elected officials whose uppermost concern is being reelected. American officials take a tough stance on crime, say the critics, merely because that is what they think American public opinion favors.

The problem, charge the critics, is that research on public opinion attitudes and information shows that the public often bases its views on sensational and atypical cases and on beliefs that punishments are less severe than they really are (Roberts et al. 2003). Franklin Zimring and colleagues accordingly argue that means be developed—they favor politically insulated sentencing commissions—to buffer punishment policies from the influence of short-term emotionalism (Zimring, Hawkins, and Kamin 2001). Michael Tonry (2004) argues that other Western countries have professionalized their justice systems, making most judges and all prosecutors career civil servants, largely in order to insulate criminal prosecutions from the influence of public opinion, and urges that American jurisdictions do likewise.

Defenders of the American approach, on the other hand, look at justice systems outside the United States and see them as under-politicized and undemocratic. One such defender, political scientist James Q. Wilson, came to that conclusion when he compared criminal punishment in the United States to that in a country—England—where scarcely any justice officials are popularly elected; none, in fact, if Parliament is excluded (Wilson 1997). According to Wilson, while deeply upset English citizens watched as crime rates soared in the 1980s, their nonelected officials were preoccupied with reducing the English prison population, whereas, in America, elected justice officials had just the opposite reaction to soaring crime and an alarmed citizenry: "Throughout the 1970s and 1980s, American prison populations grew rapidly" (Wilson 1997, p. 7). Wilson attributed the difference in response to "the wider gap between public opinion and official governance in England than in America" (Wilson 1997, p. 7).

B. Similarities with Other Systems

Countless features of America's fifty-one criminal justice systems—bail release and appellate courts, for example—are widespread, if not universal. These same features are often (not always) common in other countries as well, as comparisons with seven other countries reveal:

Australia, Canada, England, the Netherlands, Scotland, Sweden, and Switzerland.

1. *Bail Release.* In the United States, felony suspects taken into police custody are often released on bail before their trial date. Australia, Canada, England, Scotland, and Switzerland (but not the Netherlands or Sweden) also have bail release.

2. *Prosecution as a Separate Function from Police.* In all eight countries, prosecution is performed by an agency separate from the police (though until recently in England, police-employed lawyers initiated prosecutions). The separation of the two functions began in America in the seventeenth century (Jacoby 1997). Separation of these functions came much later in England (in 1986). The major exception in the United States is federal prosecution. The FBI and various other federal police belong to the same agency as federal prosecutors, the U.S. Department of Justice.

3. *Age of Adulthood.* Depending on the circumstances, an adult charged in the United States with a serious crime can be prosecuted in a state court or a federal court. Age of adulthood is eighteen in the federal system and in most states, and also in Canada, England, the Netherlands, and Switzerland. In a small number of states, it is seventeen; and in a few, sixteen. Australia is similar: age eighteen in some states and territories; seventeen in others.

4. *Juvenile Courts.* Scotland and Sweden do not have juvenile courts; the other countries mentioned do. All fifty U.S. states have juvenile courts. So, too, does the U.S. federal system, though federal juvenile court prosecutions are rare. While some countries with a juvenile court—Switzerland for one—have never adopted the practice of transferring juveniles to the adult court, in America both federal and state statutes define circumstances—the charge is a serious one, or the juvenile was previously found delinquent for a serious crime—where transfer is permissible or even automatic. Where transfer is not automatic, it is at the discretion of either the juvenile court or the prosecutor. Tens of thousands of transfers to adult court occur annually in the United States.

Once a person reaches adulthood in the United States, any crimes he or she may commit can be prosecuted only in the adult court. That makes the United States different from at least one country, the Netherlands. There, the judge can decide to handle as a juvenile a person who is between eighteen and twenty-one even though adulthood is age eighteen in the Netherlands.

5. *Federalism.* Serious crimes are violations of just national law in Canada, England, the Netherlands, Scotland, Sweden, and Switzerland. They are violations of both federal and state laws in America and Australia.

In all eight countries, persons convicted of serious crimes can be sentenced to imprisonment. In the United States, federal sentencing differs from state sentencing, and states all differ from each other. State and federal statutes specify the maximum allowable custody sentence for each type of crime. Whether the defendant (juvenile or adult, state or federal) receives a custody sentence is usually at the discretion of the judge or, occasionally, the jury. Exceptions are statutes that mandate a prison sentence.

Adult offenders sentenced to federal custody for a period longer than a year serve at least 85 percent of their sentence before they are released. With bad behavior, they might serve more. All federal sentences are considered "determinate" because release is not contingent on a parole board decision. Before 1987, federal sentences were indeterminate, meaning a parole board made the release decision.

In general, if the state court judge sentences an adult to confinement and the term is less than a year, the sentence is usually determinate and is served in a local (not state) jail. In most states, sentences of a year or longer are served in a state prison and are indeterminate; in the rest, such sentences are also served in a state prison but are determinate. Before 1975, all states had indeterminate sentences. Since 1975, a growing number of states have abolished parole in favor of determinate sentencing.

Juvenile custody sentences are usually indeterminate. A juvenile court or administrative agency decides when to release an incarcerated juvenile. Incarcerated juvenile delinquents are housed in separate institutions from adults.

6. *Jury Trials.* In the United States, persons pleading not guilty to a serious crime can choose between a jury trial and a judge trial. The same is true in Australia, Canada, England, Scotland, and Switzerland. Jury trials do not exist in Sweden and the Netherlands.

7. *Indigent Defense.* In all eight countries, persons charged with serious crimes have the right to be defended by an attorney, and if they cannot afford one, the government will provide legal defense. In America such legal defense—called "indigent" defense—is often provided through a government agency called the public defender.

Otherwise, the court assigns a private lawyer to represent the defendant.

8. *Appellate Courts.* All eight countries have appellate courts. Most (thirty-nine) state court systems in the United States are three tiered. Serious crimes are prosecuted in the state's district court. Appeals go to an intermediate court of appeals. From there, appeals are to the state supreme court. The U.S. federal court system is also three tiered. Besides hearing appeals from its intermediate appellate court (the U.S. Court of Appeals), the U.S. Supreme Court also selectively hears appeals from state supreme court decisions in cases that begin in a state court.

9. *Death Penalty.* The United States is the only one of the eight countries that has the death penalty. Capital punishment is reserved for specific forms of murder in U.S. federal law and in the laws of thirty-eight of the fifty states.

II. Trends in Crime from 1981 to 1999

This analysis summarizes crime trends over a nineteen-year period. One of the data sources is official police records, which give statistics on crimes reported to police. But since much crime goes unreported, crime trends are also summarized from a source that does not share that limitation: the National Crime Victimization Survey (NCVS), an annual nationwide survey conducted by the Bureau of Justice Statistics in which U.S. government interviewers ask the American people if they were victimized by crime. Interviewers ask about all crimes, whether or not reported to police. The victimization surveys confirm that many victims do not call the police.

Over the study period, year-to-year changes in police-recorded crime differed from changes in survey crime. The biggest differences were for rape and aggravated assault. Table 1 shows that survey-measured and police-measured rape rates had only a .182 correlation with one another over the study period. Trends in the survey aggravated assault rate bore virtually no relation to trends in the officially recorded aggravated assault rate; the correlation between the two is near zero ($r = -.008$) in table 1. Differences between the two for other offenses—robbery, residential burglary, and motor vehicle theft—were mild by comparison. Crime trend differences largely stem from year-to-year variation in the reporting of crime to police and in the recording of crime by police. Crime trend differences are investigated with measures of each.

TABLE 1

Correlations between Trends in Police-Recorded and Victim Survey Crime Rates in the United States, 1981–99

	Police-Recorded Rate						Victimization Survey Rate				
	Homicide	Female Rape	Robbery	Aggravated Assault	Residential Burglary	Motor Vehicle Theft	Female Rape	Noncommercial Robbery	Aggravated Assault	Residential Burglary	Completed Motor Vehicle Theft
Police-recorded rate:											
Homicide	...	.685**	.985**	.248	.705**	.601**	.699**	.858**	.837**	.627*	.842**
Female rape		...	.761**	.775**	.108**	.899**	**.182****	.284*	.433	-.039	.816**
Robbery			...	.363	.612**	.682**	.616**	**.809****	.776**	.520*	.878
Aggravated assault				...	-.454*	.860**	-.418	-.122	**-.008**	-.578**	.606**
Residential burglary					...	.009	.911**	.767**	.697**	**.980****	.353*
Motor vehicle theft						...	-.004	.198	.302	-.148	**.872****
Victimization survey rate:											
Female rape							...	.768**	.755**	.908**	.367
Noncommercial robbery								...	.873**	.779**	.551*
Aggravated assault									...	.697**	.601**
Residential burglary										...	.236
Completed motor vehicle theft											...

SOURCE.—Langan 2004.

NOTE.—Police-recorded rates are per 1,000 population all ages; survey rates are per 1,000 population ages twelve and older. For rape, only females are in the base. Shown in bold are correlations for trends in crimes available from both police-recorded data and victim survey data.

* Correlation is significant at the .05 level (two-tailed).

** Correlation is significant at the .01 level (two-tailed).

A. Crime Definitions Used to Describe Crime Trends

Trends in five crimes—rape, robbery, aggravated assault, residential burglary, and completed theft of motor vehicles—are documented from both victimization surveys and police records. Trends in one crime—homicide—are described with police data. Survey crime rates are based on the annual National Crime Victimization Survey. Police-recorded rates are based on data compiled by the FBI. Precise sources of survey and police-measured crime statistics used in this study are documented elsewhere by the author (Langan 2004).

1. *Residential burglary* is unlawful entry of a fixed structure used for regular residence, with or without force, to commit a felony or theft. It excludes trespassing or unlawful entry where intent is unclear, and it includes attempts. As measured here, both police-recorded and survey burglary data exclude burglary of nonresidential structures. Obtaining the number of police-recorded residential burglaries involved subtracting the number of commercial burglaries—about one-third of all burglaries on average—from police-recorded burglary totals. The one-third average was used for each year.

2. *Motor vehicle theft* is the unlawful taking of a self-propelled road vehicle (cars, trucks, and motorcycles) and includes unauthorized use of a vehicle and receiving, possessing, stripping, transporting, and reselling stolen vehicles. For measuring crime tends in this analysis, police-recorded vehicular theft includes both completed and attempted theft of both commercial and noncommercial vehicles; survey vehicular theft includes only completed theft of noncommercial vehicles, although the victimization surveys do compile data on attempted theft of noncommercial vehicles. They were excluded to facilitate international comparisons done for the larger study described above.

3. *Robbery* is the unlawful taking of property that is in the immediate possession of another, by force or threat of force, and includes attempts. Police-recorded robbery includes both commercial and non-commercial robbery against persons of any age; survey robbery excludes commercial robbery and robbery of children under twelve.

4. *Aggravated assault* is intentionally and without legal justification causing serious bodily injury or using a deadly weapon to threaten or attempt bodily injury. It includes attempted murder and attempted aggravated assault and excludes minor assault, such as assault that does not involve a deadly weapon but does involve minor injury. Police-recorded assault includes aggravated assault against persons of

any age; survey aggravated assault excludes those against children under twelve.

5. *Rape* is forcible intercourse (vaginal, anal, or oral) with a female against her will, and includes attempts. Female victims of any age are counted in police statistics; survey rape excludes female victims under twelve.

6. *Homicide* is the willful killing of one human being by another without legal justification. It excludes attempts.

B. Reported Crime versus Reported and Recorded Crime

Crime trends from official police records can differ from those based on victimization surveys because of changes either in the reporting of crimes to police or in the recording practices of police. Measures of each are described below.

1. *Percent Reported.* Based on NCVS data, this measure is defined as the number of crimes that victims said were reported to police, divided by the total number of crimes (reported and unreported) that victims experienced.

2. *Percent Recorded of Reported.* The level of crime recorded in police statistics depends not only on how often victims (and others) report crimes to police, but also on how often police record as crimes the ones that are reported to them. Police do not always record as a crime every allegation that comes to them: sometimes police find insufficient evidence that a crime occurred; alleged crimes go unrecorded because of poor record keeping; police weed out crimes they do not consider to be serious or downgrade a crime to a less serious category. "Percent recorded of reported"—defined as the number of crimes recorded by police divided by the number reported to police—measures the likelihood that a crime reported to police was recorded. The number of crimes that victims said were reported to police was based on NCVS data; the number of comparably defined crimes that police actually recorded was derived from official police statistics. Comparability was achieved (as much as possible) by excluding from police statistics the types of crimes not included in the calculation of survey crime rates (see crime definitions above).

C. Results for the Six Crimes

Criteria used to decide whether a crime rate, reporting percentage, or recording percentage rose, fell, or followed no general linear trend were the sign and magnitude of the correlation between measure and year; positive correlation over 0.4 was treated as rising; negative correlation over 0.4, falling; and correlation outside these ranges was considered trendless.

Table 2 shows that, from 1981 to 1999, three crime rates were trendless (survey vehicle theft, and police-recorded vehicle theft and rape), one crime rate rose (police-recorded aggravated assault), and seven crime rates fell (survey rape, robbery, aggravated assault, and burglary; and police-recorded homicide, robbery, and burglary).

Table 2 also shows that, over the same period, reporting of crime to police rose for four survey-measured crimes (robbery, aggravated assault, residential burglary, and completed theft of motor vehicles), and police recording of reported crimes rose for two survey-measured crimes (aggravated assault and residential burglary). These reporting and recording changes help to explain why police-recorded crime trends were not perfectly correlated with survey crime trends (see table 1).

1. *Residential Burglary.* Figure 1 shows that the victim-survey residential burglary rate fell, as did the police-recorded residential burglary rate, though less sharply. One reason for the weaker drop is an increase in the reporting rate over time. The increase is documented in table 2 with a .661correlation between the reporting rate and year. The correlation is not obvious in figure 2 because of the scale.

2. *Motor Vehicle Theft.* Figure 3 shows that the vehicle theft rate (both victim-survey and police-recorded) followed no general linear trend over the study period.

3. *Robbery.* Figure 4 shows a generally downward trend for the survey robbery rate and a less sharply downward trend for the police-recorded robbery rate. The weaker drop in the police-recorded rate is partly due to an increase in the reporting of robbery to police. Table 2 documents the increase with a .402 correlation between percent reported and year.

4. *Aggravated Assault.* Figure 5 shows that the survey aggravated assault rate generally fell, while the police-recorded aggravated assault rate generally rose. Table 2 also documents the fall in the survey aggravated assault rate ($r = -.633$) and the rise in the police-recorded rate ($r = .644$). The difference in trends is due to increases in both the aggravated assault reporting percentage (it has a .724 correlation with year, according to table 2) and the aggravated assault recording

TABLE 2

Correlations between Study Measures and Year

Study Measure	Homicide	Rape	Robbery	Aggravated Assault	Residential Burglary	Motor Vehicle Theft
Crime rates and related measures:						
Victim survey crime rates	...	**-.902**	**-.686**	**-.633**	**-.974**	-.148
Police-recorded crime rates	**-.542**	.079	**-.431**	**.644**	**-.950**	.217
Percent of crimes reported to police	...	...	**.402**	**.724**	**.661**	**.650**
Percent recorded of reported	...	...	.201	**.839**	**.828**	.292
Risk-of-punishment measure:						
Arrest rate per 1,000 offenders	-.301	**-.761**	**.532**	**.941**	**.946**	**.671**
Conviction rate per 1,000 arrested offenders	**.911**	**.885**	**.649**	**.932**	**.564**	**.809**
Conviction rate per 1,000 offenders	**.957**	**.801**	**.741**	**.954**	**.821**	**.855**
Custody rate per 1,000 offenders	**.964**	**.727**	**.695**	**.960**	**.863**	**.916**
Days served per offender	**.982**	**.733**	**.409**	**.956**	**.590**	**.724**
Severity-of-punishment measure:						
Percent custody per conviction	**.525**	-.180	-.201	**-.463**	**.409**	**.742**
Average sentence length	.151	.209	-.040	-.102	.115	-.285
Average time served	**.955**	**.605**	-.133	.003	-.123	**-.403**
Percent of sentence served	**.929**	**.504**	-.189	.255	**-.576**	-.158

SOURCE.—Langan 2004.
NOTE.—Shown in bold are correlations over 0.4 in absolute value. Correlations for crime rates and related measures are based on data for nineteen years (1981–99); correlations for punishment measures are based on eight years (1981, 1983, 1986, 1988, 1990, 1992, 1994, and 1996). Ellipses indicate not applicable (for homicide) or too few cases for analysis (for rape).

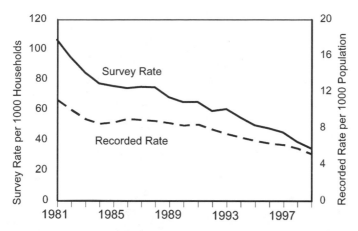

FIG. 1.—Residential burglary: survey and recorded crime rate, 1981–99. Source: Langan 2004.

percentage (a .839 correlation with year). Both increases are discernible in figure 6, particularly the increase in the percentage of aggravated assaults reported to police. In short, over the study period, once an assault occurred, its likelihood of being reported to police rose, and once reported, its likelihood of being recorded by police rose. The effect of these increases was so pronounced that year-to-year changes in the police-recorded aggravated assault rate had a correlation close to zero (table 1) with changes in the victimization survey aggravated assault rate.

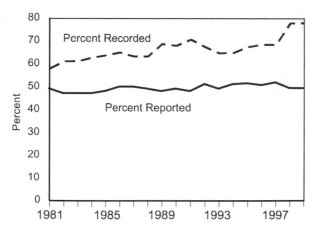

FIG. 2.—Residential burglary: percent reported to police and percent recorded of reported, 1981–99. Source: Langan 2004.

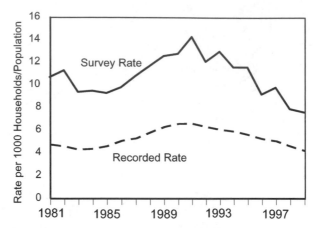

FIG. 3.—Vehicle theft: survey and recorded crime rate, 1981–99. Source: Langan 2004.

5. *Rape.* Figure 7 shows no general linear trend in the police-recorded rape rate. The absence of a trend is mirrored by the low correlation shown in table 2 ($r = .079$). By contrast, the survey rape rate fell, according to both figure 7 and table 2 ($r = -.902$). Reporting and recording changes that might explain the discrepancy were not investigated because there were too few NCVS rape cases for analysis.

6. *Homicide.* Figure 8 documents a generally falling homicide rate, as does table 2 ($r = -.542$). The homicide rate in 1999 was roughly half what it was in 1981.

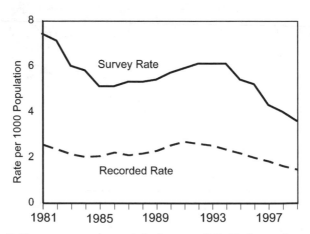

FIG. 4.—Robbery: survey and recorded crime rate, 1981–99. Source: Langan 2004.

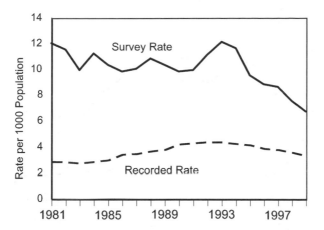

FIG. 5.—Aggravated assault: survey and recorded crime rate, 1981–99. Source: Langan 2004.

III. Trends in Punishment from 1981 to 1996

The study combines state, federal, and juvenile justice system statistics to form national measures of two types of punishment trends: in risk and in severity of criminal punishment.

A. Crime Definitions in Punishment Trends

Punishment trends are based on data for eight years (1981, 1983, 1986, 1988, 1990, 1992, 1994, and 1996) and six crimes (homicide, rape, robbery, aggravated assault, residential burglary, and motor

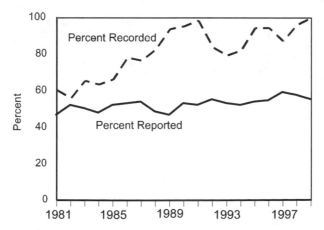

FIG. 6.—Aggravated assault: percent reported to police and percent recorded of reported, 1981–99. Source: Langan 2004.

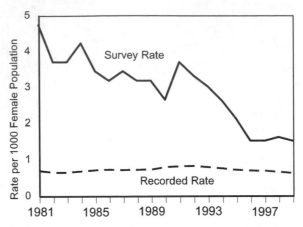

FIG. 7.—Rape: survey and recorded crime rate, 1981–99. Source: Langan 2004.

vehicle theft). Punishment data for the six conform to the crime definitions in police-recorded crime rates (see Sec. II crime definitions). The one minor exception is rape. Punishment data for rape include a small number of rapes of males; police-recorded rape is limited to female rape.

B. Punishment Measures Defined

Five risk and four severity measures were calculated for each of the six crimes. All punishment measures included juveniles and adults and used in their calculation data from across the juvenile, state, and federal justice systems. The five risk-of-punishment measures are the following:

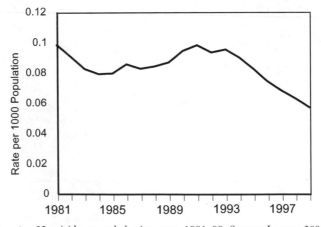

FIG. 8.—Homicide: recorded crime rate, 1981–99. Source: Langan 2004.

1. *Arrest Rate per 1,000 Offenders.* The number of arrests as a ratio to the number of persons allegedly committing the crime.

2. *Conviction Rate per 1,000 Arrested Offenders.* The number of convictions as a ratio to the number of arrested offenders.

3. *Conviction Rate per 1,000 Offenders.* The number of convictions as a ratio to the number of persons allegedly committing the crime. This measure is entirely derived from the two preceding measures.

4. *Custody Rate per 1,000 Offenders.* The number sentenced to incarceration (prison, jail, juvenile facility) as a ratio to the number of persons allegedly committing the crime. This measure is derived from the preceding measure and "percent custody per conviction."

5. *Days Served per Offender.* Total number of days incarcerated before being released divided by the number of persons allegedly committing the crime. This measure is derived from the preceding measure, "average time served," the number of offenders sentenced to incarceration, and the total number of persons allegedly committing the crime. The four severity-of-punishment measures are as follows:

1. *Percent Custody per Conviction.* The number of offenders sentenced to incarceration (prison, jail, and juvenile facility) divided by the number convicted.

2. *Average Sentence Length.* Average sentence length imposed, in months. To convert life sentences for state homicide into months, average time served by lifers released from state prisons for homicide was divided by the fraction of the sentence served by nonlifers released from state prisons for homicide that same year. A different conversion procedure was used for federal life sentences because parole is not available in the federal system. Federal life sentences for homicide were set at forty years, roughly the remaining life expectancy of these offenders.

3. *Average Time Served.* Average length of time confined before release, in months. For life sentences for state homicide, the fraction of the sentence served was set at the same fraction nonlifers released that year served for homicide. That fraction multiplied by their life sentence expressed in months gave time served. For homicide offenders with federal life sentences, their average time served was set at forty years.

4. *Percent of Sentence Served.* Number of months served divided by sentence length, in months. For incarcerated juveniles, percent of sentence served was set at 50 percent; for state prison sentences, set at the same percentage served by released state prisoners that year; for

federal prison sentence over a year, set at 85 percent (the statutory minimum); for shorter federal sentences, set at 100 percent since early release is not generally available for them; for local jail sentences, set at 50 percent.

C. Data Sources and Illustrations of Calculations

Data sources for the punishment measures and illustrations of calculations are given next.

1. *Per 1,000 Offenders and per Offender.* Certain punishment measures use "per 1,000 offenders" or "per offender" as their base. These measures relate punishments to the overall number of persons (juveniles and adults combined) committing crime. For each of the six crimes, this overall number of offenders was obtained by taking the number of crimes committed and multiplying it by the average number of offenders per crime. For each year, the same average (obtained by calculating the average over a span of years) was used: an average of 1.15 offenders per crime for homicide, 1.2 for rape, 1.8 for robbery, 1.5 for aggravated assault, 1.4 for burglary, and 1.5 for motor vehicle theft. For homicide, sources for the number of homicides and the average number of offenders per homicide were official police statistics; for rape the number of rapes was based on official police statistics, and the 1.2 rape average was from the NCVS. For robbery, aggravated assault, residential burglary, and motor vehicle theft, the number of crimes and their offender averages were from the NCVS. Precise sources of all data are given in Langan (2004). However, since certain types of robbery, aggravated assault, and vehicle theft are not measured in the NCVS, the number of offenders committing these three crimes was adjusted upward (to the extent possible) to correct for the unmeasured types (see Sec. II crime definitions for unmeasured types). Commercial burglaries are also not measured in the NCVS, but no adjustment was made for these unmeasured crimes because the study's burglary definition excluded nonresidential burglary.

For purposes of illustration, here is how one of the risk measures— conviction rate per 1,000 offenders—was calculated for residential burglary in 1996. According to the NCVS, about 4.84 million residential burglaries were committed in 1996, and the average number of offenders per burglary from 1981 to 1994 was 1.4. That makes nearly 6.8 million persons who allegedly committed burglary in 1996. That same year an estimated 108,570 juveniles and adults were

convicted of residential burglary. The 1996 residential burglary conviction rate, then, works out to about sixteen per 1,000 residential
burglars.

As for robbery—a second illustration—the NCVS estimates
1,134,300 noncommercial robberies of persons age twelve and over
in 1996, with the typical one involving 1.8 robbers (a fourteen-year
average). That makes a little over 2 million alleged robbers. Adjusting
for the unmeasured robberies (the unmeasured 2 percent of all
robberies against persons under age twelve, and the unmeasured 22
percent against commercial establishments) brings the total to 2.67
million alleged robbers. Since an estimated 63,210 juveniles and adults
were convicted of robbery in 1996, the 1996 robbery conviction rate is
twenty-four per 1,000 robbers.

2. *Per 1,000 Arrested Offenders.* The "conviction rate per 1,000
arrested offenders" used the number of arrests as the base. The
number of arrests was from official police statistics (precise data
sources are given in Langan [2004]).

3. *Postarrest Measures.* All risk and severity measures that used
postarrest data were formed by combining statistics across the juvenile,
state, and federal justice systems. The various computations and
sources for each are illustrated below with residential burglary in
1996. The year 1996 was picked because most other years in the study
are identical to it in terms of procedures and sources. Residential
burglary was picked for no special reason; that is, with one exception,
procedures and sources for calculating risk and severity measures for
residential burglary were generally the same as those for other crimes.
The exception was a procedure for obtaining the number of residential
burglary convictions. National burglary conviction statistics do not
distinguish residential from nonresidential. The residential number
had to be estimated from them by treating two-thirds of all burglary
convictions as residential, the same percentage that are residential in
police-recorded burglary statistics.

a) *Juvenile Justice System Statistics.* The federal government's *Juvenile Court Statistics 1996* (Stahl et al. 1999) reported 141,400 burglary
cases in juvenile courts nationwide that year. Assuming two-thirds
were residential, that makes 94,738 juvenile residential burglary
cases. An annual juvenile court database maintained by the National
Center for Juvenile Justice reports 76 percent of burglary cases
petitioned in 1996; 64 percent of those petitioned were convicted

("adjudicated delinquent"), and 33 percent of those convicted were sentenced to custody ("placed"). Using the three figures, and assuming that residential burglary was handled in the same way as nonresidential, that makes 46,081 juveniles convicted of residential burglary and 15,207 incarcerated. A 1997 census of juveniles in residential placement reveals that, at the time of the census, juvenile burglars had served an average of about five months. Assuming the census was taken at the midpoint of their time in custody (a reasonable assumption under steady-state conditions), doubling the five months gives ten months total time served before release. Assuming that total time served represents half the sentence length (an assumption loosely based on data the author compiled on a few jurisdictions), doubling ten months gives an average custody sentence for juvenile residential burglary of twenty months. The twenty months can be thought of as the combined amount of time in custody and on parole ("aftercare").

b) State Justice System Statistics (Adult). The publication *Felony Sentences in the United States, 1996* (Brown and Langan 1999) reports 93,197 adults convicted of burglary in 1996, 45 percent sentenced to state prison for an average of sixty months, and 26 percent sentenced to jail for an average of six months. Using these figures and making two assumptions (that two-thirds were residential burglary, and that the state system handled residential and nonresidential burglary the same), that makes 62,442 adults convicted of residential burglary, 28,099 sentenced to a state prison, and 16,235 sentenced to a local jail. Findings from the BJS *National Corrections Reporting Program* (Brown and Langan 1999) show that burglars served 42 percent of their state prison sentence before being released in 1996. Assuming that the 28,099 residential burglars sentenced to prison served 42 percent of their sixty-month sentence, average prison time served was twenty-five months. Assuming that the 16,235 residential burglars sentenced to jail served half of their six-month sentence (an assumption based on a single study of jail releases), average time served was three months for jail sentences.

c) Federal Justice System Statistics. Findings from the BJS *Federal Justice Statistics Program* (Brown and Langan 1999) reveal that federal courts convicted seventy-one persons of burglary in 1996. Of the seventy-one, 18 percent were sentenced to a short prison term (a year or less) that averaged seven months, and 56 percent were sentenced to a long prison term (over a year) that averaged thirty-four months. Using these figures and assuming that two-thirds were residential, and further assuming that residential burglary was sentenced the same as non-residential, that makes forty-eight convicted residential burglars, of whom twenty-seven got a long prison sentence averaging thirty-four months, and nine got a short prison term averaging seven months. Assuming that all nine served 100 percent of their sentence before being released (since early release is not generally available for short-sentence federal cases), and assuming that the twenty-seven served 85 percent of their sentence (the minimum for such federal terms), that makes average time served seven months for short sentences and twenty-nine months for long ones.

d) *Juvenile, State, and Federal Statistics Combined.* Collectively, juvenile, state, and federal courts convicted 108,570 persons of residential burglary in 1996. Of the 108,570, 54.9 percent—or 59,576 juveniles and adults—received a custody sentence (jail, prison, and juvenile residential facility). On average, sentence length was thirty-five months, of which 43.4 percent—15.2 months—was served before release.

D. Results for the Six Crimes

Criteria used to decide whether punishment rose, fell, or followed no general linear trend were the sign and magnitude of the correlation between punishment and year: positive correlation over 0.4 was treated as rising, negative correlation over 0.4 as falling, and correlation outside these ranges was considered trendless.

Table 2 shows that, of the thirty correlations between year and risk for the six crimes, twenty-eight indicated rising punishment risk over the study period, one showed falling risk, and one had no general linear trend. Of the twenty-four correlations between year and severity for the six crimes, seven showed rising punishment severity, three showed falling severity, and fourteen showed no general trend.

To facilitate understanding, results for one of the crimes—residential burglary—are illustrated with graphs and described at length in the text below. Residential burglary was selected because its findings are indicative of what was generally found, namely, increases in risk of punishment, however measured, but relatively few indications of generally upward or generally downward trends in punishment severity.

1. *Residential Burglary.* Table 2 and figures 9–11 show increases in all five risk-of-punishment measures. Figure 9 graphically chronicles

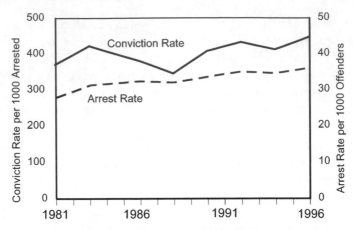

FIG. 9.—Residential burglary: arrest rate per 1,000 offenders and conviction rate per 1,000 arrested offenders, 1981–96. Source: Langan 2004.

an increase over the eight data points (1981, 1983, 1986, 1988, 1990, 1992, 1994, and 1996) in the likelihood of arrest for persons committing residential burglary ($r = .946$ in table 2) and an increase in the likelihood of burglary conviction for those arrested ($r = .564$). Figure 10 shows an increase over the same period in the likelihood of both conviction ($r = .821$) and a custody sentence ($r = .863$) among persons committing residential burglary. Figure 11 graphs the gradual rise in the cost of crime as measured by the number of days confined per each person committing residential burglary ($r = .590$).

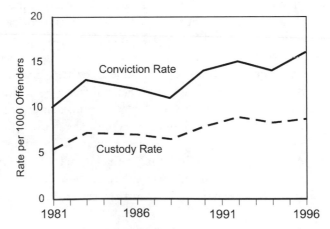

FIG. 10.—Residential burglary: conviction and custody rates per 1,000 offenders, 1981–96. Source: Langan 2004.

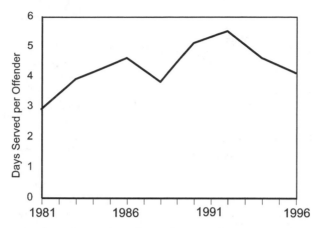

Fɪɢ. 11.—Residential burglary: days served per offender, 1981–96. Source: Langan 2004.

Turning to the four severity measures, figure 12 generally depicts a rising percentage of convicted residential burglars receiving a custody sentence ($r = .409$). Figure 12 also records a drop in the fraction of the sentence served before release from custody ($r = -.576$). Punishment severity as measured by average sentence length and average time served does not follow either a generally upward or generally downward trend in figure 13.

2. *Motor Vehicle Theft.* Table 2 shows increases in all five risk measures, a rise in one severity measure ($r = .742$ for percent custody per conviction), a decline in one severity measure ($r = -.403$ for

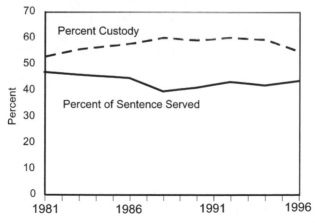

Fɪɢ. 12.—Residential burglary: percent custody per conviction and percent of sentence served, 1981–96. Source: Langan 2004.

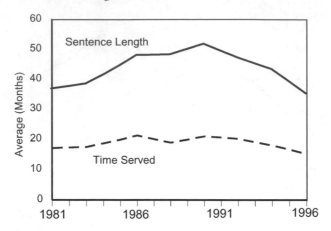

Fig. 13.—Residential burglary: average sentence length and average time served, 1981–96. Source: Langan 2004.

average time served), and no generally upward or downward trend for the other two severity measures.

3. *Robbery.* Table 2 shows increases in all five risk measures, but no generally upward or downward trend in any of the four severity measures.

4. *Aggravated Assault.* Table 2 shows increases in all five risk measures, a drop in one severity measure ($r = -.463$ for percent custody per conviction), and no generally upward or downward trend for the three other severity measures.

5. *Rape.* Table 2 shows a drop in one risk measure ($r = -.761$ for arrest rate per 1,000 offenders) and increases in the four other risk measures. Table 2 also shows increases in two severity measures ($r = .605$ for average time served, $r = .504$ for percent of sentence served) and the absence of any general linear trend for the other two severity measures.

6. *Homicide.* Table 2 shows no generally upward or downward trend in one risk measure ($r = -.301$ for arrest rate per 1,000 offenders), but increases in the four others. Also according to table 2, three severity measures rose ($r = .525$ for percent custody per conviction, $r = .955$ for average time served, $r = .929$ for percent of sentence served) and the other was trendless.

IV. Relationship between Crime and Punishment, 1981–96

For each of five offenses, changes over time in the risk of punishment for that particular crime (as measured five different ways) were compared to changes over time in the rate at which the crime was committed. Also for each of the five offenses, changes over time in the severity of punishment for that particular crime (as measured four different ways) were compared to changes over time in the rate at which the crime was committed. The comparisons were based on eight years of data: 1981, 1983, 1986, 1988, 1990, 1992, 1994, and 1996. The particular nationwide punishment data used in the analysis do not exist outside these years.

A. Crime Definitions in Crime and Punishment Trends

To study justice system effects on crime, the preferred crime measure is the one generated independently of the justice system. Victimization surveys are preferable to police statistics in this regard because they compile data on all crimes, whether or not reported to and recorded by police. Accordingly, the investigation uses survey rather than police-recorded trends as the dependent variable. The only exception is homicide, which is outside the scope of victimization surveys. The choice of survey data is further supported by findings, summarized earlier, showing that trends in police-recorded crime rates were affected by increases both in reporting of crimes to police and in police recording of crimes. Exception is made for homicide but not rape because variable reporting of crime to police and variable police-recording practices are thought to have a negligible effect only on homicide. Another reason rape is excluded from analysis of the relationship between crime and punishment trends is that some of the year-to-year changes in the volume of rape convictions are known to have resulted from changes in data-collection procedures.

In summary, punishment's effect is investigated for five crimes: police-recorded homicide, and survey robbery, aggravated assault, residential burglary, and motor vehicle theft. The five are defined the same way they were defined in computing police-recorded crime rates (see Sec. II crime definitions). Because certain forms of these crimes are not included in the surveys, survey data were adjusted (to the extent possible) to correct for the unmeasured types (see Sec. II crime definitions for unmeasured types).

B. Results for the Five Crimes

Criteria used to decide whether changes in punishment were associated with changes in crime were the sign and size of the correlation between punishment measure and crime rate: positive correlation over

0.4 indicated a positive relationship, negative correlation over 0.4 formed an inverse relationship, and correlation outside these ranges was treated as no relationship.

Altogether, twenty-five correlations were computed for the five crimes between punishment risk trends and crime rate trends, and twenty between punishment severity trends and crime rate trends. The twenty-five correlations consist of twenty-four in which the punishment-risk variable indicated rising risk over the study period (as shown in table 2, excluding rape) and one correlation in which the punishment-risk variable reflected neither generally rising nor generally falling risk. The twenty correlations consist of five in which the punishment-severity variable recorded rising severity (see table 2), three in which the punishment-severity variable recorded declining severity, and twelve in which the punishment-severity variable indicated no general trend.

Table 3 summarizes correlations between punishment and crime. In discussing table 3 correlations, frequent reference is made to all the findings summarized in table 2 except those for the crime of rape. Of the twenty-four measures from table 2 that document rising punishment risk (ignoring rape), sixteen are shown in table 3 as being associated with falling crime, and eight are shown as being unrelated to crime rate changes. The one risk measure not recorded as rising in table 2 (arrest rate per 1,000 offenders for homicide) is shown in table 3 as being unrelated to crime rate changes. Of the five measures showing rising severity according to table 2 (ignoring rape), two are associated with falling crime in table 3 and three are unrelated to crime rate changes. Of the three severity measures recorded as declining in table 2 (ignoring rape), two are shown in table 3 as being associated with rising crime, and one is shown as being unrelated to crime rate changes. Of table 2's twelve measures showing no linear trend in severity, nine are shown in table 3 as having no relationship to crime rate changes, two are associated with rising crime, and one is associated with falling crime.

The table 3 correlations between punishment measure and crime can be summarized differently by focusing just on those in which punishment rose or fell over the study period. There were twenty-four instances where risk rose (from table 2), and table 3 shows that sixteen of these twenty-four correlations are negative, indicating that as risk rose, crime fell. There were five measures where severity rose (from table 2), and table 3 correlations for two of these five correlations

TABLE 3

Correlations between 1981–96 U.S. Trends in Legal Punishment and Trends in U.S. Crime Rates

Study Measure	Homicide	Robbery	Aggravated Assault	Residential Burglary	Motor Vehicle Theft
Risk-of-punishment measure:					
Arrest rate per 1,000 offenders	-.320	-.907*	-.544*	-.992*	.152*
Conviction rate per 1,000 arrested offenders	-.33?*	-.138*	-.394*	-.607*	.301*
Conviction rate per 1,000 offenders	-.461*	-.662*	-.494*	-.863*	.274*
Custody rate per 1,000 offenders	-.439*	-.616*	-.477*	-.917*	.259*
Days served per offender	-.420*	-.528*	-.451*	-.704*	.350*
Severity-of-punishment measure:					
Percent custody per conviction	.125†	.159	.540‡	-.476†	.056†
Average sentence length	.345	-.358	.044	-.211	.688
Average time served	-.377†	-.179	-.055	-.007	.145‡
Percent of sentence served	-.513†	.605	-.255	.568‡	-.740

SOURCE.—Langan 2004.

NOTE.—Shown in bold are correlations over 0.4 in absolute value. Crime rates for homicide are based on police records; crime rates for other offenses are based on national crime victimization surveys. Also, correlations are based on eight years (1981, 1983, 1986, 1988, 1990, 1992, 1994, and 1996).

* This punishment risk rose for this crime over the study period, according to table 2 (this essay).

† This punishment severity rose for this crime over the study period, according to table 2 (this essay).

‡ This punishment severity fell for this crime over the study period, according to table 2 (this essay).

indicate that, as severity rose, crime fell. Last, there were three instances of falling severity (from table 2), and, for two of the three measures, table 3 indicates that as severity fell, crime rose.

1. *Residential Burglary.* As burglary punishment risk rose, the burglary rate fell, no matter how punishment risk was measured. That is, according to table 3, for each of the five burglary risk-of-punishment measures, rising risk was inversely associated with the falling burglary rate. The rise in punishment severity as measured by percent custody per conviction was accompanied by a drop in the residential burglary rate ($r = -.476$). But a drop in severity as measured by percent of sentence served was also associated with a falling burglary rate ($r = .568$). The two trendless burglary severity measures—average sentence length and average time served—were unrelated to drops in the burglary rate.

2. *Motor Vehicle Theft.* With two exceptions, no relationship was found over the study period between changes in risk or severity of punishment and changes in the motor vehicle theft rate. One exception shown in table 3 was a positive relationship between changes in the severity measure "average sentence length" and changes in the vehicle theft rate ($r = .688$). Another exception was an inverse relationship between the severity measure "percent of sentence served" and the vehicle theft rate ($r = -740$).

3. *Robbery.* Recall from table 2 that, however measured, risk of punishment for robbery rose. In general, as the risk of punishment for robbery rose, the robbery rate fell. More specifically, table 3 documents an inverse relationship between rising risk and the falling robbery rate for four of the five risk measures (all but conviction rate per 1,000 arrested offenders). With one exception (a positive relationship with percent of sentence served), no relationship was found between changes in severity and changes in the robbery rate.

4. *Aggravated Assault.* Recall from table 2 that risk of punishment for aggravated assault rose, however risk was measured. Table 3 shows that, as risk of punishment rose for aggravated assault, the aggravated assault rate generally fell. That is, rising risk was inversely associated with a falling aggravated assault rate for four of the five risk measures (all but "conviction rate per 1,000 arrested offenders"). Recall also from table 2 that aggravated assault severity as measured by "percent custody per conviction" generally fell over the study period. As it fell, so, too, did the aggravated assault rate ($r = .540$). Assault severity as measured three other ways was generally trendless according to table 2,

so no relationship was found between the three and the aggravated assault rate according to table 3.

5. *Homicide*. Recall from table 2 that risk of punishment for homicide rose as measured four out of five different ways (all but arrest rate per 1,000 offenders). Table 3 shows that, as punishment risk rose, the homicide rate generally fell. The one exception was that rising risk as measured by the conviction rate per 1,000 arrested offenders was unrelated to the falling homicide rate ($r = -.331$). Recall also from table 2 that severity of punishment for homicide rose as measured three different ways (all but average sentence length). These increases in punishment severity for homicide were generally unrelated to the falling homicide rate. The single exception shown in table 3 indicated that, as punishment severity rose according to the measure percent of sentence served, the homicide rate fell ($r = -.513$).

V. Discussion of Results

Periods of variation in risk and severity of criminal punishment provide natural opportunities to investigate effects on crime. Unfortunately (for research purposes), punishment severity did not generally vary over the period investigated in this study. That is, rising or falling severity characterized only eight of the study's twenty severity measures according to linear analysis of time trends. Rising risk, on the other hand, characterized twenty-four of the twenty-five risk measures, so the discussion of results mostly pertains to rising punishment risk as an explanation for the drop in crime in the United States.

A. Effect on Crime of Rising Punishment Risk

Over the study period, the size of the confined population rose. Changes in two severity measures—sentence length and time served—played no role since they did not generally rise. Factors most responsible were increases in reporting of crimes to police and increases in the five risk measures. Also contributing were increases in punishment severity as measured by the percentage of convicted offenders who received a custody sentence (percent custody per conviction). However, the latter is far less important than the others in accounting for increases in the size of the confined population. One reason is that increases in the custody percentage were small. Another is that the base for the custody percentage is much smaller than the base for the other measures. Consequently, all things being equal, a small increase in the custody percentage has considerably less impact than a small increase in one of the risk measures. (Further discussion of this by the author explaining increases in custody sentences can be found in Langan [2004].)

Growth in the size of the confined population has theoretical importance for explaining falling crime. The least difficult case to be made for a causal link between rising punishment risk and falling crime is the incapacitation effect of confinement, as opposed to its deterrent effect. As a National Academy of Sciences panel put it, "There are fewer problems in inferring the existence of effects from incapacitation than there are in establishing the existence of a deterrent effect. As long as there is a reasonable presumption that offenders who are imprisoned would have continued to commit crimes if they had remained free, there is unquestionably a direct incapacitative effect" (Blumstein, Cohen, and Nagin 1978, p. 9).

Relevant to the presumption are studies documenting the postrelease recidivism rates of prisoners. High rates imply that, had the convicted offenders remained free instead of being imprisoned, they would have continued their criminality; low rates suggest the opposite. A national study of prison releases in the United States in 1983 reported a relatively high rate, with about two-thirds being rearrested within three years (Beck and Shipley 1989, p. 1).

Still, it is possible that the growth in confined offenders over the period 1981 to 1996 was achieved by incarcerating more and more offenders who posed less and less risk of reoffending. If so, the growth in confinement would have resulted in diminishing returns in terms of crimes averted through incapacitation, and recidivism rates taken at the close of the 1981 to 1996 period would be lower than those taken at the start. No evidence of that was found, though; prisoners released toward the end of the period (in 1994) did not have a lower recidivism rate than those released near the beginning (in 1983; Langan and Levin 2002, p. 11). But these results do not adjust for the rising arrest rate documented in this study. Prisoners released late in the period may have posed less risk to public safety than those released earlier but, without the adjustment, that difference would not necessarily show up in rearrest rates. Conceivably, their lower risk to public safety was concealed in their arrest records by, say, improvements in police ability to catch criminals.

In summary, study results suggest that, when America's criminal justice system raised the risk of punishment, crime rates generally fell for residential burglary, robbery, aggravated assault, and homicide. However, results cannot be interpreted as compelling evidence that raising the likelihood of punishment reduces crime. One reason (among many) is that the study lacked controls for other factors that reduce crime. Changes in these unmeasured factors (demographic change in the population, for one), rather than rising risk of punishment, may have caused crime to fall. Even assuming a causal connection, study results cannot be interpreted as evidence that all, or even most, of the drop in crime was necessarily the result of rising legal punishment. Simply put, the study cannot say how much (if any) of the crime drop resulted from putting more people in prison. The policy relevance of the findings is further limited by the fact that the study did not investigate the costs of rising punishment, only its potential benefits in terms of reduced crime. (The impact of rising punishment on the crime rate is discussed further by the author in Langan and Farrington [1998].)

B.   Accounting for Rising Risk of Punishment

The criminal justice system of many countries—England is one of them—is highly centralized. In them, a central authority manages all (or nearly all) the nation's entire police force, all its prosecutors and courts, and all its prisons. If the central government decides too many criminals are being sent to prison, it attempts to influence the decisions of the nation's judges. If the central government becomes concerned that police are cautioning suspects rather than referring them for prosecution, it simply issues revised guidelines to the nation's police. One clear advantage of such a system is the ability to pinpoint particular governmental actions responsible for changes in the way the system processes defendants. When police cautioning rates fell in England in 1993, for example, English authorities knew precisely why: revised guidelines issued to police earlier that year (Home Office 1994).

The situation in the highly decentralized United States is quite different. The increases in punishment risk that are documented in this study are not easily attributed to particular anticrime measures adopted at specific times by specific agencies during the study period. Conceivably, any number of widely adopted measures could have contributed to the nationwide risk increases: passage of antistalking laws, legislation facilitating court issuance of restraining orders, shelters for battered women, mandatory arrest policies for domestic violence, police targeting of drugs and guns, community and problem-oriented policing, victim/witness programs, specialized prosecution units, career criminal police units, no-drop prosecution policies, abolishment of parole, the shift from indeterminate to determinate sentencing, mandatory and three-strikes sentencing laws, and so forth. Which of these actually did contribute to rising punishment risk is unknown because, in the United States, the effect of innovations on the justice system is rarely evaluated scientifically.

For two reasons, it is unlikely that federal funding of anticrime measures was the primary reason for the nationwide increases in punishment risk (though examples can probably be found where the effect of federal funding in an individual county or state was considerable). One reason is that, while hundreds of millions of dollars are funded annually by the federal government for state and local justice activities, those funds account for less than 1 percent of all local government budgets for criminal justice (Sherman et al. 1997, pp. 1–19). Another reason for downplaying the significance of federal funding on punishment risk increases over the study period 1981–96 is that the largest increases in federal funding did not occur until after 1996.

VI.   Recommendations for Future Research

This study combined state, federal, and juvenile statistics to form national estimates of various kinds at each of the major stages of the justice system, for example, estimates of the combined number of homicide convictions in state, federal, and juvenile courts. By far the biggest obstacle to forming national estimates was the absence of basic national statistics on the juvenile justice system. By "basic" is meant five offense-by-offense statistics: number convicted ("adjudicated delinquent"), percent sentenced to confinement ("placed"), sentence length, time served in custody, and time served on parole (in "aftercare"). Offense-by-offense statistics on the five are routinely published by the Bureau of Justice Statistics for adults convicted, imprisoned, or paroled in either the federal or state justice system. Since the statistics are largely nonexistent for juveniles, I had to resort to rough estimates of them. A data-collection program that routinely generates the needed numbers would close a gap in the nation's statistics on justice administration. It would also have practical value by creating benchmarks to gauge effects of juvenile justice system reforms.

Another obstacle in the study is the shortage of well-established research findings that might help to identify police and prosecution practices responsible for some of the documented increases in punishment risk. The increases essentially boil down to two key changes: first, a rising arrest rate, as measured by the arrest rate per 1,000 offenders; and, second, a rising conviction rate, as measured by the conviction rate per 1,000 arrested offenders. The two are key because all other increases in punishment risk mathematically derive from them in whole (conviction rate per 1,000 offenders) or in part (custody rate per 1,000 offenders and days served per offender). Innovations in policing in America almost certainly played a role in raising the arrest rate, and changes in prosecution almost certainly contributed to the rising conviction rate. While the research literature is somewhat helpful in identifying policing innovations that might account for the rising arrest rate, the literature is comparatively useless in identifying prosecution innovations that account for the growing conviction rate. Illustrative of the neglect are results from a 1998 survey of 500 scientific evaluations of crime prevention programs. The survey could find only one evaluation of a prosecution program (Forst 2002, p. 524). These gaps can be closed if even a small portion of the money allocated each year for federally funded anticrime programs were devoted to process evaluations of the impact of the programs on the justice system.

Finally, research—both national and cross-cultural—is also recommended on the effect (if any) of the election of criminal justice officials. In the United States, for example, felony sentences could be compared between counties where judges are elected and counties where they are appointed.

REFERENCES

Beck, Allen J., and Bernard E. Shipley. 1989. *Recidivism of Prisoners Released in 1983*. Washington, D.C.: U.S. Department of Justice, Office of Justice Programs, Bureau of Justice Statistics.

Blumstein, Alfred, Jacqueline Cohen, and Daniel Nagin, eds. 1978. *Deterrence and Incapacitation: Estimating the Effects of Criminal Sanctions on Crime Rates*. Washington, D.C.: National Academy of Sciences.

Brown, Jodi M., and Patrick A. Langan. 1999. *Felony Sentences in the United States, 1996*. Washington, D.C.: U.S. Department of Justice, Office of Justice Programs, Bureau of Justice Statistics.

Cohen, Jacqueline, and Jose A. Canela-Cacho. 1994. "Incarceration and Violent Crime." In *Understanding and Preventing Violence*, vol. 4, *Consequences and Control*, edited by Albert J. Reiss, Jr., and Jeffrey A. Roth. Washington, D.C.: National Academy Press.

DeFrances, Carol J. 2002. *Prosecutors in State Courts, 2001.* Washington, D.C.: U.S. Department of Justice, Office of Justice Programs, Bureau of Justice Statistics.

Eck, John, and Edward Maguire. 2000. "Have Changes in Policing Reduced Violent Crime? An Assessment of the Evidence." In *The Crime Drop in America*, edited by Alfred Blumstein and Joel Wallman. Cambridge: Cambridge University Press.

Farrington, David P., Patrick A. Langan, and Michael Tonry, eds. 2004. *Cross-National Studies in Crime and Justice.* Washington, D.C.: U.S. Department of Justice, Office of Justice Programs, Bureau of Justice Statistics.

Forst, Brian. 2002. "Prosecution." In *Crime: Public Policies for Crime Control*, edited by James Q. Wilson and Joan Petersilia. Oakland, Calif.: Institute for Contemporary Studies.

Gifford, Sidra Lea. 2002. *Justice Expenditure and Employment in the United States, 1999.* Washington, D.C.: U.S. Department of Justice, Office of Justice Programs, Bureau of Justice Statistics.

Home Office. 1994. *Cautions, Court Proceedings and Sentencing—England and Wales, 1993.* Statistical Bulletin no. 19. London: H.M. Stationery Office.

Jacoby, Joan. 1997. "The American Prosecutor: From Appointive to Elective Status." In *Prosecutor* 31(5).

Langan, Patrick A. 1991. "America's Soaring Prison Population." *Science* 251:1568–73.

———. 2004. "United States." In *Cross-National Studies in Crime and Justice*, edited by David P. Farrington, Patrick A. Langan, and Michael Tonry. Washington, D.C.: U.S. Department of Justice, Office of Justice Programs, Bureau of Justice Statistics.

Langan, Patrick A., and David P. Farrington. 1998. *Crime and Justice in the United States and in England and Wales, 1981–96.* Washington, D.C.: U.S. Department of Justice, Office of Justice Programs, Bureau of Justice Statistics.

Langan, Patrick A., and David J. Levin. 2002. *Recidivism of Prisoners Released in 1994.* Washington, D.C.: U.S. Department of Justice, Office of Justice Programs, Bureau of Justice Statistics.

Marvell, Thomas B., and Carlisle E. Moody. 1997. "The Impact of Prison Growth on Homicide." *Homicide Studies* 1:205–33.

Messinger, Sheldon L., John E. Berecochea, Richard A. Berk, and David Rauma. 1988. *Parolees Returned to Prison and the California Prison Population.* Sacramento: California Attorney General's Office.

Reiss, Albert, and Jeffrey A. Roth, eds. 1993. *Understanding and Preventing Violence.* Washington, D.C.: National Academy Press.

Roberts, Julian V., Loretta J. Stalans, David Indermaur, and Mike Hough. 2003. *Penal Populism and Public Opinion: Lessons from Five Countries.* New York: Oxford University Press.

Rosenfeld, Richard. 2000. "Patterns in Adult Homicide." In *The Crime Drop in America*, edited by Alfred Blumstein and Joel Wallman. Cambridge: Cambridge University Press.

Rottman, David B., Carol R. Flango, Melissa T. Cantrell, Randall Hansen, and Neil LaFountain. 2000. *State Court Organization 1998.* Washington, D.C.:

U.S. Department of Justice, Office of Justice Programs, Bureau of Justice Statistics.

Sherman, Lawrence W., and John E. Eck. 2002. "Policing for Crime Prevention." In *Evidence-Based Crime Prevention*, edited by Lawrence W. Sherman, David P. Farrington, Brandon C. Welsh, and Doris L. MacKenzie. London: Routledge.

Sherman. Lawrence W., Denise C. Gottfredson, Doris Layton MacKenzie, John Eck, Peter Reuter, and Shawn Bushway. 1997. *Preventing Crime: What Works, What Doesn't, What's Promising*. Washington, D.C.: U.S. Department of Justice, Office of Justice Programs.

Stahl, Anne L., Melissa Sickmund, Terrence A. Finnegan, Howard N. Snyder, Rowen S. Poole, and Nancy Tierney. 1999. *Juvenile Courts Statistics 1996*. Washington, D.C.: Office of Juvenile Justice and Delinquency Prevention.

Tonry, Michael H. 2004. *Thinking about Crime: Sense and Sensibility in American Penal Policy*. New York: Oxford University Press.

U.S. Department of Commerce. 1995. *1992 Census of Governments*, vol. 1, no. 2, *Popularly Elected Officials*. Washington, D.C.: U.S. Department of Commerce, Economics and Statistics Administration, Bureau of the Census.

Wilson, James Q. 1997. "Criminal Justice in England and America." *Public Interest* 126:3–13.

Zimring, Franklin E., Gordon Hawkins, and Sam Kamin. 2001. *Punishment and Democracy: Three Strikes and You're Out in California*. New York: Oxford University Press.

Catrien C. J. H. Bijleveld and Paul R. Smit

Crime and Punishment in the Netherlands, 1980–1999

ABSTRACT

According to police data, crime rates in the Netherlands increased for almost all offenses from 1980 to 1999. Victim survey data often show different patterns. Victim survey questions, however, do not always match police categorizations, and victim surveys are often too short or unstable to investigate these differences well. The system has become increasingly efficient in identifying offenses that have a greater likelihood of ending up in conviction. Sanctioning increasingly is deflected to the prosecutor's office, probably at the expense of conditional sentences. Pressure on prison space was mitigated through increasing use of community sanctions for less serious offenses. Sentence severity appears fairly stable for most offenses except rape, for which sentence lengths increased strongly.

This essay describes and tentatively explains trends in crime and justice in the Netherlands from 1980 to 1999. We focus on six offenses: residential burglary, motor vehicle theft, robbery, serious assault, rape, and homicide. We do not always have good data for each offense for each year. Only a fraction of crimes are reported and recorded by the police. Not all offenders are brought before the courts and convicted. Some convicted offenders are incarcerated to varying lengths of imprisonment.

Catrien C. J. H. Bijleveld is senior researcher at the Netherlands Institute for the Study of Crime and Law Enforcement and professor of criminology at the Free University, Amsterdam. Paul R. Smit is researcher at the Research and Documentation Center of the Ministry of Justice. Thanks to Cor Cozijn and Ad Essers, who studied burglary and motor vehicle theft in the Prosecution and Sentencing Monitor for us, and to Caspar Wiebrens and Frank van Tulder, who commented on an earlier draft. We interviewed Bert Berghuis and Bert Maan. Errors are our responsibility.

161

The analysis in this essay was conducted along with several other analyses that attempted to gather the same, and therefore comparable, information for a number of offenses for a number of countries in which two or more waves of a general victim survey were conducted in the period 1980–99. The aim is to link victimization data to police figures, prosecution and conviction statistics, and custody data and, thus, to capture the flow of offenders through the criminal justice system. The first comparative study of this kind appeared in 1992 (Farrington and Langan 1992) and presented data for England and the United States. This volume attempts to present a more in-depth and extensive analysis for several countries according to the same format and methodology. The format is dictated by the need for maximum comparability: by ensuring that as similar data as possible are collected (i.e., not comparing simply penal code entries, but comparing as similar as possible material acts), flows of offenders can be compared across countries.

For all offenses studied, we found increased numbers at the police level. Due to lack of sufficient victim survey data, it is unclear why, and more precisely whether, this rise in recorded crime was due to a real rise in crime levels or partly resulted from other factors.

Apart from quantitative changes, qualitative changes in the supply of crime may also have taken place. There are indications that more very serious offenses (perhaps even a small number) have occurred. Some writers have stressed—particularly for violent offenses—that the nature of the offenses may not have changed but rather the public perception of their seriousness. In our data, we see that reflected for rape.

The Dutch criminal justice system has coped with the increased numbers of offenses and offenders by filtering out cases, presumably including potentially successful or serious cases. Toward the end of 1990s, the criminal justice system was under heavy pressure. Prison shortages were reflected as turbulence (for some offenses). Filtering is also apparent in increasing numbers of less serious offenses not referred for prosecution (most prominently for qualified theft).

Notable changes in sentencing occurred only for rape. From 1980 to 1999, conviction probabilities decreased for rape and burglary. Chances of incarceration for rape also decreased. For other offenses, the likelihood of incarceration remained basically unaltered. We assume that the same kinds of offenses and the same kinds of offenders were entering the system—an assumption that is in all likelihood untrue—but we do not know and cannot test to what extent it is untrue.

The system coped with the increasing input by deflecting sanctioning to the prosecutor and replacing custodial with community sanctions. Such deflections have probably taken the place of conditional sentences and fines that were much more prevalent at the beginning at our research period.

Many of both our initial questions and the new questions that emerged while analyzing the data remain unanswered because of lack of data. We recommend that offenses and offenders be tracked through the system. Until results from such a tracking system emerge, studies should be carried out to link up the different sources on crime and punishment.

This essay has six sections. Section I is a brief description of the Netherlands and its population, and Section II is an overview of the organization and operation of the criminal justice system. Section III discusses the data sources on which we rely, including three separate series of victim survey data. The official data systems are not offender based, and individual offenders and cases accordingly cannot easily be traced. Instead, police records and successive series of prosecution, court, and corrections data must be consulted and various adjustments made. Sections IV and V present our findings on offending, processing, and punishment trends for burglary, motor vehicle theft, assault, robbery, rape, and homicide. Section VI summarizes and attempts to explain our main findings and offers suggestions for how data systems can be augmented to enable and improve analyses such as this one and the insights they can offer.

I. The Netherlands

The Netherlands is a small flat country in western Europe. It is a constitutional monarchy, although the monarch plays mainly a ceremonial role. The Netherlands is a parliamentary democracy, the lower house, *Tweede Kamer der Staten Generaal,* having 150 seats, and the upper house, *Eerste Kamer,* seventy-five. The lower house plays the central role; the upper house's role is smaller. Between 1994 and 2002, a coalition of labor (PvdA), conservative (VVD), and liberal democratic (D'66) parties governed the country. In 2002, a religious (CDA), conservative (VVD), and liberal democratic (D'66) coalition was formed.

The population was 16.1 million in 2002. Population density is high, and it increased from 416 inhabitants per square kilometer in 1980 to 475 in 2002. The Netherlands has experienced a large influx of labor migrants, mainly from rural regions of Turkey and Morocco in the 1960s. While their stays were intended to be temporary, most settled with their families, and their descendants make up a growing part of the population. Many second- and third-generation immigrants marry residents from their former home countries. Migrants from the former Dutch colony Surinam (Dutch Guyana) came to the Netherlands around 1975, when Surinam became independent and its inhabitants were given the choice to remain in Surinam or settle in the Netherlands. The Netherlands Antilles remain part of the kingdom of the Netherlands; while travel is not unrestricted, many Antilleans have also settled, more or less permanently, in the Netherlands. Asylum seekers from various countries (most prominently Iraq, Iran, Afghanistan, and Somalia) have augmented the nonindigenous population in recent years.

Residents are counted as nonethnic Dutch when either they or their father or mother were born outside of the Netherlands or hold a foreign nationality. By 2002, 2.97 million (18 percent) of the Dutch population was of nonethnic Dutch background, many living in the big towns (for instance, 45 percent of the population of Amsterdam was of nonethnic Dutch descent in 2002, as was 41 percent of the population of Rotterdam). Of these 2.97 million, 1.56 million (10 percent of the total population) had a non-Western background.

The population is aging rapidly, the mean age in 1999 being thirty-eight, having risen from 34.4 in 1980. Life expectancy in 2001 was 75.8 for males and 80.7 for females. About one in three marriages ends in divorce; in a sizable proportion of marriages (15 percent), at least one partner has been previously married. Since 2001, it has been possible for partners of the same sex to marry. Since the beginning of the 1990s, cohabiting partners have had effectively the same legal and fiscal status as officially married couples.

About one child in four is born out of wedlock, and about one in six lives in a single-parent household. All children ages five to fifteen receive full-time education. About 22 percent of the population between ages fifteen and sixty-four has higher education, and this figure has increased in recent years. Unemployment was historically low in the 1990s; while figures rose from 4.3 percent in 1980 to 11.7 percent in 1983, they declined thereafter, and the unemployment rate was 2 percent in 2001. Inflation, while low (falling from 6.9 percent in 1980 to 2.1 percent in 1999) for a considerable time, has increased somewhat lately. Seventy-one percent of households have one or more cars. Many people use bicycles or mopeds for transportation as the country is flat, towns are congested, and distances are small; more than 13 million people owned one or more bicycles in 2001 (Statistics Netherlands 2003).

The Netherlands has historically been perceived as a tolerant and in some ways permissive society. In recent years, abortion and euthanasia have been authorized and prostitution has been legalized. The Dutch drugs policy is (in)famous for its pragmatism, its permissiveness, and its irreconcilable elements (users may buy a certain amount of soft drugs legally in designated shops, but the owners of these shops cannot buy these drugs in a legal retail market). Sentencing until at least the mid-1980s was comparatively mild (Kommer 1994).

The Netherlands is a "welfare society": all who do not succeed in obtaining a job are entitled to welfare. Although levels have decreased somewhat in recent years and although the rules (and enforcement of these) have been tightened, it can still be said that no one in the Netherlands need go hungry or without a house to live in. Families with children receive child benefits. Much social housing is provided and health insurance is provided to people below a certain income level. Many bigger cities have concentrations of minorities and indigenous Dutch with lower incomes, but no real ghettos exist such as in the United States or the *banlieus* in Paris. Firearms are prohibited. Wim Kok, the former prime minister, often rode to work in The Hague on his bike.

II. The Criminal Justice System

Offenders who are caught are first processed through the police system. Until 1993, there were a national police force and 148 municipal police forces. A 1993 reorganization divided the police into twenty-five regional forces. Each falls under the management of the mayor of the largest city in the region. However, the public prosecutor is responsible for police investigative activities. There are also a small national force with specific tasks (e.g., motorway police, central criminal investigations, international contacts) and a military police force. Special agencies handle offenses like tax and social security fraud.

After the police decide that a suspect has committed a crime, the case, in principle, should be transferred to the public prosecutor's office. In a few cases, especially for juveniles who have committed minor offenses, the police may send the suspect home with a warning or a small fine, and no prosecution ensues. This is believed to occur in only

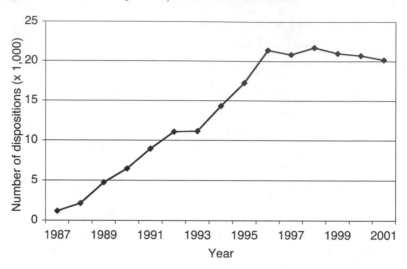

F<small>IG</small>. 1.—Number of HALT dispositions, 1987–2001

a very small proportion of cases. Since 1987, the police can deal with certain less serious offenses committed by juveniles by giving the juvenile a so-called HALT disposition, which is basically a kind of community service. See figure 1 for the development of HALT dispositions (Van der Heide and Eggen 2003). None of the offenses studied here can (officially) be dealt with by means of a HALT disposition.

The role of the prosecution is central. The prosecution is responsible for the investigation and, under the "expediency principle," decides whether to prosecute or drop the case. If the prosecutor decides to prosecute, he or she may bring the case to court or deal with it him- or herself, mostly by imposing a fine (a so-called *transactie* [transaction]). The offender must agree to the transaction (if he does not, the case will go to court), although by agreeing he does not admit guilt. One advantage for the offender is that no criminal record will show up in a background check. Only the judge can decide whether a person is guilty or not. Thus, there is no institutionalized "guilty plea" in the Netherlands, although the system by which the prosecutor and the defendant agree on a sanction resembles it. Transactions are not possible for the most serious offenses (e.g., for burglary, rape, robbery, and homicide) or in other designated circumstances (e.g., recidivism or drug addiction).

Figure 2 gives an overview of trends over time in use of the three main prosecutorial dispositions, that is, to drop the case, use a

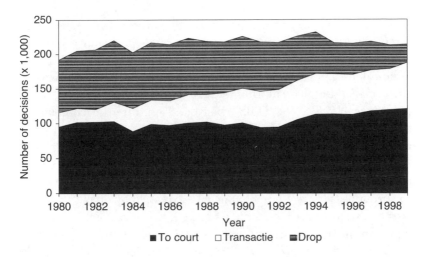

FIG. 2.—Prosecutor decisions, 1980–99

transaction, or bring the case to court. The absolute number of cases dropped has decreased, while the number of transactions has increased considerably. When comparing convictions in the Netherlands with those in other countries, transactions should be seen as equivalent to convictions, although from a strict legal point of view they are not.

Public prosecutors, though appointed directly by the minister of justice and the Crown, fall under a central office (Board of Procurators General, or *Parket-Generaal*) led by three chief prosecutors. These chief prosecutors fall directly under the responsibility of the minister of justice. Prosecutors, unlike judges, are not appointed for life.

The courts in first instance in the Netherlands consist of one judge (*politierechter*) for the less severe offenses (with a maximum custodial sentence of six months until recently) or three judges for the more serious cases (*meervoudige kamer*). Appeals courts always consist of three judges. There are no juries or lay judges. Only professional judges decide the verdict and the punishment. Judges are appointed for life by the minister of justice and the Crown.

When a case is brought to court, the offender convicted, and a punishment meted out, the punishment can assume various forms, including a fine, community service, a treatment kind of sanction (*leerstraf*), and incarceration. All can be imposed conditionally or unconditionally. In 1999, there were about 50,000 custodial sentences of which 20,000 were suspended. Almost 120,000 fines were imposed, of which

70,000 were transactions imposed by the prosecutor. There were about 20,000 community service and treatment sanctions. Sanctions can be distinguished conceptually: punishments must be proportional to the offenses; measures (such as treatment) serve different goals.

Especially for violent and sexual crimes, entrustment orders (*terbeschikkingstelling*, or "TBS") can be given, often in combination with a prison sentence (van Emmerik 1989, 1999). An entrustment order can be imposed for crimes carrying a maximum statutory penalty of at least four years of imprisonment and if hospital care is necessary to protect the safety of other people, the general public, or property. The order lasts for two years but may be extended by one or two years. Further extensions are possible (Tak 2003). In practice, the average time spent in an entrustment order is approximately five years (Leuw, Brouwers, and Smit 1999, p. 28). The average length of stay has increased in recent years, although figures are available only for those who have been released. A proportion of those upon whom treatment is imposed may end up spending the rest of their lives in confinement if their treatment does not produce the desired effect and their chances of recidivism remain high (Leuw et al. 1999).

The number of entrustment orders rose sharply during the period of our analysis, rising from fewer than 100 per year in 1980 to almost 200 in 1999. As a consequence, and presumably because of a growing reluctance by forensic staff to declare those entrusted "cured," the size of the population in entrustment facilities has also grown immensely. This means that those receiving an entrustment order must sometimes wait for years before they can be admitted and treatment can start.

A sentence is given not per offense but on the basis of the entire court case. A court case in the Netherlands always relates only to one offender. When several co-offenders have committed one crime, the cases may be combined in one court hearing, but, legally as well as statistically, they remain separate cases. About two-thirds of all court cases deal with one offense only. This is an average, however, and, especially for the less serious offenses, case files often contain more than one offense. For instance, a case may have burglary as a leading offense but also concern several other burglaries and property offenses such as motor vehicle theft or shoplifting. The less grave offenses thus do not appear in criminal and court statistics: they remain hidden behind the label of the most serious offense.

To complicate matters further, such nonleading offenses can be included in the case file in two ways: either as an offense taken into account in the verdict *(voeging ter terechtzitting)* or as an offense that is included simply to clean the slate of the defendant *(voeging ad informandum)*. The defendant can then no longer be prosecuted for this offense. Although perhaps odd at first sight, this practice is understandable if one realizes that the Netherlands has a system of non-accumulating sentence lengths. Sentence length does not relate linearly to the number of offenses: after a certain number of offenses, addition of further cases does not affect sentence severity. Adding such cases to the case file thus is done as a matter of efficiency. This practice of combining offenses into one case results in underestimation of the number of recorded crimes leading to a conviction for some offense types.

Offenders are punishable under the criminal code from twelve years of age, although prison sentences are seldom imposed on youth under fourteen. Determinate custodial sentences vary between one day and twenty years. Life sentences are rarely imposed (about one per year). Sentence length depends on the seriousness of the offense tried and the circumstances of the case. Among the latter, the foremost are the circumstances under which the crime was committed and the personal circumstances of the offender.

All prisons are state prisons. They are small; the largest has a capacity of fewer than 400 cells. The total capacity is 13,000 cells. Three-quarters are in so-called remand houses where pretrial detainees and persons with short prison sentences are held. Security levels can vary from half open (or even open) penitentiary establishments for some prisoners who have served the largest part of a long sentence to maximum security units for prisoners considered extremely high risks for escape. There are prisons especially for juveniles.

The quality of life in a Dutch prison is relatively high, at least in a material sense. Detainees may have televisions and videos in their cells (at their own expense), and activities such as sports are available. Prisoners serving long-term sentences may be granted the right to receive nonsupervised visits. The prison regime is also, however, very strict. Except for pretrial detainees, prisoners are obliged to do prison labor and contacts with the outside world are strictly regulated. The regime in the maximum security units was adjudged inhumane by the Council of Europe's Prevention of Torture Committee. The European Human Rights Court recently adjudged it a violation of the European Human Rights Convention (Tak 2003).

Dutch prisons have long provided a cell for each prisoner. Because of the fast-growing prison population, since 2003, as a test, two persons have been assigned to share a cell in some prisons. The average number of prison staff per detainee is very high, almost 1:1.

The Netherlands has a system of routine early release; prisoners are entitled to this and can lose this right only if they grossly misbehave. The calculation of the early release date varies according to sentence length (for long sentences at 67 percent, for short sentences according to a more complicated formula and generally at a relatively later point). The exception is life sentences, for which there is no early release (except when a pardon is granted). Early release is unconditional; there is no obligation that the released prisoner keep in contact with the probation service. Aftercare projects carried out by the probation service are thus entirely voluntary.

The probation service has an important role in relation to community services. It operates its own projects where community service can be done, and it has contacts with other institutions and companies in which community service sentences can be carried out. About 70 percent of the community service sentences are completed successfully. Offenders who do not finish the community service must serve a prison sentence instead. In practice, however, due to prison space shortages, the offender often is brought before a court again for imposition of a new sentence.

III. Criminal Justice Statistics

Like many countries, the Netherlands does not have an integrated system allowing an offender to be tracked from the commission of the offense through release from prison. Estimates of case processing are always based on aggregate information.

The Netherlands has a long tradition of victim surveys. The first nationwide survey was carried out in 1973 by the Research and Documentation Center (Wetenschappelijk Onderzoek- en Documentatie Centrum [WODC]) of the Ministry of Justice (Van Dijk and Steinmetz 1979). In 1980, this survey was transferred to Statistics Netherlands, which has been conducting it ever since. The sample is approximately 10,000 (Statistics Netherlands 1997).

Since 1993, victimization surveys have been carried out by the police (the Police Monitor), with much larger samples but a different sampling frame, interviewing method, and questionnaire (*Politiemonitor Bevolking* [PMB] 1999). National police figures for offenses and arrests are published yearly by the Ministry of Justice and by Statistics Netherlands (Schreuders et al. 2001). Police statistics are based on offense-level information reported to Statistics Netherlands by the police agencies. Prosecution, conviction, and sentencing information at the case level is, thanks to the central role the prosecution plays, collected by the prosecutor's offices and published yearly by both the Ministry of Justice and Statistics Netherlands (Schreuders et al. 2001). When this essay was written, conviction and sentencing statistics were available only from the district courts, where crimes are dealt with in first instance.

The yearly victimization and criminal justice data present two main comparability issues. First, definitions change. This encompasses both legal definitions and "conceptual" definitions used in victim surveys. Similar issues arise concerning recording by the police: for instance, there are indications that the police increasingly have labeled purse snatching as a violent offense, when in earlier times it was generally labeled as a property offense. At present, we have no way to test for the latter comparability issue; apart from noting it, we set it aside. The definitional issue is also hard to investigate, although one could—when a law has been changed—attempt to identify sudden statistical changes that might be by-products.

Second, victimization and criminal justice data are hard to link up. The victim survey questionnaires do not always use the same definitions as the police and other criminal justice agencies. In addition, police data contain offenses committed against companies, while the victim surveys contain only offenses against individuals. The absence of an "offender-based" tracking system and the practice of disposing of several offenses under the heading of the leading offense are other significant problems. The ancillary offenses are not sentenced separately, sentences do not add up, and these offenses do not appear in the statistics and, in a sense, "evaporate" statistically. It may thus seem as if fewer offenses are dealt with than is the case: offenses are dealt with but are not counted.

Thus, while victimization and police data are always at the offense level, from prosecution onward, we necessarily switch to the aggregate level of cases, which may contain one or more offenses. This makes for fundamental incomparability. For in-depth studies, it is therefore necessary to conduct tailored studies of special offenses. Such generalizable, in-depth information can be gathered from additional sources such as the Ministry of Justice's Prosecution and Sentencing Monitor. This monitor (which has had two waves so far) analyzes a stratified sample of first-instance criminal court cases, recording information on the defendant, the offenses, and the victims, as well as various situational and qualitative aspects of the offenses.

IV. Victimization and Police Data

Three victim surveys are conducted with some regularity in the Netherlands. The "Victim Survey" (*Slachtofferenquete*) is conducted and published by Statistics Netherlands. This survey was conducted annually from 1973 to 1979 by the WODC. From 1981 to 1985, the survey was conducted yearly by Statistics Netherlands in collaboration with the WODC. In 1983, the sampling frame was changed. From 1985 onward, the survey was conducted every odd year by Statistics Netherlands through the "Survey Victims of Crime" (*Enquete Slachtoffers Misdrijven*). In 1992, the "Survey Legal Protection and Safety" (*Enquete Rechtsbescherming en Veiligheid* [or ERV]) replaced the victim survey. With few changes, this became part of a wider survey called POLS (*Permanent Onderzoek Leefsituatie*) in 1997. The POLS survey employs continuous interviewing and therefore produces different statistics than do victim surveys administered during a short period. The parameters estimated by the POLS survey are therefore inherently incomparable to those from other such surveys and are not comparable to those produced before 1997 (Koeijers 2003). The years 1981, 1983, 1992, and 1997 thus constitute points at which some irregularities in the CBS (Centraal Bureau voor de Statistiek) victim surveys may be expected due to changes in research design, questionnaire, and frequency and periodicity in data collection.

Since 1980, samples have been drawn from the Dutch population aged fifteen and over, based on the council administrations (Gemeentelijke Basis Administratie). Information is collected in face-to-face interviews using computer-aided personal interviewing (CAPI). Approximately 10,000 respondents are interviewed in each wave for the victimization questions. The data are reweighted to match age, sex, marital status, employment status, administrative area, urbanization, and housing conditions. The response rate was approximately 55 percent in 1999.

The victim survey does not contain information on all crimes we are interested in. Apart from homicide and rape, robbery also is not a separate item in this survey. Information on assault is present from 1992 onward. Information on other offenses is present for all years.

The Police Monitor (*Politiemonitor Bevolking*) is coordinated and conducted biannually by the Dutch ministries of internal affairs and justice. Four waves were completed through 1999: in 1993, 1995, 1997, and 1999. Samples are drawn from the Dutch population aged fifteen and over. The sampling frame differs from that of the Statistics Netherlands victim surveys, as do the data collection method and reweighting procedures. The sampling frame is based on telephone registration by KPN, the former state-owned telephone company. Interviewing is done by telephone using CATI. The total sample size is around 75,000. The total response rate has steadily decreased since 1993 and was 46 percent in 1999. Questions refer to events in the preceding year. Data are reweighted to match age and sex. Respondents with unlisted phones do not appear in the sample, nor do respondents with only a mobile phone or no phone at all. It has been shown that those who refuse to be interviewed do not differ systematically from interviewed respondents, but it is widely assumed that nonethnic Dutch respondents are underrepresented or, more precisely, are more underrepresented than in other victim surveys. This and the different time frame over which victimization events are recorded make the results partly incomparable to those of the CBS victim survey. The findings of the Police Monitor over the years can be compared without reserve, however, as there have been no or only very minor changes between waves.

The International Crime Victimization Survey (ICVS) is conducted by researchers in various countries and coordinated by the United Nations Office on Drugs and Crime. The ICVS is most comparable to the Police Monitor. For the ICVS, random digit dialing is employed, which provides more representative coverage. Reweighting procedures resemble those of the Police Monitor. Response levels have varied between 58 percent and 65 percent for the years 1988, 1991, 1995, and 1999, in which the survey was carried out (each published one year later). The sample size is small, with approximately 2,000 respondents every wave.

A recent study compared differences in victimization levels among the various surveys and concluded that differences were likely due to differences in sampling frame, ordering of questions, framing of questions, and definitions employed. Some differences were very hard to explain (Schoen, Defize, and Bakker 2000).

For our victimization estimates, we used the total population size for the years 1980–99 as taken from the *Bevolkingsstatistiek*, a regular publication by Statistics Netherlands that contains demographic information and disaggregated population statistics. The population base for offending, conviction, and incarceration statistics was the population over eleven years of age. For the victim surveys, the population aged fifteen and over constituted the population base (Statistics Netherlands 1999).

The percentages of reported offenses were taken from the ICVS. Because the number of offenders per offense is not recorded for each offense on a yearly basis in the Netherlands, we drew estimates from several studies, based mainly on police data (Schreuders et al. 2001).

The number of police-recorded offenses was taken from the "Police Statistics" (*Politiestatistiek*), which are aggregated and published by Statistics Netherlands. The figures are based on police records, which are collected by the regional police departments in the Netherlands. Offenses are classified at first report. Police recording procedures have remained unaltered over the investigation period. Processing procedures have undergone numerous changes over the years; these differ among the various regions in the Netherlands. The Dutch police were reorganized in 1992, which may have caused some turbulence in the data. As part of this reorganization, specialized units dealing with youth and sex crimes were dissolved.

There may be additional differences between police-recorded offenses and victim survey results, as the police also record offenses against persons under fifteen years of age. We applied a correction factor where necessary, based on special studies (De Poot 2002) or according to the fraction of the population under age fifteen.

A. Burglary

Burglary (*inbraak*) is recorded under article 311 of the penal code ("qualified theft"). There is no separate article for burglary; article 311 covers all cases in which an item is stolen through breaking and entering plus several other "qualified" cases of theft (such as stealing cattle from a meadow or theft carried out with a group of offenders). Using the SRM (*Strafecht Monitor*), burglary is estimated to occur in one-fifth of all entries for article 311. In principle, the scope of this article is thus wider than what is popularly known as *inbraak*. This causes discrepancies between victim surveys and police records used. Burglary has been an item in the victim survey and the Police Monitor, respectively, since 1980 and 1993.

The burglary rate, according to the Statistics Netherlands victimization surveys, rose from about thirty-five per 1,000 households in 1980 to a level fluctuating between approximately fifty and sixty per 1,000 households in the period from 1985 to 1995, and then it fell back to about thirty-five per 1,000 households until 1999 (fig. 3a).

The police-recorded burglary rate behaved similarly. It started out at 2.6 per 1,000 population, rose almost threefold to 7.38 in 1995, and fell to 5.9 in 1999 (fig. 3a). There is, however, a small overall increase over time. The percentage of burglaries reported to the police varied between 85 percent and 94 percent. As data on the number of offenders per offense are available only for the years 1998 and 1999, these were averaged and held constant over the years, which resulted in a trend for the offender population exactly paralleling the victim survey rate trend.

B. Motor Vehicle Theft

Motor vehicle theft (*diefstal motorvoertuigen*) encompasses the stealing of motorized vehicles. There is no special article for this item in the Dutch penal code. In a legal sense, motor vehicle theft should be recorded under the main article for theft, article 310, under which all kinds of stealing are recorded, including shoplifting and the like. In practice, motor vehicle theft is also recorded under article 311 (qualified theft) and under less likely articles such as embezzlement (art. 321), joyriding (art. 11, Road Law), and fencing (art. 416). No statistics are available on the distribution of motor vehicle offenses under these different recording categories. Car theft data are reported by Statistics Netherlands per the number of inhabitants over age fifteen. In the Police Monitor, it is reported per the number of vehicles, which makes these statistics difficult to compare. Car theft has been an item in the victim survey since 1980 and in the Police Monitor since 1993.

Incidence data for motor vehicle theft were compiled by two separate institutions over our investigation period: until 1994, the police compiled these offenses; since 1995, the Stichting Aanpak Voertuigcriminaliteit (SAVc; Foundation for Countering Vehicle Crime) has maintained a central register. It is odd, and inexplicable, that the data differed widely at the time when police responsibility for the data was transferred to the SAVc. We were unable to correct the two curves in such a way that the resulting curve was uninterrupted, but we applied a 10 percent correction to the police data (the rationale is that the police count included company vehicles and the SAVc did not, which would account for approximately a 10 percent difference).

The victimization rate for motor vehicle theft rose from 11.8 per 1,000 households in 1980 to a peak of 16.4 per 1,000 households in 1986. It then remained, after some turbulence, at a steady level around fourteen from 1990 to 1992, then decreased to around eight from 1996 to 1999 (fig. 3b).

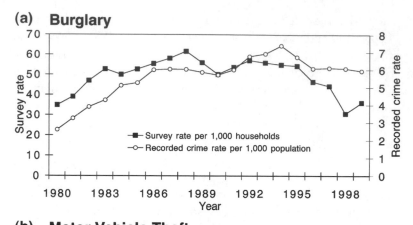

(a) Burglary

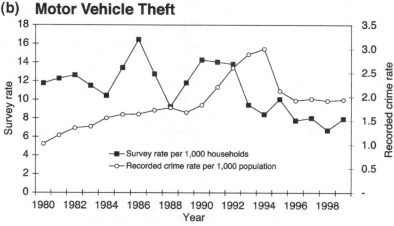

(b) Motor Vehicle Theft

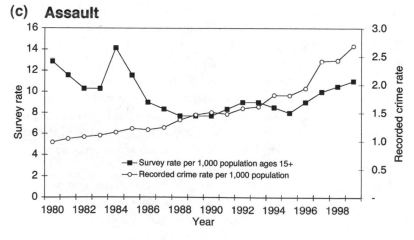

(c) Assault

Fɪɢ. 3.—Survey and recorded crime rates

(d) **Robbery**

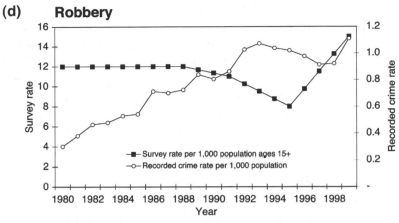

(e) **Rape**

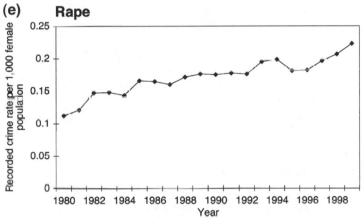

(f) **Homicide**

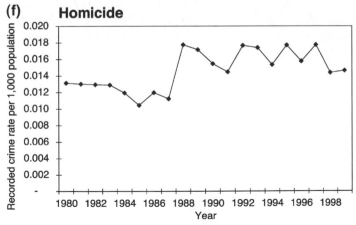

Fig. 3.—*Continued*

177

The recorded motor vehicle theft rate started out at 1.02 per 1,000 population in 1980 and rose sharply after 1990 nearly threefold to three per 1,000 population in 1994. The data, as described above, are built from two different series, however. The second series, taken from a centralized registration in effect since 1995, started out at 2.13 per 1,000 population and decreased to 1.94 per 1,000 population in 1999 (fig. 3*b*). The reporting rate for motor vehicle theft is high: between 90 and 94 percent. As with burglary, data on the number of offenders per offense were available only for the years 1998 and 1999; these were, therefore, averaged and held constant.

C. Assault

Assault can be found in articles 300–306 of the penal code. Some of these articles deal with minor intentional assaults and have subtitles for ensuing grave consequences; other articles deal with intentionally serious assaults. There are indications that a considerable number of violent offenses may be coded under an article for public order offenses (Cozijn and Essers 2002). Assault has been present as an item in the victim survey since 1992 and in the Police Monitor since 1993. The victim survey employed a much wider definition from 1980 to 1992. During this period, the victim survey asked about *handtastelijkheden*, which can be translated as "pawing" or "over-intimate unwanted touching" or as "violent interactions such as in fights." The victim survey also had a change in study design in 1997. The ICVS is not an alternative source here as it combines assault with "threats."

It was difficult to decide which series to employ for our analysis. The Statistics Netherlands victim survey provides a long series of data, and the Police Monitor, conducted since 1993 only, provides a series of much shorter length. However, the Police Monitor underwent no changes in study design, and the last three years of the Statistics Netherlands victim survey employ a different time window. A weakness of the Police Monitor is that minorities may not be represented as well as in the Statistics Netherlands survey.

We decided to use the Police Monitor series, but we hooked onto Statistics Netherlands data for the previous years by synchronizing the 1992 figure to the Police Monitor 1993 survey figure. However, looking at the results, and especially the discrepancy between the survey data and the police-recorded data in the period 1980–92, we decided that asking about *handtastelijkheden* and not "assault" caused too much disruption. Therefore, we decided to disregard the survey data for that period.

Victimization levels declined—apart from a peak in 1984, for which we have no explanation—more or less steadily from 12.9 per 1,000 population in 1981 to a low of 7.7 from 1988 to 1990, after which levels rose to eleven per 1,000 population in 1999 (fig. 3c). The Statistics Netherlands survey shows a slight increase after 1997.

Police-recorded assault levels have increased steadily (with an average annual growth of 5.1 percent) since 1980, from 0.97 per 1,000 population in 1980 to 2.68 per 1,000 population in 1999 (fig. 3c). The reporting rate was fairly constant (between 39 and 43 percent). In addition to the increase in the number of recorded assaults since the early 1990s, the number of offenders per offense increased (from 1.04 in 1989/90 to 1.32 in 1998), resulting in a considerable increase in the offender population.[1]

D. Robbery

Robbery is found in articles 312 and 317 of the penal code. Neither the victim survey nor the Police Monitor asks about this offense. The only available source is the International Crime Victimization Survey.

Figures for robbery were unavailable before 1988, so levels up to that year were set at the 1988 level. After a decrease from twelve per 1,000 population in 1988 to a low of eight in 1995, robbery levels almost doubled to fifteen per 1,000 population in 1999 (fig. 3d). These observations are based on only a few measurement points: incidence levels were taken from the ICVS, which was administered in 1988, 1991, 1995, and 1999. Given the small sample size, the low of eight may be due to instability resulting from small numbers of respondents reporting this offense.

The police-recorded robbery rate rose strongly from 0.3 per 1,000 population in 1980 to 1.07 per 1,000 in 1993, after which it decreased for a time and then increased sharply in 1999 to 1.11 per 1,000 population (fig. 3d). The average annual growth for the whole period was 6 percent. Robbery was the only offense in this analysis for which the reporting rate was not stable: reporting levels for 1988, 1991, 1995, and 1999 were, respectively, 54 percent, 59 percent, 70 percent, and 63 percent. As with assault, the average number of offenders per offense increased from 1.19 in 1989 up to a high of 1.92 in 1997, resulting in a larger offender population (Bijleveld and Smit 2004).

---

[1] We report on the number of offenders and relate our data to our estimate of the size of the offender population for specific offenses, but we draw no conclusions from these data. We assume that the police, for efficiency reasons, recorded fewer offenses than were cleared. This artificially inflates the size of the offender population.

E. Rape

Rape is defined in article 242 of the penal code as "forcing another through (threats with) violence or (threats with other facts) to undergo acts that (partly) consist of sexual penetration of the body." Since 1991, rape is not, as previously, legally excluded by marriage. Also since 1991, a rape need not entail sexual intercourse. In 1998, a rape conviction by the Appeals Chamber for a kiss that involved forcing the offender's tongue into the victim's mouth was upheld in the highest court (*Hoge Raad*). Rape is the only offense for which the legal definition changed during our study period to encompass a much wider spectrum of behaviors. We have no data that distinguish female from male rape. A number of articles covering sexual intercourse with children or minors, not necessarily forced, are not labeled as rape although they may be labeled as such in other countries (notably articles 243–45). Rape is not an item in the victim survey, the Police Monitor, or the ICVS, so we have no victimization estimates.

Recorded levels doubled from 0.1124 per 100,000 population in 1981 to 0.2228 in 1999 (an average annual growth of 2.7 percent). The data do not exhibit a sudden rise that would reflect the wider definition of rape since 1991 (see fig. 3*e*). There was no clear change in the number of offenders per offense for sexual offenses (no figure is available for rape only).

F. Homicide

The Netherlands does not have one word for homicide as is the case in the English language. *Moord* (murder) and *doodslag* (nonnegligent manslaughter) are dealt with in articles 287–91. Two separate articles for *kindermoord* entail the (premeditated) killing by a mother of her own child shortly after birth under fear of discovery of her delivery (articles 290–91). Euthanasia and abortion are punishable offenses only when prespecified conditions under which it is carried out are not met. A euthanasia law that codified existing practice was passed in 2002. After fairly similar levels of homicide incidence fluctuating around 0.012 per 1,000 population until 1987, recorded homicide levels rose to a level around .016, an overall 30 percent rise (see fig. 3*f*).

V. Conviction, Sentencing, and Incarceration

Study of offending, conviction, and sentencing processes from criminal justice information and statistics is a hazardous affair in the Netherlands. The criminal justice system is highly intricate, and criminal justice statistics grossly oversimplify reality. Court cases, as explained earlier, appear in the statistics under the article number of the leading offense, which is often (but not always) the article with the heaviest penalty attached to it.

Information on sentences was in general obtained from *OMdata* (prosecution data), an extract from the operational database containing information on all prosecuted cases and sentences by the courts of first instance. It is maintained by the Board of Procurators General. Sentencing databases contain information on sentences of first instance only; there is no centralized record of sentences passed in appeal for the period under observation. The data between 1992 and 1994 are generally considered less reliable than at other times; having no alternative, we use them.

Less serious crimes increasingly are sentenced through community service orders. In addition, under specific conditions, and increasingly often, the prosecutor may deal with the case himself or herself. For some offenses, we may expect an increase in the number of prosecutors' dispositions at the expense of judges' verdicts; given maximum sentence lengths, these are assault, some particular and rare forms of burglary, and motor vehicle theft. Berghuis (1994) showed that prosecutors' dispositions have mainly replaced conditional sentences. In addition, during the past ten years, community service orders have become increasingly popular for juveniles and first offenders, and these have become a regular type of sentence that can be combined with other sentences. One may doubt whether this popularity has been at the expense of unconditional custodial sentences, as, especially for juveniles, community service orders have mainly replaced fines. However, community service orders have become so popular and shortages of space in the prisons at times so acute that one may also assume that some selection effect must have taken place: lighter cases must increasingly have received such orders with the heavier cases or the more persistent perpetrators branching off to custodial sentences. Because of this selection effect, custodial sentences are likely to have become on average heavier for offenses for which community service orders could be meted out.

Secure hospital orders were also included in our calculations, as, while not officially a penal sanction, they are a measure that imposes custody on an offender. No centralized data are available on such orders. We obtained estimates of the percentage of such orders given for robbery, assault, homicide, and rape, and obtained an estimate of their average durations (van Emmerik 1989, 1999). For homicide, on the basis of a 1998 study by Smit et al. (2001), we added a fixed yearly percentage of 2 percent secure hospital orders to all homicides.

Early release is an entitlement. Time served is, except in the case of gross misbehavior, a fixed fraction of sentence length. When the unconditional sentence length does not exceed one year, a detainee is released when six months plus one-third of the remaining sentence has been served. When the unconditional sentence length is more than one year, a detainee is released when two-thirds has been served. We have employed this formula, interpolating for average sentences between six months and one year. In general, the time-served trend follows the trend in custodial sentence length. Very few sentences are life sentences (on average one per year), so no special estimation procedures were employed to account for this.

For rape, robbery, and assault, data on sentence length were taken from Ministry of Justice and Statistics Netherlands publications (Schreuders et al. 2001). For homicide, average custodial sentence length was estimated from the 1998 homicide study (Smit et al. 2001); no better data are available, so we have only one number for average custodial sentence length. We set the average duration of the secure hospital orders (for rape, assault, homicide, and robbery) at the current average duration of five years.

For motor vehicle theft and burglary, no statistics are available on sentence length, as the offenses have no special articles in the penal code. We estimated average sentence lengths using the SRM Prosecution and Sentencing Monitor. This database contains information on a representative sample of prosecuted criminal cases, with waves carried out approximately every four years. It specifies all offenses in the court case with the corresponding delinquent behaviors. This makes the SRM Prosecution and Sentencing Monitor uniquely appropriate for studying ancillary offenses that either have no article of their own or that may easily (because they are relatively "light" offenses) disappear behind a more serious leading article. From the SRM Prosecution and Sentencing Monitor (which had information from two waves only at the time this analysis was carried out), we estimated custodial sentence lengths as 12.7 months for burglary and 8.5 months for motor vehicle theft.

A. Burglary

The conviction rate for burglary (see fig. 4a) increased between 1980 and 1985 from about 0.4 to 0.6 per 1,000 population, after which it

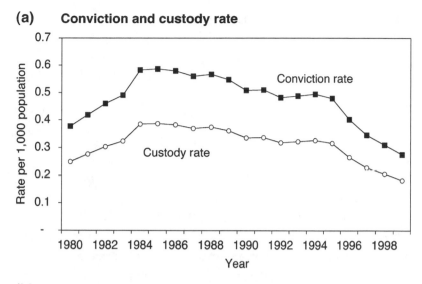

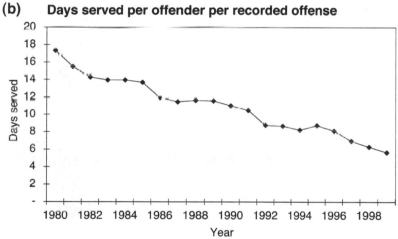

FIG. 4.—Burglary conviction and custody rates per 1,000 population and days served per offender per recorded offense.

slowly decreased to about 0.3 in 1999. Since the probability of a custodial sentence after conviction for burglary was set at an equal number of 0.66 all years, as estimated from the SRM Prosecution and Sentencing Monitor, the custody rate follows the same pattern as the conviction rate. Also, sentence length was set constant at 12.7 months per incarceration sentence, resulting also in a fixed actual time served of 11.4 months. This means that the trend in the number of days served

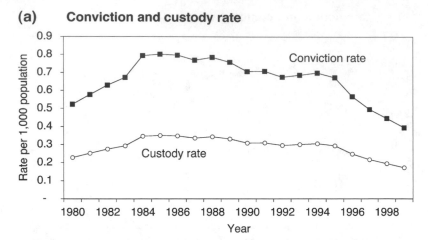

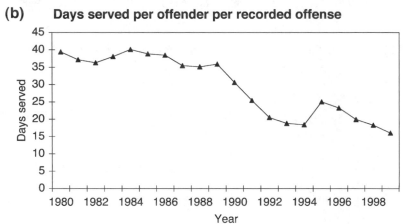

Fig. 5.—Motor vehicle theft conviction and custody rates per 1,000 population and days served per offender per recorded offense.

per offender per recorded burglary, which decreased steadily from seventeen to six (see fig. 4b), is the result of two factors only: the probability of an offender being caught and the probability of the offender being convicted.

B. Motor Vehicle Theft

For motor vehicle theft, the conviction rate per 1,000 population (see fig. 5a) followed the same overall pattern as the conviction rate for burglary, because the figures were based upon the same articles in the penal code. As with burglary, the custodial sentences after conviction

(44 percent), the sentence length (8.5 months), and the actual time served (8.1 months) were held constant over the whole period.

The number of days served per offender per recorded offense decreased from thirty-nine to sixteen, again following the same pattern as with burglary (fig. 5b). Because of the similarity with burglary due to technical reasons, we do not offer an in-depth explanation of the data for motor vehicle theft.

C. Assault

Both the conviction rate (from 0.3 to 0.8 per 1,000 population) and the custody rate (from 0.04 to 0.11 per 1,000 population) for assault increased steadily. The probability of custody given conviction decreased from 14.1 percent in 1980 to 5.9 percent in 1990, after which it jumped to 13.3 percent and remained at approximately this level until 1999, when it rose to 14.9 percent (fig. 6a).

The average sentence length increased steadily from four to six months in the period 1980–95, then decreased to about 4.5 months in 1999 (fig. 6b). Because early release seldom occurs in the case of short prison sentences, time served is almost the same as sentence length.

The average time behind bars per conviction has doubled since 1980: after declining from 11.6 days per conviction in 1980 to nine days per conviction in 1990, it nearly doubled to 17.1 in 1991 and rose some more to 21 days per conviction in 1999. Because the recorded crime rate and the conviction rate increased in roughly the same way, the number of days served per offender per recorded offense followed the same pattern (fig. 6c).

D. Robbery

The robbery conviction and custody rates also increased considerably, at factors of three and 3.5, respectively. The probability of custody after conviction has fluctuated, hovering between 60 and 65 percent during the whole period, except for a drop and subsequent rise in the period 1991–94 (fig. 7a).

Average sentence length increased from about eleven months in 1982 to seventeen months in 1994, falling back to about fourteen months in 1999. Time served followed the same pattern on a slightly lower level (fig. 7b).

Days served per conviction fluctuated between 200 and 250 days, although the level since 1995, following a big increase in the preceding two years, is somewhat higher. The number of days served per offender

Conviction and custody rates and percent custody per conviction

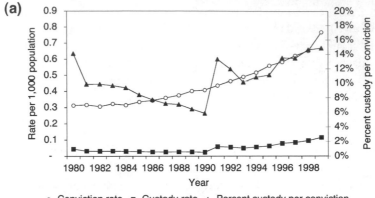

(a)

–○– Conviction rate –■– Custody rate –▲– Percent custody per conviction

Average sentence length and average time served

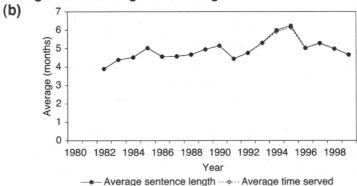

(b)

–●– Average sentence length ···◇··· Average time served

Days served per conviction and per offender per recorded offense

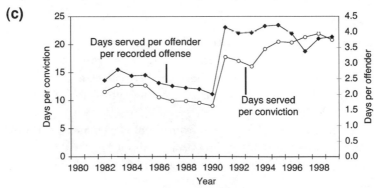

(c)

Fıɢ. 6.—Assault conviction and custody rates per 1,000 population and percent custody per conviction, average sentence length and time served, and days served per conviction and per offender per recorded offense.

Conviction and custody rates and percent custody per conviction

(a)

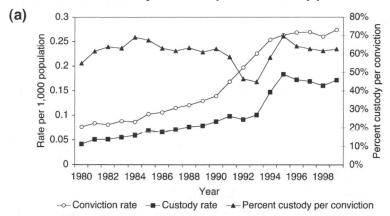

—○— Conviction rate —■— Custody rate —▲— Percent custody per conviction

Average sentence length and average time served

(b)

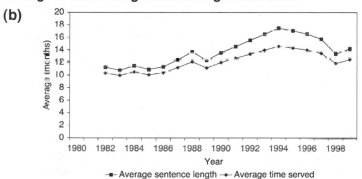

—■— Average sentence length —◆— Average time served

Days served per conviction and per offender per recorded offense

(c)

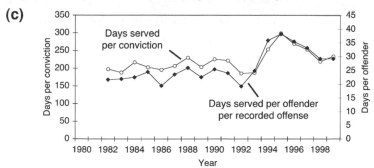

Fig. 7.—Robbery conviction and custody rates per 1,000 population and percent custody per conviction, average sentence length and time served, and days served per conviction and per offender per recorded offense.

per recorded offense increased from twenty-two to twenty-nine over the whole period, suggesting that the "cost" for robbers has definitely gone up since 1980 (fig. 7c).

E. Rape

The conviction and custody rates per 1,000 population for rape are much the same and fairly stable (except for erratic behavior in the first half of the 1990s). Only the conviction rate seemed somewhat higher at the end of the period. The custody percentage given conviction, which was over 80 percent in the 1980s, decreased to about 65 percent in the 1990s (fig. 8a).

Sentence length increased considerably, from eleven to twenty-seven months. Time served, however, because early release is used primarily for longer sentences, increased much less, from ten to seventeen months (fig. 8b).

The average number of days per conviction for rape rose from 259 to a little under 400 in 1998; the same pattern can be seen in the days served per offender per recorded offense: from about fifty in 1980 to seventy-two in 1998. The figures for 1999 for both were suddenly lower, however (fig. 8c).

F. Homicide

For homicide, only conviction data from the last five to eight years are available. Sparse data and erratic behavior of these data due to small numbers make it impossible to discern trends. Since almost all convicted offenders receive an unsuspended custodial sentence (between 90 and 95 percent), the conviction and custody rates per 1,000 population are much the same (fig. 9a). The lower values for the conviction rates in the years 1993 and 1994 are probably due to the general unreliability of the data in this period.

Average sentence length was between 100 and 120 months. The time served, however, is much lower due to early release after serving two-thirds (fig. 9b). Because most offenders are convicted and most receive unsuspended custodial sentences, days served per conviction and per offender give no extra information.

VI. Implications and Recommendations

Numerous explanations can be envisaged for cumulative crime trends. Tests of intricate hypotheses about the mechanisms generating the trends would require lots of data. Here, only (very) short

Conviction and custody rates and percent custody per conviction

(a)

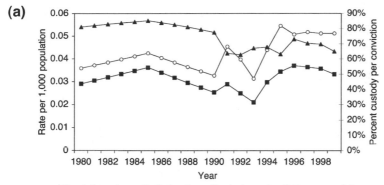

−○− Conviction rate −■− Custody rate −▲− Percentage of custody per conviction

Average sentence length and average time served

(b)

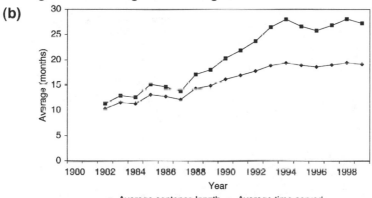

−■− Average sentence length −◆− Average time served

Days served per conviction and per offender per recorded offense

(c)

Fig. 8.—Rape conviction and custody rates per 1,000 population and percent custody per conviction, average sentence length and time served, and days served per conviction and per offender per recorded offense.

Conviction and custody rates and percent custody per conviction

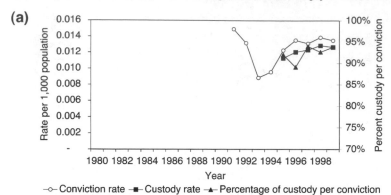

Average sentence length and average time served

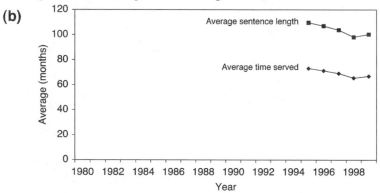

FIG. 9.—Homicide conviction and custody rates per 1,000 population and percent custody per conviction, and average sentence length and time served.

time series are available. Moreover, the data span a period in which major societal changes took place and in which public perceptions of offenses and their seriousness may have changed considerably, and trends in urbanization and immigration may have changed crime patterns. In mathematical terms, there are more unknowns than equations, so we will never be able conclusively to test explanations for trends.

While thus covering our tracks by stipulating that all explanations are tentative, at the end of this essay, we put forward a number of possible explanations for trends in crime and punishment during the period 1980–99. We attempt to explain the trend in the ultimate dependent variable, the population custody rate. The population custody rate is an ultimate outcome measure as it is the result of the cumulative forces of crime supply, police work, prosecutorial diversion, conviction probability, and custody probability. For those offenses for which we deem we have sufficient and sufficiently reliable data, we attempt to unravel whether, say, a rising custody rate is due to more crime, increased police efforts, or increased punitiveness. Our conclusions are formulated in terms of likelihood and probability. Drawing conclusions is difficult as several mechanisms will be at work, and these are not always operating in the same direction. We employ additional data where necessary.

A. Explaining Trends in Violent Crime Outcomes

We have discussed numerous trends for six offenses. We do not always consider the data to be wholly reliable. This is most notable for the motor vehicle theft police-recorded data, but it also extends to other series as well. We have sometimes presented victimization series for which the definitions of measured concepts may have changed, making the data for the various years noncomparable. For some variables, we had very limited data, so that we could not present or sensibly estimate series at all. In such cases, data have been presented for the sake of completeness, but we do not discuss such data extensively. In this subsection, we try to explain why various disposition patterns changed.

1. *Assault.* The population incarceration rate for assault, shown in figure 6a, decreased toward 1990, after which it jumped suddenly and increased further from 1996 onward. The population conviction rate rose as well, though not in the same fashion as the police figures; it picked up from 1984 onward, after which it grew almost linearly every year until a quicker rise in 1999. At first glance, it appears that more assaults were recorded by the police, that there were relatively the same but therefore absolutely more convictions for assault, and that the percentage of the population incarcerated for assault has increased. The number of convictions for assault divided by the number of police-recorded assaults remained fairly stable at about 0.25: about one in four police-recorded assaults ended up as a conviction. Up to the conviction stage, the system adapted to the increasing influx of offenses and achieved a similar fraction of the increasing numbers of recorded offenses convicted over the years.

Did the number of recorded assaults increase because there were more assaults? There has been a fierce discussion about rising police

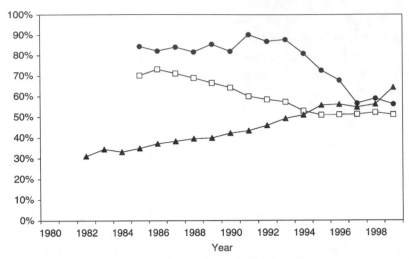

-□- Suspected per recorded -●- Prosecuted per suspected -▲- Convicted per prosecuted

Fig. 10.—Assault ratios of suspected, prosecuted, and convicted offenders

assault figures and whether these reflect a real increase or reflect increased administrative efficiency or greater attention by the police to violent crime (Wittebrood and Junger 1999; Rovers 2000). Victim survey data for assault are useful to a limited extent only. If the rising figures reflect increased efficiency, then we would expect the same rise for any serious offense; if the rising figures instead reflect increased attention to violent crime, we would expect a similar rise for all violent offenses. We leave the issue here and return to it later.

To shed more light on the assault population custody and conviction rates, we made additional calculations. First, we calculated the number of suspects per year (we have data from 1985 onward) divided by the number of recorded offenses (multiplied by the average number of offenders per assault to correct for multiple offending). This can be seen as a crude indicator of the clearance rate (see fig. 10). It appears that the clearance rate went down from about 70 percent in 1986 to about 50 percent toward 1999.

Next, we computed the number of defendants recorded per year for assault at the prosecutor's office, divided by the number of suspects for assault. This measure reflects the percentage of suspects who proceed into the criminal justice system for assault. As such, it reflects a police filtering process. As figure 10 shows, this ratio remained almost level and fairly high (around 85 percent) until 1993, after which it decreased dramatically to a little under 60 percent. By 1999, four out of ten identified assault suspects were not referred to the prosecutor's office.

As a last indicator, we computed the number of assault convictions per prosecuted defendant (see, again, fig. 10). This can be seen as an effectiveness measure, as it shows how many prosecuted cases end up in conviction. This ratio increased steadily from 1982. All in all, figure 10 is highly indicative of a filtering process: relatively fewer recorded assaults involved an identified suspect and relatively fewer of these suspects ended up in front of a prosecutor, but those who did had a doubled chance of conviction: from 30 percent to over 60 percent.

One could tentatively interpret the various trends in this figure as a filtering out of the potentially "successful" cases with a high likelihood of conviction. A different explanation is that the more serious cases were filtered out. This filtering is attributable solely to the police until 1993, after which they refer progressively fewer offenses to the prosecutor's office (as described above, sentence length does not increase beyond a certain number of offenses, and the police have often been reported to stop questioning at that number). Another simple possible explanation is that offenses are sent on but more are combined into case files at the prosecution level, so that fewer show up as separate cases (recall that offenses are counted at the police level and cases at the prosecution level).

It appears that the criminal justice system has become more efficient: faced with a rising number of assault offenses—whether or not due to a real increase in violence—relatively smaller proportions have been tried, of which larger proportions end up convicted. These countertrends do not even out the conviction rate: it more than doubled from 1980 to 1999.

Assaults can be dealt with by the prosecutor himself (a transaction). One remaining question is, therefore, whether these convictions are mainly judges' verdicts or whether the prosecution department has dealt with more assaults itself. That is what happened: in 1980, there were 3,648 assault convictions, all by judges (transactions did not exist until 1983); the 11,485 convictions in 1999 included 7,726 by judges and 3,759 transactions. It thus appears that about 50 percent of the increased volume of assault dispositions was handled by the prosecutor. The prosecutor's office announced a further policy change after the new businesslike approach (*nieuwe zakelijkheid*) started in the mid-1980s, entailing fewer dismissals and more transactions and summons. Qualitative evidence indicates that cases ending up in court are

TABLE 1

Mean Annual Growth (Percent), 1985–99

	Assault	Robbery	Rape	Qualified Theft
Population conviction rate	6.4	9.4	3.2	.8
Population custody rate	12.7	9.2	1.3	1.5*
Police-recorded offenses	8.3	7.6	3.7	1.3
Suspects per recorded offense	−2.9	−1.6	−1.3	−1.1
Prosecuted per suspect	−2.8	−1.7	−.3	−4.9
Convicted per prosecuted	4.2	5.1	1.1	5.7
Custody per convicted	5.9	−.2	−1.8	1.3*
Sentence length	.8	2.3	5.5	−1.7*

* 1990–99.

becoming increasingly more serious. As one judge said: "We see hardly any dry violence anymore, it is mostly wet violence" (i.e., involving weapons and blood; Maan 2004). At the same time, the probability that an offender will receive a custodial sentence after conviction for assault has not increased much, moving from 10 percent in 1981 to 14 percent in 1999. The population custody rate for assault peaked in the period 1990–91 due to a suddenly increased chance of a custodial sentence.

If we try to disentangle all these effects quantitatively, we can break down average annual growth of the assault custody rate. The annual growth can be written as the product of the annual increases in recorded offenses, clearance rate, prosecution probability, conviction probability, and, finally, probability of a custodial sentence given conviction:

$$\text{no. of custodial sentences} = \text{no. of recorded offenses} \times p(\text{clearance})$$
$$\times\, p(\text{prosecution}) \times p(\text{conviction})$$
$$\times\, p(\text{custodial sentence}).$$

Whether custodial sentences and recorded offenses are given in absolute numbers or as a rate makes no difference. For the period 1985–99, the average growth in these elements in the formula for assault were as follows (see table 1): The average annual growth in the custody rate was 12.7 percent. Recorded offenses grew on average by 8.3 percent, the clearance rate dropped (by 2.9 percent on average), as did the prosecution probability (by 2.8 percent on average). The probability of conviction grew on average 4.2 percent, and the incarceration probability grew on average 5.9 percent. Thus, the growth in the incarceration rate was due equally to increased numbers of convictions and increased probability of a custodial sentence. The growth in the number of convictions was mainly due to an increased likelihood of conviction; while the number of offenders fed into the criminal justice system grew, it appears as if a fairly strong police filtering process took place. The growth in convictions consists largely of dispositions by the prosecutor.

Custodial sentence lengths, however, increased only slightly over the years. Apart from a peak in 1995, they have hovered around 4.5 months since 1984 (see fig. 6b). Average assault sentences do not appear to have lengthened. Given that judges say cases are becoming more serious, this is remarkable and suggests a more lenient penal climate. One explanation could be that more and more younger offenders are tried for assault in court, but this turns out to be not the case; dramatically more juveniles enter the criminal justice system for assault (from 14 percent in 1980 to 25 percent in 1999; see Schreuders et al. 2001), but relatively fewer of these are tried by a judge. Another explanation is that a greater number of less serious cases are being given custodial sentences and that, on average, this has made sentence lengths appear to remain more or less stable.

Summarizing developments, the police are faced with more recorded assaults, are clearing relatively fewer of these cases, and are becoming more selective in referring cases to the prosecutor; the prosecution is convicting more of these, increasingly by use of transactions; and more custodial sentences of stable length are being given.

2. *Robbery*. For robbery, the picture is partly similar, partly different. The population incarceration rate for robbery, as shown in figure 7a, rose steadily, flattening a bit before 1993. From 1994 to 1995, it jumped to a much higher level (almost 80 percent in two years), after which it declined a little bit through 1999. The rise is not parallel with the trend in the conviction rate, which rose more evenly and continued to rise even while the incarceration rate was dropping during the period 1991–93. It also does not parallel the leveling off of the incarceration rate.

This means, freely formulated, that while convictions per 1,000 population increased from 1980 to 1999, the extent to which the convictions ended up in custodial sentences had two dips: a pronounced one between 1991 and 1994 and a smaller one after 1996. The first may result from a shortage of prison space during this period. Numerous offenders were turned away because there was no cell available. From 1994 onward, new prison space became available.

Although judges may not be reducing impositions of prison sentences because of lack of space, two mechanisms may have depressed the incarceration rate. First, prosecutors may have requested fewer custodial sentences knowing that these would be hard to implement. Thus, there may have been more community sanctions, fines, and so forth. There are no disaggregated data to test this; in general, the number of fines remained constant and the number of community service orders rose—although for all offenses. Transactions are not an option for serious offenses like robbery.

Second, custodial sentences are often imposed to "clean up" pretrial detention. The days in pretrial detention may be imposed plus an additional sentence. Given the acute shortages of cell space in the early 1990s, many fewer defendants were held in pretrial detention, and there was therefore less need to take account of pretrial detention through the imposition of a custodial sentence.

The reasons for the second decrease in incarceration probability are less evident. There was, during that period, once again a shortage of cell space, so this may be an explanation.

The average sentence length for robbery increased from a little over eleven months in 1980 to 17.5 months in 1994 and back to around fourteen months in 1999 (see fig. 7b). The increased sentence length for robbery may be due to a relatively small number of fairly serious cases that received proportionately severe sentences, to a larger proportion of recidivists among the offenders, and to more weapon use (Berghuis 2004). Berghuis (1994) showed that the number of armed robberies tripled between 1983 and 1993, as did the numbers of wounded and killed victims. The population conviction rate for robbery increased almost three-and-a-half-fold. Why? Is it increased supply of offenses and offenders, increased police effort, or relatively more prosecutions?

The conviction probability per recorded robbery remained fairly constant over the years, with about one in five ending up in conviction. The criminal justice system adapted its processing capacity for robbery to the increasing supply of offenses, with the police-recorded rate increasing almost fourfold—decreasing a little from the period 1993–98 and picking up sharply again in 1999. The clearance rate (see fig. 11) decreased slightly over the years, and the proportion of suspects referred to the prosecutor's office decreased suddenly after 1990. The probability of conviction given prosecution more or less mirrored this sudden change: staying relatively stable until 1990, it started rising and

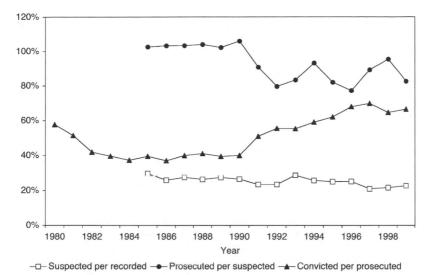

Fig. 11.—Robbery ratios of suspected, prosecuted, and convicted offenders

has risen ever since, from approximately 40 percent to almost 70 percent toward 1999.

Summarizing growth figures (see table 1): the average annual growth in the incarceration rate was 9.2 percent. The probability of incarceration given conviction decreased by 0.2 percent annually, so that the population conviction rate grew by 9.4 percent. The growth in the incarceration rate is thus an effect only of increased convictions. About half is attributable to an increased supply of offenders to the prosecutor's office (the annual growth was 4.3 percent on average) and the other half to growing probabilities of conviction (the annual growth was on average 5.1 percent). Thus, we see a similar filtering process as for assault: more offenses (average annual growth 7.6 percent), fewer clearances (on average, −1.6 percent), and fewer referrals to the prosecutor's office (−1.7 percent).

For robbery, the trends over the years show increasing numbers of convicted robbers and a system increasing its processing capacity, becoming more selective in that relatively more offenses are not cleared or not sent on to be prosecuted. Those who are prosecuted have higher chances of being convicted. While the chance of the conviction being a custodial sentence stays the same, the average length of a custodial sentence shows an upward trend.

3. *Rape.* The picture for rape is different. The conviction and custody rates show fairly similar (zigzagging) trends, although the average

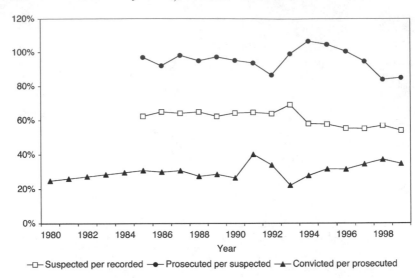

FIG. 12.—Rape ratios of suspected, prosecuted, and convicted offenders

custody rate rose a little and the conviction rate rose by 3.2 percent (see fig. 8*a*). The number of recorded rapes more than doubled. However, the changes that we saw for the two other violent offenses for which we have good data—the drop in the clearance rate, relatively fewer offenders being referred to the prosecutor's office, and more of those ending up convicted—are not evident for rape.

For rape, most lines are pretty flat (see fig. 12). Thus, the clearance rate dropped, but it did less so than for assault or robbery. The number of known offenders sent on to the criminal justice system remained pretty stable and high, hovering around 90 percent. The conviction probability also remained fairly stable (and low) at around 25–30 percent.

This is fairly low, and we analyzed available data some more to find out why. One explanation may be that the crucial element that has to be proved in a rape case is that sexual penetration occurred against the will of the victim. As most sexual offenses occur in situations where there are no witnesses, rape cases may be hard to prove. This would mean that many rape charges would end up as acquittals. This does not appear to be the case. For 1999, we found 665 rape summons, of which sixty-six ended up as acquittals and 337 as guilty verdicts. Although the number of acquittals for rape is high (usually this is about 1 percent of summoned cases), this does not explain the 40 percent conviction probability. The figures, however, show that 262 summons disappeared from the statistics! These cases likely ended up under a different label in the criminal justice statistics, for instance, under the label for sexual assault or possibly as sex with minors. When it is impossible to prove penetration, the conviction may be for a subsidiary charge, such as sexual assault (see Hendriks and Bijleveld 2004). So, it is likely that, in a sizable number of rape cases, the offender was sentenced but for a different offense. Similar mechanisms have been reported to operate for violent charges.

Working from the (clearly wrong but only available) assumption that there are as many rapes as there are offenders who could be convicted, the chances for conviction for rape must have decreased quite dramatically over the years. As our tables show, while in 1980 there were 798 police-recorded rapes and 206 convicted rapists, by 1999 this ratio had gone down to 1,775 rapes and 337 convictions. While in 1980, for every four rapes, there was one conviction for rape, by 1999 there was one conviction for every five to six rapes. Roughly speaking, the conviction chances for rape in 1999 were thus 75 percent of what they were in 1980. One explanation could be that many more cases, which have been brought into the criminal justice system by the widened definition of rape, branch off. However, the decrease occurred steadily over the years. Transactions are not an option for serious offenses like rape.

The rape incarceration rate did not change much, although it fluctuated. This can only mean that the percentage of convicted rapists sentenced to custody has decreased over the years, as figure 8a indeed shows. The decrease is quite marked: from about 80 percent (which initially climbed even higher) to about 70 percent toward the end of the 1990s. At the same time, the number of police-recorded rapes increased. Thus, an increased supply was related to an increased conviction rate. As relatively fewer of these cases over time were sentenced to incarceration, this evened out and the resulting incarceration rate remained fairly stable. Those relatively fewer incarcerations, however, were to quite spectacularly increasing sentence lengths: from an average of eleven months in 1982 to twenty-seven in 1999, a two-and-a-half-fold increase (fig. 8b). No other offense experienced such an increase (5.5 percent annually on average; see table 1).

Thus, by the late 1990s, as compared to the early 1980s, the average rapist had lower chances of being apprehended, lower chances of being convicted, and lower chances when convicted of being sentenced to custody, but if sentenced to custody, the term was much longer. It is hard to say whether these two phenomena outweigh each other for an average individual offender.

Rape is thus an offense for which it appears that dramatic shifts have taken place. Rape is increasingly viewed as a very serious offense, due perhaps to general emancipatory trends for females in the Netherlands and to generally stronger-held views toward the end of the 1990s that people's physical integrity is something to be particularly protected by the criminal justice system and that sexual offenses have particularly damning consequences.

B. Explaining Outcomes for Property Offenses

For homicide, we have only a very short series, and for burglary and motor vehicle theft, we have little usable sentencing data. This means that we ended up analyzing three violent offenses. One could thus ask whether the trends we observed are peculiar to violent offenses from 1980 to 1999 or whether they reflect more general overall trends. It is possible that the filtering process for assault and robbery may be a general response of the criminal justice system to increased numbers of offenses at the police level, but it may also be unique to violent nonsexual offenses. To shed more light on this and to circumvent problems with burglary and motor vehicle theft, we therefore examine the criminal justice system reaction to a property offense, "qualified theft." The criminal code contains one article for a collection of property offenses called qualified theft; this includes burglary, but it also covers theft of unprotected property such as cattle in a meadow and group property offenses.

The recorded qualified theft rate doubled from 1980 to 1999, from fifteen per 1,000 population to over thirty, with an interim peak of almost forty in 1994 (see fig. 13). Our crude indicator for the clearance rate (see fig. 14) decreased steadily and sizably from 1980 onward, from approximately 12 percent to 7 percent. Looking at the prosecution and conviction probabilities, we see the same filtering process and increased "efficiency" as for assault and robbery: from 1990 onward (strikingly just like robbery—an offense that also has a property element in it), the probability of a suspect being referred to the prosecutor's office decreased dramatically, from around 100 percent in 1990 to 50 percent in 1999. These 50 percent of cases simply disappear from the statistics: the cases are not dismissed officially and are not recognizable as such, but they should be counted as de facto dismissals. Van Tulder (2002) coined the term *stille sepots* for these cases, which we translate liberally as "latent dismissals."

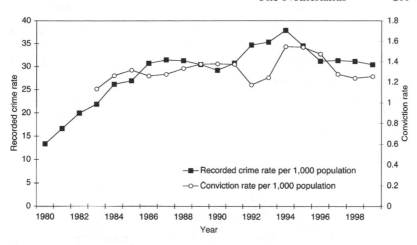

Fig. 13.—Qualified theft recorded crime and conviction rates

These dismissals are in a sense extralegal, as the expediency principle, which authorizes individualized discretionary decisions, applies to the prosecutors, not the police. One possible explanation is that these cases are being dealt with by the police themselves through so-called HALT sanctions. However, the growth in ghost dismissals has taken place mainly among nonjuvenile suspects, to whom HALT sanctions are not applicable. Other explanations are that the police have

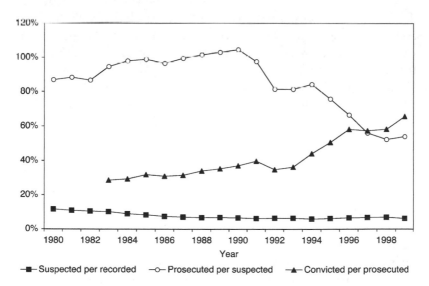

Fig. 14.—Qualified theft ratios of suspected, prosecuted, and convicted offenders

simply decided not to refer offenses, or that offenses have become hidden behind other offenses with which they were combined in a prosecutor's case. At the same time, once an offense was sent on to the prosecutor, the probability that it ended up in conviction increased—this probability increased steadily but the speed at which it happened picked up from 1992. These chances more than doubled, and this is a higher relative increase than for assault or robbery.

We have data on the conviction rate from 1983 onward and for the incarceration rate from 1990 onward. Mirroring trends of increased supply and selectivity evened out in the conviction rate. But for a few wobbles and a bigger wobble between 1991 and 1994, it was fairly stable at around 1.3 per 1,000 population. It is tempting to attribute the bigger dip and subsequent increase to the shortage of prison space around this time in the Netherlands, but it is strange that this dip did not appear much more prominently in the incarceration rate.

However, most qualified thefts cannot be dealt with by means of transactions because the maximum penalties are too long. Instead of custodial sentences, fines and community sanctions may thus have been imposed. The percentage of custody given was pretty flat at a little under 40 percent. Sentence length decreased by about 20 percent, from a little under 3.9 months on average to 3.2 months.

For qualified theft, we see basically the same mechanisms operating in the criminal justice system as for assault and robbery: even though the supply of offenses increased less than for assault and robbery, fewer cases were cleared and fewer were sent on but the likelihood of conviction increased enormously. The criminal justice system, thus, also for this offense, became more efficient.

The processing capacity of the system, however, did not keep up with the increased supply of qualified thefts, as they did not translate into a sizably increased population conviction rate (the annual average growth was 0.8 percent) or incarceration rate (the average annual growth—for a shorter time span—was 1.5 percent). While in 1980 one in eight recorded burglaries (a subset of qualified thefts) ended in conviction, by 1999 this ratio had dwindled to one in twenty-five. While the number of recorded offenses grew by 0.8 percent per year (see table 1), the clearance rate decreased (though not as strongly as for assault, robbery, or rape). By far the biggest selectivity for qualified theft occurred in referrals to the prosecutor: this proportion decreased on average almost 5 percent per year, by far the strongest decrease for any offense. This could also be translated as progressively less attention for a purely property offense. The probability of conviction once prosecuted increased on average, however. The probability of a custodial sentence also increased, on average, by 1.3 percent, second to assault (for robbery and rape, there was a decrease), with sentence lengths decreasing. The average qualified thief had, thus, by 1999, as compared to 1980, smaller chances of being caught; much smaller chances of being prosecuted; and much higher chances of being convicted once prosecuted, slightly more often receiving a custodial sentence, that was, however, shorter.

The picture for the single property and the three violent offenses for which we have sufficient data is thus a bit mixed. By 1999, the police recorded more incidents (per capita) for each offense than in 1980. The growth was strongest for robbery (more than fourfold), next came assault (almost threefold), then came burglary (more than twofold), and last came rape (almost twofold). The limited available survey data show that victim survey offenses mostly did not increase in the same fashion.

The number of convictions per recorded offense remained stable over the years for assault (approximately one in four ended up in conviction) and for robbery (approximately one in five), for burglary, this ratio decreased dramatically (from one in eight to one in twenty-five), and for rape it decreased as well (from one in four to approximately one in 5.5).

For the number of incarcerations per recorded offense, the picture is much the same: for assault, this was about one in twenty-six to twenty-seven with a slight decrease; for robbery, it was about one in eight with a slight increase; for rape, it decreased from one in five to one in eight. We have no data for burglary.

Sentence lengths increased substantially only for rape. There were slighter increases for robbery and assault, and sentence lengths decreased somewhat for qualified theft.

C. Societal and Justice System Changes

How did these changes come about? Over the period we examined, many more offenses have entered the criminal justice system. For qualified theft, assault, and robbery, we could discern clear indications of how the criminal justice system dealt with the increases. So far, we have discussed changes and trends per offense. We now adopt a different viewpoint and sketch, more broadly, a number of general societal and criminal justice system changes that may influence trends in crime and punishment. We then consider whether and to what degree these changes likely affected trends in the offenses studied.

1. *Changes in the Nature of Crime.*   When explaining trends in crime and punishment, a first obvious explanation for any changes is that crime itself has changed. Such changes may be in the number of offenses, in the nature of offenses, or in the size or composition of the offender population. Victim surveys are obvious indicators of the number of offenses, but they are only moderately helpful for our purposes. For burglary, the victim survey data span the same period and a serious break occurs only in 1997, the year when levels tail off. We cannot match these data with police-recorded data as the criminal code articles do not match the survey burglary category. For assault, we have only a short series (as the Statistics Netherlands series until 1992 asked about a different set of acts than the offense we are interested in), and, for robbery, an unstable series.

In addition to victim survey data, it is important to employ qualitative indicators of the development of crime, particularly for possible changes in the nature of offenses. From persons employed in public functions, we have heard steady complaints over a number of years that violence (threats and actual assaults) has risen considerably. This can be heard from train conductors, physicians, public service personnel, and teachers. From those working in or for institutions surrounding the criminal justice system, we have heard that increasingly younger offenders are entering the system or have been referred for screening, having committed increasingly serious offenses. Judges say that they increasingly try "wet" as compared to "dry" violence. Such signals have been interpreted by some as demonstrating increased sensitivity to violence. Such increased sensitivity is, however, not observable from reporting figures: they remained fairly stable over the years, irrespective of the particular victim survey examined. While the size of the juvenile population has decreased recently, the proportion of younger offenders entering the criminal justice system has also decreased somewhat overall, having increased (dramatically) only for violence—although, again, more juveniles were not tried in court. In addition, increasing numbers of ethnic minority offenders, to whom particular offenses are ascribed, are present among the offender population.

The picture is thus a bit mixed. Some researchers are convinced that, for some offenses, the amount of crime has remained relatively unaltered; they cite victim surveys (see, e.g., Wittebrood and Junger 1999) and propose that the growth is due to improved recording methods. By contrast, Beki, Zeelenberg, and van Montfort (1999) found no effect of improved automated recording on any offense except motor vehicle theft.

Others believe that the growth in police-recorded offenses must at least partly reflect a true rise in the volume of crime for a number of offenses (Van de Bunt and Bijleveld 2000). This leaves aside the nature of the offenses presented to the criminal justice system. It may also be that the Netherlands has experienced more serious crime (Grapendaal, Groen, and Van der Heide 1997, p. 50).

For this first explanation, there is thus little hard evidence. It is evident that the police have recorded more—many more—of our six offenses.

2. *Changes in Policy.* A second explanation is that the policy orientations of the criminal justice system institutions have changed. A number of policy documents support this contention. For instance, in the mid-1980s, the criminal justice system, which had until then operated on the assumption that it is better not to punish than to punish, started a 180-degree policy shift. A number of new sanctions were established, and the system became much more responsive in the sense that dismissals and conditional sentences were replaced with transactions and community sanctions. The policy document *Samenleving en criminaliteit* (Tweede Kamer der Staten Generaal 1985), which heralded this change, was superseded by recommendations for younger offenders from the Committee van Montfrans (Montfrans 1994).

Since the late 1990s, the police (Ministry of Interior Affairs 1998) and many other criminal justice system institutions have focused increasingly on violence. This is a focus that probably began well before the police policy document.

Chronic offenders, for a number of years, have assumed a prominent place in public debate. It is unknown and inestimable to what extent any policy changes have worked their way through quantitatively. The inertia of the criminal justice system, and particularly the police, is almost proverbial in criminal justice circles in the Netherlands. One could suppose that an increased focus on violence would result in more recorded violent offenses. Conversely—as it is hard to place such shifts in focus in time anyway—one could say that increased levels of violent offending are the cause of the shift in focus and that the police can record only so much and that any increased reporting for one offense must lead to decreased recording of other offenses. We also observed an increase in recorded qualified thefts. If there was differential attention to offenses, this is most prominent for our studied offenses at the level of police dismissal: large numbers of qualified thefts were not referred to the prosecutor toward the end of the 1990s.

3. *Capacity Problems.*   Capacity problems offer a third explanation. Two types of capacity problems can be distinguished: problems in processing cases and offenders and problems in executing sanctions. The Netherlands has experienced serious capacity problems. The prison capacity problems were quite striking just before 1994, when in a number of infamous attention-drawing cases even serious sex offenders were sent home because there was no prison space for them. Shortages have recently become more pressing in the institutions for secure hospital orders and in juvenile detention facilities. Such shortages have not been limited to the criminal justice system but, at the time of writing this report, are serious also for health care and youth care.

In general, the number of modalities to impose a sanction has increased remarkably. The imposition of those sanctions deflects pressure from the prison system. The use of HALT sanctions, community sanctions supervised by the probation service, compulsory education carried out by the Rutgers Stichting and similar institutions, and the administrative sanctioning of traffic offending all deflect pressure from the criminal justice system and its sanctions systems. Whether there are shortages in those nonprison institutions is a topic well beyond the scope of this essay.

It is surprising that we could find a presumed effect of these shortages only in the data for robbery and qualified theft, the two offenses that have a property element. Why this did not emerge for assault and rape is a question for which we have no answer.

The processing capacity of the criminal justice system has come under increasing pressure. Declining clearance rates can be seen as a failure of the system at the police level to deal with increased volume, despite increases in the size of the police force, which are believed by some to have had little effect. Wiebrens (2002) showed that police productivity has declined relative to means.

Declining rates in referring offenders to the prosecutor's office may indicate that the system is not able to deal with all offenses. Since the early 1990s, the prosecutors' and magistrates' offices have started to agree on yearly contracts about the number of cases the prosecutor will summon and transfer to the courts, something unheard of until then and met by some with incredulity. Shortages in the courts in the late

1990s were most acute in the criminal courts. Despite the yearly agreements about the supply of cases, many cases have been subject to *afwaarderen*, or devaluation as it is bluntly called. That is, for lack of sufficient staff or courtroom space, cases have been brought in front of the *politierechter*, which means that the prosecutor can ask for a maximum sentence of six months, instead of the chamber with three judges where the penalty sought is limited only by statutory maxima. This has happened regularly and not only for minor cases.

This pressure has continued, mainly because case handling at the courts over the years has become more time consuming (see Berghuis 1994). Processing times have also increased considerably, in some cases beyond limits deemed compatible with the fair trial principle as laid down in the Council of Europe's treaty on human rights. This is another indication of overburdening of the system, or stretching system capacity to the maximum.

In the preface to its 2003 yearly report, the Board of Procurators General stated that "the water has now reached up to the lips of the ... system" (Openbaar Ministerie 2003, p. 1). It is reasonable to hypothesize that cases that made it to the courts and were not filtered out earlier have special properties: the most serious and technically best cases proceed on (Grapendaal, Groen, and Van der Heide 1997; Openbaar Ministerie 2003). Many bulk cases were thus dealt with by the prosecutor and, toward the end of the 1990s, a system for automated penalty computation (called BOS/Polaris) came into effect. It served not only to speed up and make more efficient the work of prosecutors but also to synchronize prosecution across court districts.

There is no quantitative evidence on this selection process. If more serious cases are selected for the courts (something reflected by the qualitative indications from judges and prosecutors), stable sentence lengths would reflect decreased punitiveness. We have no way to test for this, and the whole topic remains something of a quagmire. One explanation for the stable sentence lengths could also be that the extent to which offenses were combined in case files has decreased since the early 1990s (fewer *voegingen*); again, however, we have no quantitative measures to test to what extent such trends could have outweighed each other.

4. *The Inflation Hypothesis.* A fourth explanation for the rise in violent crime is the so-called inflation hypothesis. Egelkamp (2002) studied two court districts and an additional prosecutor's region (*arrondissementen*) and concluded, comparing case files on assault, serious assault, attempted

homicide, violent public order offenses, and robbery from 1986 and 1996, that the summons in 1996 contained proportionally a greater number of less serious cases, those in which the victim had few or no injuries. This rise was notable mainly for barroom fights and relational violence. At the same time, Egelkamp concludes that such behavioral constellations were qualified as assault more easily in 1996 than in 1986. For that matter, Egelkamp coins the term "inflation of violence."

At the same time, Egelkamp notes that the prosecutor dismissed cases less often. As we saw, the percentages of recorded assaults and robberies that end in convictions were stable from 1980 to 1999. Sentence length remained fairly even. A strong filtering process in all likelihood operated for these two offenses.

Assuming that the most serious cases end up with a custodial sentence, Egelkamp's theory and our data seem at first sight hard to reconcile. One could posit that Egelkamp studied court cases in Groningen and Arnhem, which are not part of the central urbanized west where most of the growth in crime is presumed to have taken place, though both have active recreational areas with bars. One could argue that the issue is probably not so much inflation in the concept of violence as widening of the legal concept of "intent" (*opzet*). The violence inflation theory is not contradicted by qualitative indications, and the scrupulous reader might leaf back and see such an inflation perhaps in the increasing sentence lengths for rape. Also, if the police, the judiciary, and the public became increasingly sensitive to violence, this would have been reflected in the victim surveys (which are of limited use anyway) or in reporting figures. None of this emerges. If inflation of the concept of violence occurred, this does not preclude a real rise in crime (as we saw a rise for all studied offenses).

5. *New Sanctions.*   A fifth explanation for trends in punishment is that new and different sanctions have emerged at the lower end of the sanctioning spectrum. This is definitely the case, as was discussed extensively above.

We believe that all five explanations affected the data we have discussed. It is hard to say to what extent explanation B affected the trend in offense T. One reason is that no integrated data system exists in the Netherlands through which cases can be tracked. The best data source for studies in which it is possible to see cases entering, being processed through, and exiting the criminal justice system is the SRM Prosecution and Sentencing Monitor, although also this sample is selected and does not portray the execution of sentences. Bijleveld (2003) sketches a number of options for such a system, of which one is simply to select, say, every thousandth case that enters the police files and study each such case in detail, from beginning to end. Proper studies of this kind take ages and would shed no light in the near future. For the immediate future, linking up police, prosecution, sentencing, and execution data provides a better option. Quite a number of studies have been carried out on police data, which contain data on suspects, without anyone knowing how many of these offenders are acquitted and for what reason and how their offenses are eventually classified.

Studies on the criminal justice system will always be complex, because of its multilayered nature, the intricacies of charging and *voeging*, sometimes counterbalancing demands made on the system, and the essentially dynamic nature of the manner in which behavior is understood and qualified.

REFERENCES

Beki, C., K. Zeelenberg, and K. van Montfort. 1999. "An Analysis of the Crime Rate in the Netherlands, 1950–93." *British Journal of Criminology* 39:401–15.

Berghuis, A. C. 1994. "Punitiviteitsfeiten" (Facts on punitiveness). In *Hoe punitief is Nederland?* edited by M. Moerings. Arnhem: Gouda Quint.

———. 2004. Personal communication with author by telephone, February 13, 2004.

Bijleveld, C. C. J. H. 2003. "Mens, durf te meten!" (Measure, measure!). Inaugural speech for professorship at Free University, March 8, 2002. The Hague: Boom Juridische Uitgevers.

Bijleveld, C. C. J. H., and P. R. Smit. 2004. *Crime and Punishment in the Netherlands, 1980–1999.* In *Cross-National Studies in Crime and Justice*, edited by David P. Farrington, Patrick A. Langan, and Michael Tonry. Available at http://www.ojp.usdoj.gov/bjs/abstract/cnscj.htm. Washington, D.C.: U.S. Department of Justice, Bureau of Justice Statistics.

Cozijn, Cor, and Ad Essers. 2002. "Over de registratie van geweldsmisdrijven" (On the registration of violent offenses). Unpublished research note. The Hague: Wetenschappelijk Onderzoek- en Documentatie Centrum.

De Poot, Christianne. 2002. Personal interview with author.

Egelkamp, M. M. E. 2002. "Inflation von Gewalt? Strafrechtliche und kriminologische Analysen von Qualifikationsentscheidungen in den Niederlanden und Deutschland" (Inflation of violence? Judicial and criminological analyses of qualification decisions in the Netherlands and Germany). Ph.D. dissertation, University of Groningen.

210   Catrien C. J. H. Bijleveld and Paul R. Smit

Farrington, David P., and Patrick A. Langan. 1992. "Changes in Crime and Punishment in England and America in the 1980s." *Justice Quarterly* 9:5–46.

Grapendaal, Martin, Peter-Paul Groen, and Wieger van der Heide. 1997. *Duur en Volume: Ontwikkeling van de onvoorwaardelijke vrijheidsstraf tussen, 1985 en 1995* (Average length and volume of unconditional custodial sentences, 1985–1995). Research and Policy Series, no. 163. The Hague: Centraal Bureau voor de Statistiek, Wetenschappelijk Onderzoek- en Documentatie Centrum.

Hendriks, J., and C. C. J. H. Bijleveld. 2004. "Recidive van jeugdige zeden-delinquenten: Een onderzoek naar de algemene-, zeden- en geweldsrecidive van in JJI Harreveld behandelde jeugdige zedendelinquenten" (Recidivism of juvenile sex offenders: A study of overall sex- and violent-reoffending of juvenile sex offenders treated at JJI Harreveld). Report no. 2004–2 . Leiden: Netherlands Institute for the Study of Crime and Law Enforcement.

Koeijers, Elly. 2003. "Retrospectieve vragen naar ondervonden delicten bij POLS en de PMB" (Retrospective questions on victimizations in POLS and PMB). Internal paper. Voorburg: Centraal Bureau voor de Statistiek.

Kommer, M. M. 1994. "Het Nederlandse strafklimaat in internationaal perspectief" (The Dutch penal climate in international perspective). In *Hoe punitief is Nederland?* edited by M. Moerings. Arnhem: Gouda Quint.

Leuw, Ed., M. Brouwers, and J. Smit. 1999. *Recidive na de tbs* (Recidivism after forensic psychiatric treatment). Research and Policy Series, no. 182. The Hague: Ministry of Justice, Wetenschappelijk Onderzoek- en Documentatie Centrum.

Maan, E. A. 2004. Personal communication with author by telephone, February 13, 2004.

Ministry of Interior Affairs. 1998. *Beleidsplan Nederlandse Politie, 1999–2002* (Dutch police policy plan, 1999–2002). The Hague: Ministry of Interior Affairs.

Montfrans, G. W. van. 1994. *Met de neus op de feiten; aanpak jeugdcriminaliteit* (Facing the facts: Handling juvenile criminality). The Hague: Ministry of Justice.

Openbaar Ministerie. 2003. *Jaarverslag 2003 Openbaar Minsterie: goed beschouwd* (Annual report prosecution, 2003). The Hague: Board of Procurators General.

Politiemonitor Bevolking. 1999. *Politiemonitor bevolking 1999: landelijke rapportage; tabellenrapport* (Police Monitor population, 1999: National report; tables). The Hague; Hilversum: Politiemonitor Bevolking.

Rovers, B. 2000. "Toename van geweld leidt tot betere registratie" (Increase in violent crime leads to better registration). *Tijdschrift voor Criminologie* 42:58–70.

Schoen, E. D., P. R. Defize, and M. Bakker. 2000. *Methodologische evaluatie van de Politiemonitor Bevolking* (Methodological evaluation of the Police Monitor). Report no. FSP-RPT-000032. Delft: Toegepast Natuurwetenschappelijk Onderzoek.

Schreuders, Mike M., Frits W. M. Huls, Marja H. ter Horst-van Breukelen, and Frank P. van Tulder, eds. 2001. *Criminaliteit en Rechtshandhaving 2000* (Crime and law enforcement 2000). Research and Policy Series, no. 189. The Hague: Ministry of Justice, Wetenschappelijk Onderzoek- en Documentatie Centrum; Voorburg: Statistics Netherlands.

Smit, Paul S., Simone van der Zee, Wieger van der Heide, and Femke Heide. 2001. "Moord en doodslag in Nederland: Een studie van de moorden en doodslagen in 1998" (Homicide in the Netherlands: A study of the 1998 cases). Research Note no. 2001/8. The Hague: Ministry of Justice, Wetenschappelijk Onderzoek- en Documentatie Centrum.

Statistics Netherlands. 1997. *Veel voorkomende criminaliteit: kerncijfers, 1980–1996* (Common crime: Key figures, 1980–1996). Voorburg/Heerlen: Statistics Netherlands.

———. 1999. Bevolkingsstatistiek (Demographic statistics). Available at http://www.statline.cbs.nl.

———. 2003. *Statistisch Jaarboek, 2003* (Statistical yearbook, 2003). Voorburg/Heerlen: Statistics Netherlands.

Tak, Peter J. P. 2003. *The Dutch Criminal Justice System*. Research and Policy Series, no. 205. The Hague: Ministry of Justice, Wetenschappelijk Onderzoek- en Documentatie Centrum.

Tweede Kamer der Staten Generaal. 1985. *Samenleving en Criminaliteit: een beleidsplan voor de komende jaren* (Society and criminality: A policy plan for the coming years). The Hague: Tweede Kamer der Staten Generaal.

Van de Bunt, H. G., and C. C. J. H. Bijleveld. 2000. *Het luisterend oor van de criminoloog* (The criminologist's attentive ear). *Tijdschrift voor Criminologie* 42:55–57.

Van der Heide, W., and A. Th. J. Eggen, eds. 2003. *Criminaliteit en Rechtshandhaving, 2001* (Crime and law enforcement, 2001). Research and Policy Series, no. 211. The Hague: Ministry of Justice, Wetenschappelijk Onderzoek- en Documentatie Centrum; Voorburg: Statistics Netherlands.

Van Dijk, Jan J. M., and Carl H. D. Steinmetz. 1979. *De WODC-slachtofferenquetes, 1974–1979* (WODC Victim Surveys. 1974–1979). Research and Policy Series, no. 13. The Hague: Ministry of Justice, Staatsuitgeverij, Wetenschappelijk Onderzoek- en Documentatie Centrum.

Van Emmerik, Jos L. 1989. *TBS en recidive* (The TBS entrustment order and recidivism). Research and Policy Series, no. 95. The Hague: Ministry of Justice, Wetenschappelijk Onderzoek- en Documentatie Centrum.

———. 1999. "De last van het getal: Een overzicht in cijfers van de maatregel tbs" (The burden of numbers: An overview in numbers of the TBS secure entrustment order). *Justitiële Verkenningen* 25:9–31.

Van Tulder, F. 2002. "Stille sepots van het OM" (Hidden disposals of the PPS). *Tijdschrift voor de politie* 64(3):4–5.

Wiebrens, C. J. 2002. "Celdagen zeggen meer over doelmatigheid politie" (Days in prison are more relevant for the efficiency of the police). *Economisch Statistische Berichten*, December 19, pp. 900–903.

Wittebrood, Karin P., and Marianne Junger. 1999. "Trends in geweldscriminaliteit: een antwoord" (Trends in violent crime: An answer). *Tijdschrift voor Criminologie* 42:64–70.

Martin Killias, Philippe Lamon, and Marcelo F. Aebi

Crime and Punishment in Switzerland, 1985–1999

ABSTRACT

A recurring question in criminology has always been how the "costs of offending" (the risk of being convicted and sentenced to custody) relate to offending rates. Langan and Farrington's and Cusson's studies have renewed interest in this question. Examination of victim surveys and police and court statistics over nearly two decades produces mixed conclusions. Some of the offenses considered (burglary, motor vehicle theft, robbery, assault, rape, and homicide) show substantial variations since 1985 and are better explained by opportunity theories than in terms of changing costs of offending. The odds of an average offender being convicted and imprisoned have, depending on the indicators used, remained stable over time, or changed erratically, in ways that are difficult to relate to crime rates as the "outcome." Crime rates appear to be better explained by changes in routine activities and other opportunities than by deterrence variables.

This essay summarizes trends in crime and punishment in Switzerland between 1985 and 1999 and investigates possible explanations. Six serious offenses have been studied, namely, burglary, motor vehicle theft, robbery, serious assault, rape, and homicide. Trends over time are presented as shown by victimization surveys and police statistics. Crime trends largely follow changes in opportunity structures, including cross-national crime markets and open drug scenes in major cities. Trends in costs of offending, by contrast, are more erratic and difficult to relate to

Martin Killias and Philippe Lamon are, respectively, professor and senior researcher at the University of Lausanne, School of Criminal Sciences, Switzerland. Marcelo Aebi is professor at the University of Lausanne and the University of Seville, Spain. We thank Daniel Fink and his staff at the Swiss Federal Office of Statistics for their invaluable help.

crime trends. For reasons discussed below, however, measures of costs of offending are particularly problematic under continental sentencing systems.

Here is how this essay is organized. The first section provides some background on Switzerland and its criminal justice system. Section II describes data used in this essay with a particular focus on issues of comparability. Next, trends for all six offenses according to the several sources are presented in Section III. In Section IV, trends in probability of conviction, of being sentenced to immediate custody, and of sentence length are given for all six offenses. The conclusions are inconclusive about the hypothesis of a direct effect of costs of offending on crime rates.

I. Switzerland

Switzerland, situated in the heart of Western Europe, originates from an alliance of rural and urban republics (cantons), which dates back to the fourteenth century. Conquests during the early sixteenth century led to Switzerland developing into a multilingual country, with German-, French-, Italian-, and Romansh-speaking areas. Formally independent and neutral since 1648, Switzerland became a federal state in 1848, with a constitution heavily inspired by that of the United States. This leaves the cantons ("states") largely autonomous, particularly in matters of criminal justice. Since an occupation during the Napoleanic wars (1798–1814) and a short civil war (in 1847), Switzerland has not experienced armed conflict on its territory. With a population of 7 million in 2000, of whom 46 percent are Catholics and 40 percent protestants, Switzerland has one of the highest proportions of noncitizens in Europe. Traditionally, most immigrants have come from southern Europe and, more recently, predominantly from Balkan countries and areas outside of Europe. Although not rich in natural resources, Switzerland developed during the twentieth century and became one of the most affluent countries in Europe. Since the 1950s there has been a shift from emigration (mostly to the United States) to massive immigration. Although Switzerland's largest cities are relatively small (Zurich has a population of just over 330,000), most of the population lives in urban or suburban areas. Fewer than 5 percent are employed in agriculture, and fewer than 10 percent live in towns with a population less than 1,000.[1] The unemployment rate in 1999 was

[1] Statistical information is from *Annuaire statistique de la Suisse* (2001).

2.4 percent, and, according to the 2000 International Crime Victimization Survey (ICVS), 80 percent of households have at least one car and 29 percent have at least two.

Switzerland has at various times come under the influence of French, German, and Austrian-Hungarian criminal legislation. After having long been a cantonal matter, the substantive criminal law was unified in federal legislation in 1937. The Criminal Code, which took effect in 1942, is a fairly independent codification, combining and importing various concepts from neighboring countries (Killias 2001*b*; Trechsel and Killias, forthcoming). Some offense definitions have been modified slightly over the last twenty years, but not in a way affecting the data presented here. The federal criminal code, as with all other offenses contained in federal laws, is applied by cantonal courts. Thus, unlike in the United States, lower courts are always cantonal bodies, and no federal judiciary exists with the exception of the Federal Supreme Court. This latter court operates, however, as a court of appeals and does not usually hear cases before they are tried at cantonal courts.

Switzerland's systems of prosecution, policing, and criminal justice have remained under the authority of the twenty-six cantons. In general, the western cantons (including a few German-speaking ones) have remained under the influence of the French tradition, with an examining magistrate (*juge d'instruction*) as a central figure who operates independently of the prosecutor (*procureur*). In the majority of the German-speaking cantons and in the Italian-speaking canton of Ticino, the function of the examining magistrate is performed by a local prosecutor (*Staatsanwalt*), as in Germany and Italy (Schmid 1997; Piquerez 2000; Trechsel and Killias, forthcoming). The accusation is presented in court by the prosecutor, especially in important cases (where longer sentences are to be expected), when the canton's chief prosecutor or one of his or her deputies intervenes regularly. In minor cases, however, the court is left alone with the defendant and his or her council, and the court examines the facts on the grounds of the evidence presented by the written accusation. Usually, the interrogation of parties and witnesses is led by the court's chairperson. Although cross-examination exists in theory, it rarely plays more than a complementary role during hearings.

The way examining magistrates, prosecutors, and judges are elected or appointed is defined by cantonal law. As a general rule, prosecutors are appointed by the cantonal governments, whereas examining magistrates and judges are elected. Presiding judges and clerks always have a law degree, whereas other judges sitting on the bench may be lay judges. In cases of offenses such as those discussed in this essay, the court always includes a bench of three to five judges, if not a jury (as it still exists, under various forms, in some cantons).

In sum, the Swiss system follows the inquisitorial tradition of the European continent, with a focus on truth rather than on formal issues (see Killias 2001b; Trechsel and Killias, forthcoming). Of course, the European Convention of Human Rights (which plays a great role in the daily practice before Swiss courts) has increased respect for formal principles, but not to the extent that courts or prosecutors would accept convictions based on evidence that may have been gathered lawfully without violation of rights of the defendant, but where they doubt the alleged facts to be true.[2] In line with European jurisprudence generally, Swiss courts would not ban evidence obtained illegally if the offense at stake is too serious to accept, as an otherwise inevitable outcome, the acquittal of a clearly guilty defendant.

Examining magistrates, prosecutors, and police officers have limited discretion. Whenever they believe the facts justify a reasonable suspicion that an offense has been committed, they are, except in Geneva and a few other cantons, obliged to prosecute. These officials are also obligated to give due consideration to facts that might exonerate a suspected person. Several magistrates and prosecutors have been criminally convicted for not having disclosed evidence favorable to the defendant to the court and the defense.

A corollary of compulsory prosecution is that prosecution for some offenses is conditional, according to the Criminal Code, and requires a formal complaint of a victim (or any other party having this right according to the law). Among the offenses considered in this essay, simple assault is an example of an offense that can only be prosecuted at the victim's special request.

Suspects, once identified, are usually not arrested, except for serious offenses, if they are not permanent residents of the country, or if the defendant, if left in the community, might destroy evidence (by, e.g., contacting potential witnesses before the examining magistrate could hear them). Pretrial detention can be imposed under these

---

[2] That is true even in the case of guilty pleas, which, with the exception of minor offenses, never dispense the court from hearing the case and the evidence (see Langbein [1974] concerning German law).

circumstances by the examining magistrate and must be reviewed by a judge within a few days (according to the cantonal law).

Prisons, although heavily subsidized by the federal government, are run by the cantons. Thus, statistical systems have largely remained in the hands of cantonal authorities, although some uniformity has been developed at the levels of convictions (registered in a federal registry of records) and corrections. However, there is no system of offender-based statistics, which means that individuals cannot be traced from police through the entire system down to the correctional departments. Data collection is more complicated than in some more centralized European countries.

II. Offenses and Victimization Trends

After a short explanation of the sources of data used in this section, data are presented for trends in six offenses. Burglary nearly doubled between 1985 and 1997, with a recent drop in 1999. Motor vehicle theft decreased substantially over the entire period. Robbery and assault increased overall, although inconsistently after 1995. Rape and homicide show more erratic fluctuations. The best available explanation for these inconsistent trends is offered by opportunity theories.

A. Data on Police Recorded Crime

Federal-level police data on offenses and suspects have been available since 1981. However, statistics are limited because they are a compilation of data provided by cantonal police departments (see Killias 2001a, pp. 45–51; 2002, pp. 49–55). Furthermore, there is no standardization in data collection procedures or written rules on how to record and count offenses. It is likely that some departments count offenses at the "output" stage (when the police transfer the file to the examining magistrate), and other departments count offenses at an earlier stage. There are also discrepancies in counting procedures (as detailed in Council of Europe [1999, pp. 80–84]). For example, the thirty victims of a mass "suicide" of a sect in 1995 (many of whom were actually murdered) were counted as one "case" in the cantons of Valais and Fribourg, while the Zurich police probably would have recorded the total number of victims. Beyond these differences, some cantons have developed more detailed statistics. The canton of Zurich provides approximately one-third of the offenses that appear in the federal statistics. In the following trend analyses, the Zurich statistics are used as the bases for reasonable estimates whenever the federal statistics are insufficiently detailed.

Switzerland's definitions of the six offenses under consideration follow the continental tradition (see table 1). Police definitions by and large match legal definitions. Since certain definitions used in victim surveys are broader than corresponding legal definitions, we have included, in police counts, data relating to some other offenses in order to increase comparability.

There are several categories of homicide. However, we are concerned only with the overall concept of intentional homicide. Thus, the data used here include all forms of intentional killing of a person but exclude attempted homicide.

Robbery is defined as theft with violence. Therefore, taking something from another person without physically threatening him or her (i.e., "mugging," as in the case of bag snatching) is counted as theft and not robbery. As police statistics give data on "muggings" separately, police counts can easily be adjusted to match survey measures of robbery. Rape is similarly defined as in other European countries; it includes spousal rape and sexual intimacies resulting from use of severe psychological pressure.

B. Survey Methodology

The first national crime survey of Switzerland was conducted in two phases in 1984 (French-speaking cantons) and in 1987 (German-speaking cantons and Italian-speaking canton).[3] The overall sample comprised 6,505 respondents. The survey had a few innovative features (Killias 1989). It was one of the first major victim surveys to use computer-assisted telephone interviews (CATI). The use of CATI made it possible to collect data from a large sample of respondents, because of high telephone penetration and sophisticated computer technology. The response rates were 71 percent in the German-speaking cantons and 60 percent in the Latin cantons. The reference period was defined in a way that allowed victims to mention, in the first round of questions, any victimization that came to mind. If respondents mentioned one of the crimes listed in the screener, they were asked follow-up questions to determine more precisely the timing of

---

[3] The survey was conducted in two phases because of political difficulties. Since crime rates were fairly stable between 1984 and 1987, the impact of the split was likely to be minimal.

the incident (i.e., whether it took place during the current year, the previous year, earlier). These questions allowed telescoping to be reduced, by separating the definitional elements of questions on offenses from their temporal and spatial location. In order to test the reliability of CATI interviews, face-to-face interviews were conducted with a subsample of respondents who had already been interviewed using CATI. The CATI interviews were found to be highly reliable. The response rate was found to have a very moderate effect on the results.[4] The first survey of this type in Switzerland included many questions on lifestyle, risk, and other independent variables.

The Swiss survey was used in the development of what became the International Crime Victimisation Survey (ICVS; see Van Dijk, Mayhew, and Killias 1990), including, for example, the questions on the temporal and spatial location of incidents. The ICVS also drew on the methodology (e.g., questions) of the British and Dutch crime surveys. Respondents were interviewed using CATI, thus keeping costs relatively low and allowing the use of reasonably large samples.[5]

Criticism of the ICVS led to an extensive methodological experiment in the Netherlands. Two parallel victimization surveys (CATI vs. telepanel)[6] were conducted to determine whether they yielded similar victimization rates, and this was found to be the case (Scherpenzeel 1992). The CATI sample was also randomly split into two subsamples. This was to compare the ICVS approach in locating incidents in time[7] with the more conventional model of asking respondents directly about incidents experienced during "the last twelve months," as in many European surveys (e.g., the British Crime Survey). In the latter case, it was found that serious crimes were often telescoped into the reference period, although they had occurred long before. For robbery and burglary, the rates were 2.2 and 2.5 times higher than those observed

---

[4] As in other tests, differences were not large, since refusals were mostly related to the inconvenience of an interview and not to the theme of the survey. Due probably to higher motivation as a result of personal experience, cooperation was slightly better among victims.

[5] The cost of a CATI interview can be estimated to be at about 20–25 percent that of a personal interview.

[6] Survey completed on a computer at home. This method shares many features of mail surveys but allows higher response rates and offers better control over the way the questionnaire is completed.

[7] That is, asking first about victimizations experienced over the last five years and then only when more precisely eventual incidents had occurred (with a special focus on the current and the last year).

TABLE 1
Legal and Survey Definitions of Offenses

Offenses	International Crime Victimization Survey Definition	Swiss Criminal Code Definition
Burglary	Over the past five years, did anyone actually get into your home/residence without permission, and steal or try to steal something? I am not including here thefts from garages, sheds or lock-ups.	Not specifically defined in the Criminal Code. In practice, burglary is considered as one among several aggravated forms of theft by courts (impossible to disentangle in conviction statistics). Police use a pragmatic definition comparable to the survey definition.
Vehicle theft	Theft of cars: Over the past five years, have you or other members of your household had any of their cars/vans/trucks stolen? Please take your time to think about it. Theft of motorcycles: Over the past five years, have you or other members of your household had any of their mopeds/scooters/motorcycles/mofas stolen?	If the offender acted with the intent to keep or resell the vehicle, he will be convicted of theft (Criminal Code, sec. 139). If, however, his intention was to use it temporarily and to drop it later, he will be punishable under section 94 of the Road Traffic Act (joyriding). This section covers all kinds of motor vehicles.
Robbery	Over the past five years, has anyone stolen something from you by using force or threatening you, or did anybody try to steal something from you by using force or threatening force?	Section 140, Criminal Code. Robbery is defined as theft committed with violence, or with the threat of immediate physical violence. "Mugging" (i.e., just taking bags or other items from the victim without direct violence) is considered theft.

TABLE 1 (*Continued*)

Offenses	International Crime Victimization Survey Definition	Swiss Criminal Code Definition
Assault	Apart from the incidents just covered (sexual assaults), have you, over the past five years, been personally attacked or threatened by someone in a way that really frightened you, either at home or elsewhere, such as in a pub, in the street, at school, on public transport, on the beach, or at your workplace?	This category (as used here) includes several sections of the Criminal Code: simple bodily injury (sec. 123), serious bodily injury (sec. 122), slapping/punching (i.e., assault without injury; sec. 126), threats (secs. 180–181), extortion (sec. 156), assault against public officials (sec. 285), deprivation of liberty/hostage taking (secs. 183, 185).
Rape	…	Sexual intercourse with a female person, obtained under threat, with violence or under undue pressure (Criminal Code, sec. 190).
Homicide	…	All degrees of murder (intentional homicide, with aggravating or mitigating circumstances; Criminal Code, secs. 111–114, 116).

SOURCE.—Killias et al. 2000.

using the ICVS model.[8] Scherpenzeel's (1992) experiment provides support for the use of CATI as an interview method in victimization surveys and also for the way the ICVS and the Swiss national crime surveys had dealt with the problem of telescoping.[9]

The first Swiss national crime survey[10] was followed by the ICVS surveys of 1989 and 1996, in which Switzerland participated with sample sizes of 1,000 respondents. The response rates were 68 percent in 1989 and 56 percent in 1996. In 1998, a second national crime survey was conducted, with a sample of 3,041, followed by a third national crime survey in 2000, with a sample of 4,234 respondents. In the1998 and 2000 surveys, booster samples were taken from certain city areas, in order to overrepresent respondents from immigrant communities and, thus, allow more detailed analysis of this group of the population. The 2000 survey also formed part of the most recent ICVS. This essay uses only weighted and national data. The response rates for the 1998 and 2000 surveys were around 60 percent.[11] The screeners used in the various sweeps differed slightly for a few offenses; therefore, rates have had to be made comparable with minor adjustments (using responses to follow-up questions). The 1998 and 2000 screeners were identical, with minimal differences from the 1996 version.

The main change in the Swiss crime survey was the addition of new screening questions for domestic violence (see Kesteren, Mayhew, and Nieuwbeerta 2000). This caused an increase in the number of victim-survey offenses of assault by 29 percent. For comparability, they are not included in the crime trends given here.

C. Comparing Survey and Police Data

The number of victim-survey offenses, comparable population figures (number of households), and the probability of reporting to the police were obtained from the Swiss national crime surveys (Killias et al. 2000).

---

[8] This problem was addressed in the National Crime Victimization Survey in the United States by bounding the interviews within the panels. This expensive method has not been adopted anywhere in Europe (Killias 1993).

[9] Telescoping effects were weaker for less serious offenses, such as bicycle thefts, which tend to be more rapidly forgotten, than for serious forms of victimization.

[10] In the following trend analyses, the two parts of the first survey are related to 1985 (i.e., the year between the two waves).

[11] In 1998 and 2000, the computation is less straightforward than in former surveys due to the replacement of households with consenting respondents by new ones if the demographic characteristics of all available household members were already over-represented in the sample. According to various ways of treating these cases, the response rate in 2000 varies between 54 and 65 percent.

The 2000 national crime survey estimated that there were 34,377 robberies in 1999 and that 50 percent of these were reported to the police. Since there were an estimated 5,562,873 persons aged sixteen or over in 1999, the survey robbery rate was 6.18 per 1,000 population at risk; disregarding repeat offenses, about one in every 162 persons was robbed in 1999. All crime survey figures, of course, have confidence intervals around them. For example, the 95 percent confidence interval for the robbery rate in 1999 was 3.82 to 8.54 per 1,000 population. Confidence intervals are narrower for the other offenses, which are more prevalent.

Swiss survey crime rates for burglary and vehicle theft are per 1,000 households, while rates for robbery and assault (wounding) are per 1,000 population aged sixteen or over. Vehicle theft figures refer to completed thefts only.

III. Results

All the surveys provide prevalence data.[12] Figure 1 shows trends of survey and police crime measures. In general, changes in survey crime rates were highly correlated with changes in recorded crime rates (table 2).

Residential Burglary. Based on the national victim surveys, the residential burglary rate per household decreased between 1985 and 1988 and then more than doubled between 1988 and 1997 before decreasing by around 25 percent. Like the survey burglary rate, the police-recorded residential burglary rate almost doubled between 1985 and 1997 and decreased by 12 percent up to 1999. Burglaries reported to the police according to victims' accounts decreased from 83 percent to 74 percent between 1985 and 1997 and increased to 80 percent again in 1999.

Vehicle Theft. Based on the national victim surveys, the vehicle theft rate decreased between 1985 and 1999 by over 90 percent. Vehicle

---

[12] The number of incidents (during the last year) was recorded according to the same procedure from 1989 to 1999, but not for 1984/87. Therefore, incident rates were calculated by using estimates based on the prevalence rates for 1984/87, and the average numbers of incidents per victim derived from the other surveys. All incidents experienced abroad were excluded. For this reason, the rates given below may differ slightly from ICVS sources. The proportion of victimizations experienced in foreign countries is substantial among Swiss respondents and for certain offenses. According to the most recent data, one robbery in three and about one in ten sexual victimizations have been experienced abroad. The rate of offenses reported to the police (according to the respondent) needed to be extrapolated (i.e., multiplied by incidence/prevalence rates), since follow-up questions have been asked for the "last" incident only, as in the case of ICVS and many similar questionnaires.

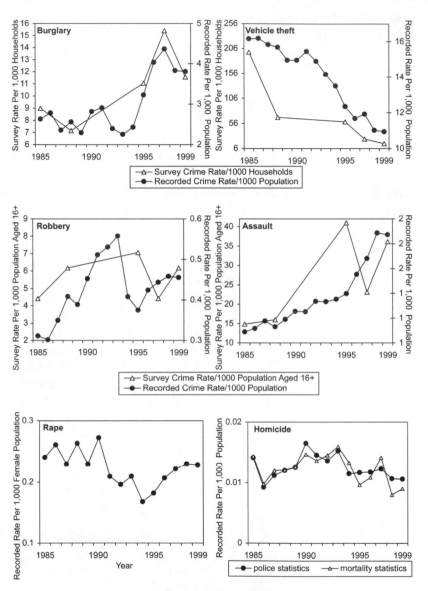

FIG. 1.—Survey and recorded crime rate for burglary, vehicle theft, robbery, assault, rape, and homicide. Sources: Swiss crime surveys (Killias et al. 2000); Swiss Federal Police Office 1985–2000.

TABLE 2

Correlations between Survey and Recorded Crime Rates

	Survey Rate			Recorded Rate					
	MVT	ROB	ASLT	BURG	MVT	ROB	ASLT	RAPE	HOM
Survey rate:									
BURG	−.52	−.31	.37	.96	−.77	.51	.75	−.51	−.24
MVT		−.43	−.58	−.71	.81	−.94	−.78	.25	.90
ROB			.69	−.19	−.28	.20	.09	−.38	−.69
ASLT				.43	−.81	.35	.62	−.81	−.73
Recorded rate:									
BURG					−.87	.72	.89	−.39	−.47
MVT						−.73	−.94	.61	.76
ROB							.81	.03	−.82
ASLT								−.34	−.73
RAPE									.26

Sources.—Killias et al. 2000; Swiss Federal Police Office 1985–2000.
Note.—BURG = burglary; MVT = motor vehicle theft; ROB = robbery; ASLT = assault; HOM = homicide.

225

thefts recorded by the police show a similar drop. Reporting to the police remained very stable over the entire period (mean 90 percent). It is possible that the decrease in victimizations mainly concerned joy-riding, that is, an offense probably less consistently recorded by the police and made largely impossible by improved safety locks and crash helmet requirements (see Sec. III.C below).

Robbery. Again, victim surveys and police counts show similar trends, with the important qualification, however, that the peak and the bottom years differ. Based on the national victim surveys, the robbery rate increased between 1985 and 1995, decreased by about one-third between 1995 and 1997, and increased again by 40 percent between 1997 and 1999. The police-recorded robbery rate increased between 1985 and 1993 by 44 percent, decreased by 32 percent until 1995, and increased again by 18 percent. Since survey estimates for robbery are based on the rates for the five years preceding each survey, it is possible that the 1995 estimate is inflated by the very high rates in 1991–93 (according to police statistics). The drop in 1995 in police-recorded offenses may be due to section 172 of the Criminal Code, which became legally effective that year. According to this provision, muggings of less than 300 Swiss francs (or US$200), which, technically speaking, are theft, were no longer recorded if the victim did not file a formal complaint. The drop in robberies (and muggings) according to both indicators may also reflect the disappearance of open drug scenes from Swiss cities once heroin and methadone prescription became officially available to addicts (from 1994).

Assault. Based on the national victim surveys, the assault rate increased between 1985 and 1995, then almost halved between 1995 and 1997, before increasing to almost 1995 levels in 1999. The police-recorded assault rate increased steadily from 1985 to 1999 by 42 percent. Reporting to the police remained very stable for assault (mean 28 percent) throughout the entire period.

Rape. The police-recorded rape rate decreased by 43 percent between 1985 and 1994 and then increased by 26 percent until 1999 (fig. 1).

Homicide. Police-recorded homicides (fig. 1) increased from 1986 to 1990 by over 70 percent and decreased by 56 percent between 1990 and 1999. The mortality statistics show a very similar trend.

A. Methodological Issues

Generally speaking, burglary and all personal offenses increased substantially between the late 1980s and 1995. When appropriate adjustments are made, the increase in police statistics by and large matches the trends in crime surveys. From 1995 to 1997, however, all crimes against the person dropped substantially; they increased again in 1999 to about the 1995 levels. This erratic change in survey trends is not matched in police data. The first question that comes to mind is, of course, whether survey methods might account for these changes.

The answer is that this is extremely unlikely. First of all, survey methods were not changed between 1995 and 1999. The screeners were identical except for a few details without interest here, all sweeps used CATI, and response rates were very similar. The surveys of 1989 and 1996 were conducted by a different company (from those in 1998 and 2000), but that would not explain why the increase from 1997 to 1999 was about as large as the drop from 1995 to 1997. The questionnaires in 1998 and 2000 were identical in all details (as far as measures of crime are concerned). Second, it should be noted that survey measures of burglary and motor vehicle theft followed, in line with police statistics, remarkably different trends from crimes against the person. Whereas theft of motorcycles continued to decrease, burglary peaked in 1997 and decreased in 1999. Finally, bicycle theft followed a trend similar to what has been observed for offenses against the person. In conclusion, it seems unreasonable to attribute these changes to methodological problems.

B. Discrepancies between Survey and Official Measures of Crime

The federal police statistics give a higher burglary rate than the survey rate, because the federal police statistics burglary category includes not only commercial burglaries but also burglary from vending machines, telephone boxes, ticket machines, parking meters, and so forth. The Zurich police statistics were used to weight the federal police data for the proportion of residential burglaries. The resulting trend is lower than what victims declared having reported to the police (as one would expect) and, by and large, follows survey trends.

The rate for vehicle theft (e.g., cars, motorcycles, and mopeds) was given per 1,000 vehicle-owning households. As surveys provided data on the number of owners, it was possible to extrapolate, using survey information and household statistics, the number of households with vehicles for all years. The dramatic drop in the survey vehicle theft rate during the late 1980s was probably influenced by a change in the law, which made wearing crash helmets compulsory. The police data show a similar trend, though it is less pronounced, possibly because minor incidents often went unrecorded, particularly during the 1980s, when many vehicles were located rapidly. The reduction in the popularity of mopeds among juveniles is likely to have affected joyriding more than actual theft; this could explain why police recording seems to have increased in recent years. Interestingly, theft of bicycles, which is not discussed here, shows a different trend, which is more similar to the trends of personal offenses (Killias et al. 2000).

The number of robberies experienced in Switzerland is not large enough to provide reliable annual rates, even with relatively large samples. In order to reduce this problem, the annual rates were based on five-year rates. This produced more stable trends, which are in line with those of other personal offenses, which are indeed very similar (Killias et al. 2000).

Survey definitions of robbery include bag snatching and other forms of "mugging." In order to adjust police measures to survey indicators, such incidents (legally considered as theft) were also included. However, commercial robberies were excluded, using detailed information from Zurich police statistics and weighting the federal data accordingly.[13] Whereas survey measures include only incidents experienced by persons aged sixteen or over, the police data (and related population figures) refer to the total population.[14]

The survey measures for assault and threats are annual rates. The police data used include first-, second-, and third-degree cases of bodily injury, plus threats, extortion, and deprivation of liberty, in order to achieve maximum consistency with survey measures of assault (which could include experiences legally qualifying for any of these other Criminal Code sections).[15] Since police measures are much lower than survey estimates for assault/threats, police data on robberies were included on the assumption that some victims may have reported attempted robberies or muggings as assaults/threats.

The gap between police data and survey measures nonetheless is dramatic. This is probably because second- and third-degree bodily injury are prosecuted only on the formal request of the victim. In

[13] Only robberies committed in public places (streets) were included.

[14] It is not possible to exclude from the police figures incidents experienced by victims younger than sixteen.

[15] Criminal Code secs. 180 (threats, menaces/Drohung), 181 (forcing somebody to do or to tolerate something, contrainte/Nötigung), 156 (extortion, extorsion/Erpressung), and 183 (deprivation of liberty, séquestration-privation de liberté/Freiheitsberaubung und Entführung).

practice, this probably leads the police to record even reported offenses only when the suspect is known and when the victim insists on prosecution.[16]

Switzerland is a country in which, for assault, the number of suspects by and large matches the number of recorded offenses (Council of Europe 1999), whereas in countries where recording occurs at an earlier stage, the number of offenses typically far exceeds the number of suspects. Research in England and Wales has shown that police record less than 40 percent of reported offenses against the person (Burrows et al. 2000). Since limited police resources do not allow an increase in output beyond certain limits within a short time, it is not surprising that massive changes in survey trends between 1995 and 1999 are not reflected in police statistics. Particularly during the years with open drug scenes (Killias 2001c), the police recorded personal offenses conservatively, according to many police sources. The 1995 rates for police-recorded offenses are, therefore, probably substantially too low.

Rape (fig. 1) is measured in this study only according to police statistics. Although survey measures for rape alone would be unreliable, survey measures of sexual offenses against females show a trend similar to those observed for assault, robbery, and bicycle theft (Killias et al. 2000). It is possible here too that police output data do not reflect real short-term trend fluctuations.

According to the federal police statistics, completed homicide remained relatively stable over the entire period. Given the unclear counting rules in the federal police statistics, homicide trends are reported according to mortality statistics (fig. 1), which overall match police counts of completed homicide well. Homicide in Switzerland, and other parts of continental Europe, it should be noted, is mostly related to conflicts in personal life, with many murderers committing suicide after the act, rather than its being an instrumental crime (Massonnet, Wagner, and Kuhn 1990; Villettaz, Killias, and Mangin 2003).

C. Alternative Explanations

The trend data are consistent with information about contextual influences on offending.

---

[16] An observational study in southern Germany some twenty-five years ago (Kürzinger 1978) showed that theft is recorded in over 90 percent of cases, whereas the recording rate drops to 30 percent in cases of assault. This may describe the situation in Switzerland as well.

1. *Property Offenses.* According to survey crime rates, residential burglary increased markedly up to 1997 and then decreased. A similar trend was seen for adjusted police-recorded residential burglary. For vehicle theft, survey crime rates and police-recorded vehicle theft were similar, showing a marked decrease up to 1999.

Burglary, motor vehicle theft, and personal crime not only follow different trends but differ in situational respects. Burglary provides access to small amounts of cash, jewelry, silver, and all kinds of household equipment. Traditionally, electronic equipment such as televisions, video recorders, and music systems were often stolen. This is reflected in the ICVS question concerning the punishment the respondent considers appropriate for a burglar who stole a color television. This pattern has, however, lost most of its importance, and in future ICVS sweeps it may be necessary to formulate that question in a more contemporary way. Televisions and other electronic household equipment have lost most of their former value on local secondhand markets (Felson 1997, 2000). However, the fall of the Berlin Wall brought the poor and the wealthy parts of Europe into close proximity. Given the short distances, various forms of exchange between the two sides were immediate. Beyond new lines of transportation for drugs and other illegal goods, exportation of prostitutes, and cheap labor, attractive markets emerged for the export of secondhand products from Western Europe, such as used cars (Gerber and Killias 2003), televisions, and personal computers (i.e., goods that were no longer as attractive as before on Western secondhand markets). Police reports also indicate increasing burglaries in factories and storehouses of boutique chains, beauty shops, and so forth, where burglars depart with the stocks of a full season.

All this shows that burglary has changed in character since 1990, moving from an occasional activity of local offenders to a large-scale transborder industry. In line with these developments, the proportion of suspects of Swiss nationality dropped, in absolute figures, by 70 percent from 1983, according to Zurich police statistics, whereas the number of suspects who are foreign nationals has increased by more than 200 percent since 1990 (Killias et al. 2000). Whereas burglary decreased in the United States and Britain over most of the 1990s, Switzerland and other European countries (Killias and Aebi 2000) continued to experience increases, along with the expansion of transborder crime, which compensated for the drop in local burglaries. The recent decrease, according to police statistics and survey measures, may reflect saturation of Eastern secondhand markets[17] and possible effects of police measures against transborder crime in several Eastern European countries seeking to join the European Union.[18]

This market explanation may apply also to car theft and, more generally, to motor vehicle theft, but some additional explanations based on routine activities may be in order. Joyriding with cars became increasingly difficult over the last twenty years due to the advances of security technology. With motorcycles and mopeds, joyriding became a riskier crime to engage in once the wearing of crash helmets became compulsory in 1987 (Dell'Ambrogio 1992). Similar trends were observed by Mayhew, Clarke, and Elliott (1989) in Germany and in England and Wales. The continuing downward trend of motorcycle and moped theft may be due then to reduced attractiveness among adolescents. Eventually, some displacement to bicycle theft may have occurred, in line with the high popularity of mountain bikes among young people in recent years. After a sharp increase (by more than 100 percent) between 1988 and 1995, bicycle thefts dropped along with crimes against the person in 1997 and increased again moderately in 1999.

2. *Personal Offenses.* According to the surveys, robbery and assault increased markedly up to 1995, decreased in 1997, and increased again in 1999. Parallel trends of police-recorded robbery have been observed. For assault, police-recorded crime rates showed a more steady increase.

Excluding cases of domestic violence (which are hard to measure with crime victimization surveys),[19] robbery, assault, sexual offenses, and bicycle theft commonly occur in public areas such as streets. It is, therefore, reasonable to look for an explanation of trends at the level of what goes on in public areas. In urban areas with a high concentration of activities related to drugs and prostitution, offenders are likely to find many potential victims, a fact that attracts more offenders (Wikström 1985). In 1999, a local crime survey in Zurich found that the rate of local resident street-crime victimization was around ten times higher in Zurich's "problem" areas than in more privileged areas

---

[17] That jewelry and silver have recently become prime targets of burglars, according to police sources, might reflect a shift in opportunity structures. Such valuables may still be in demand in Eastern Europe, and they are less difficult to transport (and conceal).

[18] According to observations in Poland, e.g., stolen cars need to be moved further and further to the east, whereas they used to be sold in western Poland a few years ago (Gerber and Killias 2003).

[19] Although the Swiss (and ICVS) questionnaires of 1998 and 2000 made special efforts to identify them.

of the city (Killias 2001*a*, 2002). Thus, the size and the deterioration of such inner city areas may play a crucial role in overall crime levels.

Furthermore, the existence of large open drug scenes was certainly among the major factors in the increase in street crime in Switzerland's cities between 1989 and 1995 (Eisner 1997). Open drug scenes were very much influenced by the extension of medical assistance to addicts in a few city centers. This led to a concentration of addicts and of dealers in city centers. According to unpublished Zurich police data (see Killias and Uchtenhagen 1996; Killias 2001*c*), 73 percent of cleared muggings and 35 percent of cleared burglaries in 1995 were committed by addicts.

In 1994, with the support of the federal government, a heroin prescription program for a small number of addicts began. A few weeks later, "needle parks" in Zurich and other cities were closed. From 1995 and 1996, the heroin prescription program was made available to 800 addicts. Simultaneously, methadone substitution was extended to roughly 15,000 addicts. The total number of regular consumers of heroin being estimated at about 20,000–25,000, a substantial proportion of all heroin addicts were, thus, admitted to substitution programs. These programs had two consequences: first, a dramatic drop in criminal involvement among recipients of heroin and, to a lesser extent, among those enrolled in methadone programs (Killias and Rabasa 1998; Killias et al. 2002), and, second, an immediate reduction in the concentration of addicts in Switzerland's urban centers.[20] Both consequences may have contributed to a reduction in crime. Reduced delinquency among addicts (i.e., at the micro-level) diminished the number of motivated offenders,[21] which is clearly borne out in the 1998 and 2000 surveys since, according to accounts of robbery victims, the proportion of addicts among offenders had dropped from 23 percent in 1993–97 to 10 percent in 1995–99.[22] Moreover, the reduced concentration of addicts may have diminished the attractiveness of offending in certain urban areas. This may have been responsible for the drop not only in robberies but also in assault and sexual aggression, two offenses in which, according to Swiss data (Killias and Rabasa 1998), addicts are

---

[20] According to police, self-report, and victimization data (collected regularly from the addicts in heroin treatment), street crime dropped by 50–90 percent, with serious offenses showing larger decreases.

[21] Drug addicts were mostly involved in drug trafficking, robbery, mugging, bicycle theft, and personal theft.

[22] Given the low absolute numbers ($n = 75$ and 110, in 1993–97 and 1995–99, respectively), the victim accounts of offender characteristics were analyzed using five-year rates. No such question was asked in the surveys conducted before 1998.

not particularly involved. Both effects may have had a major impact on macro-level crime rates between 1996 and 1997.

The recent increase in 1999 is harder to explain. Because the proportion of addicts among the offenders was lower in 1999 than in 1997, according to victim accounts, a return of the drugs-crime link is unlikely to be the cause. A possible explanation is that recent migration may have changed the shape of urban centers in 1999 and again may have led to increased concentrations of social problems in certain areas. Within Western Europe, Switzerland received by far the highest number of Balkan refugees, particularly during the winter and spring of 1999.[23] Although conviction rates have been relatively high among refugees in general over recent years (Eisner, Manzoni, and Niggli 1998; Swiss Federal Statistical Office 2000),[24] little evidence is available to support such a hypothesis. However, the proportion of offenders perceived by violent crime victims as being of foreign origin[25] increased from 33 to 63 percent in the case of robbery between 1987 and 1999, from 40 to 52 percent for sexual aggression, and from 19 to 55 percent for assault (Killias et al. 2000). These proportions more or less match police statistics. It is, thus, not impossible that recent demographic changes may be at the origin of a new deterioration in urban centers and, indirectly, of the sudden increase in crime observed in several cities—and nationwide—in 1999. An alternative (but not necessarily competing) explanation would be that youth (gang) violence increased over the last few years. Unpublished data on victimization trends show that violence against teenage boys has disproportionately increased over the last years.

IV. Trends in Costs of Offending

In order to see whether crime trends vary in response to trends in costs of offending, we try to assess in this section whether the risk of being convicted and sentenced to custody, lengths of sentence, and time served has changed over time. We also consider trends in victims' decisions to report an offense to the police (or not) and changes in

---

[23] Officially, about 160,000 people from Kosovo alone, not including illegal immigrants, in a population of about 7 million.

[24] According to conviction records, 15 percent of male asylum seekers aged eighteen to twenty-nine are convicted per year, compared to 4 percent for the resident foreign and 3 percent of the Swiss male populations of the same age.

[25] By far the most important criterion of identification was language or accent, which is not surprising in a country where accents play a central role in daily life. Thus, "foreign" origin means, in the present context, a social fact rather than legal status.

police recording of reported offenses. These two variables also affect an offender's odds of being identified, prosecuted, and convicted. The denominator is the number of offenders, respectively convicted persons. Thus, we try to establish the risk of being convicted and imprisoned, and for how long, for an average offender for each of the six offenses under consideration. Before discussing these calculations, some comments on the data used will be necessary.

A. Convictions

Since 1942, the registration of convictions has been a federal matter. A database recorded since 1984 includes full details on convictions (offenses included in the verdict) and sentences imposed.[26] As in most European countries (Council of Europe 1999), a conviction is recorded in the registers and, therefore, in the statistics only after appeal. However, conviction statistics do not include minors (people convicted for offenses committed before age eighteen). In comparison to other continental countries, Swiss data are less inclusive in this respect. Since the focus in this essay is on trends and not on cross-country comparisons of convictions, this is not a major limitation.

Since 1984, a related database contains information on every person who enters the correctional system in connection with a custodial sentence. This database provides information on how long prisoners serve under a particular conviction (Rônez 1997) and is one of the most sophisticated databases in continental Europe.

To increase comparability with other countries, the number of convictions has been related to the number of offenses. Throughout continental Europe, however, conviction statistics apply a principal offense rule, and multiple offenses are recorded only once (Council of Europe 1999). In the case of a person convicted of killing two people, only one conviction for murder is, therefore, counted in the statistics. Swiss conviction statistics compared to Germany and other countries are more detailed, as they also record convictions for secondary offenses (e.g., robbery in addition to murder). However, offenses committed by multiple offenders are counted only once for any type of offense committed. Therefore, the number of convicted robbers will not match the number of robberies cleared by the police, since multiple robberies

---

[26] The rules on registration of misdemeanors are of no concern in the present context. Convictions for the six offenses under consideration are registered under all circumstances (Killias 2001b, pp. 250–52).

committed by a particular offender (and cleared by the police) will lead to just one conviction for robbery, irrespective of the number of offenses of which the defendant has been found guilty. If the court finds an offender also guilty of rape or drug trafficking, these additional offenses will be recorded but, again, without giving the number of offenses per type of crime.

Given these features of conviction statistics in Switzerland and more generally in continental Europe, an attempt was made to relate the number of convictions to the number of suspects. Both are person measures, and both count the same person only once per offense type, although some double counts are possible in police statistics given their limited consistency.

A major problem stems from the absence, under almost all continental laws, of the concepts of burglary and motor vehicle theft. Whereas joyriding is a special offense, under the Road Traffic Act, stealing a car or any other vehicle with the intent to keep or sell it is considered theft, as is stealing valuables from premises or a closed building.[27] In the absence of a better alternative, we use conviction, custody, sentence length, and time served data concerning more general forms of aggravated theft (secs. 139.2 and 139.3, Criminal Code); because most burglars are convicted for these forms of aggravated theft, the data used here may provide an approximate measure of sentences imposed upon burglars.

There are three categories of bodily injury and assault.[28] In Swiss law (as in other continental countries), there is no equivalent to the offense of serious assault found in English law. First-degree (i.e., serious) bodily injury includes only life-threatening injuries or those that leave the victim permanently and seriously disabled. Less than fifty offenders are convicted of this offense per year, compared with more than 1,000 convictions annually for second-degree assault. Third-degree assault (slapping or punching) includes cases where the victim has suffered pain but has not been injured. For comparability with other countries, only data for first-degree bodily injury and second-degree assault have been used in connection with convictions and sentences.

[27] The police data used here refer to a national police file of "missing" motor vehicles. These data do not include cases of joyriding if the vehicle is located within one or two days.
[28] Criminal Code, secs. 122, 123, and 126.

TABLE 3

Sentence Length (in Days) for All Offenses by Cumulative
versus Simple Convictions in 1999

Burglary only	161	Burglary (among other offenses)	580
Vehicle theft only	20	Vehicle theft (among other offenses)	285
Robbery only	751	Robbery (among other offenses)	1,083
Assault only	75	Assault (among other offenses)	356
Rape only	845	Rape (among other offenses)	1,511
Homicide only	2,131	Homicide (among others offenses)	2,939

SOURCE.—Swiss Federal Statistical Office, unpublished data.

The Swiss Criminal Code has been amended many times, and some of these changes have affected the offenses under consideration in this essay. For example, in 1990, the definitions of first-degree murder and bodily injury were revised; however, as these amendments were concerned with technical details, they have no statistical impact. In 1992, the definition of rape was amended to include marital rape and rape using strong psychological pressure. In 1995, the definitions of theft and robbery were technically amended, although without any major implications for conviction statistics. However, the downgrading of minor theft (i.e., of goods below the value of US$200) to a misdemeanor (to be prosecuted upon the formal complaint of the victim only) led to a decrease of police-recorded offenses of theft (including "muggings").

B. Sentences

In Switzerland, offenders found guilty of multiple offenses at one time receive one overall sentence for all the offenses, which reflects the seriousness of the principal offense (Killias 2001b, pp. 176–77). Thus, sentences in cases in which defendants have been convicted for more than one offense at the same time are difficult to relate to any particular offense type. For example, the gross average sentence length for (serious and ordinary) assault increased in 1999 from seventy-five to 356 days if cases in which offenders were convicted of additional offenses are included. For vehicle theft alone, the average net sentence was twenty days in 1999 but increased to 285 days if cases where offenders had been convicted of other offenses were included (table 3). Assuming that patterns of multiple offending have changed little over time, it is possible tentatively to indicate overall trends despite these difficulties. For practical reasons, sentence lengths and time served in prison were

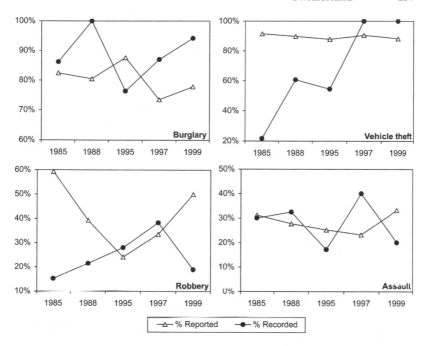

FIG. 2.—Percent reported to police and percent recorded of reported for burglary, vehicle theft, robbery, and assault. Source: Swiss crime surveys (Killias et al. 2000).

computed taking additional offenses into account in case of cumulative convictions.

C. Reporting and Recording Offenses

Figure 2 shows the percentages of crimes reported to and recorded by the police. The probability of police recording a reported residential burglary increased from 86 percent in 1985 to 100 percent in 1988, decreased in 1995 to 76 percent, and increased until 1999 to 94 percent. The probability of police recording a vehicle theft increased in two steps, from 22 percent in 1985 to 55 percent in 1995 and to 100 percent in 1999. The reporting to the police of robbery decreased sharply between 1985 and 1995 (from 59 percent to 24 percent) and then increased again to 34 percent in 1999. The probability of police recording a robbery increased from 15 percent in 1985 to 38 percent in 1997 and decreased to 19 percent in 1999. The odds of police recording an assault decreased from 30 percent in 1985 to 17 percent in 1995, increased to 40 percent in 1997, and decreased to 20 percent in 1999. Since many assaults were related to conflicts in the streets in relation to open drug scenes, the

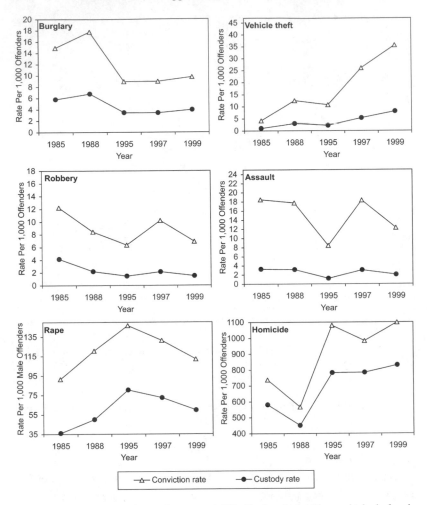

FIG. 3.—Conviction and custody rate per 1,000 offenders for burglary, vehicle theft, robbery, assault, rape, and homicide. Source: Swiss Federal Statistical Office, unpublished data.

change in drug policy may have affected assault rates in much the way it affected robbery. Given the low reporting and recording rates, it is possible that the changes in assault rates, as experienced by survey respondents, did not translate directly into police counts.

D. Trends in Conviction Rates and Sanctions

Offender-based risks of being convicted decreased for burglary and robbery, increased for homicide and motor vehicle theft, and fluctuated for rape and assault (fig. 3).

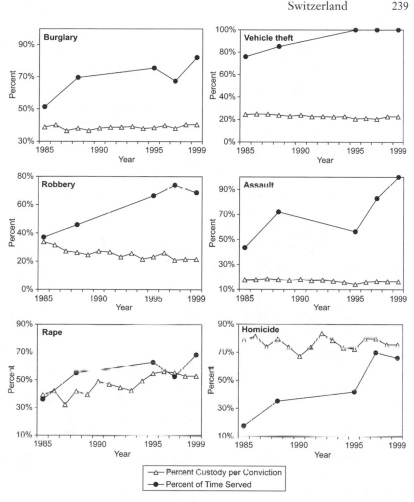

Fig. 4.—Percent custody per conviction and percent of time served for burglary, vehicle theft, robbery, assault, rape, and homicide. Source: Swiss Federal Statistical Office, unpublished data.

The probability of custody following a conviction remained fairly stable for all offenses, possibly reflecting a strong tendency toward stable sentencing patterns among judges (figs. 3 and 4; Killias et al. 2001). The reader may wonder why a rather large percentage of persons convicted of intentional homicide are not imprisoned. This is not related to therapeutic measures, since they are, in all but very exceptional and quantitatively negligible cases, counted as custodial sentences. The reason is that, under Swiss law, custodial sentences may be suspended if the defendant has killed in self-defense[29] or under mitigating circumstances.[30]

Average sentence lengths have remained stable for all offenses, despite minor fluctuations. Average time served has increased for most offenses. Average numbers of days served per conviction has fluctuated in an erratic way that is difficult to interpret (fig. 5). It should be noted, however, that sentence lengths are somewhat misleading under continental criminal law. Unlike Anglo-Saxon judges, who hand out a sentence for every offense of which the defendant has been found guilty, continental courts mete out a global sentence for all offenses together. In case of a conviction for multiple offenses, the global sentence, therefore, mostly reflects the most serious offense. Thus, sentence length will be inflated particularly for less serious offenses, as can be seen in table 3, and especially if they coincide with serious crimes.

E. Discussion

When the trends in convictions and time served per offender are related to crime rates, no clear picture emerges. It is true that robberies and assaults reached a peak in 1995 when the costs of such offenses seem to have fallen to a minimum. In terms of deterrence, however, it is not easy to explain why this drop in costs was followed by a substantial drop in robberies and assaults in 1997 rather than by an increase. In 1999, the costs associated with robbery dropped again, but not for assault; despite that, both offenses increased in 1999 (compared to 1997) to about the same extent. The costs of homicide apparently increased a lot over the years, but no similar trend is visible in recorded offenses. Rape, finally, increased somewhat over the years, although the trend in costs is essentially stable, despite a few erratic fluctuations.

Even more important may be a methodological problem, since trends in "risk of punishment" (risk of conviction/sentence length) depend also on the denominator. In this analysis and to conform to the common approach in this volume, we estimated the number of offenders using estimates derived from crime surveys. This denominator has the disadvantage of yielding lower risk rates every time survey-measured

---

[29] If self-defense is admitted, the defendant will be acquitted. However, in many cases the judge finds that the defendant's reaction was excessive. In this case, the homicide is no longer considered justified, but the self-defense situation in which the defendant acted will be a seriously mitigating circumstance.

[30] For example, the fact of having played a secondary role in the killing of the victim (notably as an accomplice).

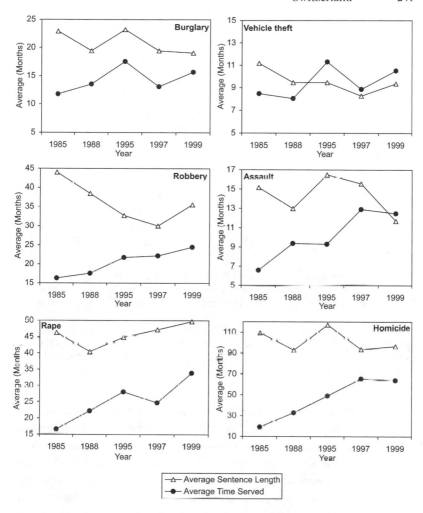

Fig. 5.—Average sentence length and average time served for burglary, vehicle theft, robbery, assault, rape, and homicide. Source: Swiss Federal Statistical Office, unpublished data.

offenses increase, and showing an apparent increase, when, according to the survey, crime is decreasing. Thus, the denominator may lead to partially circular conclusions. Indeed, if the number of convictions is divided by the number of offenders known to the police, the sometimes strong variations in costs of offending tend to disappear. Figure 6 illustrates this problem for assault, where the probability of conviction per 1,000 offenders known to the police remained remarkably stable, whereas the risks of being convicted per 1,000 offenders (derived from crime surveys) showed much higher (and erratic) variations.

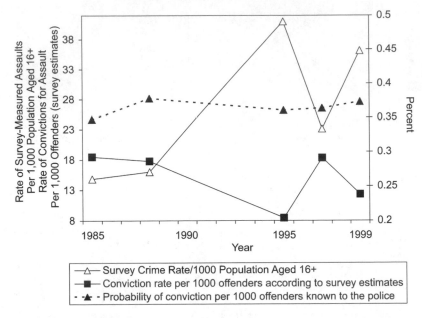

F<small>IG</small>. 6.—Differences of conviction per offender, according to survey estimates and according to offender known to the police (for assault). Sources: Swiss Federal Statistical Office, unpublished data; Swiss Federal Police Office 1985–2000; Swiss Crime Surveys (Killias et al. 2000).

Of course, it is hard to decide whether risk of conviction should be related to offenders known to the police, or to those in the population according to survey estimates. Obviously, the two denominators yield different results. Survey estimates of offenders might better reflect the actual risk of criminal behavior in a given society, whereas police-recorded offenders give a more accurate picture of the way the criminal justice system reacts to crime. As figure 6 illustrates, the criminal justice system's way of dealing with offenders might have been subject to less variation over time than the preceding analyses suggest.

F. Conclusion

Langan and Farrington (1998) raised the challenging issue of whether criminal justice system responses to crime affect crime rates. Cusson (1993) had presented a similar argument in a thought-provoking paper a few years earlier. Despite the plausibility of the "cost of crime" hypothesis, the Swiss experience is inconclusive in this regard. Although crime rates, as measured by surveys, seem to have reacted to changes in the costs of crime, several problems run counter to such a straightforward conclusion. Our measures of risk of punishment are sensitive to the choice of the denominator, being much more stable if, for example, convictions are related to offenders known to the police, than when survey-based estimates of numbers of offenders are used. These issues go beyond mere concerns about data quality but concern the logic of the deterrence argument, which easily becomes circular. Comparability of cost indicators might be increased on the continent by introducing detailed counts of sentences for each offense of which the defendant is convicted. The "summary" sentences handed down by continental courts, however, reflect more than a mere difference in data collection. European sentencing systems are much more oriented toward rehabilitation than to making the offender pay for each individual crime. Alternative, perhaps more easily comparable, sentencing data could be collected only at the price of fundamentally reshaping European sentencing systems in a more retributive way.

Beyond these methodological issues, alternative explanations can be offered to account for the observed changes in Swiss crime trends. Routine activities and changes in black markets offer competing and equally plausible explanations. For example, burglary trends are easy to explain as a result of changes in transborder crime, since the enormous demand in consumer goods after 1990 led to increasing criminal export of stolen goods from Western to Eastern Europe. Similarly, robbery, assault, and other personal crimes fluctuated in response to growing "needle" parks in Swiss cities (not only in Zurich) between 1985 and 1993 and dropped once these open scenes began to vanish (Killias 2001c). Heroin and methadone prescription became officially available to addicts from 1994. This program was extended substantially in 1995 and 1996 to include over 1,000 heroin recipients and more than 15,000 methadone patients, out of a population of 20,000–25,000 regular heroin users.

These alternative explanations suggest that changes in crime trends are sometimes more easily explained by developments outside the control of the criminal justice system. Given the problems with data comparability, the scarcity of survey data, and the relatively small national samples used, we admit, however, that the Swiss data are inconclusive to decide between these competing perspectives. Ironically, in face of the pros and cons of the cost of crime hypothesis, it seems as if our data behaved along Switzerland's long-standing policy of neutrality.

REFERENCES

Annuaire statistique de la Suisse. 2001. Zurich: Editions "Neue Zürcher Zeitung."

Burrows, John, Roger Tarling, Alan Mackie, Rachel Lewis, and Geoff Taylor. 2000. *Review of Police Forces' Crime Recording Practices.* Home Office Research Study, no. 204. London: Home Office.

Council of Europe. 1999. *European Sourcebook of Crime and Criminal Justice Statistics.* Strasbourg: Council of Europe.

Cusson, Maurice. 1993. "L'effet structurant du contrôle social." *Criminologie* 26(2):37–62.

Dell'Ambrogio, Piera. 1992. *Législation sur le port du casque et vol de motocycles.* Lausanne: IPSC-UNIL.

Eisner, Manuel. 1997. *Das Ende der zivilisierten Stadt: Die Auswirkungen von Individualisierung und urbaner Krise auf Gewaltdelinquenz.* Frankfort: Campus.

Eisner, Manuel, Patrik Manzoni, and Marcel Alexander Niggli. 1998. *Kriminalität unter Asylsuchenden.* Zurich: Schweiz Flüchtlingshilfe.

Felson, M. 1997. "A 'Routine-Activity' Analysis of Recent Crime Reductions." *Criminologist* 22(6):1–3.

———. 2000. "Trend e cicli del tasso di criminalità: I cambiamenti nella società moderna." In *Perché è diminuita la criminalità negli Stati Uniti?* edited by M. Bargabli. Bologna: Il Mulino.

Gerber, Jurg, and Martin Killias. 2003. "The Transnationalization of Historically Local Crime: Auto Theft in Western Europe and Russian Markets." *European Journal of Crime, Criminal Law and Criminology* 11(2):215–26.

Kesteren, John van, Pat Mayhew, and Paul Nieuwbeerta. 2000. *Criminal Victimisation in Seventeen Industrialised Countries: Key Finding from the 2000 International Crime Victims Survey.* The Hague: Wetenschappelijk Onderzoek-en Documentatiecentrum.

Killias, Martin. 1989. *Les Suisses face au crime.* Grüsch, Switzerland: Rüegger.

———. 1993. "How to Optimize the Use of CATI in Victimisation Surveys?" In *Fear of Crime and Criminal Victimisation,* edited by Wolfgang Bilsky, Christian Pfeiffer, and Peter Wetzels. Interdisziplinäre Beitrage zur kriminologischen Forchung (KFN). Stuttgart: Enke.

———. 2001*a. Précis de criminology.* 2d ed. Berne: Stämpfli.

———. 2001*b. Précis de droit pénal general.* 2d cd. Berne: Stämpfli.

———. 2001*c.* "Switzerland's Drug Policy as an Alternative to the American War on Drugs." In *Drug War, American Style: The Internationalization of Failed Policy and Its Alternatives,* edited by Jurg Gerber and Eric L. Jensen. New York: Garland.

———. 2002. *Grundriss der Kriminologie.* Berne: Stämpfli.

Killias, Martin, and Marcelo F. Aebi. 2000. "Crime Trends in Europe from 1990 to 1996: How Europe Illustrates the Limits of the American Experience." *European Journal on Criminal Policy and Research* 8(4):43–63.

Killias, Martin, Marcelo F. Aebi, André Kuhn, and Simone Rônez. 2001. "Sentencing in Switzerland in 2000." In *Penal Reform in Overcrowded Times,* edited by Michael Tonry. New York: Oxford University Press.

Killias, Martin, Marcelo F. Aebi, Denis Ribaud, and Juan Rabasa. 2002. *Rapport final sur les effets de la prescription de stupéfiants sur la délinquance des toxicomanes.* 3d ed. Lausanne: IPSC-UNIL.

Killias, Martin, Philippe Lamon, Christian Clerici, and Thierry Berruex. 2000. *Tendances de la criminalité en Suisse de 1984 à 2000: Risques objectifs et perceptions subjectives.* Lausanne: IPSC-UNIL.

Killias, Martin, and Juan Rabasa. 1998. "Does Heroin Prescription Reduce Crime? Results from the Evaluation of the Swiss Heroin Prescription Projects." *Studies on Crime and Crime Prevention* 7(1):127–33.

Killias, Martin, and Ambros Uchtenhagen. 1996. "Does Medical Heroin Prescription Reduce Delinquency among Drug-Addicts?" *Studies on Crime and Crime Prevention* 5(2):245–56.

Kürzinger, Josef. 1978. *Private Strafanzeige und polizeiliche Reaktion.* Berlin: Duncker & Humblot.

Langan, Patrick A., and David P. Farrington. 1998. *Crime and Justice in the United States and in England and Wales, 1981–96.* Washington, D.C.: U.S. Department of Justice, Office of Justice Programs, Bureau of Justice Statistics.

Langbein, John H. 1974. "Controlling Prosecutorial Discretion in Germany." *University of Chicago Law Review* 41(3):439–67.

Massonnet, Geneviève, Rebecca Wagner, and André Kuhn. 1990. "Etude des homicides dans les cantons de Zurich et de Vaud, en considérant plus particulièrement la relation victime-agresseur." *Bulletin de criminologie* 16(1–2):75–103.

Mayhew, Pat, Ronald V. Clarke, and Delbert Elliott. 1989. "Motorcycle Theft, Helmet Legislation and Displacement." *Howard Journal* 28(1):1–8.

Piquerez, Gérard. 2000. *Procédure pénale suisse, traité théorique et pratique.* Zurich: Schulthess.

Rônez, Simone. 1997. *Statistique pénitentiaire Suisse—1996. Flux et effectifs de la population pénitentiaire.* Berne: Office fédéral de la statistique.

Scherpenzeel, Annette. 1992. "Response effecten in slachtoffer-enquêtes: Effecten van vraagformulering en dataverzamelingsmethode." *Tijdschrift voor Criminologie* 34(4):296–305.

Schmid, Niklaus. 1997. *Strafprozessrecht: Eine Einführung auf der Grundlage des Strafprozessrechtes des Kantons Zürich und des Bundes.* 3d ed. Zurich: Schulthess.

Swiss Federal Police Office. 1985–2000. *Statistiques policières de la criminalité.* Berne: Swiss Federal Police Office.

Swiss Federal Statistical Office. 2000. *Kriminalität von Asylsuchenden: Analyse einer kleinen Gruppe von Verurteilten.* Neuchâtel: Swiss Federal Statistical Office.

Trechsel, Stephan, and Martin Killias. Forthcoming. "Criminal Law, Criminal Procedure." In *Introduction to Swiss Law*, 2d ed., edited by Francois Dessemontet and Tugrul Ansay. Dordrecht: Kluwer.

Van Dijk, Jan J. M., Pat Mayhew, and Martin Killias. 1990. *Experiences of Crime across the World: Key Findings of the 1989 International Crime Survey.* Deventer: Kluwer.

Villettaz, Patrice, Martin Killias, and Patrice Mangin. 2003. *Les constellations homicidaires et suicidaires dans quatre cantons romands.* Lausanne: IPSC-UNIL.

Wikström, P.-O. H. 1985. *Everyday Violence in Contemporary Sweden.* Stockholm: National Council for Crime Prevention.

Brandon C. Welsh and Mark H. Irving

Crime and Punishment in Canada, 1981–1999

ABSTRACT

The average Canadian enjoys a high standard of living bolstered by a social safety network that includes universal health care coverage, generous benefits for unemployed workers and families in need, and year-long maternity leave. While crime ranks among the public's top concerns nationally, Canada is viewed as a safe and peaceful country in which to live and visit. But how safe is Canada? Police records indicate that Canada experienced a substantial fall in rates of serious crimes in the 1990s. Reasons include an aging population and an improved economy. There is mixed evidence on whether the Canadian criminal justice system's response to serious crime influenced crime trends during the 1990s. There is a need for increased public investment in many facets of basic research on crime and punishment in Canada. Such an investment may go some way to bring about more informed and efficacious crime policy.

At 10 million square kilometers, Canada is the world's second largest country, surpassed only by the Russian Federation. In 2002, Canada's population was estimated at 31.4 million. The population density is very low (3.5 persons per square kilometer) when compared with other nations. With 80 percent of Canadians living in an urban center of

Brandon C. Welsh is associate professor in the Department of Criminal Justice, University of Massachusetts, Lowell. Mark H. Irving is a senior research analyst with the National Crime Prevention Centre, Department of Public Safety and Emergency Preparedness Canada. We thank Julian Roberts for helpful comments on an earlier version of this essay; Vickie Sheridan for assistance in editing; and Robert Allen, Patricia Bégin, Paul De Souza, Orest Fedorowycz, Craig Grimes, Mike Hayden, Holly Johnson, Karen Kaschube, Jean-Robert Larocque, Denise Ménard, Steven Mihorean, Chi Nguyen, Alex Smale, and Cathy Trainor for assistance in the collection of data. The views expressed herein are those of the authors and do not represent those of the Department of Public Safety and Emergency Preparedness Canada.

247

10,000 people or more, Canada is one of the most urbanized countries in the world. Canada has ten provinces and three territories, each with its own capital city. Ottawa, the nation's capital, is located in the most populous province, Ontario.

Canada's official languages are English and French. However, many Canadians have a mother tongue other than English or French, including Chinese, Italian, German, Polish, Spanish, Portuguese, Punjabi, Ukrainian, Arabic, Dutch, Cree, Inuktitut (Eskimo), and other languages, reflecting the country's multicultural and multiethnic composition.

All Canadians have access to free health care, with the exception of dental services. Canada has an extensive social safety network including old age pensions, family allowance, employment insurance, and welfare benefits. In addition, generous maternity leave is made available to working mothers. The Canada Labour Code provides up to fifty-two weeks of combined maternity and parental leave. Life expectancy is among the highest in the world. In 2000, the life expectancy at birth was 76.7 years for men and 82 years for women. Canada's unemployment rate in 2002 was 7.7 percent.

Canada's gross domestic product was US$687.7 billion in 2000, or US$28,100 per person. The average annual growth over ten years (1990–2000) was 2.7 percent. The leading industries include high technology, automobile manufacturing, pulp and paper, iron and steel work, machinery and equipment manufacturing, mining, extraction of fossil fuels, forestry, agriculture, and tourism. The United States is Canada's most important trading partner in both import and export of goods.

Canada is a constitutional monarchy, a federal state, and parliamentary democracy. The responsibility for governing at the federal level is shared by the legislative, executive, and judicial branches. In principle, all three powers flow from Queen Elizabeth II, Canada's head of state. As Queen of Canada, she is represented nationally by the governor general of Canada and provincially by lieutenant governors. By and large, Her Majesty delegates her powers to these representatives. The legislative branch consists of the Queen and two houses of Parliament: the House of Commons, whose members are elected by their constituents, and the Senate, whose members are appointed by the government of the day. The executive branch is comprised of those who propose policies and bills (prime minister and cabinet) and those who carry them out (the public service). The prime minister provides overall direction. The third branch of government is the judiciary, which is independent of the cabinet, parliament, or any other state institution. This impartiality allows the courts, especially the Supreme Court of Canada, to interpret laws in light of the nation's constitution and the Charter of Rights and Freedoms (Public Service Commission of Canada 2002).

The authority to enact criminal laws and procedures to be followed in criminal matters is assigned to the federal parliament by the Constitution Act of 1867 (formerly the British North American Act). Generally speaking, Canada's ten provinces and three territories have jurisdiction over the administration of justice, as well as responsibility for establishing and maintaining a system of provincial and territorial criminal courts. The federal government is also involved in the provision of criminal justice services, as described in more detail below.

Canada's criminal law is founded in English common law. The primary source of both substantive and procedural criminal law is the Criminal Code, which was first enacted in 1892 and has been continually revised. The Criminal Code sets out two main categories of offenses: indictable and summary conviction. The main difference is that indictable offenses (e.g., homicide, robbery) are more serious and warrant a more involved and formal trial procedure. A third, less common, group of offenses is referred to as hybrid and can be treated as either indictable or summary conviction depending on how the prosecutor elects to proceed.

The structure of the Canadian criminal justice system consists of many levels and stages of operation. Policing responsibilities are divided among many jurisdictions. Canada's federal police force, the Royal Canadian Mounted Police (RCMP), operates in all provinces and territories to enforce those federal laws for which it is responsible (e.g., Controlled Drugs and Substances Act, Food and Drugs Act). The RCMP also provides policing services, under contract, to the three territories and to some provinces and municipalities. The provinces of Ontario, Quebec, and Newfoundland have their own provincial police forces (Ontario Provincial Police, Sûreté du Québec, and Royal Newfoundland Constabulary, respectively). They are responsible for enforcing provincial laws as well as most of the provisions of the Criminal Code. Finally, regional and municipal police services are responsible for enforcing municipal bylaws, provincial laws, and the Criminal Code. Their jurisdiction tends to be restricted to the municipality. As of June 15, 2002, there were 58,414 police officers in Canada, or 186 police officers per 100,000 population (Logan 2002).

Crown attorneys are agents of the attorney general. They represent, and are responsible to, the state. These lawyers prosecute cases on behalf of the federal, provincial, or territorial governments. Once charges have been laid by the police, the crown attorney is responsible for deciding which charges the accused will face in court and for prosecuting those charges.

With respect to the hierarchy of criminal courts in Canada, the lowest level is occupied by justices of the peace who, among other things, issue summonses and warrants for arrests and hold bail hearings. The vast majority of criminal trials in Canada take place before provincial or territorial court judges in the "inferior" or provincial courts. Provincial or territorial courts may also include family and small claims divisions, as well as young offender divisions. Court structure varies from province to province, as does the number and type of divisions within each court. Next in the hierarchy are those courts in which both trials are held and appeals heard (i.e., supreme or superior court). This is the province's highest-level trial court. The second highest level in the hierarchy of criminal courts in the country is comprised of provincial courts of appeal that hear appeals from the trial courts as well as lower-level appeal courts. The highest court in the country, the Supreme Court of Canada, hears appeals from the provincial courts of appeal.

There are many options available to the sentencing court. The main types of sanctions that can be imposed include the following: a fine, probation, a conditional sentence, imprisonment, and other sentencing options, such as restitution, compensation, a conditional or absolute discharge, or a suspended sentence.

Canada has separate corrections systems for young and adult offenders. Adult correctional services in Canada are divided primarily between the provincial-territorial and federal governments on the basis of length of sentence: offenders sentenced to two years or more are placed in federal institutions, and offenders sentenced to less than two years are placed in provincial or territorial correctional centers. The various correctional services and facilities can be divided into two basic categories: custodial and noncustodial. At the federal level, two agencies provide correctional services for adult offenders. The Correctional Service of Canada (CSC) is responsible for administering custodial sentences of two years or more. The CSC is also responsible for supervising federal offenders on conditional release in the community until the end of their sentences. Decisions on the conditional release of federal offenders are the responsibility of the National Parole Board (NPB). The NPB is an independent, administrative tribunal that has exclusive authority to grant, deny, cancel, terminate, or revoke day and full parole. The NPB also makes conditional release decisions for offenders in provinces and territories that do not have their own parole boards. The provincial and territorial governments have the exclusive responsibility for offenders sentenced to probation and for young offenders.

In 1984, the Young Offenders Act (YOA) replaced the Juvenile Delinquents Act, which had been the legislative framework for youth justice in Canada since 1908. Over the past several years, academics and criminal justice practitioners alike have criticized the YOA for not providing clear legislative direction to guide appropriate implementation in several key areas. This lack of clear legislative direction was thought to be an important factor contributing to problems and deficiencies in Canada's youth justice system (Department of Justice Canada 2003). This led to the effectuation of the Youth Criminal Justice Act on April 1, 2003, which replaced the YOA. The new legislation applies to young persons between twelve and seventeen years of age. Youths who are charged with an offense are prosecuted in youth courts.

This essay examines trends in crime and punishment in Canada over the period 1981–99 and explores key (potential) explanations for important trends in these areas. Six offenses are studied: homicide, aggravated sexual assault, serious assault, robbery, motor vehicle theft, and residential burglary. We offer several main conclusions. First, police records indicate that Canada may have been safer at the end of the 1990s compared with the early 1980s. Of the six offenses studied, rates decreased for four (homicide, aggravated sexual assault, robbery, and residential burglary) and increased for the other two. Second, a much more sustained and larger change in police-reported crime rates took place in the 1990s. A substantial fall in rates of five of the six serious crimes (not motor vehicle theft) occurred from about 1991 to 1999. Third, reasons for this drop in serious crime rates in the 1990s include an aging population—a declining proportion of the age group most at risk of criminal offending (fifteen- to twenty-four-year-olds) and an increasing proportion of an age group with low involvement in criminal activity (ages fifty-five and over)—and an improved economy (falling unemployment rates). Fourth, from the available evidence on the Canadian criminal justice system's response to serious crime, through the courts and corrections agencies, during the mid-to-late

1990s, there are mixed signs about whether it could have had an impact on crime trends during this time period.

The organization of this essay is as follows: Section I looks at crime and victimization in Canada over the period 1981–99. It begins with a description of the crime and victimization data sources, presents definitions of the six offenses under study, discusses any problems of comparability over time and between crime and victimization data and any adjustments that were made to improve comparability, and examines trends in crime and victimization rates during the aforementioned time period. Section II examines changes over time in police recording practices, and Section III explores key hypotheses for trends in crime rates during the 1990s. Section IV focuses on the punishment of offenders for the six types of offenses under study; specifically, it looks at conviction rates, custody rates, the probability of custody after a conviction, and average custodial sentence length. For each of these different measures of punishment, data sources are described, any problems of comparability over time and any adjustments that were made to improve comparability are discussed, and trends for the six offenses are examined. The section ends with a brief discussion of key (potential) explanations for trends in punishment. Section V brings together the main conclusions and identifies gaps in knowledge and priorities for research.

I. Crime and Victimization

Official (police-reported) statistics on crime in Canada are collected by the Canadian Centre for Justice Statistics (CCJS), a division of Statistics Canada, through the Uniform Crime Reporting (UCR) Survey.[1] Begun in 1962, the UCR Survey measures the "incidence of crime in Canadian society and its characteristics" (Canadian Centre for Justice Statistics 1999a, p. 7). Importantly, police compliance with the UCR Survey, since its inception, has been "virtually 100 percent" (Canadian Centre for Justice Statistics 1999a, p. 69).[2]

---

[1] This term is used by the Canadian Centre for Justice Statistics to reflect the process of the police reporting those criminal incidents recorded by the police to the Uniform Crime Reporting Survey. "Police-reported" crime is identical to "police-recorded" crime, the latter being the term used by statistical agencies in other countries to refer to criminal incidents that have come to the attention of the police and have been recorded by the police. In keeping with Canadian government nomenclature, the term "police-reported" is used throughout this essay.

[2] "There are approximately 1,424 separate police locations responding to the survey, comprising about 376 different police forces. The most significant loss of information

Data collected by the UCR Survey include only "actual" incidents, both criminal and traffic. "An offence is considered to be 'actual' when, following an initial investigation, the police have confirmed that a criminal offence has occurred" (Du Wors 1997, p. 1). Another important feature is that, in the event of more than one offense occurring in an incident, the incident is classified by the most serious offense (MSO), which is "generally the offence which carries the longest maximum sentence under the Criminal Code of Canada" (Canadian Centre for Justice Statistics 1999*a*, p. 7).[3]

Unlike the United States and England and Wales, Canada's experience in carrying out national victimization surveys is more recent, and these surveys have been done on a less-frequent basis. Three national victimization surveys have been carried out: the first for 1987, the second for 1992, and the third for 1998.[4]

Each survey, a component of Statistics Canada's General Social Survey, carried out telephone interviews with persons ages fifteen years or older to gauge their experiences with crime and the criminal justice system over the previous twelve months.[5] In addition to the age limit, the sample for all three surveys was confined to households with telephones, persons not institutionalized, and inhabitants of the ten Canadian provinces (the three territories—Yukon, Northwest Territories, and Nunavut—were not included). For the 1998 survey, this

occurs in the rare situation where a police force fails to submit data to the CCJS. In this situation, estimates are calculated for that particular force" (Canadian Centre for Justice Statistics 1999*a*, p. 69).

[3] "In categorizing incidents, violent offences always take precedence over non-violent offences. For example, an incident involving both a breaking and entering offence and an assault is counted as an incident of assault. As a result of the MSO scoring rule, less serious offences are under-counted by the UCR Survey" (Canadian Centre for Justice Statistics 1999*a*, p. 7). Furthermore, "violent crime counts reflect the number of victims in the incident, whereas non-violent counts reflect the number of incidents or occurrences of crime" (Tremblay 1999, p. 3).

[4] These three surveys were administered in 1988, 1993, and 1999, respectively. In reporting on these surveys, we have used the time period in which the surveys were probing: 1987 for the 1988 survey, approximately 1992 for the 1993 survey, and 1998 for the 1999 survey. Gartner and Doob (1994), in their comparison of the 1987 and 1992 surveys, use the years that the surveys were administered. The year 1992 is approximate for the following reason: "The 1993 survey carried out over the 12 months of 1993 asked about victimizations which occurred in the previous 12 months—in this case, the one year period often spanned two calendar years, 1992 and 1993" (Gartner and Doob 1994, p. 4, n. 1).

[5] Households were the independent variable: "Once a household was chosen, an individual 15 years or older was selected randomly to respond to the survey" (Besserer and Trainor 2000, p. 15).

resulted in approximately 2 percent of the Canadian population being excluded, which, as noted by Besserer and Trainor (2000, p. 15), "is not large enough to significantly change the [victimization] estimates." A similar percentage of the Canadian population was excluded from the previous two surveys.

For each of the first two victim surveys, there were approximately 10,000 respondents; for the third survey, there was a substantial increase, to approximately 26,000. For the 1998 survey, the response rate was 81 percent. Reasons for nonresponse included refusal to participate, no answer, and could not speak English or French (Besserer and Trainor 2000, p. 16). Similar response rates were achieved for the previous two surveys. Each survey collected information on eight categories of crimes: sexual assault, robbery, assault, residential burglary, motor vehicle theft, theft of household property, theft of personal property, and vandalism.[6] (We discuss below the definitions of the first five of these offenses and any changes over time.)

Two other important issues concerning these victim surveys are scale and sampling error. In the 1998 survey, the largest of the three national victim surveys, each respondent represented about 1,000 people in the Canadian population. For the 1987 and 1992 surveys, the scale-up factor was much greater: each respondent represented approximately 2,100 and 2,200 people in the Canadian population, respectively.[7] Concerning sampling error, the measure used in reporting on estimates from the 1998 survey was the coefficient of variation (CV),[8] and any estimate that had a CV of greater than 33.3 percent was considered "too unreliable to be published" (Besserer and Trainor 2000, p. 6, box 4). We were not successful in obtaining information on the sampling error used in reporting on the findings of the 1987 and 1992 surveys.

---

[6] "Incidents involving more than one type of offence, for example a robbery and an assault, are classified according to the most serious offence. The rank of offences from most to least serious is: sexual assault, robbery, assault, break and enter, motor vehicle/parts theft, theft of personal property, theft of household property and vandalism. Incidents are classified based on the respondent's answers to a series of questions. For example, did anyone threaten you with physical harm in any way? How were you threatened?" (Besserer and Trainor 2000, p. 3, box 1).

[7] The figure for 1998 was provided by Besserer and Trainor (2000, p. 6, box 4). The figures for 1987 and 1992 were calculated by dividing the number of people ages fifteen and over—using data from Statistics Canada (2002) and adjusted for the surveys not covering 2 percent of the Canadian population—by the number of survey respondents (approximately 10,000 for each survey) and by rounding to the nearest hundred.

[8] "The CV gives an indication of the uncertainty associated with an estimate" (Besserer and Trainor 2000, p. 6, box 4).

We also report on the findings of a fourth victim survey, Canada's first large-scale victimization survey, the Canadian Urban Victimization Survey (CUVS). The CUVS was administered in 1982 to over 61,000 persons ages sixteen years or older in seven major urban centers across the country (Greater Vancouver, Edmonton, Winnipeg, Toronto, Montreal, Halifax-Dartmouth, and St. John's). Information was collected on the respondents' experiences during 1981 for the same eight crime categories included in the three national victimization surveys.

The CUVS used telephone interviews. In addition to not interviewing people under the age of sixteen, the CUVS sample excluded households without telephones, commercial premises, and institutions such as penitentiaries and psychiatric hospitals. In the seven cities where the CUVS was administered, the resident population (ages sixteen and over) was just under 5 million, so each respondent represented approximately eighty people (4,975,900 divided by 61,000). We were not successful in obtaining information about the response rate or the sampling error.

In order to make the CUVS comparable to the national victim surveys, we had to scale down the CUVS crime rates. We first calculated, for the five offenses of sexual assault, assault, robbery, motor vehicle theft, and residential burglary and the three years of national surveys (1987, 1992, and 1998), the proportion of national victim survey rates of urban victim survey rates (see table 1). We then multiplied the mean proportion (for all five crimes) by the relevant CUVS rate per 1,000 population (see table 2). The last column of table 2 lists, by crime type, the estimated 1981 national victimization rates per 1,000 population (ages sixteen and over). Not surprisingly, for each crime the estimated national rate is lower than the urban rate from the CUVS.

A. Homicide

First-degree murder, second-degree murder, manslaughter, and infanticide are included under the offense of homicide (Fedorowycz 2000). Homicide incidents, as reported throughout this essay, only include completions.[9]

[9] Official crime rates for all six offenses reported here, for the years 1981–98, are based on revised population estimates—done by the Canadian Centre for Justice Statistics (1999c)—so there may be some minor differences with past publications that have reported on these data.

TABLE 1

Proportion of National Victim Survey Rates of Urban Victim Survey Rates

Crime Type	National Rate per 1,000 Population (Ages Fifteen+)			Urban Rate per 1,000 Population (Ages Fifteen+)			Proportion of National of Urban Rate per 1,000 Population (Ages Sixteen+)		
	1987	1992	1998	1987	1992	1998	1987	1992	1998
Sexual assault		16.6	20.7[a]		18	21[a]	N.A.	.92	.99
Assault	68.4	66.8	80.7[b]	72	72	85[b]	.95	.93	.95
Robbery	13.1	9.1	9.4	14	9	11	.94	1.01	.85
Motor vehicle theft[c]	24.6	18.9	20.6	28.5[d]	23.1[e]	22.0[f]	.86	.82	.94
Residential burglary	26.3	25.2	24.2	31.3[g]	28.2[h]	26.1[i]	.84	.89	.93

SOURCES.—Canadian Centre for Justice Statistics 1990; Gartner and Doob 1994; Besserer and Trainor 2000; Statistics Canada n.d.

NOTE.—For 1987, the number of sexual assault incidents was either too low to produce statistically reliable estimates or not applicable (N.A.).

[a] Includes all incidents of spousal sexual assault. Urban incidents excluding spousal sexual assault were not available.

[b] Includes all incidents of spousal physical assault. Urban incidents excluding spousal physical assault were not available.

[c] Includes theft of motor vehicles and theft of motor vehicle parts. Urban incidents excluding theft of motor vehicle parts were not available.

[d] Calculated by dividing the urban rate per 1,000 households (fifty-nine) by the national rate per 1,000 households (fifty-one) and multiplying the quotient (1.16) with the national rate per 1,000 population (24.6). All property offenses in victim surveys are reported as rates per 1,000 households.

[e] Calculated by dividing the urban rate per 1,000 households (forty-five) by the national rate per 1,000 households (thirty-seven) and multiplying the quotient (1.22) with the national rate per 1,000 population (18.9).

[f] Calculated by dividing the urban rate per 1,000 households (forty-four) by the national rate per 1,000 households (forty-one) and multiplying the quotient (1.07) with the national rate per 1,000 population (20.6).

[g] Calculated by dividing the urban rate per 1,000 households (sixty-four) by the national rate per 1,000 households (fifty-four) and multiplying the quotient (1.19) with the national rate per 1,000 population (26.3).

[h] Calculated by dividing the urban rate per 1,000 households (fifty-six) by the national rate per 1,000 households (fifty) and multiplying the quotient (1.12) with the national rate per 1,000 population (25.2).

[i] Calculated by dividing the urban rate per 1,000 households (fifty-two) by the national rate per 1,000 households (forty-eight) and multiplying the quotient (1.08) with the national rate per 1,000 population (24.2).

TABLE 2
Estimation of National Victimization Rates for 1981

Crime Type	1981 CUVS Rate per 1,000 Population (Ages Sixteen+)	Mean Proportion of National of Urban Victim Survey Rate[a] per 1,000 Population (Ages Fifteen+)	Estimated 1981 National Rate per 1,000 Population (Ages Sixteen+)
Sexual assault	3.5	.96[b] (.92 + .99)/2	3.4
Assault	11.5	.94 (.55 + .93 + .95)/3	10.8
Robbery	9.9	.93 (.94 - 1.01 + .85)/3	9.2
Motor vehicle theft	8.2[c]	.87[d] (.86 + .32 + .94)/3	7.1
Residential burglary	45.7	.89 (.84 + .89 + .93)/3	40.7

SOURCES.—Table 1; Solicitor General Canada 1983.
NOTE.—CUVS = Canadian Urban Victimization Survey.
[a] Based on 1987, 1992, and 1998 victim surveys.
[b] Based on 1992 and 1998 victim surveys.
[c] Theft of motor vehicles.
[d] Theft of motor vehicles and theft of motor vehicle parts (from table 1).

Arguably, changes to legislation that have had the greatest impact on homicide in Canada have been those that have added further restrictions to the accessibility and availability of firearms.[10] The potential impact of firearms controls on homicide in Canada stems, in large part, from firearms accounting for about one-third of all homicides and shooting being the most common method of homicide.

Between 1981 and 1999, two major firearms laws were enacted. Bill C-17 came into effect in 1991 in response to the killing by an armed man of fourteen women at the École Polytechnique in Montreal on December 6, 1989.[11] This law introduced stricter controls on the availability and accessibility of a range of firearms (e.g., rifles, assault weapons) and increased criminal sanctions to deter offenders from using firearms in the commission of crimes (Canadian Centre for Justice Statistics 1999b, p. 8).

The second major piece of firearms legislation, Bill C-68, came into effect in 1997. It created a new firearms act and made a number of amendments to the Criminal Code of Canada, most notably introducing mandatory sentences for those convicted of using firearms in the commission of crimes. Other changes included all firearm owners having to obtain a firearms license (by January 2001), all firearms having to be registered by the end of a five-year period (1998–2003), and the prohibition of a number of different types of handguns (Canadian Centre for Justice Statistics 1999a, p. 72, 1999b, p. 8).

Between 1981 and 1999, the number of homicides in Canada dropped 17.2 percent (from 647 to 536). The 536 homicides in 1999 was the lowest number recorded in this nineteen-year period. Controlling for population increases, this decline in homicide incidents corresponds to a 33.3 percent reduction, from a rate of 0.03 to 0.02 per 1,000 population (see fig. 1). A similar reduction in homicide rates occurred in the 1990s.

During the 1980s and 1990s, the proportion of homicides caused by firearms has remained relatively stable at about one-third, ranging from a high of 37.2 percent in 1982 to a low of 29.7 percent in 1990. The year 1998 marked the first year of departure from this trend, with firearms accounting for 27.2 percent of all homicides (151 out of 555). Shooting (by firearms) has also been the most common method used in

---

[10] For an overview of Canadian and international research on the impact of the availability of firearms on homicide, see Gabor (1994, 1995).

[11] For writings on this killing, see Malette and Chalouh (1991).

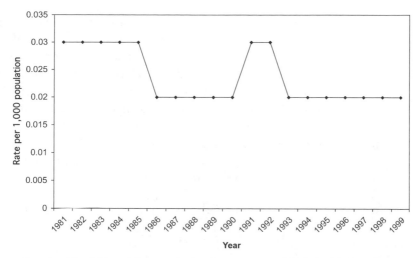

FIG. 1.—Homicide: police-reported crime rate per 1,000 population. Sources: Canadian Centre for Justice Statistics 1999*b*; Fedorowycz 2000.

homicides in Canada since 1961, with the exception of three years in the 1990s (1990, 1995, and 1998), when stabbing—most often by knives—was most common. In 1998, the breakdown of homicides by cause of death was as follows: stabbing (33.2 percent), shooting (27.2 percent), beating (22.7 percent), strangulation (10.8 percent), fire (burns-suffocation, 2.2 percent), poisoning (1.1 percent), shaking (Shaken Baby Syndrome, 1.1 percent), other (0.7 percent), and unknown (1.1 percent; Fedorowycz 1999, p. 8, table 5).

B. *Aggravated Sexual Assault*

This offense "results in wounding, maiming, disfiguring or endangering the life of the victim" (Integration and Analysis Program 1999, p. 3). Police-reported incidents include both completions and attempts.

Bill C-127, a new statute enacted under the Criminal Code of Canada in 1983, introduced three new offenses to address sexual assault, abolishing the previous offenses of rape, attempted rape, and indecent assault: "sexual assault (s. 271); sexual assault with a weapon, threats to a third party or causing bodily harm (s. 272); and aggravated sexual assault (s. 273)" (Mohr and Roberts 1994, p. 6). The three new offenses corresponded with different levels of severity of victimization: level 1, level 2, and level 3, respectively.

The purpose of these changes was to de-emphasize the sexual nature of the offence, to stress the violent and assaultive nature of such crimes, to encourage victims to report incidents to the police, and to improve police and court handling of cases, thereby reducing the trauma to victims and increasing the number of convictions. In addition, as a result of the changes, both men and women can now be victims of sexual assault and "spousal immunity" no longer exists. Prior to 1983, a victim of what was then rape could only be a woman and a man could not be charged with raping his wife. (Integration and Analysis Program 1999, p. 2)

Because of the substantial differences between pre- and post-1983 definitions of this offense, our examination of police records begins with 1983.

Turning to the victim surveys, only the CUVS of 1981 measured rape or aggravated sexual assault. The definition of aggravated sexual assault used in this survey was the following: "sexual assault includes rape, attempted rape, molesting or attempted molestation" (Solicitor General Canada 1984, p. 12).

Because the CUVS was administered prior to the changes of the sexual assault laws in 1983, its definition of sexual assault differed substantially from the definitions used in the subsequent national victimization surveys. For the three national surveys, respondents were asked if they had been the victim of sexual assault in general, which is more comparable with the legal definition that includes all three levels of the offense category. We were not able to make adjustments to either set of victim surveys (pre- and post-1983) to make this offense comparable over the full complement of years (1981–98).

Disappointingly, but to the benefit of the information elicited, the 1987 questions on sexual assault were changed in the two subsequent surveys of 1992 and 1998, thus making this offense not completely comparable over this period of time. The most drastic change occurred between 1987 and 1992. Gartner and Doob (1994, p. 4) summarized the changes to the sexual assault questions, which also had implications for the assault questions:

In the 1988 survey, respondents were asked about being "attacked." They were told that an "attack can be anything from being hit, slapped, pushed or grabbed, to being shot, raped or beaten." In 1993, a similar question was asked but the word "raped" was omitted from the list of examples of an "attack." However, in addition, two further questions were asked: "... has anyone forced you or attempted to force you into any sexual activity when you did not want to, by threatening you, holding you down or hurting you in some way ..." and "... has anyone ever touched you against your will in any sexual way? By this I mean anything from unwanted touching or grabbing to kissing or fondling."

In the 1992 survey, sexual assault was described as "sexually assaulted, molested or attempt to sexually assault or molest" (Gartner and Doob 1994, p. 3). In the 1998 survey, the definition of sexual assault was slightly altered to "forced sexual activity, an attempt at forced sexual activity, or unwanted sexual touching, grabbing, kissing or fondling" (Besserer and Trainor 2000, p. 2, box 1). Another change to the 1998 survey was the addition of a "specialized series of questions to measure sexual and physical assault by a current or former spouse/partner" (Besserer and Trainor 2000, p. 6, box 3). Fortunately for our purposes, Besserer and Trainor (2000), in their report on the 1998 survey, excluded, in most cases, incidents of sexual and physical assault obtained from the specialized and more general series of questions, thus making the 1992 and 1998 findings on sexual assault (and assault) more comparable. In all four victim surveys, data available on sexual assaults only included completed incidents.

Between 1983 and 1999, the total number of aggravated sexual assaults recorded by the police declined by 61.3 percent, from 550 to 213. Controlling for population increases over this time, this translates to a one-half reduction, from a rate (per 1,000 population) of 0.02 to a rate of 0.01. An even greater reduction in aggravated sexual assaults was evident when only the Canadian female population, ages fifteen years and older, was considered: 66.7 percent, from a rate per 1,000 females, fifteen and older, of 0.06 in 1983 to a rate of 0.02 in 1999 (see fig. 2).[12] The overwhelming majority of incidents recorded by police involved a male perpetrator and a female victim. According to the Revised Uniform Crime Reporting (UCRII) Survey,[13] for 1997, for

---

[12] We have used this age category instead of ages sixteen years and older, because Canada's national victimization surveys interviewed persons ages fifteen years and older.

[13] The UCRII Survey "collects detailed information on criminal incidents reported to a sample of police departments. The data are not nationally representative. In 1997, data were collected from 179 police departments in six provinces (New Brunswick, Quebec,

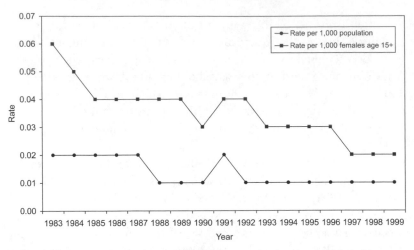

FIG. 2.—Aggravated sexual assault: police-reported crime rate. Major changes to legislation governing crimes of a sexual nature came into effect in 1983, hence affecting comparability with data in previous years. Sources: Canadian Centre for Justice Statistics 1999*b*; Tremblay 2000; Statistics Canada 2002.

example, 98 percent of all individuals accused of sexual assault (levels 1–3 combined) were male (Integration and Analysis Program 1999, p. 6), and 84 percent of all victims were female (Kong 1998*b*, p. 7).

In contrast, national rates (both per 1,000 population and per 1,000 females ages fifteen years and older) of sexual assault victimization increased substantially over the eighteen-year period of 1981–98 (see fig. 3).[14] In 1981, the rate (per 1,000 population) of sexual assault was 3.4, and in 1998 it was 20.5. Over the same time period, the rate of sexual assault per 1,000 females increased from 10.6 to 33.2. (It is important to remember that the definition of sexual assault used in the 1998 survey was much broader than that used in the 1981 survey; see above.)

C. Serious Assault

Bill C-127, the same law that introduced revised sexual assault statutes in 1983, also produced, in the same year, several different

---

Ontario, Saskatchewan, Alberta, and British Columbia) and represented about 48 percent of the national volume of crime" (Integration and Analysis Program 1999, p. 6).

[14] Throughout this essay, population-based rates for all crimes in the 1981 victim survey use the age range of sixteen years and older. This is because the survey questioned respondents in this age range.

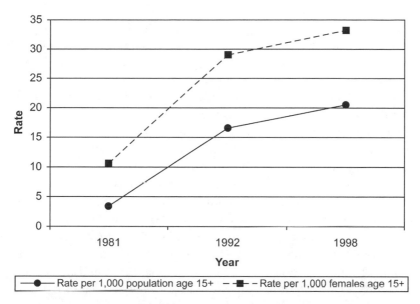

Fig. 3.—Sexual assault: victim survey rate. Rates for 1981 are per 1,000 population ages sixteen and older and per 1,000 females ages sixteen and older, calculated following procedures in tables 1 and 2. The number of sexual assault incidents in 1987 was too low to produce statistically reliable estimates. Sources: table 2; Gartner and Doob 1994, p. 6, table 2; Roberer and Trainor 2000, pp. 19, 23, tables 3, 7; Canadian Centre for Justice Statistics 2000; Statistics Canada 2002.

categories of assault: "common assault (level 1), assault with a weapon or causing bodily harm (level 2), aggravated assault (level 3), and other assaults (i.e., assault on a peace officer, unlawfully causing bodily harm, discharge of firearm with intent and all other assaults)" (Tremblay 1999, p. 7). Aggravated assault, the most serious category of assault offenses (level 3), is defined as "any of a variety of serious assaults or particularly reprehensible behaviour calling for a more severe punishment" (Yogis 1983, p. 20).

To produce a measure of serious assault, we have combined assault levels 2 and 3. Police-reported incidents of serious assault include both completions and attempts. Prior to 1983, serious assaults were not recorded separately from other assaults; therefore, our examination of police records begins with 1983.

Not all of the victim surveys used comparable definitions of assault, and the definitions used are more comparable with the legal definition that includes all three levels of the offense category (total assaults). However, we were able to adjust survey records of assault so that they would be comparable with police records. This involved multiplying total victim survey assault incidents by 0.2, which is the mean percentage of levels 2 and 3 of the total (levels 1–3) police-reported assaults for the years 1983–99.

As noted above, the most extensive changes to the definition of assault, which corresponded with the changes to the definition of sexual assault, were for the 1992 survey. Assault was described as an incident where "a weapon was present or there was an attack (anything from being hit, slapped, grabbed or knocked down to being shot or beaten up) or threat of an attack" (Gartner and Doob 1994, p. 3). (See above for the definition of assault used in the 1987 survey.) The definition of assault used in the CUVS of 1981 was as follows: "Assault involves the presence of a weapon or an attack or threat. Assault incidents may range from face-to-face verbal threats to an attack with extensive injuries" (Solicitor General Canada 1984, p. 12). For the 1998 survey, the definition of assault was as follows: "An attack (victim hit, slapped, grabbed, knocked down, or beaten), a face-to-face threat of physical harm, or an incident with a weapon present" (Besserer and Trainor 2000, p. 3, box 1). Importantly, this definition differs slightly from that used in the 1992 survey, by the coverage of only "face-to-face" threats; in the 1992 survey, "all threats, including those that were not face-to-face, were included in the definition of assault" (Besserer and Trainor 2000, p. 2). In all four victim surveys, data available on assaults only included completed incidents.

Between 1983 and 1999, police-reported rates of serious assault increased by 18.2 percent, from 1.1 to 1.3 per 1,000 population (see fig. 4). The 1990s witnessed a decline in serious assault rates (-13.3 percent), from a high of 1.5 in 1991 to a low of 1.3 in 1995, which was sustained for the next four years.

Between 1981 and 1998, national rates (per 1,000 population) of serious assault victimization decreased slightly (4.6 percent; from 10.8 to 10.3). As shown in figure 4, serious assault victimization rates over this time can be characterized by three periods: a period of growth between 1981 and 1987 (from 10.8 to 13.7), a stable period between 1987 and 1992 (from 13.7 to 13.4), and a period of decline between 1992 and 1998 (from 13.4 to 10.3).

D. Robbery

The legal definition of robbery is "theft with violence or the threat of violence against persons" (Du Wors 1992, p. 2) and, for police

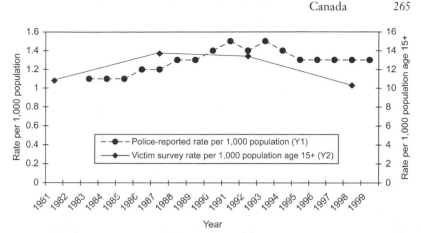

Fig. 4.—Serious assault: victim survey and police-reported crime rate. Major changes to legislation governing crimes of assault came into effect in 1983, hence affecting comparability with data in previous years. Victim survey rate for 1981 is per 1,000 population ages sixteen and older. Sources: table 2; Gartner and Doob 1994, p. 6, table 2; Canadian Centre for Justice Statistics 1999b, 2000; Besserer and Trainor 2000, p. 23, table 7; Tremblay 2000; Statistics Canada 2002.

records, includes robberies committed with firearms, other weapons (e.g., knives), or no weapons. Police-reported incidents of robbery include both completions and attempts.

Over the period under study (1981–99), there have been no changes to the specific laws governing robbery; however, as with the offense of homicide, the legislative changes (during this period) that have had potentially the greatest impact on robbery in Canada have been those that have added further restrictions to the accessibility and availability of firearms (see above). The potential impact of firearms controls on robbery stems, in part, from their use in the commission of robberies, although the majority of all robberies do not involve firearms.

For victim survey reports, the definition of robbery has remained relatively stable. For example, in the 1981 survey, an incident was recorded as a robbery if "something is taken and the offender has a weapon or there is a threat or an attack" (attempts were also included; Solicitor General Canada 1984, p. 12). In the 1998 survey, robbery was described as "theft or attempted theft in which the perpetrator had a weapon or there was violence or the threat of violence against the victim" (Besserer and Trainor 2000, p. 2, box 1). Victim survey incidents of robbery include both completions and attempts.

Over the period 1981–99, the total number of police-reported robbery incidents increased by 9.3 percent (from 26,292 to 28,745),

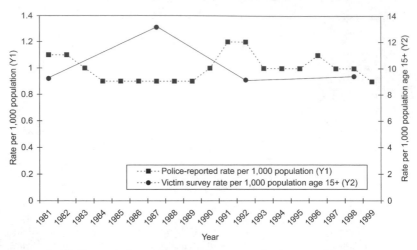

FIG. 5.—Robbery: victim survey and police-reported crime rate. Victim survey rate for 1981 is per 1,000 population ages sixteen and older. Sources: table 2; Gartner and Doob 1994, p. 6, table 2; Canadian Centre for Justice Statistics 1999*b*, 2000; Besserer and Trainor 2000, p. 19, table 3; Tremblay 2000; Statistics Canada 2002.

but the more accurate measure of change over time—rate per capita—shows that police-reported robberies have in fact declined by 18.2 percent (from a rate of 1.1 to 0.9 per 1,000 population; see fig. 5). Following an increase in the late 1980s, robbery rates peaked in 1991 and 1992, at 1.2 per 1,000 population, and then fell to their lowest level in the decade in 1999, at 0.9 per 1,000 population, a 25 percent reduction.

National rates (per 1,000 population) of robbery victimization remained fairly stable between 1981 and 1998. As shown in figure 5, only 1987 marked a departure from this stable situation, with a robbery rate of 13.1 per 1,000 population. Rates of robbery victimization in the other three years were as follows: 9.2 in 1981, 9.1 in 1992, and 9.4 in 1998.

E. Motor Vehicle Theft

For police records, motor vehicle theft "consists of taking a vehicle without the owner's authorization. A motor vehicle is defined as a car, truck, van, bus, recreational vehicle, semi-trailer truck, motorcycle, construction machinery, agricultural machinery or other land-based motorized vehicle such as an all-terrain vehicle, a go-kart, a dune buggy or a snowmobile" (Sauvé 1998, p. 2). Police-reported incidents of motor vehicle theft include both completions and attempts. For the

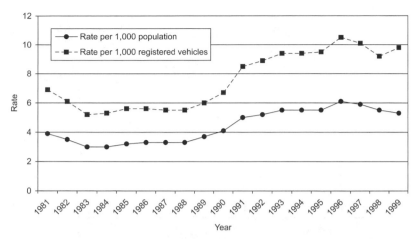

FIG. 6.—Motor vehicle theft: police-reported crime rate per 1,000 population and per 1,000 registered vehicles. Sources: Canadian Centre for Justice Statistics 1999*b*; Tremblay 2000; Statistics Canada 2002.

period under study, there have been no changes to the laws governing motor vehicle theft.

The definition of motor vehicle theft from victim survey reports is identical to the definition used for police records, with the exception that the former includes theft or attempted theft of motor vehicle parts or accessories, for example, wheels, hood ornaments, and steering wheels (Sauvé 1998, p. 5). Of the four victim surveys, only the 1981 survey did not include in its definition theft of motor vehicle parts. We were able to remove incidents of thefts of parts for the victim surveys of 1987, 1992, and 1998, thus making all four victim surveys and police-reported and victim survey incidents comparable.[15] Victim survey incidents of motor vehicle theft include both completions and attempts.

In 1999, according to police reports, there were 5.3 motor vehicle thefts for every 1,000 Canadians. This represented a 35.9 percent increase over the 1981 police-reported rate of 3.9 per 1,000 population. When expressed as a rate per 1,000 registered motor vehicles, between 1981 and 1999, police-reported motor vehicle thefts increased by 42 percent, from 6.9 to 9.8 (see fig. 6).

[15] For the 1987 victim survey, data were not available to enable us to remove incidents of attempted thefts of motor vehicle parts. We were, however, able to produce an estimate of the number of attempted thefts of motor vehicles for the 1987 survey (58,789), which was done by multiplying the mean proportion of attempted thefts of motor vehicles and parts for the 1992 and 1999 surveys (0.64) by the total number of incidents of attempted thefts of motor vehicles and parts for the 1987 survey (91,858).

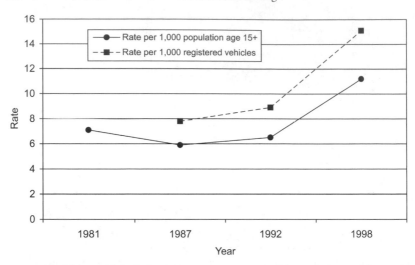

Fig. 7.—Motor vehicle theft: victim survey rate per 1,000 population and per 1,000 registered vehicles. Victim survey rate for 1981 is per 1,000 population ages sixteen and older. Data for the 1981 rate per registered vehicles are not available. Sources: table 2; Besserer and Trainor 2000; Canadian Centre for Justice Statistics 2000; Mihorean 2001; Statistics Canada 2002.

Similarly, for victim reports, national rates (per 1,000 population) of motor vehicle theft (excluding theft of motor vehicle parts) increased by more than half (57.7 percent; from 7.1 in 1981 to 11.2 in 1998). When expressed in rates per 1,000 registered motor vehicles, motor vehicle thefts between 1987 and 1998 increased by 93.6 percent (from 7.8 to 15.1; see fig. 7). Rates of motor vehicle theft per 1,000 registered motor vehicles could not be calculated for the 1981 survey.

F. Residential Burglary

There are three categories of police-reported burglary, also referred to as "break and enter" in Canada: residential, commercial or business, and other. Residential, the focus of this essay, refers to "the breaking and entering of a private residence, including single homes, garden homes, apartments, cottages, mobile homes, rooming houses, etc." (Kong 1998a, p. 3, box 2). Commercial refers to "the breaking and entering of a facility used for commercial or public affairs. These include, for example, financial institutions, stores, and non-commercial enterprises such as government buildings, schools, churches, and non-profit agencies" (Kong 1998a, p. 3, box 2). Other types of burglary refer to "the breaking and entering of private property structures (e.g.,

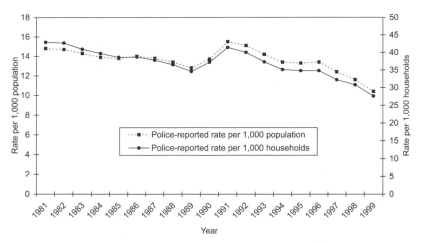

FIG. 8.—Residential burglary: police-reported crime rate per 1,000 population and per 1,000 households. Sources: Canadian Centre for Justice Statistics 1999*b*; Tremblay 2000; Statistics Canada n.d.

shed, detached garages) or storage and transport facilities" (Kong 1998*a*, p. 3, box 2). Police reported incidents of residential burglary include both completions and attempts. For the period under study, there have been no changes to the laws governing residential burglary or burglary in general.

The four victim surveys focused on residential burglary, and the definition has not changed over time. Importantly, the definition of residential burglary is identical for police records and victim survey reports. Victim survey incidents of residential burglary also include both completions and attempts.

As illustrated in figure 8, between 1981 and 1999, police-reported rates of residential burglary per 1,000 population decreased by 25.3 percent, from 8.7 to 6.5. Over the same time period, rates of residential burglary per 1,000 households decreased by 32.4 percent, from 25.3 to 17.1. Residential burglary rates (for both measures) declined for most of the 1990s, from a peak in 1991 to the lowest recorded level in 1999.

From its peak in 1981, the national rate of residential burglary victimization, whether expressed as per 1,000 population or per 1,000 households, was much lower and changed very little in the last three survey years (see fig. 9). In 1981, the rate (per 1,000 population) of residential burglary was 40.7, and in the next survey year (1987) the rate was 26.3, a decrease of more than one-third (35.4 percent). The

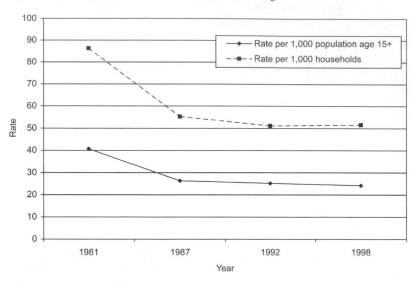

Fig. 9.—Residential burglary: victim survey rate per 1,000 population and per 1,000 households. Sources: table 2; Gartner and Doob 1994, p. 11, table 6; Besserer and Trainor 2000, p. 22, table 6; Canadian Centre for Justice Statistics 2000; Statistics Canada n.d.

residential burglary rate (per 1,000 population) in the two subsequent survey years was marginally lower, at 25.2 in 1992 and 24.2 in 1998.

In 1981, the residential burglary rate (per 1,000 households) was 86.3, and in 1987 the rate was 55.2, a decrease of 36.0 percent. The residential burglary rate (per 1,000 households) in the two subsequent survey years was marginally lower, at 51.1 in 1992 and 51.6 in 1998.

II. The Probability of Police Recording a Reported Offense

Langan and Farrington (1998, p. 11) define the measurement of police recording of crime as follows: "Comparison of the volume of crime that victims said they reported to police during the year with the volume that police actually recorded that year reveals how often police record as crimes those incidents that come to their attention." This section examines the important issue of the probability of police recording a reported offense for four offenses (sexual assault, assault, robbery, and residential burglary), and for the four years for which victim survey data were available (1981, 1987, 1992, and 1998).[16]

---

[16] It was not possible to calculate the probability of police recording a motor vehicle theft, because data were not available on the total number of motor vehicle thefts reported to police by victims separate from thefts of motor vehicle parts reported to police by victims.

Police records and victim survey reports for the four offenses were highly comparable. For robbery and residential burglary, no further adjustments (than those already noted above) were required to make police records and victim survey reports comparable. However, for sexual assault and assault, we were faced with having to use these aggregate offense categories instead of the desired subcategories of aggravated sexual assault and serious assault. This coverage of police-reported sexual assaults and assaults is very similar to the types of sexual assaults and assaults included in the victim surveys.

It is also important to note that for 1981, the year of the CUVS, both victim survey reports and police records were based on an urban sample, the seven cities involved in the survey. With the exception of the offense of robbery, there appear to be no substantial differences in the probability of the police recording reported offenses for 1981 compared with the other three years, which are based on national samples. In 1981, the probability of the police recording a reported robbery was 0.71, and in the other three years (1987, 1992, and 1998) it was 0.27, 0.36, and 0.28, respectively. Whether this difference in probability represents an urban effect could not be investigated based on the data available at the time of writing.[17]

Of the four crimes, sexual assault had the highest mean probability of police recording a reported offense: 0.78. The probabilities for the different years are as follows: 0.71 for 1981, 0.95 for 1992, and 0.67 for 1998.[18] The mean probabilities, from highest to lowest, for the three other offenses are as follows: 0.60 for residential burglary, 0.42 for assault, and 0.41 for robbery.

III.   Explaining Trends in Crime

This section looks at key (potential) explanations of the main trends in crime rates, focusing on the 1990s. Our discussion is limited to trends in crime rates from police records. This has been done for two main reasons: first, police records were available for all of the years of interest, and there were clearly distinguishable trends in crime rates from police records; and, second, only a small number of victim surveys were conducted over the period of interest.

[17] "Urban effect," in this instance, refers to robberies in cities or urban areas being more likely to be recorded by police than robberies in the nation as a whole.

[18] The number of sexual assault incidents in the 1987 national victim survey was not available because the number of incidents was too low to produce statistically reliable estimates.

Research on why crime went down in Canada during the 1990s is limited. The earliest piece we found on the subject attempted to explain a downward trend in police-reported crime rates in Edmonton, a large city in western Canada, beginning in 1992 and continuing through 1994, the latest year for which crime figures were available (Kennedy and Veitch 1997). The authors examined a number of factors that could have had an effect on crime over this period, including the number of male youths ages fifteen to twenty-four years, unemployment, social service usage, the number of police personnel, police workload (e.g., calls for service) and corresponding organizational changes to police recording of crimes, and new community policing and problem-solving policing initiatives. Between 1991 (the peak year of crime) and 1994, in Edmonton, rates (per 100,000 population) of violent crime declined by 26.4 percent (from 1,305 to 961), while rates of property crime declined by 37.4 percent (from 8,934 to 5,589; Kong 1997). The authors concluded that the drop in overall crime rates, driven largely by lower property crime rates, was the result of "increases in private security and new crime prevention practices, including proactive policing which seeks to solve problems rather than simply reply to calls for service" (Kennedy and Veitch 1997, p. 66).

More recent research has attempted to explain the national crime drop over the full decade of the 1990s. Hartnagel (2001) looked at three main factors: prison admissions, demographics, and the economy. He observed that it was very unlikely that the use of incarceration played any role in the decline of crime in Canada in the 1990s, because incarceration rates were going down during this time. Hartnagel found some support for demographic and economic explanations, because of a declining proportion of the population ages fifteen to twenty-four and falling unemployment rates, respectively. He cautioned that other economic variables also need to be considered (e.g., income inequality, part-time work).

Ouimet (2002) investigated the role of the economy, demographics, and the criminal justice system for the drop in crime rates in Canada during the 1990s (1991–99). To assess whether a tougher or more punitive criminal justice system may explain some of the crime drop, Ouimet looked at changes in the incarceration rate and the number of police per capita. In both instances, there was negative growth: −3 percent for the incarceration rate (from 110 to 106 per 100,000 population) and −11 percent for the number of police per capita (from

2.0 to 1.8 per 1,000 population). Although the numbers do not support a "get-tough-on-crime" hypothesis for Canada's crime drop in the 1990s, Ouimet notes that policing may have played a role because of "greater use of computers and databases and the creation of specialized units or task forces" (2002, p. 43). This is consistent with Kennedy and Veitch's (1997) view for why crime rates declined in Edmonton during the early part of the 1990s crime drop.

Ouimet (2002), like Hartnagel (2001), finds some support for economic (i.e., falling unemployment rates) and demographic (i.e., aging youth population) explanations for Canada's crime drop in the 1990s, and Ouimet considers these areas to be the most promising in explaining the crime drop. Ouimet (2002, p. 45) calls for further research into two other important trends in Canada that may shed light on the crime drop during the 1990s: an increase in the proportion of young people going on to university or college and a decrease in the public consumption of alcohol.

In the following discussion of some possible explanations for the decline in police-reported crime rates in Canada that began in 1991 and 1992 and continued through 1999, crime rates are sometimes aggregated into the categories of "total," which includes all violent, property, and other (e.g., prostitution, arson) offenses, excluding traffic incidents, and "selected," which includes the six offenses examined here.[19] Rates for five of the six police-reported crimes (except motor vehicle theft) matched very closely the downward trend for total police-reported crime rates during the 1990s.

A. Demographics

Two important demographic trends were evident in Canada during the 1990s. The first was a decline in the proportion of the population ages fifteen to twenty-four years, the age group most at risk for criminal offending. The second important demographic trend was an increase in the proportion of the population ages fifty-five years and over, an age group characterized by very low involvement in criminal activity. Both of these trends continued through 1999.

[19] In reporting on what is known as Canada's "police-reported crime rate," the CCJS does not include traffic violations, "as these data have proven to be volatile over time. This volatility is the result of changes in police procedures that allow for some traffic violations to be scored under either a provincial statute or the Criminal Code (e.g., failure to stop or remain at an accident)" (Tremblay 1999, p. 14).

Between 1991 and 1999, the proportion of young people in the fifteen- to twenty-four-year-old age group (of the total population) dropped by 5.6 percent, from 14.3 percent to 13.5 percent (Statistics Canada 2002). This modest decrease was characterized by year-to-year declines for the better part of the time period, with the years 1997–99 remaining stable at 13.5 percent. For Canadians ages fifty-five and over, between 1991 and 1999, their proportion of the total population increased by 6.5 percent, from 20.1 percent to 21.4 percent (Statistics Canada 2002).

Despite the popularity of the demographic explanation for the recent crime drop in Canada (see Foot with Stoffman 1996, 1998), two issues are noteworthy. First, evidence of a decline in the proportion of the most crime-prone age group is modest, particularly when compared with the decline in total and selected police-reported crime rates for the same time period: −25.2 and −26.5 percent, respectively. Second, the demographic trends for both age groups began well before the 1990s crime drop. The younger age group, as a proportion of the total population, "began to decline in 1978, [while] the crime rate was still increasing until 1991" (Canadian Centre for Justice Statistics 1999a, p. 9). As noted by Tremblay (2000, p. 5), "variations in the size of the high-risk offender age group have had some effect on the crime rate, but the amount of this influence is not clear, and other factors have also influenced the crime rate trend."

B. Economy

As noted above, consideration of economic conditions is important in any attempt to explain Canada's crime drop in the 1990s. We have used national unemployment rates as an indicator of Canada's economy. As noted by Becsi (1999, p. 47), "The unemployment rate measures reduced legitimate earnings opportunities that are particularly important for the population segment most at risk for engaging in criminal activities."

Between 1991 and 1999, the Canadian unemployment rate fell by more than a quarter (−26.9 percent), from 10.4 to 7.6 percent (Sharpe 1996; Statistics Canada 2002). The beginning of the drop in the rate of unemployment did not, however, correspond exactly with the beginning of the drop in crime rates. In 1992 and 1993, the unemployment rate reached its highest points of the 1990s: 11.3 and 11.2 percent, respectively. The first real drop in the unemployment rate was from 1993 to 1994, at −7.1 percent (from 11.2 to 10.4 percent). For the

most part, year-to-year declines characterized the fall in unemployment rates between 1993 and 1999.

With the exception of a small time lag in the start of the fall in
unemployment rates, there appears to be some general congruence
with the downward trends in unemployment rates and total and
selected police-reported crime rates during the period of 1992–99.
As important as understanding the amount of influence of employment
on crime, future research should also investigate why, during 1992–93,
unemployment rates and crime rates were going in opposite directions.
Seemingly, factors other than the economy were influencing the drop
in crime rates during this period.

C. Spending on Policing

Government spending on police services "measure[s] public efforts
to reduce crime and raise the expected cost to criminals" (Becsi
1999, p. 47).[20] The effect on crime from spending on policing, as well
as on other criminal justice sectors (e.g., courts, corrections), has
received some scholarly attention in recent years (see Spencer 1993,
MacLean 1996; LaFree 1998; Becsi 1999).

In Canada, policing accounts for the majority of expenditure that is
spent on the criminal justice system. (Six sectors are included in the
accounting of Canada's criminal justice budget: policing, courts, legal
aid, criminal prosecutions, adult corrections, and youth corrections.) In
1996 (the most recent year that data on the full amount spent on
criminal justice were available at the time of writing), policing
accounted for 59 percent of criminal justice spending, or $5.9 of $10
billion in 1996 Canadian dollars (Besserer and Tufts 1999). This share
of criminal justice expenditures has changed very little over the last ten
years (Young 1994; Besserer and Tufts 1999).

In 1992, spending on policing in Canada peaked at $223 per person
(in 1999 Canadian dollars).[21] Between 1992 and 1999, spending on
policing declined by 5.8 percent, from $223 to $210 per person. There
were year-to-year declines in per capita spending on police services for

---

[20] In his analysis of variables that may explain the recent crime drop in the United
States, Becsi looked at both police expenditures (per capita) and police employment ("as a
share of state population") but found them to be "qualitatively very similar" (1999, p. 47).
We focus only on police expenditures.
[21] All expenditures are reported in 1999 Canadian dollars, using the (annual average)
Consumer Price Index.

1993–97, with small increases in 1998 and 1999 (year-to-year changes of 2 and 0.5 percent, respectively). From 1985 to 1992, spending on policing increased by 10.4 percent, from $202 to $223 per person (Dunphy and Shankarraman 2000).

The downward trend in (inflation-adjusted and per capita) police expenditures between 1992 and 1997 compares with what was happening to total and selected police-reported crime rates over the same time period. (With only two years of increasing police expenditures per capita and declining crime rates, 1998 and 1999, it is difficult to characterize this departure from the downward trends between 1992 and 1997.) The one notable difference between the two downward trends is the respective starting points for the declines: 1992 for total and most selected crime rates and 1993 for per capita police expenditures.

The finding that declining spending on policing coincided with declining crime rates seems rather illogical, but this noneffect on crime rates has been demonstrated previously. For an earlier period in Canada (1950–66), MacLean found that increased spending on policing, as well as on the criminal justice system as a whole, had no effect on crime or conviction rates, leading him to note that "criminal-justice efficiency is not increased by expenditures" (1996, p. 145). In the United States, for the two periods of 1971–94 and 1990–94, Becsi (1999) found mostly positive relationships between per capita spending on policing and rates of Index crimes. As to why this finding may be produced in study after study, Becsi suggested a number of possible explanations, one of which is that, "it might be that the regressions do not capture the exogenous component of police efforts very well and mostly capture the endogenous response of police activity to changes in crime. In other words, the regression might not be controlling for simultaneity bias" (1999, p. 51).

D. Incarceration

Our analysis of custody rates for the six offenses under study supports Ouimet's (2002) finding that incarceration did not seem to be an important factor in the decline of crime rates in the 1990s. Our analysis of average custodial sentence length for the six offenses under study provides further support against a punitive hypothesis in explaining Canada's crime drop during this period of time. Average time served in custody per offense provides another important measure to investigate the punitive hypothesis. As noted below, we were not able to obtain time served data, but our previous analysis of average time served in custody for residential burglary, robbery, serious assault, aggravated sexual assault, and homicide (Welsh and Irving 2001), which relied solely on federal corrections data (Kaschube and Hayden 2000), showed that there was very little change in these five offenses over the period 1994–99.

E. Alternative Crime Prevention Approaches

In Canada today, alternative or noncriminal justice approaches to preventing criminal offending and crime have come to be synonymous with "crime prevention through social development" (Standing Committee on Justice and the Solicitor General 1993; Sansfaçon and Waller 2001), which is essentially a mix of developmental (e.g., Tremblay and Craig 1995) and community (e.g., Hope 1995) crime prevention approaches. Indeed, the recent history of crime prevention in Canada has been dominated by the notion of investing in children and young people to ameliorate individual- and family-level risk factors for delinquency and later offending, as well as strengthening families and communities (Canadian Criminal Justice Association 1989; Sansfaçon and Waller 2001). Recent federal government initiatives have included the establishment in 1994 of a national strategy on crime prevention spearheaded by a council of community leaders and social advocates; the setup of a permanent structure—the National Crime Prevention Centre—in 1998 to replace the council and manage crime prevention funding, policy development, and evaluation; and, at the same time, the start of a $32 million (Canadian) annual budget, for five years, to fund crime prevention programs, partnerships, and research across the country.

Despite the recent policy and programmatic attention given to crime prevention through social development nationally, it is difficult to say whether this form of crime prevention has had any effect on police-reported crime rates during the latter part of the 1990s. For the most part, this is because increased spending on crime prevention began only in 1997 and, with the focus being on children and youths, it is expected that there would be some lag time before any benefits are realized. Moreover, there has been very little evaluation research published on the effectiveness of crime prevention programs in Canada. It is of course conceivable that the increased spending on crime prevention programs may have an effect on youth crime rates in the short-term, but this may be more likely to occur in the years following the period of time covered in this essay.

IV. Punishment

Besides the collection of official crime statistics, CCJS is also respon-sible for the collection, analysis, and dissemination of youth and adult court statistics. In the present study, the number of persons convicted for each offense is derived from the Youth Court Survey (YCS) and the Adult Criminal Court Survey (ACCS).

The YCS maintains a national database of statistical information on charges, cases, and persons involving accused who are twelve to seventeen years of age.[22] Youth court data were available for the years 1991–99. Similarly, the ACCS provides a national database of statistical information on the processing of adult criminal court cases. There are, however, several limitations with the ACCS. First, three of the ten provinces (British Columbia, Manitoba, and New Brunswick) do not participate in the survey. The jurisdictions that do report to the ACCS represent approximately 80 percent of the national adult criminal court caseload. Second, data from "Quebec's 140 municipal courts, which account for approximately 20 percent of federal statute charges in that province, are not yet collected. Finally, with the exception of [the province of] Alberta, no data are provided from the superior courts" (Roberts and Grimes 2000, p. 18). This last limitation has the effect of underestimating the severity of sentences. "The reason for this," according to Roberts and Grimes (2000, p. 18), "is that some of the most serious cases, which are likely to result in the most severe sanctions, will be processed in superior courts." Because the data that were available— adult criminal court data were only available for the years 1994–99— suffered from the same limitations, comparisons over time are not affected.

To allow for comparisons with other countries represented in this volume, court data from both the YCS and the ACCS were aggregated (except for sentence length). It should be noted, however, that there are several definitional and methodological differences between the two microdata surveys. For example, according to the Canadian Centre for

[22] Canadian Centre for Justice Statistics (1998, p. xiv). The YCS collects data from all youth courts in Canada. However, "these data must be interpreted as *indicators* of caseload and case characteristics rather than precise caseload measures" (Canadian Centre for Justice Statistics 1998, p. xvii). Although jurisdictions do their best to inform the YCS of suspected reporting problems and/or anomalies, the level of underreporting (i.e., charges not reported to the survey) is simply not known. For example, in 1991–1992, the Province of Ontario reported a 15 percent undercoverage (Canadian Centre for Justice Statistics 1998, p. vi).

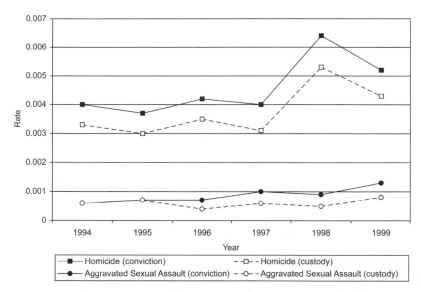

Fig. 10.—Conviction and custody rates per 1,000 population (ages twelve and over): homicide and aggravated sexual assault. "Aggravated sexual assault" is the conviction rate and custody rate per 1,000 male population (ages twelve and older) only. Sources: De Souza 2002*b*; Grimes 2002; Statistics Canada 2002.

Justice Statistics (2001, p. 1), "one of the most difficult issues arising when comparing statistics [from the YCS and ACCS] is that, regardless of data quality, the use of different 'units of count' complicates the interpretation of outputs." As a result, CCJS stresses that end users of its data must exercise caution when comparing statistics from the YCS and ACCS. This caveat seems to apply even more when aggregating data from both court surveys.

Two other limitations with these data sets exist. First, unlike the UCR survey, the YCS and ACCS do not distinguish among the different categories of burglary (i.e., residential, commercial, and other). As such, all burglaries are reported in the courts data. Second, for the offense of motor vehicle theft, court records are not limited to theft of motor vehicles that operate on land but also include theft of boats.

A. Conviction Rates

Expressed as a rate per 1,000 population ages twelve or over, the total (youths and adults combined) homicide conviction rate increased and decreased slightly throughout the period between 1994 and 1997, with a substantial increase reported in 1998 (see fig. 10). As shown in

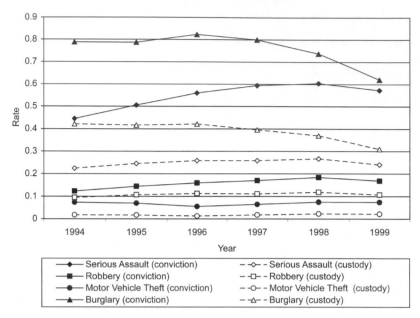

F<small>IG.</small> 11.—Conviction and custody rates per 1,000 population (ages twelve and older): serious assault, robbery, motor vehicle theft, and burglary. "Motor vehicle theft" includes thefts of all motor vehicles operated on land and water. "Burglary" includes all burglaries (i.e., residential, commercial, and other). Sources: De Souza 2002*b;* Grimes 2002; Statistics Canada 2002.

figure 10, the conviction rate of males (ages twelve and over) for aggravated sexual assault increased by 117 percent between 1994 and 1999. The serious assault conviction rate increased steadily between 1994 and 1998 (a 36 percent increase) before declining in 1999 (see fig. 11). The conviction rate for robbery increased by 50 percent between 1994 and 1998 (see fig. 11) but dropped to 0.17 per 1,000 population in 1999. As shown in figure 11, between 1994 and 1999, the total motor vehicle theft conviction rate remained fairly constant, with the exception of a 21.4 percent decrease between 1995 and 1996 (from 0.070 to 0.055 per 1,000 population). As shown in figure 11, burglary conviction rates declined from 1996 to 1999, with the most significant year-to-year change (a 15.9 percent decrease from 0.74 to 0.62) observed between 1998 and 1999.

B. Custody Rates

The population custody rate (persons sentenced to custody per 1,000 population ages twelve and over) for homicide closely resembles the patterns found in the homicide conviction rate (see fig. 10), with increases and decreases between 1994 and 1997, a sizeable increase in 1998, followed by a notable decrease in 1999. As shown in figure 10, the custody rate per 1,000 male population (ages twelve and over) for aggravated sexual assault fluctuated between 1994 and 1999, reaching its highest point in 1999 (0.0008 per 1,000 male population). The custody rate for serious assault remained fairly constant between 1994 and 1999 (see fig. 11). The total custody rate for robbery increased slightly between 1994 and 1998 and then declined in 1999 (see fig. 11). As shown in figure 11, between 1994 and 1996, the total custody rate for motor vehicle theft decreased slightly, followed by a brief period (1996–98) of small, gradual increases and then a decrease again in 1999. Burglary custody rates gradually decreased between 1996 and 1999 (see fig. 11), with the largest year-to-year decrease occurring between 1998 and 1999 (0.37 to 0.31).

C. The Probability of Custody after Conviction

The number of persons sentenced to custody for each offense is derived from the YCS and ACCS. The probability of an offender receiving a custodial sentence on conviction was calculated by dividing the number of offenders sentenced to custody for a particular offense by the number of persons convicted for that offense.

In 1996, several sentencing reforms came into force. One of the key elements of this initiative was the creation of a new sentencing option: the conditional sentence of imprisonment. "Judges in Canada now have the discretion to allow some offenders sentenced to terms of imprisonment to spend the sentence in the community under supervision. . . . The ACCS is currently being adapted to include the [future] collection of data on conditional sentences of imprisonment" (Roberts and Grimes 2000, p. 3).

The probability of custody after a conviction for homicide was fairly high between 1994 and 1999 (around 82 percent; see fig. 12). The probability of custody for males after a conviction for aggravated sexual assault was 100 percent in 1994 and 1995 (see fig. 12) but dropped off significantly in 1996 (63 percent) and continued to decline until 1998, where it reached its lowest point (55 percent). As shown in figure 12, the probability of custody after a conviction for serious assault showed a consistent, slight downward trend between 1994 (51 percent) and 1999 (42 percent). Similarly, the probability of custody after a conviction for robbery decreased gradually from its highest level in 1994

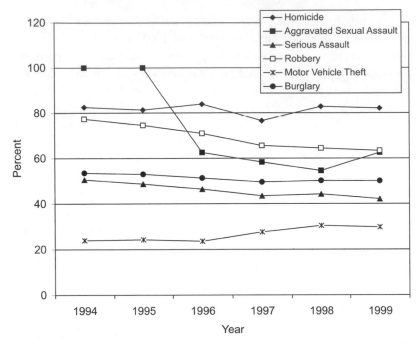

Fig. 12.—Percent custody per conviction. "Aggravated sexual assault" is the conviction rate and custody rate per 1,000 male population (ages twelve and older) only. "Motor vehicle theft" includes thefts of all motor vehicles operated on land and water. "Burglary" includes all burglaries (i.e., residential, commercial, and other). Sources: De Souza 2002*b*; Grimes 2002; Statistics Canada 2002.

(77 percent) to its lowest level in 1999 (63 percent; see fig. 12). The probability of custody following a conviction for motor vehicle theft remained constant between 1994 and 1996 (24 percent) but then increased to 30 percent in 1998 and 1999 (see fig. 12). The probability of receiving a custodial sentence after a conviction for burglary decreased slightly over the period 1994 (54 percent) to 1999 (50 percent; see fig. 12).

D. Sentence Length and Time Served

Sentence length data are derived from the YCS and ACCS. Data from YCS and ACCS pertaining to average sentence length were not aggregated since the sentencing guidelines for judges are very different when it comes to youths and adults convicted of a particular offense. Consequently, comparative data analysis of sentence length between the two offender populations is difficult to undertake.

In this essay, custodial sentence length for young offenders was obtained by calculating the mean between the average number of days of secure custody sentences and the average number of days of open custody sentences. Secure custody refers to facilities designated for secure restraint, while open custody refers to placement in a residential center or group home setting (Sanders 2000, p. 3).

In Canada, young offenders generally can receive a maximum custodial sentence length of two years. "However, this sentence can be three years if the crime would normally carry a maximum penalty of life imprisonment in adult court. In addition, the most serious crimes . . . carry higher sentences. [For example], first-degree murder carries a maximum custodial sentence of six years followed by four years of conditional supervision" (De Souza 2002a, p. 7). In the ACCS, adult cases sentenced to life imprisonment are recoded to 9,125 days (or twenty-five years) for the calculation of sentence length's means and medians.

With respect to time served, the Youth Custody and Community Services (YCCS) survey collects data related to young offenders serving a custodial and/or community-based disposition. Similarly, the Adult Correctional Services (ACS) survey collects aggregate case-load and case characteristics data for custodial and noncustodial correctional services at both the federal and provincial levels. However, both the YCCS and the ACS are limited in that they cannot provide detailed offense-specific information (e.g., offense-specific time served data). In an attempt to overcome this limitation, we obtained offense-specific provincial youth and adult corrections data from two of the largest jurisdictions (British Columbia and Ontario) and corrections data pertaining to adults serving a federal sentence (two years or more) from the Correctional Service of Canada. Disappointingly, we were not able to produce an accurate estimate of time served. This is because there are many definitional and methodological differences between "time served" data from these jurisdictions.

With respect to definitional issues, some of the offense categories varied from jurisdiction to jurisdiction. For example, one particular jurisdiction had only one offense entitled "breaking and entering" related to the average time served data for burglary. In contrast, another jurisdiction had more than five disaggregated offense categories related to burglary. Without having access to, and being able to study in greater detail, the scoring rules and offense classification systems of the various jurisdictions where corrections data are available,

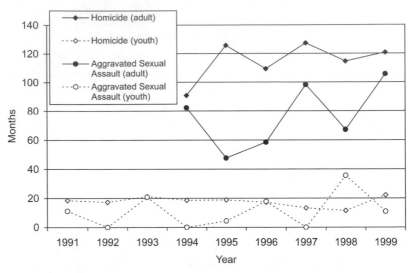

Fig. 13.—Average custodial sentence length (in months): homicide and aggravated sexual assault. "Aggravated sexual assault" is the average custodial sentence length for male adults and male youths only. Sources: De Souza 2002*b*; Grimes 2002.

it is very difficult to say whether some or all of the burglary-related offenses included by the latter jurisdiction are included by the other jurisdictions.

An example of one of the methodological problems is that one of the provincial jurisdictions differentiates its adult corrections data by time served on a provincial sentence and time served in provincial facilities on a federal sentence, while the other provincial jurisdiction does not make this same differentiation. As a result, double counting may be occurring where the same case is being included in both the provincial jurisdiction's database and the federal jurisdiction's database.

There were also difficulties present in comparing the corrections-based time served data and the courts-based sentence length data. For example, in many instances, the average time served by offenders for a particular offense ended up being substantially more than the custodial sentence length handed down by the courts. As a result, we could not use the corrections data obtained from CSC or the two provinces.

As shown in figure 13, the average custodial sentence length for homicide for young offenders changed very little between 1991 and 1998 but increased between 1998 (349.5 days, or 11.5 months) and 1999 (675 days, or 22.2 months). For adult offenders, the average

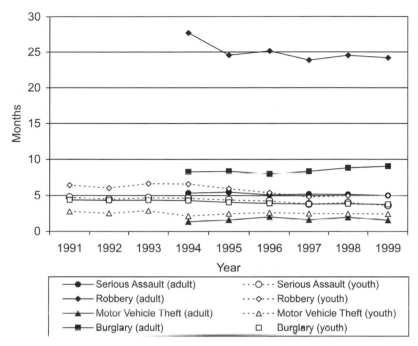

FIG 14 —Average custodial sentence length (in months). serious assault, robbery, motor vehicle theft, and burglary. "Motor vehicle theft" includes thefts of all motor vehicles operated on land and water. "Burglary" includes all burglaries (i.e., residential, commercial, and other). Sources: De Souza 2002b; Grimes 2002.

custodial sentence length for homicide reached its highest point in 1997 (3,872 days, or 127 months). It should be noted, however, that because of life sentences for adult murderers, the estimation of average sentence length for the offense of homicide is problematic. The average custodial sentence length for aggravated sexual assault for male young offenders showed no discernible pattern between 1991 and 1999, although it was highest in 1998 (1,080 days, or 35.5 months; see fig. 13). In 1992 and 1994, there were no recorded cases of male youths being convicted for aggravated sexual assault, and in 1997 there was only one case, but the young offender was not sentenced to custody. For male adults, the average custodial sentence length for aggravated sexual assault increased from 2,500 days (82 months) in 1994 to 3,211 days (106 months) in 1999, but between these years there were some sizeable fluctuations.

As shown in figure 14, the average custodial sentence length for serious assault for young offenders decreased irregularly, from 144 days

(4.7 months) in 1991 to 110 days (3.6 months) in 1999. For adult offenders, the average custodial sentence length for serious assault reached its highest level in 1995 (166 days or 5.5 months). The average custodial sentence length for robbery for young offenders peaked in 1993 (202 days, or 6.6 months), while the average custodial sentence length for adult offenders reached its highest level (842 days, or 27.7 months) in 1994 (see fig. 14). The average custodial sentence length for motor vehicle theft for young offenders decreased between 1993 (eighty-eight days, or 2.9 months) and 1994 (sixty-five days, or 2.1 months), increased slightly the year after, and then showed little change over the period 1996–99 (see fig. 14). For adults, the average custodial sentence length for motor vehicle theft increased between 1994 and 1996, followed by slight year-to-year increases and decreases in the subsequent years. As shown in figure 14, the average custodial sentence length for burglary for young offenders decreased slightly from 1991 to 1999, reaching a low of 114 days (3.8 months) in 1999. For adults, the average custodial sentence length for burglary increased slightly between 1996 and 1999, reaching a high of 275 days (nine months) in 1999.

E.   *Explaining Trends in Punishment*

Unlike for police-reported crime rates, few data points were available for conviction rates, custody rates, the probability of custody after conviction, and average custodial sentence length. This, along with a number of definitional and methodological limitations, makes it less than ideal to try to explain any trends in punishment. But there were some interesting events that took place in the 1990s that are deserving of comment.

In 1996, sentencing reform Bill C-41 was enacted, which created a new sanction. Sentencing judges were given the discretion to allow some offenders sentenced to terms of imprisonment to serve their sentences in the community under supervision and strict conditions. A major impetus for this new sanction was to reduce the adult incarceration rate. Some observers have noted, however, that custody rates in Canada have actually risen since the enactment of the conditional sentence portion of this law (John Howard Society of Alberta 2000). While this observation is not consistent with recent (1996–99) trends in custody rates for most of the offenses examined in the present study (aggravated sexual assault is the one exception), the law does not appear to have had the intended effect of lowering incarceration rates.

The failure of Bill C-41 to reduce incarceration rates, at least in the short-term, may have to do with a more punitive Canadian judiciary. Some sentencing policy experts have argued that "judges have become harsher in response either to pressure from prosecutors or perhaps from judicial perception that society favors the imposition of harsher punishments" (Roberts et al. 2002, p. 18). National public opinion polls conducted in 1994 and 1998 found that 66 percent and 63 percent, respectively, supported increased sentences for most offenders; 72 percent and 65 percent believed that offenders should serve their full sentences; and 82 percent and 77 percent supported the imposition of harsher sentences for violent young offenders (Stein 2001, p. 13).

One factor that may have contributed to lower custody rates during the 1990s was a change in administrative procedures concerning custody admissions. In the case of the Province of Ontario, for example, "the decision to no longer place offenders guilty of 'fine default' in custody" was reported as a possible contributing factor to a decline in custody rates (Hendrick, Martin, and Greenberg 2003, p. 20).

V. Conclusions, Gaps in Knowledge, and Research Priorities
This essay examines trends in crime and punishment in Canada over the period 1981–99 and explores key explanations for important trends in these areas. Six offenses are studied: homicide, aggravated sexual assault, serious assault, robbery, motor vehicle theft, and residential burglary.

Police records indicate that Canada may be safer at the end of the 1990s compared with the early 1980s. Of the six offenses studied, rates decreased for four (homicide, aggravated sexual assault, robbery, and residential burglary) and increased for the other two. Victim survey reports over this time period present a slightly different picture: sexual assault and motor vehicle theft rates increased, serious assault and residential burglary rates decreased, and robbery rates stayed about the same.

A much more sustained and larger change in police-reported crime rates took place in the 1990s. A substantial fall in rates of five of the six serious crimes occurred from about 1991–99. The one exception was motor vehicle theft, which showed an upward trend in rates from the early 1980s to a peak in 1996, followed by a few years of decline. With only two victim surveys conducted during the 1990s, it is not possible to comment on trends.

Reasons for this drop in serious crime rates in the 1990s include an aging population—a declining proportion of the age group most at risk of criminal offending (fifteen- to twenty-four-year-olds) and an increasing proportion of an age group with low involvement in criminal activity (ages fifty-five and over)—and an improved economy (falling unemployment rates). Declines in robbery and residential burglary rates during this time period may be partly explained by police recording a slightly smaller fraction of these crimes reported to them by victims. Government spending on policing (which actually declined during the 1990s), punishment in the form of incarceration, and increased policy and programmatic attention to social crime prevention approaches did not appear to have an effect on crime rates during this period of time.

From the available evidence on the Canadian criminal justice system's response to serious crime, through the courts and corrections agencies, during the mid- to late 1990s, there are mixed signs about whether it could have had an impact on crime trends during this time period. The risk of punishment, as measured by conviction rates and custody rates, increased for homicide, aggravated sexual assault, and robbery; decreased for burglary (all types); and changed little or did not change for serious assault and motor vehicle theft. The severity of punishment, as measured by the probability of convicted offenders being sentenced to custody and average custodial sentence length, provides perhaps a clearer statement about the criminal justice system's inability to have a desirable impact on crime trends during this period of time. Only for motor vehicle theft did the probability of custody after conviction increase during the mid- to late 1990s; for aggravated sexual assault, serious assault, robbery, and burglary (all types), it decreased. Only for aggravated sexual assault did the average custodial sentence length increase over this period of time; for serious assault and robbery it went down.

Future comparisons of crime and punishment in Canada over time (and with other Western nations) would benefit from a number of improvements in the collection and dissemination of statistics on sentencing and corrections. Limited data on punishment variables (custody or prison rates, probability of custody on conviction, etc.) over time precluded a detailed examination of (potential) explanations of trends in punishment, as well as possible relationships between changes in punishment and changes in crime. A rigorous program of research should be initiated to test explanations for the crime drop of the 1990s.

The main aim of this part of the essay is to contribute to improving future comparisons of crime and punishment in Canada over time. In discussing gaps in knowledge, we do not revisit all of the data imperfections that have been noted throughout this essay, but instead we will draw attention to those we consider to be the most pressing.

Clearly, the most important deficiencies in Canadian statistics on crime and punishment pertain to the latter, that is, statistics on sentencing and corrections. Roberts (1999, p. 231) summarizes some of the most important limitations with the best available source on sentencing statistics, the ACCS: "No information is available regarding superior courts (or even all provincial courts); the data lack any indication of important sentencing related variables such as the criminal history of the offender, or details of the crime of conviction (e.g., value of property stolen or damaged, extent of harm inflicted, etc.)." Again, we turn to Roberts (1999, p. 231), this time to note the importance of research on sentencing in Canada: "National sentencing statistics are an indispensable element of a rational and comprehensive sentencing research programme. ... Unless and until greater resources are devoted to the issue of research on sentencing, we shall remain behind other nations in terms of understanding this critical component of the criminal process."

Concerning crime statistics, future national victimization surveys should be conducted on a more frequent basis. In the three national surveys that have been carried out, the most recent being for 1998, there has been a five- and a six-year gap between the surveys. Large time periods between surveys may miss important parts of, or entire, trends. Large samples are also needed for future surveys. The most recent survey used the largest sample to date, 26,000 persons. This meant that each respondent represented about 1,000 people in the Canadian population. This was a significant improvement over the two previous surveys, and future surveys should replicate this scale-up factor. We do not, of course, take issue with changes that were made to definitions of crimes or survey questions for some of the crimes of interest to this essay (i.e., sexual assault and assault), as these changes were no doubt made to improve the information elicited. Importantly, the practice of reporting separately the findings from the new and old questions, as was done in the 1998 survey, should be continued in publications of future surveys. This allows for like-with-like crime comparisons over time, as well as the ability to advance knowledge in specialized areas of victimization.

Finally, a program of research should be initiated to test explanations for the crime drop in Canada during the 1990s. We examined some of the key (potential) explanations (demography, economy, spending on policing, incarceration, and alternative crime prevention approaches) for the decline in police-reported crime rates during this time period. Future research should expand the number of explanatory variables; examine how these variables hold up in different regions of the country, especially because of regional variation in crime rates across the country; and assess how key explanations compare between Canada and the United States (see Ouimet 2002), in light of the United States experiencing similar trends in national crime rates during the 1990s (Blumstein and Wallman 2000). When sentencing and corrections statistics become available for a longer time frame, research should be conducted to test explanations for any trends in national rates of convictions and custody, as well as the probability of custody on conviction and average custodial sentence length and time served for the six offenses covered here.

As many before us have noted (e.g., Doob 1999; Roberts 1999), there is a need for increased public investment in many facets of basic research on crime and punishment in Canada. Such an investment offers to improve future comparisons of crime and punishment in Canada over time and with other Western nations and may go some way toward bringing about more informed and efficacious crime policy, whether it be in addressing sentencing disparity, reducing the use of prisons for nonviolent offenders, or implementing early intervention programs for at-risk children and families.

REFERENCES

Becsi, Zsolt. 1999. "Economics and Crime in the States." *Economic Review* (First Quarter):38–56.

Besserer, Sandra, and Catherine Trainor. 2000. "Criminal Victimization in Canada, 1999." *Juristat*, vol. 20, no. 10. Ottawa: Statistics Canada, Canadian Centre for Justice Statistics.

Besserer, Sandra, and Jennifer Tufts. 1999. "Justice Spending in Canada." *Juristat*, vol. 19, no. 12. Ottawa: Statistics Canada, Canadian Centre for Justice Statistics.

Blumstein, Alfred, and Joel Wallman, eds. 2000. *The Crime Drop in America*. New York: Cambridge University Press.

Canadian Centre for Justice Statistics. 1990. "Criminal Victimization in Canada: The Findings of a Survey." *Juristat*, vol. 10, no. 16. Ottawa: Statistics Canada, Canadian Centre for Justice Statistics.

———. 1998. *Youth Court Statistics, 1996–1997*. Ottawa: Statistics Canada, Canadian Centre for Justice Statistics.

———. 1999a. *Canadian Crime Statistics, 1998*. Ottawa: Statistics Canada, Canadian Centre for Justice Statistics.

———. 1999b. *A Graphical Overview of Crime and the Administration of Criminal Justice in Canada, 1998*. Ottawa: Statistics Canada, Canadian Centre for Justice Statistics.

———. 1999c. "Uniform Crime Reporting Survey." Unpublished tables. Ottawa: Statistics Canada, Canadian Centre for Justice Statistics.

———. 2000. Statistical tables, national criminal victimization surveys. Available at http://ccjsccsj.statcan.ca.

———. 2001. *The Impact of Using an End-Date Case Definition for the Youth Court Survey*. Ottawa: Courts Program, Statistics Canada, Canadian Centre for Justice Statistics.

Canadian Criminal Justice Association. 1989. "Safer Communities: A Social Strategy for Crime Prevention in Canada." *Canadian Journal of Criminology* 31:359–401.

Department of Justice Canada. 2003. "Improving the Youth Justice System." Available at http://www.canada.justice.gc.ca/en/ps/yj/repository/2overvw/2010001b.html. Last accessed on June 20, 2003.

De Souza, Paul. 2002a. "Youth Court Statistics, 2000–2001." *Juristat*, vol. 22, no. 3. Ottawa: Statistics Canada, Canadian Centre for Justice Statistics.

———. 2002b. "Youth Court Survey Cases and Custody Rates, 1991–1992 to 1999–2000, Selected Offences by Sex," and "Youth Court Survey Custody Sentence Lengths, 1991–1992 to 1999–2000, Selected Offences by Sex." Unpublished data from the Youth Court Survey. Ottawa: Statistics Canada, Canadian Centre for Justice Statistics.

Doob, Anthony N. 1999. "Youth Justice Research in Canada: An Assessment." *Canadian Journal of Criminology* 41:217–24.

Du Wors, Richard. 1992. "Robbery in Canada." *Juristat*, vol. 12, no. 10. Ottawa: Statistics Canada, Canadian Centre for Justice Statistics.

———. 1997. "The Justice Data Factfinder." *Juristat*, vol. 17, no. 13. Ottawa: Statistics Canada, Canadian Centre for Justice Statistics.

Dunphy, Robert, and Gayatri Shankarraman. 2000. *Police Resources in Canada, 2000*. Ottawa: Statistics Canada, Canadian Centre for Justice Statistics.

Fedorowycz, Orest. 1999. "Homicide in Canada—1998." *Juristat*, vol. 19, no. 10. Ottawa: Statistics Canada, Canadian Centre for Justice Statistics.

———. 2000. "Homicide in Canada—1999." *Juristat*, vol. 20, no. 9. Ottawa: Canadian Centre for Justice Statistics, Statistics Canada.

Foot, David K., with Daniel Stoffman. 1996. *Boom, Bust and Echo: How to Profit from the Coming Demographic Shift*. Toronto: Macfarlane Walter & Ross.

———. 1998. *Boom, Bust and Echo 2000: Profiting from the Demographic Shift in the New Millennium*. Rev. ed. Toronto: Macfarlane Walter & Ross.

Gabor, Thomas. 1994. *The Impact of the Availability of Firearms on Violent Crime, Suicide, and Accidental Death: A Review of the Literature with Special Reference to the Canadian Situation.* Ottawa: Department of Justice Canada.
———. 1995. "The Proposed Canadian Legislation on Firearms: More Symbolism than Prevention." *Canadian Journal of Criminology* 37:195–213.
Gartner, Rosemary, and Anthony N. Doob. 1994. "Trends in Criminal Victimization: 1988–1993." *Juristat,* vol. 14, no. 13. Ottawa: Statistics Canada, Canadian Centre for Justice Statistics.
Grimes, Craig. 2002. "Cases Convicted in Adult Criminal Court by Type of Offences, Selected Provinces and Territories, 1994–1995 to 1999–2000." Unpublished data from the Adult Criminal Court Survey. Ottawa: Statistics Canada, Canadian Centre for Justice Statistics.
Hartnagel, Timothy F. 2001. "Crime and Punishment in Canada." Paper presented at the fifty-third annual meeting of the American Society of Criminology, Atlanta, November 7–10.
Hendrick, Dianne, Michael Martin, and Peter Greenberg. 2003. *Conditional Sentencing in Canada: A Statistical Profile, 1997–2001.* Ottawa: Statistics Canada, Canadian Centre for Justice Statistics.
Hope, Tim. 1995. "Community Crime Prevention." In *Building a Safer Society: Strategic Approaches to Crime Prevention,* edited by Michael Tonry and David P. Farrington. Vol. 19 of *Crime and Justice: A Review of Research,* edited by Michael Tonry. Chicago: University of Chicago Press.
Integration and Analysis Program. 1999. "Sex Offenders." *Juristat,* vol. 19, no. 3. Ottawa: Statistics Canada, Canadian Centre for Justice Statistics.
John Howard Society of Alberta. 2000. "Conditional Sentences." Available at http://johnhoward.ab.ca/res-pub.htm. Accessed on June 20, 2003.
Kaschube, Karen, and Mike Hayden. 2000. "Federal Inmates—Admissions/Releases." Unpublished data. Ottawa: Correctional Service of Canada.
Kennedy, Leslie W., and David Veitch. 1997. "Why Are Crime Rates Going Down? A Case Study in Edmonton." *Canadian Journal of Criminology* 39:51–69.
Kong, Rebecca. 1997. "Canadian Crime Statistics, 1996." *Juristat,* vol. 17, no. 8. Ottawa: Statistics Canada, Canadian Centre for Justice Statistics.
———. 1998*a.* "Breaking and Entering in Canada, 1996." *Juristat,* vol. 18, no. 5. Ottawa: Statistics Canada, Canadian Centre for Justice Statistics.
———. 1998*b.* "Canadian Crime Statistics, 1997." *Juristat,* vol. 18, no. 11. Ottawa: Statistics Canada, Canadian Centre for Justice Statistics.
LaFree, Gary. 1998. *Losing Legitimacy: Street Crime and the Decline of Social Institutions in America.* Boulder, Colo.: Westview.
Langan, Patrick A., and David P. Farrington. 1998. *Crime and Justice in the United States and in England and Wales, 1981–1996.* Washington, D.C.: Bureau of Justice Statistics, U.S. Department of Justice.
Logan, Ron. 2002. *Police Resources in Canada, 2002.* Ottawa: Statistics Canada, Canadian Centre for Justice Statistics.
MacLean, Brian C. 1996. "State Expenditures on Canadian Criminal Justice." In *Crime and Society: Readings in Critical Criminology,* edited by Brian C. MacLean. Toronto: Copp Clark.

Malette, Louise, and Marie Chalouh, eds. 1991. *The Montreal Massacre.* Translated by Marlene Wildeman. Charlottetown, Canada: Gynergy.

Mihorean, Stephen. 2001. "The 1988, 1993, and 1999 General Social Surveys: Selected Tables." Unpublished tables. Ottawa: Department of Justice Canada, Research and Statistics Division.

Mohr, Renate M., and Julian V. Roberts. 1994. "Sexual Assault in Canada: Recent Developments." In *Confronting Sexual Assault: A Decade of Legal and Social Change,* edited by Julian V. Roberts and Renate M. Mohr. Toronto: University of Toronto Press.

Ouimet, Marc. 2002. "Explaining the American and Canadian Crime 'Drop' in the 1990s." *Canadian Journal of Criminology* 44:33–50.

Public Service Commission of Canada. 2002. "How Government Works." Available at http://www.edu.psc-cfp.gc.ca/tdc/learn-apprend/psw/hgw/index.htm. Accessed on June 20, 2003.

Roberts, Julian V. 1999. "Sentencing Research in Canada." *Canadian Journal of Criminology* 41:225–34.

Roberts, Julian V., and Craig Grimes. 2000. "Adult Criminal Court Statistics, 1998–1999." *Juristat,* vol. 20, no. 1. Ottawa: Statistics Canada, Canadian Centre for Justice Statistics.

Roberts, Julian V., Loretta J. Stalans, David Indermaur, and Mike Hough. 2002. *Penal Populism and Public Opinion: Lessons from Five Countries.* New York: Oxford University Press.

Sanders, Trevor. 2000. "Sentencing of Young Offenders in Canada, 1998–1999." *Juristat,* vol. 20, no. 7. Ottawa: Statistics Canada, Canadian Centre for Justice Statistics.

Sansfaçon, Daniel, and Irvin Waller. 2001. "Recent Evolution of Governmental Crime Prevention Strategies and Implications for Evaluation and Economic Analysis." In *Costs and Benefits of Preventing Crime,* edited by Brandon C. Welsh, David P. Farrington, and Lawrence W. Sherman. Boulder, Colo.: Westview.

Sauvé, Julie. 1998. "Motor Vehicle Theft in Canada—1996." *Juristat,* vol. 18, no. 1. Ottawa: Statistics Canada, Canadian Centre for Justice Statistics.

Sharpe, Andrew. 1996. *The Canada-U.S. Unemployment Rate Gap: An Assessment of Possible Causes.* Ottawa: Human Resources Development Canada, Applied Research Branch, Strategic Policy.

Solicitor General Canada. 1983. "Victims of Crime." *Canadian Urban Victimization Survey Bulletin 1.* Ottawa: Solicitor General Canada, Programs Branch/Research and Statistics Group.

———. 1984. "Reported and Unreported Crimes." *Canadian Urban Victimization Survey Bulletin 2.* Ottawa: Solicitor General Canada, Programs Branch/Research and Statistics Group.

Spencer, Jon. 1993. "Criminal Justice Expenditure: A Global Perspective." *Howard Journal of Criminal Justice* 32:1–11.

Standing Committee on Justice and the Solicitor General. 1993. *Crime Prevention in Canada: Toward a National Strategy.* Ottawa: Supply and Services Canada.

Statistics Canada. N.d. "Estimated Number of Households for Canada and Provinces." Unpublished tables. Ottawa: Statistics Canada, Households Surveys Division.

———. 2002. Canadian population statistical tables. Available at http://www.statcan.ca.

Stein, Karin. 2001. *Public Perception of Crime and Justice in Canada: A Review of Opinion Polls.* Ottawa: Department of Justice Canada.

Tremblay, Richard E., and Wendy M. Craig. 1995. "Developmental Crime Prevention." In *Building a Safer Society: Strategic Approaches to Crime Prevention,* edited by Michael Tonry and David P. Farrington. Vol. 19 of *Crime and Justice: A Review of Research,* edited by Michael Tonry. Chicago: University of Chicago Press.

Tremblay, Sylvain. 1999. "Crime Statistics in Canada, 1998." *Juristat,* vol. 19, no. 9. Ottawa: Statistics Canada, Canadian Centre for Justice Statistics.

———. 2000. "Crime Statistics in Canada, 1999." *Juristat,* vol. 20, no. 5. Ottawa: Statistics Canada, Canadian Centre for Justice Statistics.

Welsh, Brandon C., and Mark H. Irving. 2001. "Crime and Punishment in Canada, 1981–1999." Paper presented at "Cross-National Crime and Punishment Trends," New Hall College, University of Cambridge, Cambridge, England, June 28–30.

Yogis, John A. 1983. *Canadian Law Dictionary.* Woodbury, N.Y.: Barron's Educational Series.

Young, Gail. 1994. "Trends in Justice Spending—1988–199 to 1992–193." *Juristat,* vol. 14, no. 16. Ottawa: Statistics Canada, Canadian Centre for Justice Statistics.

Carlos Carcach

Crime and Punishment in Australia, 1980–2000

ABSTRACT

Over the twenty years from 1980 to 2000, Australia experienced sustained increases in the incidence of robbery, serious assault, and rape; declines in motor vehicle theft; and stability in homicide and burglary. Persons convicted of homicide, serious assault, burglary, and motor vehicle theft received longer sentences. The exceptions were robbery and rape. Limited access to uniform national crime statistics and time-series data on crime-related socioeconomic factors makes explaining these trends difficult. Differences in the responses of states and territories to crime and lack of uniform court and prison statistics make identification of the factors underlying the risk of offending complicated. The risk of punishment seems to be negatively associated with crime rates, but trying to explain this apparent relationship is adventurous. Development of uniform and integrated national crime statistics systems remains a priority.

Australia has experienced sustained increases in the incidence of robbery, serious assault, and rape; declines in motor vehicle theft; and stability in the incidence of homicide and burglary over the twenty-year period 1980–2000, as indicated by both crime survey and recorded crime trends. In addition to socioeconomic factors, these increases are attributable to changes in legislation, organizational and technological innovations in policing, and changes in crime-recording policies and

Carlos Carcach is professor of statistics and econometrics at the Escuela Superior de Economía y Negocios in El Salvador. This work was completed while he was head of the Communities and Crime Analysis Program at the Australian Institute of Criminology, Canberra, Australia. The author is grateful to Ibolya Losoncz for assistance with data collection and to Peter Grabosky, Toni Makkai, Gloria Laycock, and Pat Mayhew for critical comments and editorial assistance with earlier versions. The author claims sole responsibility for any remaining errors.

crime-counting rules. Assessing the exact contribution of each of these factors to the observed trends was not possible due to data problems.

With the exception of rape, reporting rates for the other personal and property offenses remained stable. The factors underlying reporting rates include the seriousness of the offense, the victim-offender relationship, changes in the tolerance of crime in the community, and changes in perceptions of police performance. Stable reporting rates suggest that crime incidents may have remained unchanged in nature over time and that, for some offenses, the observed increases in crime rates might have resulted from increases in crimes recorded by police.

Clearance rates seem to be declining within a framework of stable to increasing crime rates and increasing police numbers per 1,000 population.[1] This suggests that, contrary to what is suggested by the results from crime surveys, crime has increased in Australia over the past twenty years.

Australian data seem to confirm Farrington, Langan, and Wikström's 1994 finding of a negative correlation between crime rates and risk of conviction.[2] Except for robbery, the average arrested criminal faced a lower risk of conviction in 1998 than in 1983. For robbery, the probability of conviction has remained stable.

Imprisonment rates for offenders convicted of burglary, vehicle theft, and serious assault were higher in 1998 than in 1983. The rates for robbery and rape did not change significantly, but there was a decline for homicide. There is a negative correlation between the risks of conviction and incarceration, which suggests a tendency toward using alternative forms of punishment.

Sentence lengths increased for homicide and vehicle theft but decreased for robbery and rape. Sentence lengths for the remaining offenses have not experienced significant changes over the period investigated.

Sentenced offenders spent longer times in prison in 1998 than in 1983. Robbery and rape are the exception. Among those serving terms of imprisonment for robbery, the time served in prison has declined, and for rape the average time served in prison has remained stable.

The overall risk of punishment associated with the commission of burglary, vehicle theft, serious assault, and homicide has increased.

---

[1] The number of "sworn" police officers has increased from 216.5 per 1,000 resident total population in 1983 to 229.5 in 1998 (Australian Institute of Criminology 2000). This is an average increase of 0.4 percent a year.

[2] Spearman correlation coefficients were negative and above 0.8 for burglary, vehicle theft, serious assault, rape, and homicide.

Burglary and vehicle theft have the lowest clearance rates, so the results give support to the argument by Becker (1968) that sentences should be longer when arrest rates are lower. Homicide is the most serious offense against the person, followed by serious assault. This explains the high risk of incarceration associated with these crimes.

This essay describes and provides the analyses on which the preceding conclusions are based. Here is how it is organized. Section I provides background information about Australia, together with a brief overview of the Australian criminal justice system and major significant changes over the last twenty years. Section II describes the method of estimation and discusses the data used for analysis. This discussion focuses on limitations with the data and the steps undertaken to minimize their impact on the analyses. Section III analyzes the flow of offenders through the criminal justice system for each of the crimes included in the study. Emphasis is placed on significant changes to the risk of offending, as measured by the following three key measures: the probability of arrest, the probability of conviction, and the probability of imprisonment. Section IV explores possible reasons for the observed variations in the risk of offending. Section V outlines major data issues that need to be addressed to support research on change in the Australian criminal justice system.

I. Australia

Australia is an island in the southern hemisphere with a land area of about 7,692,030 square kilometers.[3] This is almost as large as the United States (excluding Alaska), about 50 percent larger than Europe (excluding Russia and the former European Soviet republics), and thirty-two times greater than the United Kingdom. Six states and two territories together constitute the Commonwealth of Australia.

The Australian population was 19.2 million in June 2000, with a rate of growth of 1.2 percent. Indigenous peoples make up about 2.2 percent of the population. Most of Australia's population is concentrated in two widely separated coastal regions. The larger of these two regions lies in the southeast and east. Half of the area of the continent contains only 0.3 percent of the population, and the most densely populated 1 percent of the continent contains 84 percent of the population. The population is concentrated in urban centers, particularly in the state and territory capital cities (64 percent of the population).

[3] Unless otherwise stated, this section is based on data extracted from the *2002 Year Book Australia* (Australian Bureau of Statistics 2002).

Australians live in a multicultural society. Twenty-three percent of Australians were born elsewhere, in about 125 different countries. The proportion of the population born in the United Kingdom and Northern Ireland declined from 7.3 percent in 1989 to 6.5 percent in 1998. The proportion born in eastern and southern Asia increased from 3.5 percent to 5.5 percent.

Australia has an aging population, with the median age projected to increase from the current 34.9 years in 2000 to forty-six years in 2051. Life expectancy is 76.2 years for males and 81.8 years for females. Patterns of family formation changed over the ten-year period 1988–98. The number of marriages declined by 5.5 percent between 1988 and 1998, and the number of divorces increased by 25 percent. In 1998, 19 percent of children younger than fifteen years lived in one-parent families, compared to 12.7 percent in 1990. Nineteen percent of all births occurred outside marriage in 1988. This increased to 28.7 percent in 1998.

The Australian economy experienced unprecedented prosperity during the 1990s. The GDP per capita increased by 23 percent, and household disposable income increased by 35 percent between 1989 and 1998. Household final consumption expenditure grew by 20 percent. About 30 percent of all household units derive their main source of income from government payments,[4] with 7 percent of the GDP being spent on income support (Australian Bureau of Statistics 2000a).

Australians have universal access to health care through the Medicare system. In 1998, health expenditure represented 8.3 percent of total GDP. Full-time education is compulsory for children ages five through fourteen. Education participation rates increased over the ten-year period 1988–98 by an annual 1.2 percent for persons ages fifteen to twenty-four years. Year 12 retention rates have also increased, with females staying longer at school than males (Australian Bureau of Statistics 2000a).

Australia is a constitutional monarchy with a parliamentary democratic system based on a federal division of powers. The national constitution is found in the Commonwealth of Australia Constitution Act 1990. Each state and territory has its own constitution. Commonwealth legislative power is vested in the Commonwealth Parliament,

---

[4] Eleven percent of all couples with dependent income units had government payments as their main source of income; 62 percent of one-parent income units derived their main income from this source (Australian Bureau of Statistics 2000a).

consisting of the House of Representatives (150 members) and the Senate (seventy-six members). The powers of the Commonwealth Parliament are limited to areas of national importance.[5] As in the United States, crime and justice are the responsibility of the states and territories.

National crime data are generated by aggregation of information about individual events taking place within contexts characterized by specific historical, legal, cultural, social, and economic conditions. Public values regarding crime and responses by the criminal justice system are in continuing evolution. Changes in legislation, policing approaches, and sentencing policies, as well as new developments in corrections, result in temporal and jurisdictional variations in crime statistics. The nature of these changes and their consequences at the national level must be understood to assist in the correct interpretation of cross-national differences.

Nine criminal justice systems coexist in Australia (seven states, two territories, and a federal jurisdiction). Each state or territory has its own legislature, police force, criminal courts, and correctional system.

In Australia, the power to legislate for most criminal matters is vested in the states. In Queensland and Western Australia, the criminal law is codified. In Tasmania, common law offenses are retained within a codified system. In New South Wales, Victoria, and South Australia, the common law is applicable unless it is excluded by statute. The Northern Territory has had a separate code since 1983. The Australian Capital Territory applies the New South Wales Crimes Act 1900 with some modifications. There are significant variations between the jurisdictions, not only in the definition of offenses but also in the existence and scope of particular offenses (Fairall 2000).

The standards and classifications applicable to crime statistics have undergone major change over the last twenty years. The Australian Standard Offence Classification (ASOC; Australian Bureau of Statistics 1997a) came into effect in 1997 and replaced the Australian National Classification of Offences (ANCO), which was released in 1985. A draft ANCO classification had been in place since June 1980 until it was replaced with ANCO in 1985. Use of a common classificatory scheme has helped in the development of uniform national crime statistics, which have been available since 1993. The ANCO and ASOC classifications are not very

[5] Among the powers granted by the constitution are trade and commerce, taxation, postal services, foreign relations, defense, immigration, naturalization, quarantine, currency and coinage, weights and measures, copyrights, and patents and trademarks.

different in terms of definitions and classifications for the six offenses covered in this essay.

All Australian police services have moved toward adoption of models of policing that move beyond the traditional "reactive" approach. Community policing, problem-oriented policing, and information-driven policing have been adopted at different times by police services (Brereton 2000).

Introduction of new technologies that enhance the clerical capacity of police services had a major impact on the volume of recorded crime in all jurisdictions beginning some time around the mid-1980s. Most police services implemented computerized crime-recording systems in the mid-1980s, which resulted in increased volumes of recorded crime.[6]

There is a hierarchy of criminal courts at the commonwealth and state or territory levels. Magistrates' courts deal with minor or summary criminal offenses. Intermediate courts (district/county courts) hear the majority of cases involving indictable crimes. The supreme courts are the highest within a state or territory. They deal with the most serious crimes. Children's courts deal with offenses committed by persons under the jurisdiction of the juvenile justice system.[7]

Diversionary mechanisms for adult and juvenile offenders, increased use of infringement notices, and changes to the content of summary jurisdiction have substantially affected the workloads of courts over the last two decades.[8] The large number of minor matters being dealt with outside the summary courts by means of infringement notices have been replaced by a substantial number of serious offenses that were formerly heard in the higher courts. The courts of summary jurisdiction hear the great majority of all criminal cases in Australia.[9]

---

[6] A test for structural change in the time series of police-recorded crime rates confirmed this hypothesis for all offenses except homicide ($p < .01$).

[7] In all Australian jurisdictions, the statutory minimum age of criminal responsibility is now ten years (Urbas 2000). The maximum age of treatment as a child/juvenile is eighteen years in all jurisdictions except Victoria and Queensland, where it is seventeen.

[8] According to Freiberg and Fox (1994), in Victoria in 1990–91, over 2,300,000 infringement notices were issued, and in New South Wales, in 1992–93, the police alone issued 1,988,746 infringement notices. In Victoria, driving offenses contributed 70 percent of all the convictions recorded in the magistrates' courts during 1971. Twenty years later, driving offenses accounted for less than 30 percent of all offenses charged in the magistrates' courts (Fox 1995).

[9] In New South Wales, the summary jurisdiction for many indictable property offenses has increased over recent years. Prior to 1983, these offenses could be heard summarily only if the property value did not exceed $1,000. This was increased to $10,000 in 1983, to $15,000 in 1987, and in 1995 the upper limit was removed (Willis 2000).

This transfer of cases from higher courts to summary courts has had a major effect on the workload of the latter. Since a majority of penalties imposed in the intermediate courts result in short terms of imprisonment, the transfer of cases to the summary courts must affect not only the volume of convictions but the numbers of short prison sentences.

Recent developments in sentencing include mandatory sentencing laws, judicial sentencing guidelines, and sentencing grids. In the words of Zdenkowski (2000, p. 173), "the genesis of these developments lies not, primarily, in ... notions of consistency and fairness ... but rather from a perception that sentence severity should be escalated."[10]

Community penalties include postcustodial programs, under which prisoners released into the community continue to be subject to correctional supervision (including parole, release on license, prerelease orders, and some forms of home detention). They also include orders imposed by the court as a sentencing option, such as suspended sentences, court-imposed home detention, community service orders, probation, intensive supervisions, and release on recognizance. In most jurisdictions, fine default orders fall under community corrections, as does bail supervision in some jurisdictions. Each jurisdiction has reparation, supervision, and restricted orders.

There is huge variation in the use of community corrections in the states and territories. In 2000, community corrections rates ranged from 175 offenders per 100,000 adults in Victoria to 971 offenders per 100,000 adults in the Northern Territory (Steering Committee for the Review of Commonwealth/State Service 2002, p. 531). Nationally, the community corrections rate has remained stable since 1994–95, around an average value of 480 offenders per 100,000 adults (Steering Committee for the Review of Commonwealth/State Service 1999, p. 573). Restorative justice schemes to deal with juvenile offenders were introduced in New South Wales, Victoria, Queensland, and Western Australia around 1996, and, more recently, in the Australian Capital Territory.

A number of developments have contributed to alter the numbers of offenders processed by Australian criminal justice systems over time. Despite increases in police-recorded crime, clearance rates have declined,

---

[10] Mandatory sentencing laws have included New South Wales's mandatory life sentence laws in 1989, Western Australia's "three strikes" legislation in 1992, and the Northern Territory's mandatory minimum imprisonment laws for property offenders in 1997 (Zdenkowski 2000). In Western Australia, legislation authorizing the referral of cases to the Court of Criminal Appeal for the purpose of the formulation of sentencing guidelines and authorizing a sentencing matrix system were introduced in 1995 and 1998.

and a number of mechanisms have been put in place to divert individuals away from prison-based sentences. For those offenders sentenced to imprisonment, the average sentence length has remained stable, but incarcerated offenders are serving a longer proportion of their sentence now than they did twenty years ago. However, except for the offenses of homicide and rape, the cost of offending remains low in Australia. The average offender might expect to be held in prison for less than one day if caught for burglary, less than two days if caught for motor vehicle theft, and less than one week if caught for robbery.

II. Data and Methods

In this essay, I discuss changes in crime and punishment in Australia from 1980 to 2000. I analyze national estimates for the flow of offenders through different stages of the criminal justice system and examine estimates for six offenses: residential break and enter, motor vehicle theft, robbery, serious assault, rape, and homicide.

The analysis follows the approach of Farrington, Langan, and Wikström (1994) and Langan and Farrington (1998) as closely as possible. This methodology relies heavily, although not exclusively, upon crime victim surveys as the main source of data on total numbers of offenses occurring during a given period. Three national crime victim surveys were conducted during the period covered (1983, 1993, and 1998). Data for the remaining years are national estimates derived from annual crime victim surveys conducted in the state of New South Wales since 1990. Previous to 1990, numbers of survey offenses were estimated using a synthetic method (Carcach 2003, app. D).

The analysis combines crime survey data on total numbers of incidents with national data on recorded crime, numbers of individuals coming into courts and their associated outcomes, and correctional statistics. The Australian Bureau of Statistics has published uniform national crime statistics for the crimes included in this study only since 1993. Before that, the Australian Institute of Criminology published national crime data (Mukherjee and Dagger 1990). No uniform court statistics exist, and data have only recently been published for higher courts. National correctional statistics providing data necessary to perform the analyses described in this essay are not readily available. The national correctional statistics are restricted to quarterly average daily numbers of prisoners and to a prison census that has been available since 1982.

As a consequence, the data and results in this essay are subject to a number of limitations and assumptions. In most cases, estimates were obtained by aggregating data published by the police services or the crime statistics offices in the states and territories. A number of adjustments were made to crime survey data and police-recorded crime data to ensure consistency in crime definitions and validity of the estimates (Carcach 2003, app. D).

These estimates are used to address the following key questions: Are crime rates increasing or decreasing? Are crimes being reported at higher or lower rates to police? Are police recording more or less crime? Are conviction rates increasing or decreasing? Is imprisonment being used more or less frequently as punishment for crimes? Is the sentence length increasing or decreasing? Are sentenced prisoners spending longer or shorter times in prison? Is the average time served per offender increasing or decreasing?

A. Data Sources and Data Problems

The data come from several sources (see app. A). With the exception of homicide, the total numbers of offenses during each of the years considered were obtained from crime victim survey data and official recorded crime statistics published by police services.[11] The National Homicide Monitoring Program (NHMP) at the Australian Institute of Criminology was the main source of homicide data.[12]

1. *Crime Victim Survey Data.* The national crime survey conducted by the Australian Bureau of Statistics has undergone several changes since 1983, the most important relating to use of different data collection methods and changes to the wording of survey questions. Appendix B in Carcach (2003) summarizes the main characteristics of the surveys, as well as the questions used in each of them to assess the victimization status of respondents. These changes have not had a major impact on the comparability of survey estimates with the exception of the offenses of robbery and assault.[13]

---

[11] Data showing full distributions of victims according to the number of incidents experienced during the surveys' reference periods were not available, and the estimates included in this study were based on truncated versions of such distributions as published by the Australian Bureau of Statistics (1986, 1991–2001, 1994a, 1999b). Therefore, the total numbers of offenses reported here are lower bounds for the true levels of crime during the twelve months prior to the surveys.

[12] Data on numbers of homicides recorded between 1983 and 1989 were obtained from Mukherjee and Dagger (1990). Data for the years 1991–2000 came from the National Homicide Monitoring Program held at the Australian Institute of Criminology (James and Carcach 1997; Mouzos 2000).

[13] According to data from national crime surveys, robbery rates were five per 1,000 in 1983, twelve per 1,000 in 1993, and six per 1,000 in 1998. The 1998 survey asked two

Data from the crime victims survey conducted annually in New South Wales since 1990 (Australian Bureau of Statistics 1991–2001) were used to derive estimates of numbers of offenses for the periods 1990–92, 1994–97, and 1999–2000.[14] Before 1990, the numbers of survey offenses were estimated using the method described in Carcach (2003).

To maintain consistency with other countries participating in the project, my analysis deals with the offenses of rape and serious assault rather than the generic offenses of sexual assault and assault that are included in the crime victim surveys. For serious assault, I included only assaults in which actual violence was used against the victim.[15]

The crime victim survey question on sexual assault is asked only of females ages eighteen years and over, and it includes any incident of a sexual nature (Carcach 2003, table B1). Therefore, sexual assaults as defined in crime victim surveys are not strictly equivalent to the offense of rape, or even to the offense of sexual assault in the Australian Standard Offence Classification or its predecessor the Australian National Classification of Offences (Carcach 2003, app. B). Rape, defined as having sexual intercourse with a woman against her will, is but one of several offenses included within the generic offense of sexual assault.

The national crime survey does not ask questions aimed to differentiate among types of sexual incidents. Data are, however, available from an alternative source, the Australian component of the International Crime Victims Survey (ICVS). The ICVS is based on a much smaller sample than the national crime survey, but it gives reliable

---

separate questions relating to robbery, whereas a single question was asked in the 1983 and 1993 surveys (see app. A). Data from crime surveys in New South Wales show robbery rates between sixteen per 1,000 during 1990–91 and 1995–96, twelve per 1,000 during 1992–94 and 1999, and five per 1,000 during 1997–98. The rates of assault were thirty-four per 1,000 in 1983, twenty-five per 1,000 in 1993, and forty-three per 1,000 in 1998. The change to a self-completing questionnaire in 1993 required the assault question to be modified; this may explain the decline in the victimization rate in 1993 compared to 1983 (see app. A). National estimates from New South Wales survey data suggest that the assault rate has increased steadily from twenty-two per 1,000 in 1990 to thirty-nine per 1,000 in 2000.

[14] Unlike the national crime survey, the New South Wales crime survey, which has been conducted every year since 1990 with the exception of 1993 and 1998, uses the same questionnaire and data collection method and has as its main objective the generation of time-series data.

[15] Crime survey data show that the number of victims of serious assault increased from 1983 to 1993 and has remained stable since then. Twenty-seven percent of assaults in the 1983 crime surveys involved actual violence on the victim as compared to 38 percent reported in the 1993 and 1998 surveys (Australian Bureau of Statistics 1986, 1994a).

national estimates (Carcach and Makkai 2003). More important, the estimates from the ICVS are comparable to the estimates from the national surveys used in this essay. The ICVS data show that rape and attempted rape accounted for 19 percent, 36 percent, and 25 percent of incidents of sexual assault recorded in 1988, 1991, and 1999, respectively.[16] The average 27 percent from these surveys was applied to the national survey estimates of sexual assault to derive estimates of the numbers of rapes for this analysis (Kesteren, Mayhew, and Nieuwbeerta 2001, p. 188).

2. *Reporting Rates.* Crime victim surveys were the source of data on percentages of incidents reported to police. Information on reporting behavior is gathered only for the most recent victimization, and therefore the reporting rate estimated from survey data may not necessarily apply to all crimes experienced by respondents. Repeat victims report crimes to the police at lower rates than do single-occasion victims (Carcach 1997). The reporting rates used in this analysis may thus overestimate the probability that victims report crimes to the police. Reporting rates for years with no national crime surveys were assumed to be at the same level as for the most recent national survey.

3. *Recorded Crime.* The total numbers of offenses recorded by police since 1993 were obtained from crime statistics published by the Australian Bureau of Statistics (1994c, 1995, 1997b, 1998, 1999c, 2000c, 2001). Statistics for the years 1983–92 were obtained from official statistics published by police services.[17] Except for rape, recorded-crime rates were calculated relative to the estimated total population on June 30 of each year.[18] Rape rates were calculated relative to female population ages eighteen years and over.

Recording practices and procedures vary among police services, divisions within police services, and police officers (see, e.g., Burrows

---

[16] Australia has participated in three waves of the ICVS (1988, 1992, and 2000). The sample sizes have averaged 2,005 respondents with a 52 percent response rate. The ICVS uses computer-assisted telephone interviewing as the data collection method. It collects data about experiences of victimization during the calendar year previous to the survey (Kesteren, Mayhew, and Nieuwbeerta 2001).

[17] The Australian Bureau of Statistics started to publish data for assault only in 1995. Data used to obtain the estimates for serious assault during 1995 were obtained from Australia-wide official statistics published by police services. Data for homicide came from the National Homicide Monitoring Program (NHMP) at the Australian Institute of Criminology, except for 1983. Homicide data for this year were obtained from Mukherjee and Dagger (1990).

[18] Data on the population as of June 30 of each year come from estimates of residential population published by the Australian Bureau of Statistics (1994b, 2000b).

et al. 2000). I am unaware of any comprehensive research assessing differences in recording practices and procedures among the Australian police services. According to the only two published studies on the topic, in 1992 in Queensland, police recorded only one-third of the incidents that came to their attention (Criminal Justice Commission 1996), and in 2001 in Victoria, 26 percent of police activities resulted in a crime record being created (Carcach and Makkai 2002). State comparisons of crime survey offenses reported to the police and recorded-crime statistics for 1998 suggest that there may be significant variations in police recording practices across both jurisdictions and types of offenses. There is evidence of a tendency toward classifying crimes at first report; however, this cannot be substantiated from data currently available.[19]

4. *Crime Survey Equivalent (CSE) Offenses Recorded by Police.*   Crime definitions in the official statistics sometimes differ from operational definitions used in crime survey questionnaires. Two standards for the classification of offenses (ANCO and ASOC) have been developed during the period covered by this essay. Appendix A in Carcach (2003) contains a summary of the definitions of offenses included in this essay as stated in the official classifications (Australian Bureau of Statistics 1997*a*).

Numbers of CSE offenses recorded by police were obtained from several sources. The Australian Bureau of Statistics (1999*c*, p. 84) published data on numbers of CSE offenses recorded during the twelve months prior to the 1998 survey. Similar data were not published for the 1983 and 1993 surveys, so indirect estimates were developed. Appendix D in Carcach (2003) details the assumptions and processes followed to obtain these estimates.

5. *Crimes Cleared and Numbers of Offenders.*   Data on numbers of crimes cleared by arrest and on numbers of distinct offenders involved in these crimes are not published by all the police services in Australia. Only Victoria and South Australia publish such data for the period covered by this essay. Data from these two states were used to obtain

---

[19] Data in Carcach (2003, app. C) show that, for burglary, robbery, and assault, New South Wales and South Australia had an above-average proportion of reported crimes that were recorded as such by police. Above-average robberies were also recorded in Victoria, whereas in Queensland police recorded an above-average proportion of reported sexual assaults. Western Australia was the only state with a below-average proportion of reported car thefts recorded by police. Above-average recording probabilities may also indicate a tendency toward classifying crimes at first report.

estimates of numbers of distinct offenders involved in each incident.[20] The average number of offenders per offense was calculated from the ratio of numbers of offenders recorded by police to the number of crimes cleared by arrest. Clearance rates were estimated using averages of published numbers of crimes cleared for the states of New South Wales (New South Wales Bureau of Crime Statistics and Research 1995–98, 1999b), Victoria (Victoria Police 1994, 1995, 1998, 1999), Queensland (Queensland Police Service 1995/96–1999/2000), Western Australia (Ferrante and Loh 1996a, 1996b; Ferrante, Loh, and Fernández 1998, 1999, 2000; Ferrante, Loh, and Maller 1998), and South Australia (South Australia Police 1994, 1995, 1998, 1999).

6. *Persons Convicted.* The term "convicted persons" applies to those who, for at least one offense charged, pled guilty or were found guilty by trial.[21]

Uniform court statistics are not available for Australia. Therefore, national estimates must be derived from state and territory court statistics. These data are not available in published form in all jurisdictions. A major problem with court data is that they do not always refer to distinct offenders or distinct offenses. In most cases, and when available, court statistics refer to court appearances. A court appearance may involve multiple offenders or multiple offenses.

Data on numbers of distinct offenders dealt with by courts and court outcomes were available for New South Wales and South Australia.[22] The conviction rates used in this analysis for the years 1993 and 1998 were averages of the New South Wales and South Australia rates, whereas the South Australia rates were used as a proxy for the national estimates during 1983.[23]

Conviction rates per 1,000 population were calculated relative to the total population aged ten years and over. This includes juvenile and

[20] For the offense of homicide, starting from 1993, data on numbers of offenders were obtained from the NHMP, whereas data prior to that year were obtained from Mukherjee and Dagger (1990).

[21] When a person faces several charges, the conviction is recorded for the most serious offense.

[22] Data for New South Wales existed over the period 1989–98, and for South Australia data were available over the period 1982–98. Data for 1983, 1993, and 1998 were used to derive estimates of persons convicted for each offense and year included in this study (Office of Crime Statistics 1984a, 1984b, 1984c, 1984d, 1994, 1999a, 1999b; New South Wales Bureau of Crime Statistics and Research 1994b, 1999b).

[23] These data were used to calculate conviction rates for each year within the two jurisdictions. The correlation coefficient between the conviction rates of New South Wales and South Australia was over 80 percent for most offenses. For homicide and assault, the correlation between the series was 57 percent.

adult convictions. Another set of conviction rates was calculated on the basis of numbers of adult convictions and total population aged eighteen years and over. This was required because offense-specific data on length of prison sentences and times served in prison were available for adults only.

7. *Persons to Imprisonment.*   Data for estimation of numbers of persons sentenced to imprisonment, both juvenile and adults, came from the same sources as data on convictions, and therefore they were affected by problems similar to those faced when estimating numbers of persons convicted. The imprisonment ratios obtained from these data were applied to the national estimates of persons convicted to derive estimates of persons sentenced to imprisonment.[24]

8. *Sentence Length and Time Served.*   Estimates of average sentence length and average time served were derived from prison census data (Australian Institute of Criminology 1983–1995; Australian Bureau of Statistics 1996–2001). The National Prison Census collects data on adults held at Australian corrective institutions on June 30 each year. No similar collection is available for persons in juvenile correctional institutions.[25] Juveniles cannot be sentenced to periods of imprisonment longer than three months; therefore, it was assumed that the average length of stay for juveniles was 1.5 months, both across offenses and over time.

Prison census data are problematic in many respects. First, they refer to the characteristics of prisoners counted on June 30 each year. Census data, therefore, do not contain information about all the persons who were admitted to, and released from, prison between census dates.

Second, prison census data are biased toward the characteristics of persons sentenced to longer periods of imprisonment. Further, census estimates of lengths of sentence and times served may overestimate the true magnitudes.

Third, sentence lengths from prison censuses refer to an average aggregate sentence, which may include periods of imprisonment for

[24] Lack of published data prevented inclusion of the states of Queensland and Western Australia, as well as the Northern Territory, in these calculations. These three jurisdictions have the highest rates of imprisonment in the country (Carcach and Grant 1999), and their exclusion can be assumed to result in underestimation of imprisonment rates and associated probabilities.

[25] No data on length of sentence and time served in prison for juveniles were available. The majority of juvenile offenders are sentenced to short periods of imprisonment. For instance, data from South Australia showed that 1,134 persons were admitted to a juvenile detention center in 1998. The average daily occupancy was 36.79 during the same year, giving an average length of detention of 30.8 days per person (Office of Crime Statistics 1999a).

several offenses. When this is the case, the estimated aggregate sentence is related to the most serious offense for which the individual is serving a period of imprisonment.

Fourth, data on the effective time served by the prisoners released during specific periods are not available from the prison census, nor are they easy to obtain from other sources. Instead, the prison census collects data on the expected time to serve for each sentenced prisoner. This variable relates to all offenses for which a person may be imprisoned; however, it is published in relation only to the most serious offense.

Despite these problems, and due to limitations with data availability, expected times to serve for prisoners counted on census night were used as a proxy for the time served by those released between census dates. Aggregate sentence was used as a proxy for sentence length of all prisoners coming through the corrections system during the periods included in this study.

B. Methodological Approach

I followed the approach in Farrington, Langan, and Wikström (1994) and Langan and Farrington (1998). The aim was to obtain estimates of three key measures for the cost of offending: the probability of arrest, the probability of conviction conditional on the event of arrest, and the probability of imprisonment conditional on arrest and conviction. According to the deterrence hypothesis, increases in these probabilities should cause crime rates to drop. Current research suggests that this may not always be the case.[26]

The criminal justice system also potentially affects crime rates by incapacitating offenders. Individuals who are convicted and sentenced to terms of imprisonment are precluded from committing further crimes. Incapacitative effects depend on factors such as rates of offending, frequency and patterns of offending, lengths of criminal careers, the probability of incarceration, and the length of incarceration (Spelman 2000). Results on the relationship between crime rates and time served in

---

[26] Criminal justice sanctions are interdependent. Arrest is not a pure sanction. When arrested, an individual faces a stochastic distribution of outcomes, which range from dismissal of charges to conviction and imprisonment. Court decisions have an effect on the relationship of risk of arrest, clearance rates, and crime rates. Prospective offenders may lack knowledge about changes in the risk of punishment. Unless information about sanctions is communicated to potential offenders, a variation in sanctions has no deterrent effect (Greenberg, Kessler, and Logan 1979).

prison are mixed, so there is no certainty that incapacitation acts to reduce crime rates (Blumstein, Cohen, and Nagin 1978).

The results presented here are subject to a number of assumptions and data adjustments. Appendix D in Carcach (2003) details calculations performed for each offense.

III. Results

Both victimization and official data document increases in robbery, serious assault, and rape between 1980 and 2000, declines in motor vehicle theft, and stability in homicide and burglary.[27] Clearance rates for most offenses declined over that period and, for most but not all offenses, the likelihood of a prison sentence and sentence lengths increased.

A. Survey Crime Rates

Crime survey data and estimates indicate that the residential burglary rate per 1,000 households declined from 118 per 1,000 in 1983 to ninety-six per 1,000 in 1994, increased up to 122 per 1,000 in 1998, and then declined to 109 per 1,000 in 2000 (fig. 1a). The motor vehicle theft rate increased by about 20 percent between 1983 and 1987, then remained relatively stable around an average twenty-two per 1,000 until 1991, when it started to drop to a stable level around seventeen per 1,000 since 1993 (fig. 1b). The number of survey serious assaults per 1,000 persons aged fifteen years and over remained relatively stable around fifteen per 1,000 between 1983 and 1993, when it started to increase until 1998. It seems to have stabilized since then at around an average twenty-five per 1,000 (fig. 1c). The robbery rate increased from four per 1,000 in 1983 to seven per 1,000 in 1998, and it has declined since then (fig. 1d). The rape rate declined until 1989, then increased until 1994, when it resumed its declining trend up to 1996, to increase again until 2000 (fig. 1e).

The correlation coefficient between the survey rates and the year was used to assess whether crimes were increasing markedly over time. A positive correlation coefficient of 0.5 or greater indicated a strong relationship. Data in Carcach (2003, table 7) indicate that serious assault ($r = 0.72$) and robbery ($r = 0.61$) increased markedly between 1983 and 2000. By contrast, motor vehicle theft declined over the same period ($r = -0.75$). The survey rates for burglary and rape did

---

[27] Refer to Carcach (2003) for details concerning the graphs and tables.

not trend strongly in any definite direction ($r = 0.18$ and $r = -0.24$, respectively).

B. Recorded Crime Rates

Trends in recorded crime rates are similar to those for survey rates (fig. 1a, b). This was confirmed by the correlation of recorded rates with time, all of which exceeded the 50 percent threshold (Carcach 2003, table 7), and the correlation coefficients between the survey and recorded rates (Carcach 2003, table 9). Rape was the only offense for which there was an apparent discrepancy between the generally parallel trends in the survey and recorded crime rates. This was due to the sharp decline in survey rates between 1994 and 1996, a year after which the survey rate resumed its increasing trend. The correlation between the rape survey and recorded rates was 0.72 prior to 1996.

C. Reporting Crime to the Police

The percentage of victims who report crimes to the police tends to remain stable over time. The police are informed about 60 percent of burglaries, 97 percent of vehicle thefts, 50 percent of robberies, and 30 percent of serious assaults and rapes (see fig. 2a–e).

D. Police Recording Crime

The probability of police recording a reported incident increased for all offenses except robbery, for which it remained stable ($r - 0.40$). The correlation of the recording probability with time was positive and greater than 50 percent for the other offenses. The highest correlation was observed for serious assault ($r = 0.93$), followed by residential burglary ($r = 0.84$), rape ($r = 0.78$), and motor vehicle theft ($r = 0.74$; Carcach 2003, table 7, fig. 2a–e).

E. Conviction Rates Relative to Population

The correlation of the number of convictions per 1,000 population with time indicates that conviction rates increased markedly for serious assault ($r = 0.92$), robbery ($r = 0.93$), and rape ($r = 0.78$); for residential burglary, they remained stable (Carcach 2003, table 7). On the other hand, conviction rates for motor vehicle theft have declined since 1983 ($r = -0.69$; Carcach 2003, fig. 3a–e, table 7).

F. Conviction Rates per Offender

Conviction rates per offender followed the same trend as conviction rates in the general population, with the exception of residential

Residential burglary

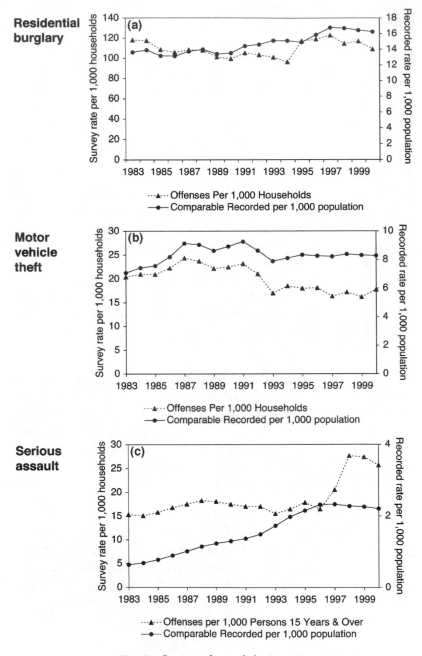

Motor vehicle theft

Serious assault

FIG. 1.—Survey and recorded crime rates

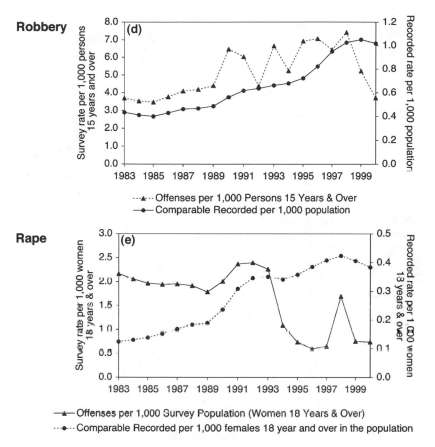

Robbery

(d)

····▲··· Offenses per 1,000 Persons 15 Years & Over
——●—— Comparable Recorded per 1,000 population

Rape

(e)

——▲—— Offenses per 1,000 Survey Population (Women 18 Years & Over)
····●··· Comparable Recorded per 1,000 females 18 year and over in the population

Fig. 1.—*Continued*

burglary, for which conviction rates per offender declined markedly ($r = -0.75$; see fig. $2a–f$). The correlation coefficients of the conviction rates per offender with time for serious assault, robbery, and rape were all positive ($r = 0.63, 0.49,$ and $0.72,$ respectively). As with conviction rates for the general population, the offender-based conviction rate of motor vehicle theft declined ($r = -0.75$; fig. 2; Carcach 2003, table 7).

G. Custody Rates Relative to Population

Custody rates followed the same trend as conviction rates in the general population, with the exception of residential burglary, for which the former increased markedly ($r = 0.51$; see fig. $2a–f$). The correlation

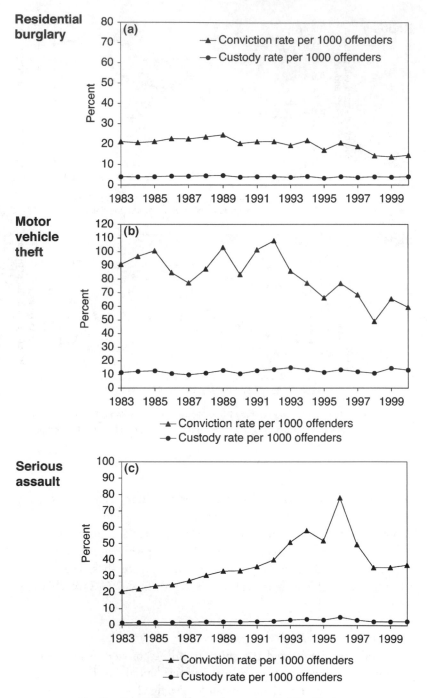

Fig. 2.—Conviction and custody rates per 1,000 offenders

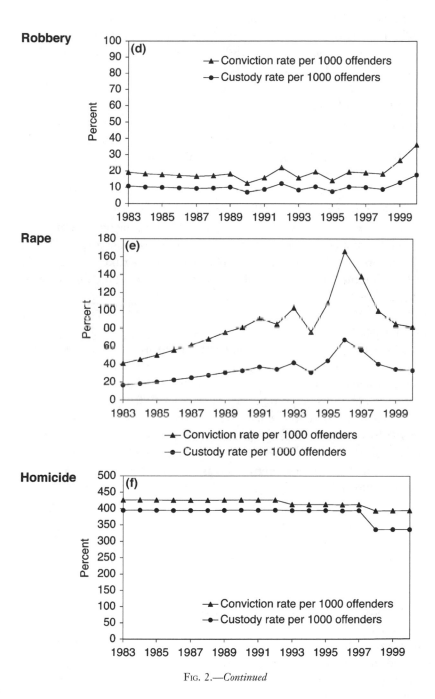

FIG. 2.—*Continued*

coefficients of the custody rates with time for serious assault, robbery, and rape were positive ($r = 0.92, 0.49$, and 0.78, respectively). The conviction rate for motor vehicle theft remained stable according to the criteria used in this study (fig. $2b$).

H. Custody Rates per Conviction

The risk of imprisonment (given conviction) increased for the offenses of residential burglary ($r = 0.68$) and motor vehicle theft ($r = 0.89$), and remained stable for the remaining offenses (refer to Carcach 2003, fig. $5a–d$, table 7).

I. Probability of an Offender Receiving a Custodial Sentence

Serious assault ($r = 0.63$) and rape ($r = 0.72$) are the only offenses for which there was an increase in the risk of a prospective offender being sentenced to a term of imprisonment over the period from 1983 to 2000. This measure shows stability over time for the remaining offenses (fig. $2a–e$).

J. Average Sentence Length

The average length of a prison sentence has increased over time for burglary ($r = 0.59$), serious assault ($r = 0.70$), and homicide ($r = 0.79$), has declined for robbery ($r = -0.72$), and has remained stable for motor vehicle theft and rape (see fig. $3a–f$; Carcach 2003, table 7). For burglary, the average sentence length increased from twenty-four months in 1983 to thirty-six months in 2000. For serious assault, the increase was from thirty-two months in 1983 to thirty-eight months in 2000. For homicide, sentence length increased from 160 to 186 months between 1986 and 2000 (fig. 3).

K. Average Time Served per Conviction

The average time served has followed a trend similar to length of sentence, except for motor vehicle theft and serious assault, for which it has remained stable ($r = -0.18$ and $r = 0.44$, respectively), and rape, for which it recorded a marked increase between 1983 and 2000 ($r = 0.85$; Carcach 2003, table 7). Time served for rape offenders sentenced to prison increased from forty to sixty-two months. An imprisoned burglar spent at least twenty-one months in prison before being released in 2000, compared to thirteen months in 1983. For homicide, time served increased from 104 months in 1983 to 132 months in 2000 (fig. 3).

L. Percentage of Sentence Served in Custody

Robbery and rape were the only offenses that recorded an increase in this measure during the period 1983–2000 ($r = 0.75$ and $r = 0.79$, respectively; Carcach 2003, table 7). Rapists served 66 percent of the sentence in custody in 2000 as compared to 47 percent in 1983. Robbers served 58 percent of the sentence in prison in 2000 as compared to 42 percent in 1983 (Carcach 2003, fig. 5a–f). The percentage time served remained stable for the other offenses.

M. Average Time Served per Conviction

The average time served per conviction increased for all offenses except robbery and serious assault (Carcach 2003, table 7). For burglary ($r = 0.78$), time served per conviction was stable between 1983 and 1994 at around thirty-seven days, increased from 1995, to reach over ninety days in 2000. Motor vehicle theft recorded step increases over the study period and rose from fifteen days in 1983 to thirty-three days in 2000. The average time served per conviction for serious assault has remained stable around an average of thirty days over the study period. For robbery, the length of time served oscillated around 410 days between 1983 and 1988, since which it has oscillated from around 340 to 350 days. Rape and homicide have both recorded increases in the average time served per conviction: for rape, from 370 days in 1983 to 527 days in 2000, an increase of 42 percent; for homicide, from 2,955 to 3,447 days, or 17 percent (Carcach 2003, fig. 7a–f).

N. Average Time Served per Offender

Average time served per offender has followed the same trend as average times served per conviction. An offender sentenced to imprisonment can expect to spend more time now than in 1983 for all offenses, except serious assault and robbery (Carcach 2003, fig. 7a–f).

IV. Explaining the Results

Trends in crime, as shown by national data, are difficult to explain, particularly in countries with a federal system of government. In Australia, national crime statistics mask significant variations within the states and territories, which sometimes cancel each other out.

Many factors can affect crime trends. These include changes in legislation that criminalize or decriminalize certain behaviors or modify police powers or modify the severity and nature of penalties; organizational and technological innovations in policing; changes to crime

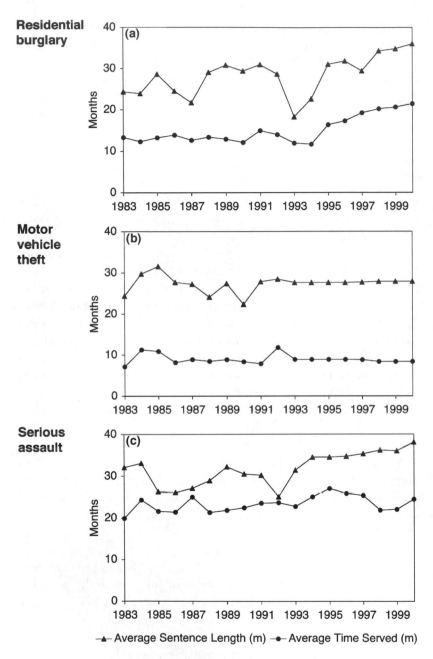

Residential burglary

Motor vehicle theft

Serious assault

-▲- Average Sentence Length (m) -●- Average Time Served (m)

Fig. 3.—Average sentence length and average time served

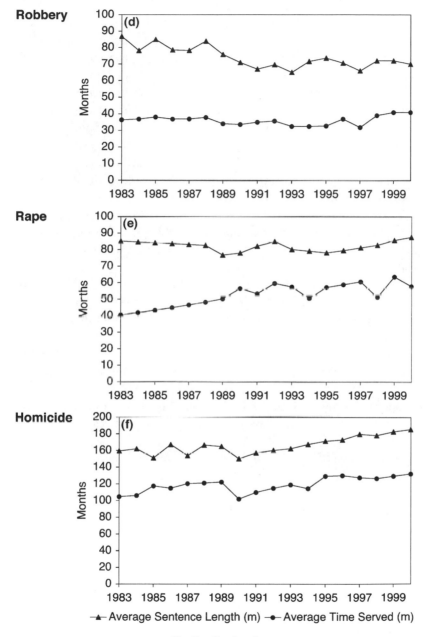

Fig. 3.—*Continued*

classifications, crime-recording policies, and crime-counting rules; and demographic and socioeconomic changes.

In a federal country, these factors may operate differently within each state or territory. Even if two states follow similar policies, crime data would still not be strictly comparable because of factors such as differences in timing and method of implementation or interpretation.

In general, changes in survey crime rates in this analysis were highly correlated with changes in recorded crime rates, either over the seventeen years spanning from 1983 to 2000 or over shorter periods. This suggests that there is relatively good agreement between crime rates as measured from police statistics and from victimization rates from crime surveys, provided that proper adjustments are made to the data to improve their comparability (refer to Carcach 2003, table 8).

The data indicate that the general trend is toward increasing crime rates for burglary, serious assault, and robbery; declining rates for motor vehicle theft; and stable rates for rape and homicide (refer to Carcach 2003, table 7).

Unlike in the United Kingdom and other developed countries, there are no recent studies on the determinants of crime rates in Australia. The only research on the topic (Mukherjee 1990) found that variables such as urbanization, unemployment, GDP per capita, and numbers of cars registered correlated well with crime rates over the period 1900–1980. At the regional level, variables such as economic transformation, accessibility to services, income inequality, residential stability, family structure, economic stress, and child neglect have been found to explain variation in Australian crime rates (Carcach 2001; Weatherburn and Lind 2001).

It is impossible to control for all factors underlying national crime rates without using proper econometric or statistical methods, and any attempt simply to correlate these rates with socioeconomic variables may result in spurious relationships. Data aggregation imposes additional constraints to performing any analysis aimed at uncovering the socioeconomic drivers of the crime rates discussed in this study.

Survey data findings generally support the views of authors like Indermaur (1995, 2000) that crime in Australia has remained stable over the recent past. This holds for motor vehicle theft and homicide but not for burglary, robbery, assault, and rape. Burglary has increased, but the component measured by crime surveys (i.e., residential burglary) remained stable between 1983 and 1998. The upward trend in total burglary has been driven by increases in burglaries on nonresidential premises. Personal robbery has remained stable over the fifteen years covered by this analysis, but robberies perpetrated on organizations seem to have increased (Mouzos and Carcach 2001).

Assault and rape are the two offenses for which the trends from victim surveys and data do not seem to be consistent, with the most likely reality being an increase over time. Before 1993, the survey rate for serious assault was stable, but the recorded crime rate increased. From 1994 onward, this pattern reversed; the survey rate increased, and the recorded crime rate stabilized. For rape, both the survey rate and the recorded crime rate followed a similar upward trend until 1993, the year after which the survey rate dropped sharply and then stabilized. However, the recorded crime rate continued to increase.

National crime rates based on crime surveys or on official counts of recorded crime are subject to large variation over time and across spatial entities. As an example of this, data from the 1998 National Crime and Safety Survey show rates of residential burglary varying between fifty-three per 1,000 households in Victoria and 124 per 1,000 households in Western Australia.

At the regional level, in Victoria, the rate of residential burglary ranged from twenty-six per 1,000 in Goulburn-Ovens-Murray and North-Eastern Melbourne to 110 per 1,000 in North-Western Melbourne. In Western Australia, the rate varied between ninety-six per 1,000 in lower Western Australia and 136 in the Central Metropolitan Region (Australian Bureau of Statistics 1999b).

Regional data on police-recorded crime show that national crime rates have high variances, which suggests that any observed difference in recorded crime rates may not appear as statistically significant.[28] Differences in police recording practices and procedures are other sources of local variation in police-recorded crime rates. The magnitude of such variation cannot be assessed with the data used in this analysis.[29]

National crime data from surveys or official statistics mask an important reality: crime is unevenly distributed among regions within a country, among localities within regions, and among individuals in

[28] Local-area data on police-recorded crime for the 1994–98 period held at the Australian Institute of Criminology show that crime rates have large coefficients of variation. Coefficients of variation for the rates of burglary, robbery, and vehicle theft were 96 percent, 700 percent, and 383 percent, respectively.

[29] Burrows et al. (2000) found that, in the United Kingdom, 47 percent of crime allegations were recorded as crimes but that this varies across police forces, from a low of 33 percent to a high of 55 percent. Similar data are not available in Australia.

different socioeconomic groups. Studies based on national data are often unsuccessful in controlling for the effects that factors associated with crime, delinquency, and victimization have on aggregate crime rates. The causes of crime are multidimensional and include biological factors, family factors, schooling-related factors, relational networks, poverty and unemployment, substance abuse, public attitudes toward crime, criminal opportunities, weak informal social controls, police activity, levels of punishment, and economic fluctuations (Weatherburn 2001).

Australian homicide rates exhibit remarkable stability. This is due to the small number of homicides in Australia (the rate has never exceeded 2.5 per 100,000 population). The distribution of homicides by type has remained stable over the ten-year period 1988–98.[30] There has been a decline in the number of homicides committed with firearms, but this has been counterbalanced by an increase in the use of knives and other sharp instruments (Mouzos 2000).

It is difficult to identify the myriad of factors underlying victims' reporting behavior. Depending on the type of crime, higher reporting rates can be associated with increases in the seriousness of offenses or more offenses involving offenders known to victims. Increases in crimes reported to police may reflect less tolerance of crime in the community, increased concern that crime is on the rise, or improved perceptions of police performance. The influence of these factors varies across regions and social groups. It is impossible to identify which factors drove the reporting behavior of victims during the 1983–98 period.

Clearance rates in 1998 were lower than in 1983 for all the offenses. Research shows that, in general, clearance rates are negatively associated with crime rates and relative size of police forces (Phillips 1978; Vandaele 1978; Carr-Hill and Stern 1979; Gyimah-Brempong 1986).

Changes in crime and punishment are no doubt related to social and economic conditions. Does the sustained economic growth experienced by the Australian economy during the 1990s explain the observed stability in crime rates? In what ways does this stability relate to the many factors in the literature? Lack of appropriate data prevented examination of these issues.

---

[30] Intimate-partner homicides account for 23 percent of total homicides, and family homicides contribute around 12 percent to total homicides. There has been a decline in stranger homicide at the expense of an increase in homicides involving friends and acquaintances.

V. Conclusion

This essay provides national estimates for the flow of offenders through the Australian criminal justice system, from the commission of crimes through police recording and conviction to imprisonment, for six offenses and for the period 1983–2000. Despite being the best source of comparable statistics across states and territories, available crime survey data in Australia are not adequate to perform comparisons over time, in particular due to lack of consistency in methodology and changes to the wording of questions across surveys.

Trends in crime survey data are not always consistent with trends in crime recorded by police. This essay has identified differences in the crime definitions used in national crime surveys and those used in the development of statistical collections as a factor likely to explain discrepancies between these sources.

Due to the presence of sampling error, incidence rates estimated from different crime surveys are not statistically different. The same occurs with estimates of the proportion of crimes reported to the police. In the cases of residential burglary and motor vehicle theft, police statistics suggest that incidence rates remained stable over the last twenty years.

For robbery, assault, and rape, crime survey estimates are at odds with the trends in recorded-crime statistics. My analysis suggests that the incidence of these offenses increased between 1983 and 1998, given the relatively large increases in the rates of crimes recorded by police.

Homicide is an offense for which problems of simultaneously dealing with survey and recorded crime data are not present. The incidence of homicide remained stable over the 1983–98 period.

Crime rates are primarily the outcome of offender decision making. A stable crime rate results from stability in the number of active offenders or in the number of crimes committed by offenders during a given period of time, or both. Consequently, increases in crime rates can reflect an increase in the pool of active offenders or in the activity rate of these offenders, or both. The supply of offenders is affected by the supply of opportunities to offend.

The decisions made within each of the interconnected (but autonomous) components of the criminal justice system may have different effects on the achievement of the goals of reducing opportunities for crime, incapacitating active offenders, and deterring offending among the crime free. Measurement of these effects requires access to uniform crime statistics across all the components of the criminal justice system.

In Australia, uniform statistics on recorded crime have been collected only since 1993. Correctional statistics are limited to annual inmate counts from the prison census (available since 1982) and monthly statistics on average daily numbers of prisoners and sentenced admissions (available since 1977). Data on released prisoners and data on times served are not readily available. National court statistics are practically nonexistent apart from a limited collection on higher courts. All these limitations with existing national data systems make it difficult to study the flow of offenders through the criminal justice system in order to answer questions relative to crime and punishment.

Underlying analyses of flows of offenders through the criminal justice system in relation to the probability of conviction and punishment is the notion that individuals weigh the costs and benefits of engaging in criminal behavior. This translates into rational judgments about the risk of offending. This essay used three indicators for the risk of offending. The probability of apprehension, in particular apprehension by arrest, is one measure of the risk of offending (Becker 1968; Ehrlich 1973). The clearance rate is used as a proxy for the risk of arrest. Clearance rates have declined across all offenses between 1983 and 1998. The exact nature of observed changes in clearance rates over time is a topic requiring further research.

The other two indicators relate to the overall risk of offending. One is the average time served in prison per convicted offender. This measure is calculated conditional on a criminal being arrested, then convicted, and, finally, sentenced to a term of imprisonment. The other is the average time served per offense, which measures risk of crime for any offender, whether processed by the criminal justice system or not.

In general, the most serious crimes of homicide and serious assault, together with burglary and motor vehicle theft, experienced increased risks of punishment. For the offenses of robbery and rape, the overall risk of punishment has not changed between 1983 and 1998.

Given the lack of knowledge about variation in outcomes and severity of the criminal justice system, potential criminals might perceive that the risks of punishment following offending are low. However, little is known in Australia about offending behavior, decision making, and criminal careers. Enhancing knowledge on these issues is crucial to the conduct of research on the deterrent and incapacitative effects of the criminal justice system.

At a more fundamental level, the main purpose of a criminal justice system is not to punish those who transgress the law but to deliver justice. In the same way, to the eyes of citizens, the purpose of police is not to arrest more criminals but to enhance community safety. More police do not necessarily produce more arrests or lower crime rates. Identifying and understanding factors that drive perceptions of public safety is the key to the developing cost-efficient alternatives to increasing police expenditure.

The lack of comprehensive uniform statistics has negative consequences for research on crime and justice. There is the need to develop integrated statistical collections to gather data across the whole criminal justice system and over time. Ideally, these collections should use longitudinal or panel designs to enable the study of interrelationships between the different components of the criminal justice system and the testing of causal theories of crime and punishment.

APPENDIX A

Data Sources

Data used in this study came from the following sources:

1. *Crime Victimization.* National crime victim surveys conducted in 1983, 1993, and 1998 (Australian Bureau of Statistics 1986, 1994a, 1999b, 1999c). Crime victim surveys conducted annually in New South Wales in 1990–92, 1994–97, and 1999–2000 (Australian Bureau of Statistics 1991–2001).

2. *Recorded Crime.* Data for 1983 were obtained from Mukherjee and Dagger (1990). Data for 1993 and 1998 were obtained from annual reports published by police services, except for New South Wales, for which data are published by the New South Wales Bureau of Crime Statistics and Research (1994b, 1999b).

3. *Crimes Reported to Police.* National crime victim surveys conducted in 1983, 1993, and 1998 (Australian Bureau of Statistics 1986, 1994a, 1999a, 1999c) and official crime statistics as specified in item 2 above.

4. *Population Data.* Estimated resident population on June 30 of each year (Australian Bureau of Statistics 1994b, 2000b).

5. *Cleared Offenses.* Derived from official crime statistics published in the states (refer to text for an explanation of the process followed to derive these data).

6. *Convictions and Imprisonment Sentences.* Court statistics published in New South Wales (New South Wales Bureau of Crime Statistics and Research 1994a, 1999a) and South Australia (Office of Crime Statistics 1984a, 1984b, 1984c, 1984d, 1994, 1999a, 1999b). (Refer to the text for an explanation of the process followed to derive these data.)

7. *Length of Sentence and Time Served.* National Prison Census (Australian Institute of Criminology 1983–95; Australian Bureau of Statistics 1996–2001).

8. *Homicide Data.* Australian Institute of Criminology, National Homicide Monitoring Program (Unit Record File).

REFERENCES

Australian Bureau of Statistics. 1986. *Victims of Crime, Australia, 1983.* Canberra: Australian Bureau of Statistics.

———. 1991–2001. *Crime and Safety, New South Wales, April.* Sydney: Australian Bureau of Statistics.

———. 1994*a*. *Crime and Safety, Australia, April 1993.* Canberra: Australian Bureau of Statistics.

———. 1994*b*. *Estimated Resident Population by Sex and Age, States and Territories of Australia, June 1992 to Preliminary June 1997.* Canberra: Australian Bureau of Statistics.

———. 1994*c*. *National Crime Statistics, January to December, 1993.* Canberra: Australian Bureau of Statistics.

———. 1995. *National Crime Statistics, January to December, 1994.* Canberra: Australian Bureau of Statistics.

———. 1996–2001. *Prisoners in Australia.* Canberra: Australian Bureau of Statistics.

———. 1997*a*. *Australian Standard Offence Classification, 1997.* Canberra: Australian Bureau of Statistics.

———. 1997*b*. *Recorded Crime Australia, 1996.* Canberra: Australian Bureau of Statistics.

———. 1998. *Recorded Crime, Australia, 1997.* Canberra: Australian Bureau of Statistics.

———. 1999*a*. *Crime and Safety, Australia, April 1998.* Canberra: Australian Bureau of Statistics.

———. 1999*b*. *Crime and Safety: Supplementary National and Standard Tables, Australia, 1998.* Canberra: Australian Bureau of Statistics.

———. 1999*c*. *Recorded Crime, Australia, 1998.* Canberra: Australian Bureau of Statistics.

———. 2000*a*. *Australian Social Trends, 2000.* Canberra: Australian Bureau of Statistics.

———. 2000*b*. *Estimated Resident Population by Sex and Age, States and Territories of Australia, June 1998 to Preliminary June 1999.* Canberra: Australian Bureau of Statistics.

———. 2000*c*. *Recorded Crime, Australia, 1999.* Canberra: Australian Bureau of Statistics.

———. 2001. *Recorded Crime, Australia, 2000.* Canberra: Australian Bureau of Statistics.

———. 2002. *2002 Year Book, Australia.* Canberra: Australian Bureau of Statistics.

Australian Institute of Criminology. 1983–95. *Australian Prisoners.* Canberra: Australian Institute of Criminology.

———. 2000. *Composition of Australia Police Services.* Canberra: Australian Institute of Criminology.

Becker, Gary S. 1968. "Crime and Punishment: An Economic Approach." *Journal of Political Economy* 78:169–217.

Blumstein, Alfred, Jacqueline Cohen, and Daniel Nagin, eds. 1978. *Deterrence and Incapacitation: Estimating the Effects of Criminal Sanctions on Crime Rates.*

Panel on Research on Deterrent and Incapacitative Effects. Washington, D.C.: National Academy of Sciences.

Brereton, David. 2000. "Policing and Crime Prevention: Improving the Product." In *Crime and the Criminal Justice System in Australia: 2000 and Beyond*, edited by Duncan Chappell and Paul Wilson. Sydney: Butterworths.

Burrows, John, Roger Tarling, Alan Mackie, Rachel Lewis, and Geoff Taylor. 2000. *Review of Police Forces' Crime Recording Practices*. Research Study no. 204. London: Home Office, Research, Development, and Statistics Directorate.

Carcach, Carlos. 1997. *Reporting Crime to the Police*. Trends and Issues in Crime and Criminal Justice, no. 68. Canberra: Australian Institute of Criminology.

———. 2001. *Regional Variation in Crime*. Paper presented at the fifty-third annual meeting of the American Society of Criminology, Atlanta, Georgia, November 7–10, 2001.

———. 2003. "Australia." In *Cross-National Studies in Crime and Justice*, edited by David P. Farrington, Patrick A. Langan, and Michael Tonry. Washington, D.C.: Bureau of Justice Statistics.

Carcach, Carlos, and Anna Grant. 1999. *Imprisonment in Australia: Trends in Prison Populations and Imprisonment Rates, 1982–1998*. Trends and Issues in Crime and Criminal Justice, no. 130. Canberra: Australian Institute of Criminology.

Carcach, Carlos, and Toni Makkai. 2002. *Review of Victoria Police Crime Statistics*. Research and Public Policy Series, no. 45. Canberra: Australian Institute of Criminology.

———. 2003. *The Australian Component of the 2000 International Crime Victim Survey (ICVS)*. Technical and Background Series Paper, no. 3. Canberra: Australian Institute of Criminology.

Carr-Hill, R. A., and N. H. Stern. 1979. *Crime, the Police, and Criminal Statistics: An Analysis of Official Statistics in England and Wales Using Econometric Methods*. London: Academic.

Criminal Justice Commission. 1996. *The General Nature of Police Work*. Research Paper Series, vol. 3, no. 2. Brisbane: Criminal Justice Commission.

Ehrlich, Issac. 1973. "Participation in Illegitimate Activities: A Theoretical and Empirical Investigation." *Journal of Political Economy* 81:521–65.

Fairall, Paul. 2000, "The Reform of the Criminal Law." In *Crime and the Criminal Justice System in Australia: 2000 and Beyond*, edited by Duncan Chappell and Paul Wilson. Sydney: Butterworths.

Farrington, David P., Patrick A. Langan, and Per-Olof H. Wikström. 1994. "Changes in Crime and Punishment in America, England, and Sweden between the 1980s and the 1990s." *Studies on Crime and Crime Prevention* 3:104–31.

Ferrante, Anna, and Nini Loh. 1996a. *Crime and Justice Statistics for Western Australia, 1994*. Statistical Reports. Perth: University of Western Australia, Crime Research Centre.

———. 1996b. *Crime and Justice Statistics for Western Australia, 1995*. Statistical Reports. Perth: University of Western Australia, Crime Research Centre.

Ferrante, Anna, Nini Loh, and John Fernández. 1998. *Crime and Justice Statistics for Western Australia, 1997*. Statistical Reports. Perth: University of Western Australia, Crime Research Centre.

———. 1999. *Crime and Justice Statistics for Western Australia, 1998*. Statistical Reports. Perth: University of Western Australia, Crime Research Centre.

———. 2000. *Crime and Justice Statistics for Western Australia, 1999*. Statistical Reports. Perth: University of Western Australia, Crime Research Centre.

Ferrante, Anna, Nini Loh, and Max Maller. 1998. *Crime and Justice Statistics for Western Australia, 1996*. Statistical Reports. Perth: University of Western Australia, Crime Research Centre.

Fox, Richard. 1995. "On Punishing Infringements." In *Sentencing: Some Key Issues*, edited by Andros Kapardis. Melbourne: La Trobe University Press.

Freiberg, Arie, and Richard Fox. 1994. *Enforcement of Fines and Monetary Penalties*. Working Paper no. 16. Canberra: National Road Transport Commission.

Greenberg, David F., Ronald C. Kessler, and Charles L. Logan. 1979. "A Panel Model of Crime Rates and Arrest Rates." *American Sociological Review* 44:843–50.

Gyimah-Brempong, Kwabena. 1986. "Production of Public Safety: Are Socioeconomic Characteristics of Local Communities Important Factors?" *Journal of Applied Econometrics* 4:57–71.

Indermaur, David. 1995. "Are We Becoming More Violent? A Comparison of Trends in Violent and Property Crime in Australia and Western Australia." *Journal of Quantitative Criminology* 11:247–70.

———. 2000. "Violent Crime in Australia, Patterns, and Politics." *Australian and New Zealand Journal of Criminology* 33:213–29.

James, Marianne, and Carlos Carcach. 1997. *Homicide in Australia, 1989–96*. Research and Public Policy Series, no. 13. Griffith, ACT: Australian Institute of Criminology.

Kesteren, John van, Pat Mayhew, and Paul Nieuwbeerta. 2001. *Criminal Victimisation in Seventeen Industrialised Countries: Key Findings from the 2000 International Crime Victims Survey*. Onderzoek en beleid, no. 187. The Hague: Ministry of Justice, Wetenschappelijk Onderzoek- en Documentatie Centrum.

Langan, Patrick A., and David P. Farrington. 1998. *Crime and Justice in the United States and in England and Wales, 1981–96*. Washington, D.C.: United States Department of Justice, Office of Justice Programs, Bureau of Justice Statistics.

Mouzos, Jenny. 2000. *Homicidal Encounters: A Study of Homicide in Australia 1989–1999*. Research and Public Policy Series, no. 28. Canberra: Australian Institute of Criminology.

Mouzos, Jenny, and Carlos Carcach. 2001. *Weapon Involvement in Armed Robbery*. Research and Public Policy Series, no. 38. Canberra: Australian Institute of Criminology.

Mukherjee, Satyanshu K. 1990. *Crime Trends in Twentieth-Century Australia*. Sydney: Allen & Unwin.

Mukherjee, Satyanshu K., and Dianne Dagger. 1990. *The Size of the Crime Problem in Australia*. 2d ed. Canberra: Australian Institute of Criminology.

New South Wales Bureau of Crime Statistics and Research. 1994a. *New South Wales Criminal Court Statistics, 1993.* Statistical Report Series. Sydney: New South Wales Bureau of Crime Statistics and Research.

———. 1994b. *New South Wales Recorded Crime Statistics, 1993.* Statistical Report Series. Sydney: New South Wales Bureau of Crime Statistics and Research.

———. 1995–98. *New South Wales Recorded Crime Statistics, 1995–1998.* Local Government Area Supplementary Tables. Sydney: New South Wales Bureau of Crime Statistics and Research.

———. 1999a. *New South Wales Criminal Court Statistics, 1998.* Statistical Report Series. Sydney: New South Wales Bureau of Crime Statistics and Research.

———. 1999b. *New South Wales Recorded Crime Statistics, 1998.* Statistical Report Series. Sydney: New South Wales Bureau of Crime Statistics and Research.

Office of Crime Statistics. 1984a. *Courts of Summary Jurisdiction, 1 January–30 June 1983.* Series A, Crime and Justice, no. 9. Adelaide: Department of the Attorney General.

———. 1984b. *Courts of Summary Jurisdiction, 1 June–31 December 1983.* Series A, Crime and Justice, no. 10. Adelaide: Department of the Attorney General.

———. 1984c. *Crime and Justice in South Australia, 1 January–30 June 1983.* Series A, Crime and Justice, no. 4. Adelaide: Department of the Attorney General.

———. 1984d. *Crime and Justice in South Australia, 1 June–31 December 1983.* Series A, Crime and Justice, no. 6. Adelaide: Department of the Attorney General.

———. 1994. *Crime and Justice in South Australia 1994.* Series A, Crime and Justice, no. 30. Adelaide: Department of the Attorney General.

———. 1999a. *Crime and Justice in South Australia 1998: Juvenile Justice.* Series A, Crime and Justice, no. 35. Adelaide: Department of the Attorney General.

———. 1999b. *Crime and Justice in South Australia 1998: Police, Adult Courts and Corrections.* Series A, Crime and Justice, no. 34. Adelaide: Department of the Attorney General.

Phillips, Lliad. 1978. "Factor Demand in the Provision of Public Safety." In *Economic Models of Criminal Behaviour,* edited by J. M. Heincke. Amsterdam: North Holland.

Queensland Police Service. 1995/96–1999/2000. *Annual Statistical Review.* Brisbane: Queensland Police Services.

South Australia Police. 1994. *South Australia Police Annual Report, 1992–93: Statistical Review Supplement.* Adelaide: South Australia Police.

———. 1995. *South Australia Police Annual Report, 1993–94: Statistical Review Supplement.* Adelaide: South Australia Police.

———. 1998. *South Australia Police Annual Report, 1996–97: Statistical Review Supplement.* Adelaide: South Australia Police.

———. 1999. *South Australia Police Annual Report, 1998–99: Statistical Review Supplement.* Adelaide: South Australia Police.

Spelman, William. 2000. "What Recent Studies Do (and Don't) Tell Us about Imprisonment and Crime." In *Crime and Justice: A Review of Research,* vol. 27, edited by Michael Tonry. Chicago: University of Chicago Press.

Steering Committee for the Review of Commonwealth/State Service. 1999. *Report on Government Services Provision.* Melbourne: Productivity Commission.

——. 2002. *Report on Government Services Provision.* Melbourne: Productivity Commission.

Urbas, Gregor. 2000. *The Age of Criminal Responsibility.* Trends and Issues in Crime and Criminal Justice, no. 181. Canberra: Australian Institute of Criminology.

Vandaele, Walter. 1978. "An Econometric Model of Auto Theft in the United States." In *Economic Models of Criminal Behavior,* edited by J. M. Heineke. Amsterdam: North Holland.

Victoria Police. 1994. *Crime Statistics, 1992–93.* Melbourne: Victoria Police.

——. 1995. *Crime Statistics, 1993–94.* Melbourne: Victoria Police.

——. 1998. *Crime Statistics, 1997–98.* Melbourne: Victoria Police.

——. 1999. *Crime Statistics, 1998–99.* Melbourne: Victoria Police.

Weatherburn, Don. 2001. *What Causes Crime?* Crime and Justice Bulletin, no. 54. Sydney: New South Wales Bureau of Crime Statistics and Research.

Weatherburn, Don, and Bronwyn Lind. 2001. *Delinquent-Prone Communities.* Cambridge: Cambridge University Press.

Willis, John. 2000, "The Processing of Cases in the Criminal Justice System." In *Crime and the Criminal Justice System in Australia: 2000 and Beyond,* edited by Duncan Chappell and Paul Wilson. Sydney: Butterworths.

Zdenkowski, George. 2000. "Sentencing Trends: Past, Present and Prospective." In *Crime and the Criminal Justice System in Australia: 2000 and Beyond,* edited by Duncan Chappell and Paul Wilson. Sydney: Butterworths.

Philip J. Cook and Nataliya Khmilevska

Cross-National Patterns in Crime Rates

This volume contains detailed reports on crime and punishment for six types of crime in each of seven nations. The nations were selected by the criterion that during the period 1981–89 they all had conducted several representative national crime-victimization surveys, which provide the basis for comparison of time trends in survey data with time trends in official recorded data. Sweden, not among the seven nations but also meeting this criterion, was included in an earlier publication stemming from this project (Farrington, Langan, and Tonry 2004); in this essay, we include Sweden in some comparisons. Five of the nations are English-speaking and are, or were at one time, British (England and Wales, Scotland, the United States, Canada, and Australia); the remainder are Western European (the Netherlands, Sweden, and Switzerland). These nations have in common that they are part of the "first world" of wealthy countries with stable governance and similarly advanced technological infrastructure. But they have substantial differences with respect to criminal codes and administrative procedures for recording data on crime and punishment. Considerable effort was devoted by the authors of the studies included in this volume to adjust available data to make them as comparable as possible. Here we use these data to explore crime patterns across the nations and over time, based on both recorded data and survey data, and to take some modest steps toward explaining the observed patterns.

Philip J. Cook is ITT/Sanford Professor of Public Policy at Duke University in Durham, North Carolina. Nataliya Khmilevska is a doctoral student in the Duke University Department of Economics.

We begin by summarizing some of the cross-national patterns in recorded crime rates and comparing the recorded rates with survey-based estimates, which often differ dramatically not only in level but also in trend. We then sketch a possible analytical use of multinational trend data; comparisons between closely related pairs of nations (England and Scotland, Canada and the United States) may be helpful in ruling out some explanations for observed trends. Subsequently we present evidence relevant to the deterrent effects of punishment, comparing trends in crime rates to trends in the relative frequency of custodial sentences. A brief conclusion sums up these exercises.

I. Changes in Crime Rates

Crime data were provided for each nation. In each case, considerable effort was devoted to adjusting available statistics to bring them into line with a set of standard definitions. These definitions are given in the earlier publication from this project (Farrington, Langan, and Tonry 2004).

Tables 1 and 2 provide summary statistics for the recorded crime rates. Table 1 is devoted to the violent crimes of homicide, assault, and

TABLE 1

Crimes of Violence: Growth in Recorded Crime
Rates per 1,000 Population, Eight Nations

Nation	Rate in Last Year			Percentage Change, First Year to Last		
	Homicide	Assault	Rape	Homicide	Assault	Rape
England and Wales (1981, 1999)	.014	4.2	.29	57	111	588
Scotland (1981, 1999)	.023	11.9	.28	31	93	145
Australia (1983, 2000)	.017	1.9	.39	−15	280	115
Canada (1981, 1998)	.018	1.3	. . .	−31	18	. . .
United States (1981, 1999)	.057	3.4	.64	−42	16	−10
Netherlands (1980, 1999)	.015	2.7	.22	12	176	98
Sweden (1980, 1998)	.019	5.5	.37	36	100	85
Switzerland (1985, 1999)	.011	1.9	.23	−21	73	−5

SOURCE.—Farrington, Langan, and Tonry 2004.

TABLE 2

Property Crimes: Growth in Recorded
Crime Rates, Eight Nations

Nation	Rate in Last Year per 1,000 Population			Percentage Change, First Year to Last		
	Burglary	MVT	Robbery	Burglary	MVT	Robbery
England and Wales						
(1981, 1999)	8.6	8.6	1.5	22	7	266
Scotland						
(1981, 1999)	10.5	5.8	1.0	−43	−7	22
Australia						
(1983, 2000)	22.8	7.3	1.2	43	24	300
Canada						
(1981, 1999)	6.5	5.3	.9	−25	36	−18
United States						
(1981, 1999)	5.2	4.2	1.5	−53	−11	−42
Netherlands						
(1980, 1999)	5.9	1.9	1.1	127	90	270
Sweden						
(1980, 1998)	3.5	6.3	.7	−5	46	85
Switzerland						
(1985, 1999)	3.8	11.0	.5	46	−32	48

SOURCE.—Farrington, Langan, and Tonry 2004.
NOTE.—MVT = Motor vehicle theft.

rape, and table 2 to the property crimes of burglary, motor vehicle theft, and robbery. (Robbery, a violent crime and a property crime, is classified with the latter group as a convenience in balancing the sizes of the two tables.) In each table the first three data columns display the recorded rate in the most recent available year (1998, 1999, or 2000), while the remaining three columns display the percentage growth from the first available year (early 1980s).

These data tell a story of remarkable diversity. For each type of crime the highest rate exceeds the lowest by a factor of five or more. The highest rates are usually outliers, more than twice the second highest for homicide (where the United States rate is highest), assault (Scotland), and burglary (Australia). A wide range of crime rates is not a new phenomenon but rather is characteristic of the eight nations throughout the two decades under observation.

We also find wide diversity in growth rates over this period. The most muted changes are for homicide, which range from a reduction of

42 percent (United States) to an increase of 36 percent (Sweden). Recorded assaults increased in all countries, and in half of them had more than doubled by the late 1990s. Robbery also exhibited large increases in three countries (England, the Netherlands, and Australia).

Comparing the overall experience of the eight countries, it appears from these recorded data that the United States enjoyed the most favorable trends, placing first or second in every crime category when the countries are ranked from lowest (or most negative) to highest growth rate. Canada was in the top three in all but motor vehicle theft. At the other end of the spectrum, we see that England ranked in the bottom (least favorable) three for each of the violent crimes, including robbery. Australia had the worst performance of all eight for assault and robbery, while the Netherlands fared worst for burglary and motor vehicle theft.

The trends and general volatility in rates of recorded crime may be due in part to changes in administrative procedures and practices by law-enforcement agencies for compiling the crime statistics. Survey-based estimates provide an alternative look at levels and trends for these countries. Table 3 provides a summary of the survey results for four of the six crime types. (Homicide is not included in victimization surveys for obvious reasons, and rape is not included in most surveys, perhaps because it is too rare to be accurately estimated.) It turns out that the survey estimates are several times higher than the recorded estimates and sometimes exhibit quite different trends.

The "Ratio" column of table 3 reports the ratio of the average survey-based estimate over all years in which survey data are available to the average recorded rate for the same years, for each country and crime type. The survey estimates are at least twice the recorded figure (with one exception) and are an order of magnitude higher for assault and robbery in some nations. Among the four crime types, motor vehicle theft appears to have the lowest ratio, which is to say the highest percentage of crimes recorded by the police.

The fact that survey estimates of crime rates are higher than rates indicated by police records is no surprise. Crimes may be missing from the official statistics because they are never reported to the authorities or because the authorities fail to record them in crime reports. On the other hand, survey estimates may be inflated: respondents may tend to report crimes to the interviewers that did not occur during the reference period, a phenomenon called "telescoping." To help the respondent place events in time, the U.S. National Crime Victimization

TABLE 3

Comparison of Survey and Recorded Crime Data, Eight Nations

Crime Type by Country	Range	No. of Data Points	Growth (Percent) Survey Data	Growth (Percent) Recorded Data	Correlation	Ratio
Assault:						
England and Wales	1981–99	8	7	111	.68	4.5
Scotland	1981–99	5	21	93	.23	4.3
Australia	1983–2000	9	67	280	.74	14.9
Canada	1987–98	3	−25	8	−.08	9.6
United States	1981–99	19	−44	16	0	2.8
Netherlands	1980–99	20	−15	176	−.18	6.3
Sweden	1980–98	19	36	100	.77	8.0
Switzerland	1985–99	5	144	73	.63	18.2
Burglary:						
England and Wales	1981–99	8	38	22	.91	6.3
Scotland	1981–99	5	2	−43	.74	2.8
Australia	1983–2000	9	−8	43	−.10	5.5
Canada	1981–98	4	40	16	.51	7.4
United States	1981–99	19	−68	−53	.98	8.2
Netherlands	1980–99	20	4	127	.49	8.9
Sweden	1980–98	19	19	−5	.23	9.9
Switzerland	1985–99	5	29	46	.96	3.3
Motor vehicle theft:						
England and Wales	1981–99	8	−4	7	.97	2.3
Scotland	1981–99	5	−43	−7	.61	1.9
Australia	1983–2000	9	−13	24	.34	2.8
Canada	1981–98	4	55	11	.67	3.7
United States	1981–99	19	−29	−11	.87	2.0
Netherlands	1980–99	20	−33	90	−.28	6.0
Sweden	1980–98	19	109	46	.91	8.3
Switzerland	1988–99	4	−77	−30	.83	3.3
Robbery:						
England and Wales	1981–99	8	95	266	.95	6.1
Scotland	1981–99	5	61	22	0	3.6
Australia	1983–2000	9	0	300	.43	7.9
Canada	1981–98	4	2	−9	−.81	9.7
United States	1981–99	19	−51	−42	.82	2.5
Netherlands	1980–99	20	25	270	−.34	14.8
Sweden	1980–98	19	NA	85	NA	9.0
Switzerland	1985–99	5	41	48	.25	14.2

Source.—Farrington, Langan, and Tonry 2004.

Note.—NA = not available. Only one of the Swedish crime surveys during this period included robbery.

Survey (NCVS) interviews the same households every six months over seven cycles, encouraging the respondent to use the previous interview as a cognitive bracket for the survey reference period. The NCVS practice is to throw out the results of the first interview since it lacks this bracket. But other nations do not use this costly procedure for creating a bracket and hence may have more telescoping. (We note in this regard that for two of the four crimes, the United States has the lowest ratio of survey-to-recorded crime, and it is close to the lowest for a third.)

A more disturbing result from the comparisons in table 3 is the large difference in trends. It is logically possible for the recorded crime rate to be a fraction of the true crime rate each year but still provide an accurate indication of trend—so long as that fraction remains constant over time. This possibility is not realized in practice. Recorded data and survey-based data often exhibit very different growth rates. Among the notable disparities are Netherlands for assault (survey, −15 percent; recorded, +176 percent) and Australia for robbery (survey, 0 percent; recorded, +300 percent). Still, it should be said that the intertemporal correlation between recorded and survey data exceeds 0.5 in a majority of cases. Comparing countries, we see that the United States has high positive correlations for three of the four crimes (the notable exception being assault), while the correlations for England are high for all four crimes.

There is no clear conclusion from these comparisons about whether the survey data or recorded data are more reliable for estimating trends or even levels in crime. Both sources are flawed but for entirely different reasons. As a result, it may be reasonable to conclude that when the two sources of information do tell the same story (such as the sharp decline in burglary rates in the United States or the large increase in Canadian motor vehicle theft rates), then there is a good chance that that story is true.

II. Possible Explanations

The data that have been assembled and refined for this volume have several evident uses. One is simply to compare the nations in terms of levels and growth in crime. The comparisons then suggest questions that might not otherwise arise. For example, why does the United States have such a high homicide rate, especially given that its rate of assaults (which, in a sense, are potential homicides) is nothing out of the ordinary? What is it about Australia that produces such a (relatively) high burglary rate? What accounts for the near tripling of the robbery rate in England during a period when Scotland's rate remained relatively flat?

A second use of these data is to provide an empirical basis for answering such questions. There are a wide variety of factors thought to affect crime rates and trends. A systematic comparison of nations with respect to these causal factors and crime-rate outcomes may provide, if not clear answers, at least some limits to the array of plausible answers (Cook and Laub 2002). The difficulty of the task is suggested by James Q. Wilson: "Social scientists have made great gains in explaining why some people are more likely than others to commit crimes but far smaller gains in understanding a nation's crime rate" (Wilson 2002, p. 537).

There are two relevant traditions of social science here. The first is what might be called "social-science historiography," or "ex post analysis," or, maybe, "statistical detective work." The task is made especially difficult because, like Hercule Poirot in Agatha Christie's *Murder on the Orient Express*, we are not necessarily looking for just one villain. Given a historical fact (e.g., a large increase in recorded robbery rates in England since 1981), the task is to sort through available explanations and decide which ones to credit and how much. For example, there has been much interest in the recent criminology literature in explaining the dramatic crime drop during the 1990s in the United States (Blumstein and Wallman 2000; Cook and Laub 2002; Levitt 2004). Comparisons with other countries that are in some sense similar may provide a basis for assessing various explanations. One method is to analyze pairs of nations that are closely linked economically and culturally. The plausible explanations for England's robbery experience are limited by the fact that Scotland did not share it; the plausible explanations for the drop in homicide rates in the United States are limited by the fact that Canada did share in it, though to a much lesser extent.

The second tradition is to assess the influence of one or more variables on crime rates, holding all else constant. This tradition is grounded in the experimental method, where the factor or factors of interest are artificially isolated through the experimental intervention. While controlled experiments are rarely possible in criminology, under some circumstances it is possible to assess the effect of a variable from nonexperimental data, controlling for other factors through multivariate statistical methods. The availability of comparable data from a number of jurisdictions is helpful in this regard.

A. Explanatory Variables

There is a fairly well established list of "usual suspects" in criminology that should be considered in developing an explanation for a historical trend or in analyzing the partial effect of a particular variable (Land, McCall, and Cohen 1990; Blumstein and Wallman 2000; Levitt 2004; Soares 2004). These "suspects" have been assessed in studies of data at all levels of aggregation, from the neighborhood to the nation. This is not the place to provide an in-depth account of this tradition. Here we simply offer some examples of variables in common use under a fairly arbitrary set of categories: population composition with respect to age, sex, urbanicity, ethnicity and race, immigration, "wantedness" of children (as mediated by abortion law); child welfare, as indicated by household structure, adult-child ratio, investments in children; educational attainment; economic structure and legitimate opportunity, including average income, the degree of income inequality, employment and unemployment, social mobility; criminal opportunities, associated with technology, routine activities, legal restrictions on economic activity (with accompanying black markets); criminogenic commodities and toxins, such as guns, alcohol and other intoxicating drugs, and environmental lead; social influence, structured by institutional arrangements that shape social intercourse, and mediated through popular culture and the efficacy of neighborhoods and other groups to exert control, represented by such variables as church attendance, residential mobility, exposure to popular media of various kinds; and law and law enforcement, including the resources devoted to policing and sanctioning offenders, the de facto severity of punishment, and the extent of incapacitation of crime-prone individuals.

Much of the systematic evidence available on the relationship between crime rates and environmental or "ecological" (the more common term) characteristics derives from multivariate regression analysis on cross sections of data on jurisdictions. A recent example gives the flavor of these studies. Morgan Kelly (2000) analyzed crime rates in 1991 for the 200 largest United States counties, using the following clusters of explanatory variables: population, population per square mile, percent black, percent of households headed by females; percent of adults with college degree; income per capita, income inequality (measured by the Gini coefficient);[1] percent of the population that moved in the previous five years; and number of police per capita.

Comparing this list to the generic list of causes, it is clear that Kelly could have added a number of other variables, covering the missing

---

[1] The Gini coefficient is a general measure of inequality in a population. It ranges from zero (when all households are equal) to one (when one household has everything and the others have nothing).

categories and elaborating on the others with additional measures. The choice of variables to be included in a multivariate regression analysis entails a trade-off between thoroughness and statistical feasibility. With a data set that includes a finite number of observations and limited variation along some dimensions, it is not statistically possible to sort out the effects of all possible influences on crime, and fortunately it is not necessary to do so if the goal is to estimate the effects of particular variables (the experimental tradition referred to above) rather than to give a complete account. The technical condition for generating unbiased estimates is this: omission of an influential variable does not bias the estimates of the effects of the variables that are included in the specification if that omitted variable is orthogonal to (uncorrelated with) the included variables. Unfortunately, this condition is unlikely to be satisfied in practice.

Since we have only a handful of nations in our data set, and the time series is fairly short and incomplete, there is insufficient evidence to identify the separate effects of a long list of variables. But it is possible to learn something by comparing crime trends for natural pairs of nations.

B. Natural Pairings

A regression analysis estimates the effects on crime of specified variables. One necessary assumption if the results are to be believed is that the myriad of other variables that are omitted from the analysis are not confounding the estimates. Another approach is to limit the comparison to pairs of nations that are closely linked economically, culturally, and demographically. Canada and the United States, for example, or England and Scotland, are pairs for which it is reasonable to presume that there is much in common with respect to variation in the causal factors listed above.[2]

Consider the 1990s drop in crime rates in the United States. There was a dramatic reduction in homicide rates (42 percent) between 1991 and 1999, which has been the subject of extensive speculation (Blumstein and Wallman 2000; Levitt 2004). Any satisfactory explanation would

---

[2] Tapio Lappi-Seppälä (2001) used a similar approach in assessing the effects of Finland's remarkable drop in imprisonment rates over the past half century. He compared crime trends in Finland with those of three other Scandinavian countries that all had steady imprisonment rates. The curves for all four countries are close to parallel, with similar peaks, troughs, and direction changes and with Finland maintaining the same rank—second lowest—throughout the forty to fifty years, suggesting that the drop in imprisonment rates had little effect on Finnish crime rates.

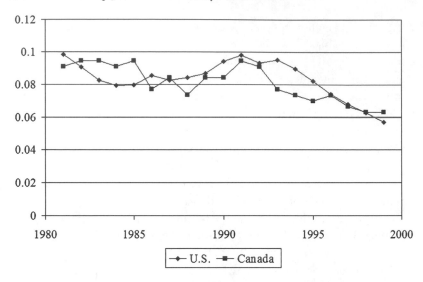

FIG. 1.—Recorded homicide rates per 1,000 population, United States and Canada. Source: Farrington, Langan, and Tonry 2004. Canadian homicide rates have been multiplied throughout by 3.5 for the sake of comparison with United States rates.

have to account for the fact that Canada also exhibited the same general pattern, albeit in more muted form (see fig. 1): the Canadian homicide rate dropped 33 percent during this period. One common explanation for the crime drop in the United States, the economic boom of the 1990s, becomes dubious in the face of the fact that the Canadian unemployment rate remained high throughout this period (8.1 percent in 1990, 7.6 percent in 1999; U.S. Census Bureau 2000, p. 838).

Another popular explanation, the large growth in the prison population during the 1990s, fares no better, since Canada's imprisonment rate did not change much during this decade (Tonry 2004). Other candidate explanations for the U.S. drop, such as abortion legalization (Levitt 2004) or removal of lead from gasoline (Cook and Laub 2002) could also be fruitfully explored by comparison with the corresponding circumstance in Canada. Of course, this approach does not provide definitive results—it simply serves as one check on strong claims for particular causes.

Another natural pairing is England with Scotland. Since these two nations have much in common, the fact that they exhibited such different trends in crime during the 1980s and 1990s provides an intriguing mystery. Figure 2 tracks the trends in recorded robberies, which do not look much alike. In England, robbery rates grew 366 percent,

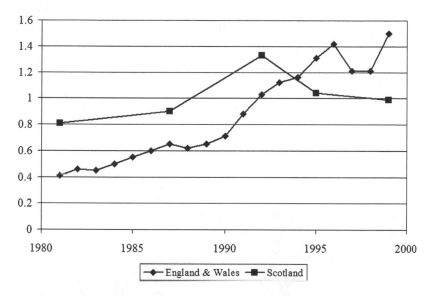

FIG. 2.—Recorded robbery rates per 1,000 population, England and Wales and Scotland. Source: Farrington, Langan, and Tonry 2004. Correlation = 0.47.

compared to a meager 22 percent growth in Scotland. A search for an explanation in terms of underlying criminogenic factors may well provide useful insights, although in part the difference may be an artifact of the data—robbery trends in the survey data for England and Scotland are more similar.

C. Effects of Law-Enforcement Sanctions

All nations seek to control crime by sanctioning criminal behavior. Economists and criminologists have conducted myriad empirical studies of the extent to which punishment, and the threat thereof, is effective in reducing crime rates. The first comprehensive analyses used data from the United States or Britain and found that after controlling for other factors, rates of both theft and violence were negatively related to both the probability of punishment and the average severity of punishment (Carr-Hill and Stern 1973; Ehrlich 1973). These studies were subjected to a devastating critique by an expert panel of the National Academy of Sciences (Blumstein, Cohen, and Nagin 1978), which concluded that the statistical methods being used were unreliable. Since then, other, more reliable, methods have been employed to analyze deterrence and incapacitation effects of legal sanctions (Cook 1980; Levitt 1996; Nagin 1998). But the discredited approach may still have some allure. Here we illustrate

TABLE 4

Correlation between Crime Rates and Custodial
Punishment/Crime Ratio, Seven Nations

Country	Range	No. of Data Points	Assault	Burglary	MVT	Robbery
Recorded data:						
England and Wales	1981–99	8	−.30	−.88	−.81	−.94
Scotland	1981–99	5	.51	−.54	−.29	.27
Australia	1983–2000	9	.74	−.68	−.18	.46
United States	1981–99	8	.80	−.90	.71	.07
Netherlands	1980–99	20	.87	−.70	.28	.78
Sweden	1980–98	19	.04	.43	−.81	−.65
Switzerland	1985–99	5	−.40	−.83	−.78	−.80
Survey data:						
England and Wales	1981–99	8	−.82	−.93	−.71	−.98
Scotland	1981–99	5	−.68	−.80	−.89	−.75
Australia	1983–2000	9	.11	−.41	.49	−.57
United States	1981–99	8	−.48	−.92	.29	−.61
Netherlands	1980–99	20	−.29	−.10	−.60	−.66
Sweden	1980–98	19	−.56	−.29	−.86	N.A.
Switzerland	1985–99	5	−.97	−.87	−.93	−.72

SOURCE.—Farrington, Langan, and Tonry 2004.
NOTE.—MVT = Motor vehicle theft. N.A. = Not applicable.

the simplest version of that approach and discuss some of the statistical problems.

Table 4 reports the correlations over time between a crime rate and one measure of the likelihood of punishment, for each of seven nations (the relevant data for Canada are not available) and four types of crime. The indicator of punishment likelihood used here is the number of custodial sentences in a year for that crime, divided by the number of offenses.[3] Thus we are reporting the correlation between the crime rate (offenses divided by population) and the ratio of custody sentences to offenses. The table reports these correlations for both measures of crime—recorded and survey.

If the threat of punishment has a deterrent effect on crime, then we expect to find a negative relationship between the crime rate and the

[3] One problem with this indicator is that it takes no account of the number of offenders involved in an offense. If the average number of offenders per offense remains constant over time, then our indicator (the ratio of sentences to offenses) bears a constant relationship to the ratio of sentences to offenders.

likelihood of punishment, other things equal. The correlations reported in table 4 do not control for other variables that may be influencing crime, so there is no reason to believe that "other things" are in fact equal. Nonetheless, it is intriguing to note that most of the correlations with the survey measure (twenty-four out of twenty-seven) are negative; while the pattern is not so strong for the recorded measure, it is still true that a majority of the correlations with the recorded measure (sixteen out of twenty-seven) are also negative. It is tempting to believe that this represents evidence in support of a deterrent effect. But there are serious statistical problems with this sort of analysis.

First, the estimated number of offenses is the numerator of the crime rate and the denominator of the custody-sentence rate. Consider how errors in measurement of offenses affect the two variables. A positive error will inflate the crime rate and reduce the custody rate. A negative error will have the opposite effect. Thus errors in measurement of the number of offenses will generate an artifactual negative correlation between the two variables. Given that offense rates tend to be measured with considerable error, this effect may account for even a strong negative correlation.

Second is the issue of causal ordering. While a negative correlation could result from deterrence, it could also result from a quite different process. Suppose that criminal-justice resources for investigating crimes and meting out sentences are scarce. An increase in the crime rate will then result in a reduction in the fraction of criminals who are arrested, convicted, and sentenced. This "resource congestion" process will produce a negative correlation but one due to the effect of crime on the custody rate rather than vice versa.

Third is the possibility of coincidence. A negative correlation between crime and custody rates could be generated if there are other trends in the nation that are correlated with both. For example, suppose that there is a cultural trend toward greater permissiveness in public attitudes toward deviance. That trend may in turn lead directly to higher rates of crime and to a more lenient criminal-justice response.

Given that there are compelling alternative explanations for the predominance of negative correlations, any conclusion regarding the deterrence mechanism is unwarranted.[4]

---

[4] It should be noted that the early econometric investigations were a good deal more sophisticated in their approach and sought to address these three problems in particular. But their solutions were not adequate in the judgment of many experts, as developed in the National Academy of Sciences report (Blumstein, Cohen, and Nagin 1978).

III. Conclusion

The path to wisdom concerning crime causation and prevention is paved with good data. Crime data that are not only of good quality but comparable across nations would provide criminologists with a chance to ask new questions and get a new handle on answering the old ones. We are particularly intrigued by the possibilities of comparing crime trends in pairs of nations that are closely linked with respect to economy and culture but which, at least sometimes, follow different paths with respect to policies that influence (or may influence) crime. Canada may provide a useful "control group" for the United States, and vice versa; and similarly for England and Scotland.

The data from this volume also provided us with an opportunity to analyze the deterrent effect of punishment in seven different countries and four different crime types by computing the correlation of crime rate with the ratio of prison sentences to crimes in each case. But the results are subject to multiple interpretations, and even if they had been more consistent across countries and crimes, it still would have been impossible to draw any firm conclusion regarding the deterrent effect. This exercise illustrates a less sanguine lesson, that a weak statistical method applied to data from several nations still produces weak results.

The quest for stronger multinational evidence on deterrence should be focused on finding natural experiments—circumstances in which a nation abruptly changed its punishment-related practices for one or more types of crime. Examples might include a nationwide strike by the police or the introduction of a powerful new technology for solving crimes (such as Lojack for vehicle theft). The resulting trajectory in relevant crime rates could be compared with one or more other nations (pairs) that are comparable in some sense but did not experience the same change in practice.

REFERENCES

Blumstein, Alfred, Jacqueline Cohen, and Daniel Nagin, eds. 1978. *Deterrence and Incapacitation: Estimating the Effects of Criminal Sanctions on Crime Rates.* Washington, D.C.: National Academy of Sciences.
Blumstein, Alfred, and Joel Wallman, eds. 2000. *The Crime Drop in America.* New York: Cambridge University Press.

Carr-Hill, R. A., and H. H. Stern. 1973. "An Econometric Model of the Supply and Control of Recorded Offenses in England and Wales." *Journal of Public Economics* 2(4):289–318.

Cook, Philip J. 1980. "Research in Criminal Deterrence: Laying the Groundwork for the Second Decade." In *Crime and Justice: An Annual Review of Research*, vol. 2, edited by Norval Morris and Michael Tonry. Chicago: University of Chicago Press.

Cook, Philip J., and John H. Laub. 2002. "After the Epidemic: Recent Trends in Youth Violence in the United States." In *Crime and Justice: A Review of Research*, vol. 29, edited by Michael Tonry. Chicago: University of Chicago Press.

Ehrlich, Isaac. 1973. "Participation in Illegitimate Activities: A Theoretical and Empirical Investigation." *Journal of Political Economy* 81(3):521–65.

Farrington, David P., Patrick A. Langan, and Michael Tonry, eds. 2004. *Cross-National Studies in Crime and Justice*. Washington, D.C.: U.S. Department of Justice, Office of Justice Programs.

Kelly, Morgan. 2000. "Inequality and Crime." *Review of Economics and Statistics* 82(4):530–39.

Land, Kenneth C., P. McCall, and L. Cohen. 1990. "Structural Covariates of Homicide Rates: Are There Any Invariances across Time and Space?" *American Journal of Sociology* 95:922–63.

Lappi Seppälä, Tapio. 2001. "Sentencing and Punishment in Finland: The Decline of the Repressive Ideal." In *Sentencing and Sanctions in Western Countries*, edited by Michael H. Tonry and Richard S. Frase. New York: Oxford University Press.

Levitt, Steven D. 1996. "The Effect of Prison Population Size on Crime Rates: Evidence from Prison Overcrowding Litigation." *Quarterly Journal of Economics* 111(2):319–51.

———. 2004. "Understanding Why Crime Fell in the 1990s: Four Factors That Explain the Decline and Six That Do Not." *Journal of Economic Perspectives* 18(1):163–90.

Nagin, Daniel S. 1998. "Criminal Deterrence Research at the Outset of the Twenty-First Century." In *Crime and Justice: A Review of Research*, vol. 23, edited by Michael Tonry. Chicago: University of Chicago Press.

Soares, Rodrigo Reis. 2004. "Development, Crime, and Punishment: Accounting for the International Differences in Crime Rates." *Journal of Development Economics* 73(1):155–84.

Tonry, Michael H. 2004. *Thinking about Crime: Sense and Sensibility in American Penal Culture*. New York: Oxford University Press.

U.S. Census Bureau. 2000. *Statistical Abstract of the United States: 2000*. Washington, D.C.: U.S. Census Bureau.

Wilson, James Q. 2002. "Crime and Public Policy." In *Crime: Public Policies for Crime Control*, edited by James Q. Wilson and Joan Petersilia. Oakland, Calif.: ICS Press.

*Alfred Blumstein, Michael Tonry,
and Asheley Van Ness*

Cross-National Measures of Punitiveness

Dealing with criminal offenders is a fundamental governmental process in a democratic society. Maintenance of public safety that allows citizens to get on with their lives is a core responsibility of government. Sanctioning of offenders, whether for preventive or moral reasons, provides the paradigm case of conflict between the state's interests in pursuing collective goals and the individual's interests in preserving liberty and autonomy.

Societies vary substantially in the severity of the penalties they impose for various kinds of crimes and criminals, but it is not obvious by what metric to make such comparisons. Most such claims rely on cross-national comparisons of the average number of people held in prison per 100,000 population, but arguably equally valid measures include the number of people sent to prison per year per 100,000 population, average lengths of prison sentences, and the probability of imprisonment or average sentence length per crime committed, recorded, prosecuted, or resulting in a conviction. Results are likely to vary substantially depending on which measure is used. If average imprisonment rates in Western countries early in the twenty-first century are compared, the United States' approximately 700 per 100,000 in 2005 is much the

Alfred Blumstein is J. Erik Jonsson University Professor of Urban Systems and Operations Research, H. John Heinz III School of Public Policy and Management, Carnegie Mellon University. Michael Tonry is Sonosky Professor of Law and Public Policy, University of Minnesota, and Senior Fellow, Netherlands Institute for the Study of Crime and Law Enforcement, Leiden. Asheley Van Ness is a 2005 recipient of a Master of Science degree in Public Policy and Management, H. John Heinz III School of Public Policy and Management, Carnegie Mellon University. Catrien Bijleveld, David P. Farrington, Paul Smit, and Brandon Welsh commented on earlier drafts; their help is greatly appreciated.

highest, and those in Scandinavia, typically around sixty per 100,000, are the lowest. If annual rates of admission to prison are compared, Scandinavian rates in the 1990s were among the highest (Young and Brown 1993; Kommer 1994, 2004), but Scandinavian imprisonment rates and average sentence lengths are among the lowest.

Relative to the most common measure of national differences in punitiveness—the number of prisoners per 100,000 population—there is considerable variation among the eight nations considered in the analyses in this and the related Bureau of Justice Statistics (BJS) publication (Farrington, Langan, and Tonry 2004). In 2002, the United States had the highest incarceration rate, 686 per 100,000 (including prisoners in local jails). The seven other nations had much lower national rates in 2002 (Walmsley 2003): Sweden (68 per 100,000), Switzerland (69), Netherlands (93), Canada (102), Australia (116), Scotland (126), and England and Wales (139).

The analyses reported in this essay indicate that the high U.S. imprisonment rate results primarily from much greater lengths of prison sentence by every punitiveness measure we were able to use—years of imprisonment per recorded crime or conviction, or average sentence length given a commitment—than are imposed in other countries. The high American imprisonment rate is also partly explained by comparatively high probabilities of imprisonment given a conviction. Sweden, however, also had consistently high probabilities of imprisonment, but these were offset by the shortest average sentences of the eight countries. By contrast, Switzerland had imprisonment rates and average times served relative to recorded offenses similar to Sweden's, but these were due to low probabilities of imprisonment per recorded crime or conviction coupled with moderately severe average sentences rather than because of short sentences.

To the extent that crime rates or patterns might be affected if penalties are made more or less severe, it is important to try to learn to what extent national differences in punishment patterns affect national differences in crime. The essays published in this volume and the related BJS volume provided a potential opportunity to do that. It turned out, however, not to be possible to draw conclusions about the crime prevention or control effects of national differences in punishment practices or policies. This is partly because of the complexity of estimating these effects in even a single country with well-defined measures of crime and punishment. Efforts to estimate these effects cross-nationally are made even more difficult because of national differences in how

crimes are defined and in crime reporting and recording and changes in
the latter over time.

It is also, however, as James Q. Wilson has observed, because "social
scientists have made great gains in explaining why some people are more
likely than others to commit crimes but far smaller gains in understanding
a nation's crime rate" (Wilson 2002, p. 537). Cross-national differences
in legal and political culture, institutional arrangements, and constitutional traditions and values shape both crime and punishment in ways
that no one has yet figured out how to quantify credibly (Zimring and
Hawkins 1991; Whitman 2003; Tonry 2004).

It is possible, however, to draw cross-national conclusions about the
comparative severity of countries' punishment practices as measured in
diverse ways (the imprisonment rate per 100,000, the probabilities of
conviction or prison commitment per recorded offense, the probabilities of imprisonment per offense or per conviction, and average prison
sentence lengths per offense or per commitment). We have made as
many of these calculations in this essay as the available data allow.

Countries with high incarceration rates may have such high rates not
simply because they send relatively more people to prison, or for relatively longer times, or both, but because they have higher crime rates.
If so, the crime rate rather than punitiveness would be driving the high
incarceration rate.

Alternatively, a country with a low incarceration rate per crime might
have that low rate not because it is not punitive but because of its limited
ability to solve its crimes and find and convict their perpetrators. Because of that possibility, it might be better to explore the magnitude of
punishment per conviction.

It is also likely that some countries are highly punitive concerning
some types of crime, say interpersonal violence, but much less so for
other types, say property crimes. Examining this possibility calls for
examination of various measures of punitiveness by crime type.

To explore these issues, we use data collected for this volume on
crimes, convictions, commitments to prison, and time served for six types
of crime in the eight countries. Five of these countries are English-
speaking, common-law countries on three continents, and the other
three are civil law countries in Europe. All are wealthy, developed
Western societies with broadly similar criminal justice systems. Although there are some well-known differences between inquisitorial
civil law and adversarial common law procedures, the criminal justice
systems of the eight countries are much more similar than different. All

have professional police forces and established prosecutorial, judicial, and correctional systems. All afford defendants a common core of broadly similar procedural and human rights protections under relevant constitutional documents and traditions. All rely on imprisonment as the principal sanction for serious crimes (only the United States still uses capital punishment), though they vary considerably in the other punishments commonly imposed.

The biggest differences between countries for our purposes are found in the details of criminal law definitions and the organization of information systems. Countries vary widely in classification of crimes. Residential and commercial burglaries, for example, are sometimes recorded as one offense and sometimes as two separate offenses. In some places, though, there is no separate burglary offense at all, and crimes that would be counted as burglaries in the United States or England and Wales are counted under various other property offense classifications. Offense definitions and recording practices for motor vehicle crimes are another example of wide divergence. Private automobiles, commercial vehicles, and motorized two-wheeled vehicles are classified together in some places and separately in others. In some places, joyriding is not counted as motor vehicle theft, which means that those offenses that are counted are on average more serious than are motor vehicle thefts in other countries that do include joyriding.

There are also differences affecting violent offenses. Most continental European civil law countries, for example, include attempts among homicides; common-law countries do not. Concerning assaults generally and sexual assaults in particular, there are significant differences between countries in offense definitions, reporting thresholds, and recording practices. In all eight countries, including the United States (see, e.g., Blumstein and Wallman 2000), reporting and recording practices changed in the final decades of the twentieth century, reflecting reduced tolerance of violence generally and domestic and sexual violence in particular. As a result, significant components of apparent increases in assault, sexual assault, and rape in all countries probably result from changes in reporting and recording; this no doubt varies between countries.

As the introduction to this volume describes, considerable effort has been made to make the data as comparable between countries as possible by disaggregating data into subcategories, combining data into new categories, and using various estimation techniques. All such adjustments are spelled out in the individual essays. Sometimes, however, for reasons we understand and try to explain, some data from some countries appear anomalous, and for this reason we sometimes exclude them from our analyses.

In the body of this essay, we consider criminal justice system responses to six kinds of crime: homicide, rape, robbery, residential burglary, assault, and motor vehicle theft (MVT). For each crime type, we begin with an overall measure of punitiveness as the expected time served per recorded crime.[1] This measure takes account of the operations of the entire criminal justice system. It starts with recorded crimes and average sentence lengths, thereby reflecting in aggregate the outcome of decisions by police, prosecutors, and judges. We also examine a more narrowly focused definition of punitiveness, the post-conviction expected time served per crime. Arrests and convictions are not necessarily signs of punitiveness, but committing a convicted offender to prison and specifying a particular prison term explicitly are.

We first examine these measures averaged across the countries to see the differences in how the different crime types are treated. For some crime types, one or two of the countries are significantly different from the others, and so we calculate the group averages, both with and without these "outliers."[2] We then consider the country-specific measures for each crime type, which permits us to examine how countries vary in punitiveness generally and for particular crime types.

For each country and each crime type, we calculate the average values over that period for each of our parameters. Because punishment trends varied widely among the eight countries in the final two decades of the twentieth century, average values may over- or underestimate current values. In the United States and the Netherlands, for example, imprisonment rates rose continuously and sharply throughout the period,

---

[1] The essays on individual countries in this volume emphasize victim reports of crime. We focus on crimes recorded by the police because our emphasis is on analysis of processing within the criminal justice system, and only the recorded crimes are processed.

[2] In our calculations, we omitted "outliers" where they were higher than the mean of all eight countries by a factor of two or more. Since it is the high outliers rather than the low ones that distort the mean, we recalculate the means without the high outliers. Values above or below the recalculated mean (the mean without the high outliers) by a factor of two or more were recorded as "outliers." In table 1, e.g., motor vehicle theft in the Netherlands had a value of 297.77 convictions per 1,000 crimes, well more than twice the eight-country average of 78.60 (see table 1). Hence, the Netherlands was not included in this aggregated result for MVT because it is an "outlier" by this definition.

and in England and Wales from the early 1990s onward; average sentences calculated over a twenty-year period will significantly underestimate average sentences in 1999.[3] For other countries, including Sweden, Switzerland, and Canada, imprisonment rates were broadly stable, and twenty-year averages may more closely approximate current averages.[4] Australia's imprisonment rates also were broadly stable, though rising somewhat in the late 1990s and fluctuating throughout.[5]

We also examine trends in some of the patterns of criminal justice response. Since the time series in many cases are quite erratic, we seek to identify only those trends that are both "statistically significant" (i.e., a clear trend that can be seen through the fluctuations in the time series) and "operationally significant" (i.e., trends that are sufficiently large compared to the mean of the series).[6] Issues relating to time trends are discussed at the end of the essay.

Besides this introduction and a conclusion, this essay has four sections. Section I sets out our analytical framework and presents basic data and estimates. It then examines two measures of punitiveness: expected time served per 1,000 recorded crimes and per 1,000 convictions for each type of offense in each country. By these measures, the United States is substantially more punitive than the other countries. The Netherlands and Switzerland are the least punitive. Section II looks at probabilities of conviction and commitment per 1,000 recorded offenses. The Netherlands has the highest conviction rates per 1,000 recorded crimes and the United States and Switzerland the lowest. The Netherlands also has the highest prison commitment rates per 1,000 recorded crimes, the United States is among the highest, and Switzerland is the lowest. Section III examines average sentence lengths given a conviction. The United States is highest for all offenses except homicide (for which it is second highest), and Sweden and the Netherlands are lowest. Section IV examines national trends in prison

---

[3] Conversely, were Finland one of the countries covered, twenty-year averages would likely overstate severity in 1999 because Finnish imprisonment rates declined substantially during that period (Lappi-Seppälä 2001).

[4] Stable imprisonment rates do not mean that punishment patterns have not changed; the mix of offenses receiving prison sentences may have changed, as may have commitment probabilities and average sentence lengths for particular offenses.

[5] Data on national imprisonment rates over time can be found in Kuhn (2003) and in the individual country essays in Tonry and Frase (2001).

[6] The data may be erratic as a consequence of inherently erratic patterns, long intervals between the reporting of the measures, changes in definitions and recording practices, or large shifts in the underlying measures.

commitments and average sentence lengths given a conviction. The only country showing consistent increases in severity was England and Wales, where the probability of receiving a prison sentence significantly increased for assault and MVT and average sentence lengths increased for homicide, rape, robbery, and burglary.

I. Measuring Punitiveness

The following basic components of criminal justice processing are combined later in developing various measures of punitiveness: convictions per crime, commitments per conviction, and average time served per commitment.

The basic recorded data from which we calculate these measures are

CRIM = number of recorded crimes,
CONV = number of convictions for that crime in a year,
COM = number of persons committed to prison for that crime, and
TS = average time served by offenders committed to prison for that crime.

With only a few exceptions, CRIM, CONV, COM, and TS were available by year for the twenty years 1980 to 1999 for each crime type and for each country.[7] With these data, we calculated three basic components to be used in various measures of punitiveness: first, convictions per crime (CONV/CRIM); second, commitments per conviction (COM/CONV); and third, time served per commitment (TS). These components are averaged over the reported years for each country and crime type. These basic components are presented in table 1 (convictions per 1,000 recorded crimes), table 2 (commitments per conviction), and table 3 (average time served per commitment). We present these tables here, even though the contents of tables 1 and 3 are presented again in somewhat different form in tables 11 and 13, because they set out basic data used in calculations in all the following tables, and we frequently refer to them to explain formulas and illustrate calculations.

A. Overall Punitiveness: Expected Time Served per 1,000 Recorded Crimes

The first measure of punitiveness is the expected time served per 1,000 recorded crimes. This broad measure encompasses the interacting effects of actions of all the functionaries who make up the criminal justice system, including police solving crimes and arresting

[7] Not all countries had reports for every year. Australia provided data for the year 2000.

TABLE 1

Convictions per 1,000 Recorded Crimes
by Country and Crime Type

	Residential Burglary	MVT	Robbery	Assault	Rape	Homicide
England and Wales	38.05	50.69	109.41	240.26	65.14	685.34
United States	59.23	29.46	106.51	74.95	96.69	542.75
Sweden	48.58	39.27	92.55	170.97	54.42	789.84
Australia	69.68	94.71	177.36	156.18	97.97	442.74
Scotland	66.29	74.83	127.64	263.40	62.40	720.04
Canada	85.61	13.24	139.96	17.58	...	169.29
Switzerland	40.54	28.82	212.77	131.37	66.11	883.21
Netherlands	71.55	297.77	185.59	245.25	102.60	737.71
Mean of all eight	59.94	78.60	143.97	162.50	77.90	621.37

NOTE.—MVT = motor vehicle theft.

perpetrators, prosecutors securing convictions, judges sentencing people to prison, and various actors making decisions that determine how long people stay there. Postconviction actions that produce commitments and time served, more explicitly indicative of punitiveness, are considered in Section II.

This analysis allows us to characterize this measure of punitiveness by crime type and by country. It also provides an opportunity to explore explanations of national differences. Some countries might be very

TABLE 2

Probability of Commitment per Conviction
by Country and Crime Type (in percent)

	Residential Burglary	MVT	Robbery	Assault	Rape	Homicide
England and Wales	46.7	23.1	73.1	19.9	95.5	91.8
United States	57.7	51.9	78.9	61.0	81.4	94.5
Sweden	54.1	28.4	77.6	32.6	91.4	97.1
Australia	27.6	22.5	61.7	8.2	42.7	91.7
Scotland	39.8	24.4	62.6	13.2	84.7	87.1
Canada	20.0	20.0	40.0	12.0	...	76.0
Switzerland	38.8	22.3	25.1	16.6	48.8	77.2
Netherlands	66.0	44.0	61.0	10.5	77.3	92.4
Mean of all eight	43.8	29.6	60.0	21.8	74.5	88.5

NOTE.—MVT = motor vehicle theft.

TABLE 3

Average Time Served (in Months) per Conviction
by Country and Crime Type

	Residential Burglary	MVT	Robbery	Assault	Rape	Homicide
England and Wales	7.28	3.83	18.00	6.66	34.05	88.33
United States	18.65	11.94	41.60	23.40	59.78	113.63
Sweden	5.23	2.47	15.20	3.07	15.41	86.95
Australia	15.18	8.71	36.20	23.08	50.91	120.33
Scotland	3.56	2.66	17.60	7.00	36.40	94.70
Canada	15.40	3.00	25.90	27.95	...	72.39
Switzerland	14.30	9.46	20.50	10.13	25.14	46.16
Netherlands	11.40	8.10	12.14	4.91	15.80	69.20
Mean of all eight	11.38	6.27	23.39	13.28	33.93	86.42

NOTE.—MVT = motor vehicle theft.

efficient at solving crimes and convicting offenders but less aggressive
than others at sending them to prison and doing so for shorter times.
The factors contributing to such differences might then be explored.

We calculate the expected time served per 1,000 recorded crimes
(ETS) by the following formula:

$$ETS = (1,000 \times CONV/CRIM) \times (COM/CONV) \times TS, \quad (1)$$

where:[8]

ETS = expected time served per 1,000 recorded crimes,[9]
CRIM = number of crimes of a particular type recorded annually by
the police,[10]
CONV = number of convictions for that crime type in a year,
COM = number of persons sent to prison for that crime, and
TS = average time served by offenders sentenced for that crime.

The first factor in formula (1) represents the conviction rate per 1,000
recorded crimes, the second the commitment probability per conviction (a measure of certainty of punishment), and the third the average
time served by those committed to prison (a measure of severity). Thus,

[8] More technically, there should be a subscript under each of the terms in formula 1,
where ETS_{ij} represents the expected time served for crime type "i" in country "j," and
similarly for the other terms in the formula. We omit this technicality.

[9] We use a base of 1,000 crimes simply to avoid small decimals.

[10] Although victim surveys were available for all the countries, we use only crimes
reported to the police and recorded by them because only those crimes find their way
into the criminal justice system.

TABLE 4

Expected Time Served per 1,000 Recorded Crimes (in Months and Years) for Six Offenses, Averaged across Time and Country

	Raw Mean		Mean without High Outliers		Countries Excluded as High Outliers
	Months	Years	Months	Years	
Homicide	47,073	3,923	...	...	None
Rape*	1,936	161.3	1,500	125	United States
Robbery	1,914	159.5	1,622	135	Australia
Residential burglary	289.7	24.1	240	20	United States
Assault	313.1	26.1	205	17	United States
Motor vehicle theft	202.4	16.9	79.7	6.6	Netherlands

* No data provided for rape in Canada.

ETS/1,000 is the average time served multiplied by the probability that a crime will be followed by a conviction and a commitment to prison.

The calculation of ETS is based on the reports of CRIM, CONV, COM, and TS by year for each crime type and each country.[11] These results averaged over time and across the countries are summarized in table 4.

This overall measure of punitiveness across all eight countries is reasonably consistent with commonly held perceptions of the comparative seriousness of the various offenses. Homicide has the highest value, rape and robbery are next, followed by burglary and assault, with MVT the lowest. In particular, the expected time served for 1,000 murders (using the raw mean) is 47,073 months or 3,923 years, or an average of about four years per recorded murder. The expected time served per 1,000 recorded crimes is nearly twenty-five times higher for homicide than for robbery and rape; this results from the much higher likelihood (see table 1) compared with other crimes that a conviction will follow a recorded homicide and the substantially higher average time served for homicide (see table 3). Times served for rape and robbery per 1,000 recorded crimes are about equal and result from the

[11] Not all the countries provided all the requested data for all the years. We were able, however, to calculate average values across the reported years, and most of our analyses here are based on those averages. When there are important trends in the data that are reliably reported, we examine those trends in Section IV. Also, in some specific crime type-country combinations (e.g., rape in Canada), no data were reported.

interaction of lower conviction probabilities for rape but longer average sentences.

The similarity in times served per recorded offense could be misleading if it were not deconstructed. In most countries, the probability that a recorded rape will result in a conviction (mean: seventy-eight per 1,000) is about half that for a recorded robbery (144 per 1,000), but convicted rape defendants are more likely to be sentenced to prison (means: 75 percent compared to 60 percent) and to stay there longer (means: thirty-four months compared to 23.3 months).

Table 5 presents the analysis of ETS by country and crime type. The analysis of expected time served per crime (ETS) by individual country contributes to the aggregate estimates of ETS averaged over the countries in table 4. Comparing across countries by crime type shows that all of the countries impose severe punishments for homicide, but this is much less so concerning property crimes.

For homicide in the United States, for example, the product of a mean time served of 9.5 years (113.63 months; see table 3) multiplied by a probability of commitment per conviction (0.945; see table 2) and the probability of conviction per recorded crime (0.54275; see table 1) yields 58.57 months or an average of 4.9 years per recorded murder.[12] For another example, the expected time served for burglary in Switzerland, 0.22 months, or about seven days, is the product of a mean of 14.3 months time served (see table 3) multiplied by the probability of commitment given conviction (0.388; see table 2) and 40.54 convictions per 1,000 burglaries (see table 1). This value of ETS is so low because property crimes (MVT and burglaries) are hard to clear (only 6 percent of burglaries and 8 percent of MVTs lead to a conviction), thereby keeping the expected time served low.

Expected time served per 1,000 crimes (ETS) is reasonably consistent across the countries, in the sense that differences in time served relative to various offenses accord with widely shared views about offense seriousness, albeit with important outliers. We focus first on the high outliers because they have an important influence on the aggregate mean across the countries.[13] The United States is the most frequent

[12] ETS = (CONV/CRIM) × (COM/CONV) × TS or (0.54275) × (0.95) × 113.63 = 58.57 months or about 4.9 years per murder.

[13] The Netherlands is a high outlier only for MVT, which results from a definitional anomaly in what crimes are recorded as MVT. According to Paul Smit of the Netherlands Ministry of Justice, Research, and Documentation Centre (personal communication, January 13, 2004), joyriding (temporarily stealing a vehicle for the "thrill" or for temporary transportation) is excluded from the recorded MVT crime rate.

TABLE 5

Expected Time Served (in Years) per 1,000 Recorded Crimes by Country and Crime Type

	Homicide	Rape	Robbery	Residential Burglary	Assault	MVT
England and Wales	4,631	176.5	120.0	10.8	26.5	3.7
United States	4,857	391.9	291.3	53.1	89.2	15.2
Sweden	5,551	63.8	91.0	11.5	14.3	2.3
Australia	4,071	177.5	330.1	24.4	24.6	15.5
Scotland	4,949	160.3	117.2	7.8	20.3	4.0
Canada	775	N.D.	120.8	22.0	4.9	.7
Switzerland	2,617	67.6	91.2	18.8	18.4	5.1
Netherlands	3,931	104.4	114.5	44.9	10.5	88.4
Mean of all Eight	3,923	163.1	159.5	24.1	26.1	16.9
High outliers	...	United States	Australia	United States	United States	Netherlands
Mean without high outliers	3,923	125.0	135.1	20.0	17.1	6.6
Low outliers	Canada	Sweden	...	Scotland	Canada	Sweden Canada
Mean without low outliers*	4,372	207.1	135.1	22.0	19.1	8.7

NOTE.—MVT = motor vehicle theft. N.D. = no data provided.

* There are two steps involved in calculating the overall mean without outliers. First, we calculated the aggregate mean to determine the high outliers. As stated earlier, high outliers are values that are above the aggregate mean by a factor of two or more. Second, the aggregate mean was then recalculated without these high outliers and the low outliers were those cases that were below half this new mean.

outlier, exceeding the aggregate mean by a factor of more than two for rape, burglary, and assault. Australia is an outlier in robbery. The single offense for which there is no high outlier is the most serious crime of homicide, where ETS is reasonably consistent across the countries (with the exception of Canada, which is a low outlier).[14] The United States is by this measure the most punitive country, based on its high values of expected time served per recorded crime in three crime types.

The high outliers result primarily from high values of time served. For rape, the United States and Australia have the highest values of time served and convictions per crime. Similarly, the United States has the highest time served for burglary and for assault (with the exception of Canada, which has 15.4 months, compared to 15.2 for the United States). For robbery, Australia has a high time served and a high rate of convictions per crime.

Canada is most often a low outlier, probably for the reasons of unreliability of court and corrections data sketched in note 14 and in Welsh and Irving (in this volume). Sweden is a low outlier for rape and MVT, and it is low for time served for both these offenses. Scotland is a low outlier for residential burglary because it has the lowest value of time served.

Two conclusions from table 5 stand out. One reason why the United States has the world's highest imprisonment rate is that, when sentence severity is calculated relative to recorded offenses, much harsher aggregate prison sentences (expected time served) are doled out than elsewhere. For rape, burglary, and assault, aggregate years' imprisonment per 1,000 recorded offenses is substantially higher than elsewhere; aggregate imprisonment for robbery is exceeded only by Australia, and for MVT only by the Netherlands and Australia.[15] Only for homicide are aggregate U.S. imprisonment years in the mainstream.

Conversely, Sweden and Switzerland, both countries with relatively comprehensive and reliable data systems, are consistently at the low end in aggregate years' imprisonment per 1,000 recorded crimes. Except

[14] Welsh and Irving (in this volume) and Brandon Welsh privately (private communication, January 18, 2005) indicate that failures in integration of provincial and national information systems for court and corrections data result in substantial undercounting of convictions and sentence durations.

[15] See n. 13 regarding the Netherlands. Australia, a federal country like Canada, also has problems of poor integration of court and corrections data systems between state and federal governments, and the data in table 5 depend heavily on estimates (see Carcach, in this volume).

for homicide, for which Sweden tops the field, both countries are among the lowest for every offense.

B. Narrow Punitiveness: Expected Time Served per Conviction

The preceding section examined expected time served per 1,000 recorded crimes as an overall measure of punitiveness. A narrower measure focuses on the expected time served per 1,000 convictions. This measure is not affected by the number of convictions per recorded crime, which results from the abilities of the police to solve crimes and arrest perpetrators and prosecutors to convict. Expected time served per 1,000 convictions more narrowly reflects punishment in terms of commitment to prison and time served by those found guilty.

We calculate the expected time served per 1,000 convictions (EC) by the following formula:

$$EC = (1,000COM/CONV) \times TS, \tag{2}$$

where:

EC = expected time served per 1,000 convictions,
CONV = number of convictions for that crime type in a year,
COM = number of persons committed to prison for that crime, and
TS = average time served by offenders sentenced for that crime.

The first factor in formula (2) represents the commitment probability given conviction (a measure of the risk and certainty of incarceration by those convicted; see table 2), and the second factor is the average time served by those committed to prison (a measure of the severity of punishment; see table 3). Thus, EC, the expected time served per 1,000 commitments, represents the product of the average time served by those convicted and the probability that a person convicted will be committed to prison.

The results averaged over time and across the countries are summarized in table 6. Like the broad punitiveness measure of aggregate years' imprisonment per 1,000 recorded crimes (ETS, or expected time served per 1,000 crimes), this measure also is consistent with widely shared views of the seriousness of the various crimes. Homicide has the highest value, followed by rape and robbery. Burglary and assault are comparable, and MVT is the lowest.[16] The expected time served for 1,000 convictions for murder is 77,508 months or 6,459 years, or an

---

[16] Assault is probably the crime type with the greatest range of seriousness among the convictions.

TABLE 6

Expected Time Served per 1,000 Convictions for Six Crime Types, Averaged across Time and Country

	Raw Mean		Mean without High Outliers		
	Months	Years	Months	Years	Countries Excluded as High Outliers
Homicide	77,508	6,459	...	...	...
Rape*	24,611	2,051	20,61⁻	1,718	United States**
Robbery	14,255	1,189	11,61⁻	968	United States
Residential burglary	4,844	403.7	3,99⁻	333	United States
Assault	3,121	260.1	1,52⁻	127	United States
Motor vehicle theft	2,083	173.6	1,49⁻	124	United States

* No data provided for rape in Canada.

** Outlier measure just under 2, so included as an outlier.

average of about 6.5 years per murder conviction (calculated for the raw mean). For MVT, the mean value of EC is 2.1 months. EC is a stronger indication of the societal interest in punishment for the particular crime type than ETS, since there is no discounting for the difficulty of clearing the crime, which importantly affects the measure of time served per crime.[17]

The United States is the only outlier in table 6 and is an outlier for all the crime types except homicide, which has no outliers.[18] In contrast to the broader measure of punitiveness shown in table 4, where a number of countries show up as outliers, when this narrower measure is used, the United States is consistently high.

Table 7 provides measures of EC by crime type for each individual country. In this table, for example, the value for homicide in the United States is the product of a mean time served of 9.5 years (113.63 months; see table 3) multiplied by a probability of commitment given conviction (0.945; see table 2); this yields 107,352 months or 8,948 years per 1,000 murders, or an average of about nine years per individual murder conviction.

Table 7 highlights the degree to which the United States is the outlier in the expected time served per 1,000 convictions (EC). Aside from homicide, the United States is generally higher than the mean of all the countries by a factor of two to three and has the highest value of EC. Only Australia is higher for homicide, and not by much. The ratio of the United States to the mean of all eight countries is highest for assault with a value of 4.6.

There are a number and variety of low outliers. For motor vehicle theft, there are three low outliers (Canada, Scotland, and Sweden, all of which have values of EC in the fifties, well below the overall mean or the means without high and low outliers) for MVT. These are low outliers even when the influence of the United States, which is high by a factor of three, is eliminated.

The Netherlands, Scotland, Canada, and Switzerland are each a low outlier for two crime types: the Netherlands for rape and assault, Switzerland for rape and robbery, Scotland for burglary and MVT, and

---

[17] Indeed, one of the important confounding factors in the analysis of ETS was potential differences across countries in the counting of the crimes. Different definitions could well affect EC also, since a country with a broader crime definition (say, including attempts as well as completions) could well display lesser punitiveness for that crime.

[18] For rape, the value of EC for the United States was 1.98 times the mean of the other six countries (Canada did not report on rapes), and so round-off warranted classifying it here as an outlier.

TABLE 7

Expected Time Served (in Years) per 1,000 Convictions by Country and Crime Type

	Homicide	Rape	Robbery	Residential Burglary	Assault	MVT
England and Wales	6,757	2,709	1,097	283.3	110.4	73.6
United States	8,948	4,053	2,735	896.4	1,189.5	515.9
Sweden	7,028	1,173	982	235.9	83.4	58.4
Australia	9,195	1,812	866	349.5	157.7	163.5
Scotland	6,874	2,569	918	118.1	77.0	54.1
Canada	4,578	N.D.	865	256.7	279.5	50.0
Switzerland	2,963	1,023	437	462.6	140.1	176.1
Netherlands	5,328	1,017	615	627.0	43.0	297.0
Mean of all eight	6,459	2,051	1,189	403.7	260.1	173.6
High outliers	...	United States	United States	United States	United States	United States
Mean without high outliers	6,459	1,718	968	333.3	127.3	124.7
Low outliers	Canada	Netherlands Switzerland	Switzerland	Scotland	Netherlands	Sweden Scotland Canada
Mean without low outliers	6,958	2,463	1,057	369.2	141.4	177.6

NOTE.—MVT = motor vehicle theft. N.D. = no data provided.

Canada for homicide and MVT. Thus, the Netherlands and Switzerland seem to be relatively less severe for the violent crimes, Scotland for the property crimes, and Canada for both the most and least serious of the crime types.

II.   Certainty of Punishment

Expected time served measures reflect the strong influence of severity of punishment (sentence length). For both theoretical and practical reasons, it is important also to look at certainty of punishment. "Certainty" is typically measured as the probability that incarceration will be imposed, and "severity" is measured by the duration of the prison sentence, or time served. The previous section combined these two aspects of punishment. They can be disentangled by looking at commitments per 1,000 recorded offenses as a measure of the certainty of punishment, leaving aside the issue of severity. This section looks at commitments per 1,000 crimes recorded by the police and then per 1,000 convictions. Dropping time served from the formula for expected time served per offense (formula [1]) provides a measure of the rate of commitment to prison per 1,000 crimes. This rate is based on the product of the probability that a crime will lead to a conviction (reflecting police and prosecutorial effectiveness in producing convictions) and the probability that the conviction leads to a prison commitment by the judge. Thus, we can calculate the certainty of incarceration (CER) as

$$CER = (1,000CONV/CRIM) \times (COM/CONV), \qquad (3)$$

where:

CER = rate of commitment per 1,000 crimes (i.e., certainty of incarceration),
CRIM = number of crimes of a particular type recorded by the police in each country,
CONV = number of convictions for that crime type in a year, and
COM = number of persons committed to prison for that crime.

A.   Commitments per 1,000 Recorded Crimes

The measures of certainty of punishment, CER, are displayed in table 8 by crime type averaged over time and country. Certainty of punishment is by far the highest for homicide, both because suspects are more often identified and because convictions are very likely to lead to imprisonment. Robbery and rape are next highest, but lower than

TABLE 8

Commitments per 1,000 Recorded Crimes for Six Crime Types, Averaged across Time and Country

	Raw Mean	Mean without High Outliers	Countries Excluded as High Outliers
Homicide	554.3	...	...
Rape*	56.7	...	...
Robbery	81.0	...	...
Residential burglary	25.5	...	...
Assault	30.8	...	...
Motor vehicle theft	27.2	12.4	Netherlands

* No data provided for rape in Canada.

homicide by a factor of between seven and ten. The other crimes are of still lesser seriousness, but are plausibly ordered as assault, residential burglary, and motor vehicle theft.

There are no high outliers here other than the Netherlands, which has an anomalous rate of convictions for MVT, probably because of definitional differences that excluded joyriding from the count of MVT.

The country-specific analyses are shown in table 9. Here again, there is only one outlier, Canada, which is very much a low outlier for homicide (one-fourth the aggregate mean) and assault (one fourteenth the aggregate mean). Canada is also a low outlier for MVT, about one-quarter the aggregate mean without the Netherlands. Most likely the Canadian outliers are the result of data problems rather than nominal commitment rates that are facially implausible.

Setting aside Canada generally and the anomalous Netherlands MVT sentencing, the commitment rates per 1,000 crimes (CER) are much more consistent across the countries. Two findings stand out. First, the United States, though consistently in the upper half of commitment probabilities, is not the highest for any offense in commitments per 1,000 recorded crimes and, by this measure, is not demonstrably more punitive than other Western countries. Second, Switzerland conspicuously is the most parsimonious user of prison commitments, with the lowest rates for rape, robbery, and burglary, and among the lowest for assault and MVT.[19]

---

[19] If the seemingly anomalous Canadian data are disregarded, Switzerland is also lowest for MVT and second lowest for assault.

TABLE 9

Commitment Rates per 1,000 Recorded Crime Types
by Country and Crime Type

	Homicide	Rape	Robbery	Residential Burglary	Assault	MVT
England and Wales	629.1	62.2	80.0	17.8	47.8	11.7
United States	512.9	78.7	84.0	34.2	45.7	15.3
Sweden	766.9	49.7	71.8	26.3	55.7	11.1
Australia	406.0	41.8	109.4	19.3	12.8	21.3
Scotland	627.2	52.9	79.9	26.4	34.8	18.3
Canada	128.7	N.D.	56.0	17.1	2.1	2.7
Switzerland	681.8	32.3	53.4	15.7	21.8	6.4
Netherlands	681.7	79.3	113.2	47.2	25.8	131.0
Mean of all eight	554.3	56.7	81.0	25.5	30.8	27.2
High outlier	...	...	...	...	...	Netherlands
Mean without high outliers	...	...	...	...	...	12.4
Low outliers	Canada	...	...	...	Canada	Canada
Mean without low outliers	615.1	...	...	...	34.9	14.0

NOTE.—MVT = motor vehicle theft. N.D. = no data provided.

B. *Convictions per 1,000 Recorded Crimes*

Even without a commitment to prison, convictions entail punishment. Part of it is intangible and consists of the stigma associated with a conviction and others' reactions to it. Many convictions, however, involve restrictions on freedom of liberty and autonomy associated with probation, community service, or risks of being sent to prison for violations of conditions of community penalties.

To address this more limited aspect of certainty, we calculate the conviction rate (CONVR) by the following formula:

$$CONVR = (1,000CONV/CRIM), \qquad (4)$$

where:

CONVR = convictions per 1,000 crimes (i.e., certainty of conviction),
CRIM = number of crimes of a particular type recorded by the police, and
CONV = number of convictions for that crime in a year.

This conviction rate, CONVR, is the risk of conviction faced by someone who commits a crime that gets recorded by the police. Table 10

TABLE 10

Convictions per 1,000 Recorded Crimes for Six Crime Types,
Averaged across Time and Country

	Raw Mean	Mean without High Outliers	Countries Excluded as High Outliers
Homicide	621.4	...	...
Rape*	77.9	...	...
Robbery	144.0	...	...
Residential burglary	59.9	...	...
Assault	162.5	...	...
Motor vehicle theft	78.6	47.3	Netherlands

* No data provided for rape in Canada.

presents the aggregate raw mean averaged over all countries. There was only one high outlier, the Netherlands, for motor vehicle theft. The risk of conviction is by far the highest for homicide; there are often likely suspects. The violent crimes of robbery and assault are next highest, but lower than homicide by a factor of about four; these crimes involve face-to-face confrontations, so identification of offenders is easier than for typically more anonymous property crimes. The other violent crime of rape is lower than these by an additional factor of two. The property crimes are the lowest, largely because of the difficulty of identifying perpetrators.

Table 11 displays conviction rates by crime type and country. As with commitment rates, Canada is a low outlier in conviction rates for several crimes, which we attribute to the unreliability of the Canadian data. The United States and Sweden, an odd couple given that they hold top and bottom rankings for prison sentence lengths given a conviction, both appear to be significantly less efficient in securing convictions than are other countries.[20] Both are below the means in conviction rate for at least four of six offenses. Otherwise there are no distinctive patterns for particular countries.

C. Commitments per Conviction

A third measure of certainty is the probability of commitment given a conviction. Like the expected time served per conviction, this is a

[20] The United States somewhat unexpectedly is a low outlier in assault. This is probably a consequence of reclassification of domestic assaults as "aggravated" at the time of arrest, and these rarely end up being prosecuted as assaults, leading to a low ratio of convictions per recorded crime (see Blumstein and Beck 1999).

TABLE 11

Convictions per 1,000 Recorded Crimes by Country and Crime Type

	Homicide	Rape	Robbery	Residential Burglary	Assault	MVT
England and Wales	685.3	65.1	109.4	38.1	240.3	50.7
United States	542.8	96.7	106.5	59.2	75.0	29.5
Sweden	789.8	54.4	92.6	48.6	171.0	39.3
Australia	442.7	98.0	177.4	69.7	156.2	94.7
Scotland	720.0	62.4	127.6	66.3	263.4	74.8
Canada	169.3	N.D.	140.0	85.6	17.6	13.2
Switzerland	883.2	66.1	212.8	40.5	131.4	28.8
Netherlands	737.7	102.6	185.6	71.6	245.3	297.8
Mean of all eight	621.4	77.9	144.0	59.9	162.5	78.6
High outlier	...	...	...	...	...	Netherlands
Mean without high outlier	...	...	...	...	...	47.3
Low outlier	Canada	...	...	...	Canada/United States	Canada
Mean without low outliers	685.9	...	...	...	201.2	53.0

NOTE.—N.D. = no data provided.

TABLE 12

Average Time Served (in Months and Years) for Six Crime Types, Averaged across Time and Country

	Raw Mean		Mean without High Outliers (Months)	Countries Excluded as High Outliers
	Months	Years		
Homicide	86.4	7.2	...	...
Rape*	33.9	2.8	...	...
Robbery	23.4	2.0	...	...
Residential burglary	11.4	...	...	...
Assault	13.3	1.1	11.2	Canada
Motor vehicle theft	6.3	...	...	...

* No data provided for rape in Canada.

more direct measure of punitiveness than convictions or commitments per offense because it ignores variations in clearance and conviction.

Commitments per conviction are presented in table 2. There is striking consistency in these measures. Since these values are inherently constrained to be less than 100 percent, and the aggregate means for three crime types are over 50 percent, there cannot be high outliers. Of the other three, burglary (44 percent) and MVT and assault (both in the twenties) do not generate high outliers. There are some low outliers (burglary in Canada, robbery in Switzerland, and assault in Australia), but no consistent pattern emerges that justifies discussion.

III. Severity of Punishment: Time Served

The typical indicator of severity of punishment is the average time served by those committed to prison, with longer time served indicating more severe punishment. All the uncertainty about clearance of a crime through arrest, uncertainty of conviction, and even the discretion associated with a decision to commit to prison is eliminated. The focus here is on those sent to prison and how long they spend there. The results for severity of punishment are reported in table 12 for averages across all countries and in table 13 for the country-specific values (which are basically drawn from table 3).

Severity of punishment is certainly consistent with the relative seriousness of the offenses—highest for homicide, next for rape, then robbery, then for assault and residential burglary, and lowest for MVT. The striking observation from table 13 is the consistency with which Sweden is a low outlier for four offenses—rape, residential burglary,

TABLE 13
Average Time Served (in Months) by Country and Crime Type

	Homicide	Rape	Robbery	Residential Burglary	Assault	MVT
England and Wales	88.33	34.05	18.00	7.28	6.66	3.83
United States	113.63	59.78	41.60	18.65	23.40	11.94
Sweden	86.95	15.41	15.20	5.23	3.07	2.47
Australia	120.33	50.91	36.20	15.18	23.08	8.71
Scotland	94.70	36.40	17.60	3.56	7.00	2.66
Canada	72.39	N.D.	25.90	15.40	27.95	3.00
Switzerland	46.16	25.14	20.50	14.30	10.13	9.46
Netherlands	69.20	15.80	12.14	11.40	4.91	8.10
Mean of all eight	86.42	33.93	23.39	11.38	13.28	6.27
High outlier	...	...	...	...	Canada	...
Mean without high outlier	...	...	...	...	11.20	...
Low outlier	...	Sweden Netherlands	...	Sweden Scotland	Sweden Netherlands	Sweden Scotland Canada
Mean without low outliers	...	41.30	...	13.70	14.10	8.40

NOTE.—MVT = motor vehicle theft. N.D. = no data provided.

assault, and MVT.[21] Sweden imposes relatively short sentences, moving offenders relatively quickly out of prison back into the community. Scotland and the Netherlands are low outliers in two crime types each, Scotland for the property crimes of MVT and burglary, and the Netherlands for the personal crimes of rape and assault. For the more serious crimes of homicide and robbery, there are no outliers, and there is substantial consistency across the countries.

IV.   Trends in Punitiveness

So far, we have ignored time trends, presenting averages over time for each crime type in each country. In this section we focus briefly on trends in punitiveness,[22] focusing on the certainty and severity of punishment. We measure certainty by the rate of commitments per conviction and severity by time served.

We assess the time trend by an annual "trend ratio." This is the time regression coefficient over the period 1980–99 divided by the mean of the time series.[23] Positive (or negative) trend ratios equal to or greater than 2 percent change per year that were statistically significant were taken as evidence of an upward (or downward) trend. Trend ratios less than 2 percent were interpreted as evidence of stability.

A.   Certainty of Punishment: Probability of Commitment per Conviction

The analysis of trends in certainty of commitment per conviction is displayed in table 14 by crime type and country. The dominant pattern is more one of stability than of consistent trends. The crime type with the most consistent trend is MVT with an upward trend in three countries (England and Wales, Scotland, and Australia). One country,

---

[21] There are three low outliers for MVT. This is largely a consequence of the bimodality of the sentence distribution. Four countries (United States, Switzerland, Australia, and Netherlands) are at the high end, with a mean of 9.55 months, and the other four countries (England and Wales, Scotland, Sweden, and Canada) are at the low end, with a mean of 2.99 months. Thus, the outliers are more interesting for identifying those at the low end of the distribution (England and Wales just missing the cut-point of the outlier criterion) than for suggesting they are anomalous.

[22] Some countries used the same figure year after year as the time served, thereby precluding any meaningful trend analysis; thus, we did not include such repetitive estimates in our analysis. Furthermore, it is difficult to detect long-term trends that may exist within a country if only a few years of data were submitted. This could be the case with Canada for burglary and Scotland for robbery.

[23] Concerning the time regression coefficient, if Y is the measure of concern, then in the regression formula, $Y = a + bt$, the estimated value of b is the relevant time regression coefficient.

TABLE 14

Trend Ratios (Trend Coefficient/Mean Value), Commitments per Conviction by Crime Type

	Rape	Trend	Robbery	Trend	Burglary	Trend	Assault	Trend	MVT	Trend
England and Wales	.1**		−.6**		1.5*		.4**	Up	2.3*	Up
United States	−.4**		−.2		0		−.2		.8	
Sweden	.3		−1.8**		−.9**		−.1		−.2	
Australia	...		−.9*		1.3		0		2.2**	Up
Scotland	.6		.8		3.4*	Up	1.3		3.5*	Up
Canada	...		...		...		...		...	
Switzerland	2.5		−1.8*		.4		−.8		−.8	
Netherlands	−1.7**		−.4		...		3.0*	Up	...	

Note.—Countries with the same entry for every year were not included. A trend of "up" or "down" is noted when the trend ratio exceeds 2 percent per year and is statistically significant at least at a 5 percent level of confidence. In this table, there were no "down" trends. MVT = motor vehicle theft.

* $p < .05$ (two-tailed).

** $p < .01$ (two-tailed).

Scotland, has an upward trend in burglary, and two, England and Wales and the Netherlands, in assault. We do not include homicide in table 14 because the probability of custody per conviction is consistently high everywhere, and trends would be difficult to identify.

Across countries, the trends are most consistent in England and Wales, with two upward trends in assault and MVT. Scotland had upward trends in burglary and MVT. Perhaps because of its large value in the denominator of the trend ratio, the United States was the only country to display no trends over this period.

B. Severity of Punishment: Time Served

Table 15 presents trends in time served by country and by crime type. Trends in time served vary with the seriousness of the offense. In light of growing international concern about violent offenses, an upward trend in average time served for the violent offenses might be expected. Indeed, though table 15 does not identify many trends in average time served, the few trends apparent were more often upward and more often associated with violent offenses. The trend was upward in England and Wales for homicide and rape, for homicide in Switzerland, and for rape in the Netherlands. Time served was also up for robbery and burglary in England and Wales and for homicide and robbery in Switzerland. England and Wales displayed the most consistent upward trend in four of the six offenses, with Switzerland showing an upward trend in two offenses. Motor vehicle theft and assault displayed no trends.

V. Conclusions

There have been few serious efforts cross-nationally to compare punishment practices and policies generally or the severity of punishment in particular. Well-known impediments of variations in institutional arrangements and procedures, in criminal law definitions, and in the comprehensiveness and reliability of data systems explain why. The project of which this volume is a part has tried to address and to minimize those difficulties, and some interesting conclusions or, more modestly, hypotheses, can be drawn from the analyses set out in this essay. First, in general, there are more similarities than differences in how countries responded to the various kinds of crimes. "Punitiveness," variously measured, was consistent with widely shared views about the comparative seriousness of crimes and, in most cases, broadly similar across countries. There were often, however, "outliers" that deviated from the group norms, but usually there was only one high outlier and

TABLE 15

Trend Ratios (Trend Coefficient/Mean Value) in Average Time Served by Crime Type by Country

	Hom.	Trend	Rape	Trend	Rob.	Trend	Burg.	Trend	Assault	Trend	MVT	Trend
England and Wales	3.4**	Up	5.5**	Up	3.3**	Up	2.6*	Up	1.1		-1.1	
United States	1.6**		2.1		-.4		-1.0		-.6		-1.3	
Sweden	1.2**		1.4		.1		1.7**		1.1*		1.5*	
Australia	.8	Up	1.6*		.5		3.9**	Up	.4		-1.2	
Scotland	.9		4.8		-5.4**	Down	1.5		3.6		-1.3	
Canada	2.3	Down	...		1.1		-4.2**	Down	0		...	
Switzerland	6.6*	Up	3.3		2.9**	Up	.9		3.1		2.0	
Netherlands	-2.4	Up	3.7**		1.9**		...		1.0*			

NOTE.—No data provided for rape in Canada. A trend of "up" or "down" is noted when the trend ratio exceeds 2 percent per year and is statistically significant at least at a 5 percent level of confidence. Hom. = homicide. Rob. = robbery. Burg. = burglary. MVT = motor vehicle theft.

* p < .05 (two-tailed).

** p < .01 (two-tailed).

sometimes a low outlier. Even in those cases, the outliers seemed likelier to result from definitional and data problems than from real differences.

The analyses showed that inferences drawn from incarceration rate comparisons that the United States is the most punitive country in the world can be supported by data on average time served relative to recorded crimes, convictions, and average sentence lengths. The United States was the most punitive country for nearly all the crime types, especially when punitiveness is defined narrowly as expected time served per conviction.

Depending on the punitiveness measure used, Sweden and Switzerland are the least punitive countries, though their dynamics differ. The Swedes use imprisonment often but for short terms and the Swiss use prison comparatively seldom but for longer terms. It has been the announced policy of the Swedish criminal justice system to limit the duration of prison sentences, and the effect of that policy is demonstrated in the time-served analysis. The Swiss have been creative in the use of community penalties and appear to be diverting a large fraction of less serious offenders and imposing relatively longer prison sentences on the more serious offenders not diverted.

The analyses in this essay have been based on the time average over the twenty years of each of the parameters characterizing criminal justice processing in each of the eight countries being examined. A separate examination of time trends suggests that there have been a limited number of strong trends in various aspects of punitiveness. These have occurred more often in severity of punishment than in its certainty, and primarily in the violent offenses. Only one country, England and Wales, appears to have increased punitiveness markedly over time, more for severity than for certainty.

The conclusions drawn here are necessarily tentative, but they illustrate that such analyses are possible and that they can be improved as techniques for standardizing and calibrating data across national boundaries improve. The main conclusions, that the United States by multiple measures is substantially more punitive than other Western countries, that, for different reasons, the Swiss and the Swedes are among the least punitive, and that England and Wales is rapidly moving in an American direction are not in themselves very surprising, but they are more firmly bedded in data than such conclusions usually are.

REFERENCES

Blumstein, Alfred, and Allen Beck. 1999. "Population Growth in U.S. Prisons, 1980–96." In *Prisons*, edited by Michael Tonry and Joan Petersilia. Vol. 29 of *Crime and Justice: A Review of Research*, edited by Michael Tonry. Chicago: University of Chicago Press.

Blumstein, Alfred, and Joel Wallman. 2000. *The Crime Drop in America*. New York: Cambridge University Press.

Farrington, David P., Patrick Langan, and Michael Tonry, eds. 2004. *Cross-National Studies in Crime and Justice*. Washington, D.C.: U.S. Bureau of Justice Statistics.

Kommer, Max. 1994. "Punitiveness in Europe—A Comparison." *European Journal on Criminal Policy and Research* 2:29–43.

———. 2004. "Punitiveness in Europe Revisited." *Criminology in Europe* 3(1), 8–12.

Kuhn, André. 2003. "Prison Population Trends in Western Europe." *Criminology in Europe* 2:1, 12–16.

Lappi-Seppälä, Tapio. 2001. "Sentencing and Punishment in Finland: The Decline of the Retributive Ideal." In *Sentencing and Sanctions in Western Countries*, edited by Michael Tonry and Richard S. Frase. New York: Oxford University Press.

Tonry, Michael. 2004. *Thinking about Crime: Sense and Sensibility in American Penal Culture*. New York: Oxford University Press.

Tonry, Michael, and Richard S. Frase, eds. 2001. *Sentencing and Sanctions in Western Countries*. New York: Oxford University Press.

Young, Warren, and Mark Brown. 1993. "Cross-National Comparisons of Imprisonment." In *Crime and Justice: A Review of Research*, vol. 17, edited by Michael Tonry. Chicago: University of Chicago Press.

Walmsley, Roy. 2003. *World Prison Population List*. 4th ed. Home Office Findings Report no. 188. London: Home Office.

Whitman, James Q. 2003. *Harsh Justice: Criminal Punishment and the Widening Divide between America and Europe*. New York: Oxford University Press.

Wilson, James Q. 2002. "Crime and Public Policy." In *Crime: Public Policies for Crime Control*, edited by James Q. Wilson and Joan Petersilia. Oakland, Calif.: ICS Press.

Zimring, Franklin E., and Gordon Hawkins. 1991. *The Scale of Imprisonment*. Chicago: University of Chicago Press.

David P. Farrington and Darrick Jolliffe

Cross-National Comparisons of Crime Rates in Four Countries, 1981–1999

The main aims of this essay are to compare changes in crime rates over time in different countries and to assess the plausibility of some explanations of these changes. We do not attempt to explain differences between countries in levels of crime. We compare four countries: England and Wales (hereafter referred to as England), the United States, the Netherlands, and Switzerland. We choose these countries because the essays on the United States, the Netherlands, and Switzerland most closely followed the template of the original England chapter in the Bureau of Justice Statistics report (Farrington, Langan, and Tonry 2004), both in documenting changes in crime and punishment over time and in investigating correlations between crime rates and other possibly influencing factors. We analyze victim survey crime rates for residential burglary, vehicle theft, robbery, and assault because we believe that they are more accurate than police-recorded crime rates, but we have to use police-recorded crime rates for rape and homicide.

Despite efforts to collect comparable data in different countries, many problems remain. In particular, the methodology used in victim surveys in the four countries differed, and serious assault was not very comparable. Burglary and vehicle theft were not explicitly distinguished from other types of theft in the criminal codes of the Netherlands and Switzerland, rapes included male victims in the Netherlands, and there were no convictions of persons under age eighteen in Switzerland. (For more

David Farrington is professor of psychological criminology, Institute of Criminology, Cambridge University, from which institution Darrick Jolliffe recently received his Ph.D. We are very grateful to Matthew Durose, Martin Killias, Philippe Lamon, and Patrick Langan for providing additional information and carrying out additional analyses.

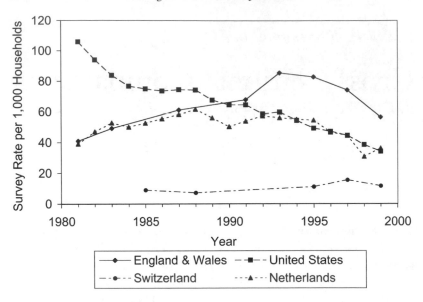

FIG. 1.—Burglary: survey crime rate

detailed information about these countries, see the other essays in this volume.)

This essay has a very simple organization. Section I compares changes in crime rates over time in the four countries. Section II assesses the plausibility of some explanations for these changes by investigating correlations between crime rates and sociodemographic and criminal justice factors in the four countries. Section III summarizes the main conclusions and makes recommendations about future research that is needed to advance knowledge about changes in crime rates over time in different countries.

I. Changes in Crime Rates over Time

This section presents comparative figures describing trends in crime rates over time in England, the United States, the Netherlands, and Switzerland. Trends in residential burglary, vehicle theft, robbery, serious assault, rape, and homicide are compared between 1981 and 1999.

A. Burglary

Figure 1 shows changes in residential burglary rates over time in the four countries as shown by national victimization surveys. In 1981, the United States had the highest burglary rate: 106 per 1,000 households, compared with forty-one in England and thirty-nine in the Netherlands. By 1999, the U.S. rate had decreased by two-thirds, to thirty-four per 1,000 households, compared with thirty-six in the Netherlands and fifty-seven in England. In 1981, the American burglary rate was 2.6 times the English rate and three times the Dutch rate. In 1999, the English burglary rate was 66 percent higher than the American, and the Dutch rate was 6 percent higher.

The English burglary rate more than doubled between 1981 (forty-one per 1,000 households) and 1993 (eighty-six) but then decreased by one-third to fifty-seven in 1999. Similarly, the Dutch burglary rate increased from 1981 (thirty-five per 1,000 households) to 1988 (sixty-two) but then decreased back to thirty-six in 1999. The burglary rate in Switzerland was consistently the lowest, at between seven and fifteen burglaries per 1,000 households; survey burglary rates were not available in Switzerland before 1985. The Swiss burglary rate showed some tendency to increase over time.

B. Vehicle Theft

In contrast to burglary, the rate of vehicle theft (including taking and driving away vehicles) in Switzerland was consistently the highest before 1999, although it decreased remarkably from 198 per 1,000 households in 1985 to sixteen per 1,000 households in 1999 (see fig. 2; the 1985 figure was too high to show on the graph without using a logarithmic scale). The main reason for this decrease was dramatically reduced numbers of thefts of motorcycles, mopeds, and scooters, partly caused by a new law in 1987 requiring all riders of motorcycles, mopeds, and scooters to wear crash helmets (Killias, Lamon, and Aebi, in this volume). In 1984, in the French-speaking parts of the country, the survey rates of vehicle theft per owner were 14.9 percent of mopeds, 8.7 percent of motorcycles, and 0.4 percent of cars. In 1986, in the remaining parts of the country, the survey rates were 10.0 percent of mopeds, 1.1 percent of motorcycles, and 0.4 percent of cars. In 1999, in the whole of Switzerland, the survey rates were only 1 percent of motorcycles and mopeds and 0.4 percent of cars. Recorded vehicle theft in Switzerland also decreased during this time period, but by only about one-third (Killias, Lamon, and Aebi, in this volume).

The English vehicle theft rate varied in the same way as the English burglary rate, increasing from sixteen per 1,000 households in 1981 to twenty-six in 1993, and then decreasing to fifteen in 1999. The American and Dutch vehicle theft rates were generally similar and low during this

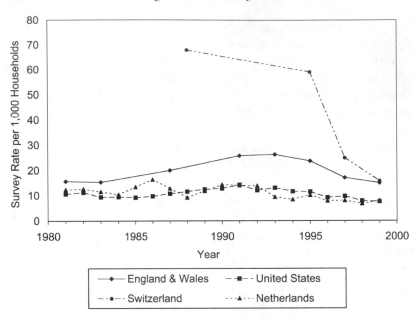

Fɪɢ. 2.—Vehicle theft: survey crime rate

time period, although both tended to decrease in the 1990s. The American rate was eleven per 1,000 households in 1981 and eight in 1999; the Dutch rate was twelve per 1,000 households in 1981 and eight in 1999. In 1999, the English and Swiss vehicle theft rates (fifteen and sixteen per 1,000 households, respectively) were about twice as high as the American and Dutch rates (both eight).

C. Robbery

The Netherlands consistently had the highest robbery rate (fig. 3; survey robbery rates were not available before 1988). In 1988, the Dutch robbery rate was twelve per 1,000 persons, compared with seven in the United States, six in Switzerland, and four in England. The Dutch robbery rate then decreased up until 1995 but increased again up until 1999. In 1999, the Dutch robbery rate was fifteen per 1,000 persons, compared with eight in England, six in Switzerland, and four in the United States. The American robbery rate decreased from seven per 1,000 persons in 1981 to four in 1999, while, conversely, the English robbery rate increased from four per 1,000 persons in 1981 to eight in 1999. The Swiss rate showed no clear trend, fluctuating between four and seven robberies per 1,000 persons. The rate was seven in 1995, four in 1997, and six in 1999 (see below).

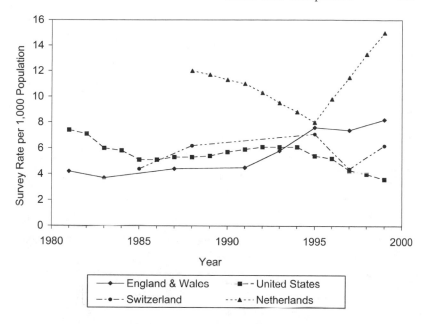

FIG. 3. Robbery. survey crime rate

D. Serious Assault

Serious assault was the least comparable offense between countries. However, figure 4 shows that assault rates were consistently highest in Switzerland, where the rate increased from fifteen per 1,000 persons in 1985 to forty-one in 1995, twenty-three in 1999, and thirty-six in 1999. It seems likely that the decreases in robbery and assault between 1995 and 1997, and the increases between 1997 and 1999, were real.

Between 1995 and 1996, a heroin prescription program was introduced and methodone substitution was extended to about 15,000 of Switzerland's 25,000 heroin addicts. Since these addicts were heavily involved in street crime, this program probably caused a decrease in robbery and assault (Killias, Lamon, and Aebi, in this volume). In 1998–99, the situation in Kosovo worsened considerably, and about 150,000 refugees (mainly young males) came to Switzerland within a short time period, which had a big impact in a country of 7 million people. This immigration led to many young males hanging about on the streets with few structured activities and probably caused a large increase in street crime. The proportion of offenders perceived by Swiss victims to be of foreign origin increased between 1987 and 1999 from 33 to 63 percent for robbery and from 19 to 55 percent for assault (Killias, Lamon, and Aebi, in this volume). The increases in street crime were less apparent

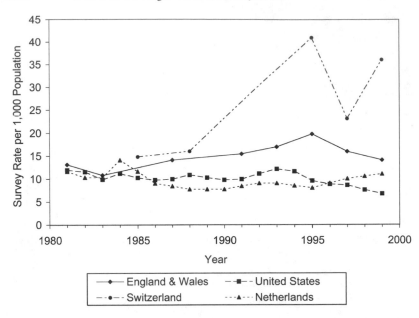

FIG. 4.—Assault: survey crime rate

in police figures because the police were cautious about recording robberies and assaults.

The English assault rate increased from eleven per 1,000 persons in
1983 to twenty in 1995, before decreasing to fourteen in 1999. In contrast, the American assault rate decreased from twelve per 1,000 persons
in 1981 to seven in 1999. The Dutch assault rate fluctuated over time
between eight and thirteen per 1,000 persons. In 1999, the serious assault rate was highest in Switzerland (thirty-six), followed by England
(fourteen) and the Netherlands (eleven), and lowest in the United States
(seven). All the assault rates were quite similar in 1985.

E. Rape

The recorded rape rate was consistently highest in the United States
(fig. 5); between 1981 and 1992, it increased from seventy-one to eighty-
four rapes per 100,000 females, before decreasing to sixty-four in 1999.
The rape rate in England increased dramatically, from four per 100,000
females in 1981 to twenty-nine in 1999. The rape rate in the Netherlands
also increased, from eleven per 100,000 females in 1981 to twenty-two
in 1999. The rape rate in Switzerland fluctuated between eighteen and
twenty-six per 100,000 females. In 1999, the American rape rate was
2.2 times the English rate, 2.8 times the Swiss rate, and 2.9 times the

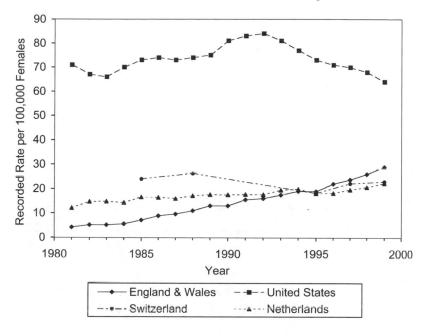

FIG. 5.—Rape: survey crime rate

Dutch rate. However, in 1981 the American rate had been 16.9 times the English rate and 6.3 times the Dutch rate.

F. Homicide

As with rape, the homicide rate was consistently highest in the United States (fig. 6); however, it decreased irregularly from 9.8 per 100,000 persons in 1981 to 5.7 in 1999. The homicide rates were similar in the other three countries. However, the English rate increased slightly from 1.1 per 100,000 in 1981 to 1.4 in 1999, while the Swiss rate decreased slightly from 1.4 per 100,000 in 1985 to 1.1 in 1999. The Dutch rate fluctuated between 1.0 and 1.8 per 100,000. In 1999, the American homicide rate was 3.9 times the Dutch rate, 4.1 times the English rate, and 5.2 times the Swiss rate. However, in 1981 the American rate had been 7.5 times the Dutch rate and 8.9 times the English rate.

II. Explaining Changes in National Crime Rates

As we pointed out in another essay in this volume (Farrington and Jolliffe, in this volume), it is difficult to test explanations of changes in national crime rates over time, because of the difficulty of isolating particular factors and controlling statistically for other possible influences

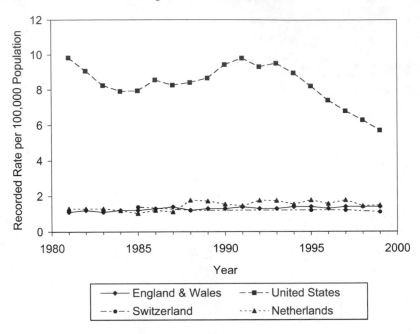

Fig. 6.—Homicide: survey crime rate

on crime rates. Different factors may influence different types of crimes in different time periods and different countries, possibly depending on the magnitude of change in the explanatory factor. Nevertheless, we analyze data from the four countries to see if we can identify factors that might have similar effects on crime rates in different countries. Our modest aim is to assess some possible influencing factors as more or less plausible, on the basis of their correlations with crime rates in different countries.

A. Explanatory Factors

Correlations are available for the following explanatory factors in the four countries.

The Percentage of the Population Ages Fifteen to Twenty-Four.   It might be expected that crime rates would be higher when there are relatively more young people in the population, because young people are more likely than older people to commit crimes (see, e.g., Farrington 1986).[1]

The Percentage of Males Seeking Work Who Are Unemployed.   It might be expected that property crime rates would be higher when unemployment rates were higher, because males commit more property crimes (but not

---

[1] The U.S. figures refer to the percentage of the population ages thirteen to twenty-four.

more violent crimes) during periods of unemployment than during periods of employment (Farrington et al. 1986).[2]

The Gross Domestic Product (GDP) per Population, Adjusted for Retail Price Inflation.   This is a measure of economic prosperity. According to Field (1990), increases in prosperity mean that people in marginal economic groups are better able to obtain income legitimately and hence have less need to commit property crimes in order to obtain income. However, increases in prosperity also mean that people in marginal economic groups go out more and drink more alcohol, both of which are likely to cause increases in violence and sex crimes. According to these theories, periods of high prosperity should cause low rates of property crimes and high rates of violent crimes.

Alcohol Consumption per Population.   As stated above, high rates of alcohol consumption might be expected to cause high rates of violence and sex crimes.[3]

Police Strength per Population.   To the extent that police are effective, increases in police strength (i.e., in the number of police officers per population) should cause decreases in crime rates.

Conviction Rate per Offender.   If the risk of being convicted deters a potential offender from committing crimes, increases in this risk should cause decreases in crime rates. However, this theory assumes that offenders make rational decisions. To the extent that offenders are irrational (e.g., in committing violent crimes) or compulsive (e.g., in committing sex crimes), the risk of conviction will not be effective as a deterrent. On the assumption that property crimes are more likely than violent crimes to involve a rational calculation, it might be expected that the risk of conviction would be negatively correlated with property crime rates but not with violent crime rates.

The risk of being convicted was measured by comparing the number of convictions with the number of crimes, with appropriate corrections for co-offending and for differences between survey crimes and crimes leading to conviction (see Farrington and Jolliffe, in this volume). However, as Cook and Khmilevska (in this volume) point out, when this risk is correlated with the crime rate, there is a methodological problem, because the number of crimes is the numerator of the crime measure and the denominator of the risk measure. Therefore, errors of measurement

---

[2] The U.S. figures refer to the percentage of adults seeking work who are unemployed.

[3] The England figures refer to beer consumption.

in estimating the number of crimes will generate an artifactual negative correlation between the risk of conviction and the crime rate.

In order to avoid this problem, we used the number of survey crimes in estimating the risk of conviction and correlated it with the police-recorded crime rate. We could only do this for burglary, vehicle theft, robbery, and assault; for rape and homicide, the risk of conviction also had to be based on the police-recorded crime rate. To the extent that the police-recorded crime rate is a worse measure of the true crime rate than is the survey crime rate, this procedure has disadvantages. We return to this issue later.

Probability (Custody per Conviction) and Average Time Served.   If the severity of punishment deters a potential offender from committing crimes, increases in severity should cause decreases in crime rates. Again, since this theory assumes that offenders make rational decisions, the severity of punishment may be negatively correlated with property crime rates rather than with violent or sex crime rates.

Problems of Causal Order.   Establishing a correlation does not, of course, establish a causal relationship, partly because of the problem of uncontrolled influences that has already been mentioned, but also because of problems of causal order. In particular, if the probability of an offender being convicted is negatively correlated with the crime rate, this may be because increases in the numbers of crimes cause decreases in the risk of conviction (given constant resources in the criminal justice system), rather than the reverse.

We attempted to address the problem of causal order by calculating lagged correlations. When the crime rate in one time period was used to predict the risk of conviction in the next time period, this was termed "conviction rate/offender A" (crime rate first). When the risk of conviction in one time period was used to predict the crime rate in the next time period, this was termed "conviction rate/offender B" (conviction rate first).

Unfortunately, because of long gaps between surveys in England (up to four years) and Switzerland (up to seven years), this attempt to throw light on causal order had severe limitations. Even in the Netherlands, which had yearly surveys, this analysis would only be useful if the gap between cause and effect were at least one year. If changes in the risk of conviction influenced changes in the commission of crime (or vice versa) within one year, the two types of lagged correlations would produce identical results and hence would throw no light on causal order.

TABLE 1

Correlations with Survey Burglary Rates

Correlate	England	United States	Netherlands	Switzerland
Year	.67	−.97	.10	.75
Recorded burglary rate	.91	.98	.65	.96
Percent population ages 15–24	−.65	.94	−.06	−.80
Percent males unemployed	.48	.77	.81	.91
GDP/population	.67	−.97	−.13	.60
Alcohol consumption/population	−.69	.92	−.65	−.80
Police strength/population	.56	−.95	−.29	.65
Conviction rate/offender	−.75	.89	−.70	−.83
Probability (custody/conviction)	.12	−.48	−.05	.03
Average time served	.10	−.01	N.A.	.13
Conviction rate/offender A	−.86	−.59	−.70	−.38
Conviction rate/offender B	−.42	−.72	−.71	−.77

NOTE.—GDP = gross domestic product, corrected for price inflation; conviction rate/offender is correlated with recorded crime rates; A = crime rate first; B = conviction rate first; N.A. = not available.

B. Burglary

Table 1 shows correlations between survey burglary rates and the various explanatory factors. It also shows correlations among the survey burglary rate, the year, and the police-recorded burglary rate. The correlations with the year show that survey burglary rates generally increased in England and Switzerland, decreased in the United States, and showed no clear trend the Netherlands (see also fig. 1). The correlations with the recorded burglary rate show that the victim survey largely agreed with the police records in all four countries in revealing trends in burglary.

In regard to sociodemographic factors, correlations with the number of young people in the population, prosperity (GDP), alcohol consumption, and police strength were clearly inconsistent between the United States and other countries, suggesting no consistent causal relationships between these factors and the burglary rate. In the United States (where burglary was decreasing), the burglary rate was positively correlated with the fraction of young people in the population and with alcohol consumption and negatively correlated with prosperity and police strength, as expected. Most notably, the unemployment rate was positively correlated with the burglary rate in all four countries.

In regard to measures of legal punishment, the probability of custody and the average time served were not consistently correlated with the

TABLE 2

Correlations with Survey Vehicle Theft Rates

Correlate	England	United States	Netherlands	Switzerland
Year	.22	−.15	−.48	−.87
Recorded vehicle theft rate	.97	.87	−.15	.81
Percent population ages 15–24	−.20	−.24	.37	.84
Percent males unemployed	.73	.17	.08	−.60
GDP/population	.25	−.21	−.54	−.93
Alcohol consumption/population	−.27	−.45	.29	.87
Police strength/population	.86	−.22	−.57	.42
Conviction rate/offender	−.67	.70	.28	−.82
Probability (custody/conviction)	−.50	.06	.02	.66
Average time served	−.88	.15	N.A.	−.42
Conviction rate/offender A	−.74	.59	−.02	−.96
Conviction rate/offender B	−.40	.80	.32	−.83

NOTE.—GDP = gross domestic product, corrected for price inflation; conviction rate/offender is correlated with recorded crime rates; A = crime rate first; B = conviction rate first; N.A. = not available.

burglary rate; almost all correlations were very low. The probability of an offender being convicted was consistently negatively correlated with the burglary rate. However, the lagged correlations were not consistently higher in the "crime rate first" condition as opposed to the "conviction rate first" condition.

C. Vehicle Theft

Correlations with the year indicated that vehicle theft generally decreased in the Netherlands and Switzerland but did not show linear trends in England or the United States (table 2). The survey crime rate was highly correlated with the recorded crime rate in three countries but not in the Netherlands. This was because, in the Netherlands, the survey crime rate increased to a peak in 1986 and then decreased, while the recorded crime rate kept on increasing to a peak in 1994 before decreasing. Since at least 90 percent of survey offenses were reported to the police in all years, the later peak in recorded vehicle theft was probably caused by the increasing probability of a reported crime being recorded. Hence, in the Netherlands, survey crimes probably provide a more accurate indication of crime trends over time.

Vehicle theft was not consistently correlated with any of the sociodemographic factors. In Switzerland, where vehicle theft was decreasing, the vehicle theft rate was positively correlated with the fraction of young

TABLE 3
Correlations with Survey Robbery Rates

Correlate	England	United States	Netherlands	Switzerland
Year	.91	−.69	.23	.29
Recorded robbery rate	.94	.81	−.19	.20
Percent population ages 15–24	−.94	.56	.35	−.29
Percent males unemployed	−.41	.76	−.69	.01
GDP/population	.90	−.77	.38	.40
Alcohol consumption/population	−.93	.49	.37	.19
Police strength/population	−.43	−.68	.29	−.46
Conviction rate/offender	−.91	−.02	.85	−.77
Probability (custody/conviction)	−.56	.17	.15	−.38
Average time served	.79	−.18	−.74	.34
Conviction rate/offender A	−.96	−.29	.78	−.54
Conviction rate/offender B	−.76	.20	.90	−.11

Note.—GDP = gross domestic product, corrected for price inflation; conviction rate/offender is correlated with recorded crime rates; A = crime rate first; B = conviction rate first.

people in the population and with alcohol consumption and negatively correlated with prosperity, as expected. It was highly positively correlated with the unemployment rate only in England. Nor was vehicle theft consistently negatively correlated with any of the measures of punishment. In the United States, the peak in the recorded crime rate (between 1988 and 1994) coincided with high probabilities of an offender being convicted. Hence, the correlation between the vehicle theft rate and the risk of punishment was positive in the United States. In England, the risk of conviction, the risk of custody, and the average time served were all negatively correlated with the vehicle theft rate.

D. Robbery

Correlations with the year indicated that robbery generally increased in England, decreased in the United States, and showed no clear trend in the Netherlands or Switzerland (table 3). The survey robbery rate was highly correlated with the recorded robbery rate in England and the United States but not in the Netherlands or Switzerland. In the Netherlands, the probability of a reported crime being recorded peaked in 1994–95, at a time when survey crime rates were low. Hence, survey crime rates are probably more accurate. In Switzerland, the number of recorded crimes tended to increase, but the survey crime rate fluctuated considerably, from 7.1 robberies per 1,000 persons in 1995 to 4.4 in 1997 and 6.2 in 1999. As mentioned earlier, Killias, Lamon, and Aebi (in this

TABLE 4

Correlations with Survey Assault Rates

Correlate	England	United States	Netherlands	Switzerland
Year	.62	−.63	−.41	.77
Recorded assault rate	.51	−.01	.92	.62
Percent population ages 15–24	−.67	.44	−.13	−.79
Percent males unemployed	.28	.63	−.83	.57
GDP/population	.64	−.69	.88	.70
Alcohol consumption/population	−.69	.28	.19	−.70
Police strength/population	.35	−.66	.63	−.52
Conviction rate/offender	−.88	.79	.69	−.35
Probability (custody/conviction)	.49	.54	.82	−.88
Average time served	.33	−.06	−.19	.41
Conviction rate/offender A	−.82	.81	.68	−.02
Conviction rate/offender B	−.90	.82	.69	−.32

Note.—GDP = gross domestic product, corrected for price inflation; conviction rate/offender is correlated with recorded crime rates; A = crime rate first; B = conviction rate first.

volume) considered that the survey crime rates indicated real changes in the robbery rate.

Like vehicle theft, robbery was not consistently correlated with any of the sociodemographic factors. In the United States, the robbery rate was positively correlated with the fraction of young people in the population, with the unemployment rate, and with alcohol consumption and negatively correlated with prosperity and with police strength. Vehicle theft was not consistently correlated with any of the measures of punishment. In the Netherlands, high recorded robbery rates (in 1992–95) coincided with the highest probabilities of an offender being convicted. However, the fluctuations in recorded robbery rates were not very great, from 0.80–0.86 per 1,000 population in 1989–91 to 1.02–1.07 in 1992–95 and 0.91–0.98 in 1996–98. Hence, the correlation between the robbery rate and the risk of conviction was positive in the Netherlands. It was highly negative in England and Switzerland. The average time served was negatively correlated with the robbery rate in the Netherlands but positively correlated in England.

E. Assault

Correlations with the year indicated that assault generally increased in England and Switzerland and decreased in the United States and (to a lesser degree) in the Netherlands (table 4). The survey assault rate was highly correlated with the recorded assault rate in all countries except

TABLE 5

Correlations with Recorded Rape Rates

Correlate	England	United States	Netherlands	Switzerland
Year	.99	−.08	.93	−.53
Percent population ages 15–24	−.96	−.49	−.51	.65
Percent males unemployed	−.29	.40	−.66	−.74
GDP/population	.99	.03	.87	−.31
Alcohol consumption/population	−.90	−.63	−.73	.48
Police strength/population	−.06	.01	.51	.37
Conviction rate/offender	−.92	.80	−.66	−.66
Probability (custody/conviction)	.62	−.56	−.53	−.75
Average time served	.96	.76	.42	−.43
Conviction rate/offender A	−.91	.62	−.52	.33
Conviction rate/offender B	−.93	.45	−.43	−.49

NOTE.—GDP = gross domestic product, corrected for price inflation; A = crime rate first: B = conviction rate first.

the United States. Langan and Farrington (1998, pp. 10–11) noted that the probability of a reported assault being recorded in the United States increased considerably (from 60 percent to 100 percent) between 1981 and 1991. Hence, in the United States, survey assaults probably provide a more accurate indication of crime trends over time.

Assault was not consistently correlated with any of the sociodemographic factors. High prosperity coincided with high assault rates in England, the Netherlands, and Switzerland, but not in the United States. Police strength was negatively correlated with the assault rate in the United States and Switzerland but positively correlated in the Netherlands. Assault was highly positively correlated with the unemployment rate in the United States and Switzerland but negatively correlated in the Netherlands. The assault rate was not consistently correlated with any of the measures of punishment. In the United States and the Netherlands, both the recorded assault rate and the probability of an offender being convicted tended to increase over time. The probability of custody was negatively correlated with assault only in Switzerland.

F. Rape

Correlations with the year show that rape increased in England and the Netherlands, decreased in Switzerland, and showed no linear trend in the United States (table 5). The rape rate was not consistently correlated with any of the sociodemographic factors, and neither was it

TABLE 6

Correlations with Recorded Homicide Rates

Correlate	England	United States	Netherlands	Switzerland
Year	.81	−.54	.61	−.81
Percent population ages 15–24	−.71	.24	−.52	.74
Percent males unemployed	−.12	.55	.53	−.35
GDP/population	.80	−.61	.55	−.94
Alcohol consumption/population	−.68	.10	−.52	.80
Police strength/population	.17	−.58	−.03	1.00
Conviction rate/offender	−.43	−.46	−.72	−.55
Probability (custody/conviction)	.56	.13	.75	.49
Average time served	.58	−.38	−.99	−.76
Conviction rate/offender A	.13	−.16	.17	−.91
Conviction rate/offender B	.01	.01	−.24	−.07

NOTE.—GDP = gross domestic product, corrected for price inflation; A = crime rate first; B = conviction rate first.

consistently correlated with any of the measures of punishment. In England and the Netherlands, periods of high prosperity coincided with high rape rates. In agreement with the deterrence hypothesis, rape was negatively correlated with the probability of an offender being convicted and with the probability of an offender being sentenced to custody in three out of four countries. However, it was positively correlated with the average time served in three out of four countries.

G. *Homicide*

Correlations with the year indicated that homicide generally increased in England and the Netherlands and decreased in the United States and Switzerland (table 6). However, fluctuations in three of these countries (all except the United States) were relatively small (fig. 6). The homicide rate was not consistently correlated with any of the sociodemographic factors. It was correlated with the fraction of young people in the population in Switzerland, with the unemployment rate in the United States and the Netherlands, and with alcohol consumption in Switzerland. Homicide was positively correlated with prosperity in England and the Netherlands and negatively correlated in the United States and Switzerland. Homicide was negatively correlated with police strength in the United States but positively correlated in Switzerland. (The perfect correlation between the homicide rate and police strength in Switzerland is based on only five years.)

TABLE 7
Summary of Correlations

Correlate	.40 or higher	.39 to −.39	−.40 or lower	Total
Year	10	6	8	24
Recorded crime rate	12	4	0	16
Percent population ages 15–24	6	8	10	24
Percent males unemployed	11	7	6	24
GDP/population	11	6	7	24
Alcohol consumption/population	6	7	11	24
Police strength/population	7	9	8	24
Conviction rate/offender	5	3	16	24
Probability (custody/conviction)	8	9	7	24
Average time served	6	10	6	22
Conviction rate/offender A	5	8	11	24
Conviction rate/offender B	5	8	11	24

NOTE.—GDP = gross domestic product, corrected for price inflation; A = crime rate first; B = conviction rate first.

The homicide rate was negatively correlated with the probability of an offender being convicted in all four countries. It was positively correlated with the probability of an offender being sentenced to custody in three out of four countries and negatively correlated with the average time served in the Netherlands and Switzerland.

H. Summarizing the Results

Table 7 summarizes the main results by counting the number of substantial positive correlations (.40 or higher), the number of substantial negative correlations (−.40 or less), and the number of smaller correlations (between .39 and −.39). Over six offenses in four countries in 1981–99, there was no marked tendency for crime rates to increase, since the number of substantial increases (ten) was only slightly greater than the number of substantial decreases (eight). However, recorded crime rates were usually substantially positively correlated with survey crime rates (in twelve out of sixteen cases). In most cases, therefore, the survey and recorded crime rates indicated the same conclusions about crime trends.

There was little tendency for crime rates to be consistently correlated with the number of young people in the population, prosperity (GDP), or police strength. Crime rates tended to be negatively correlated with alcohol consumption, but this is a counterintuitive result. As expected, crime rates were somewhat more likely to be substantially positively

TABLE 8

Summary of Correlations with the Unemployment Rate

	.40 or Higher	.39 to −.39	−.40 or Lower	Mean
Burglary	4	0	0	.74*
Vehicle theft	1	2	1	.10
Robbery	1	1	2	−.08
Assault	2	1	1	.16
Rape	1	1	2	−.32
Homicide	2	2	0	.15
Total	11	7	6	.12
England	2	3	1	.11
United States	5	1	0	.55*
Netherlands	2	1	3	−.13
Switzerland	2	2	2	−.03

* $p < .05$.

correlated with unemployment rates than substantially negatively correlated (eleven, compared with six, cases).

There was little tendency for crime rates to be consistently correlated with measures of the severity of punishment. However, crime rates were more likely to be substantially negatively correlated with the risk of conviction than substantially positively correlated (sixteen, compared with five, cases). There was no tendency for lagged correlations to be greater for "crime rate first" or "conviction rate first." One possible implication of this is that any effects of changes in the risk of punishment on offending (or vice versa) occur relatively quickly, perhaps within one year.

Table 8 summarizes correlations between the crime rate and the unemployment rate in more detail. These correlations were significantly positive for burglary and for the United States but not in any other case.

Table 9 summarizes correlations between the crime rate and the risk of conviction in more detail. These correlations were significantly negative for burglary and homicide and for England and Switzerland.

Unlike the sociodemographic factors, we can also calculate these correlations using the spreadsheets of Scotland (Smith 2004) and Sweden (Wikström and Dolmen 2004; robbery is not included). Over six countries, the significant negative correlation between the homicide rate and the risk of conviction is maintained, but the correlation for burglary is now not quite significant ($p < .10$), nor is the correlation for rape. Of course, it must be remembered that the correlations for homicide and rape

TABLE 9

Summary of Correlations with Conviction Rate/Offender

	.40 or Higher	.39 to −.39	−.40 or Lower	Mean
Burglary	0	0	4	−.79*
Vehicle theft	1	1	2	−.13
Robbery	1	1	2	−.21
Assault	2	1	1	.06
Rape	1	0	3	−.36
Homicide	0	0	4	−.54*
Total	5	3	16	−.33
Adding Scotland and Sweden				
Burglary	1	1	4	−.43+
Vehicle theft	1	1	4	−.34
Robbery	1	2	2	−.13
Assault	2	3	1	−.02
Rape	1	0	5	−.52+
Homicide	0	1	5	−.52*
Total	6	8	21	−.33*
England	0	0	6	−.76*
United States	3	1	2	.15
Netherlands	2	1	3	−.04
Switzerland	0	1	5	−.66*
Scotland	0	3	3	−.36+
Sweden	1	2	2	−.31

* $p < .05.$
+ $p < .10.$

are subject to the methodological problem mentioned earlier, namely, that the recorded crime rate also contributes to the estimate of the risk of conviction. There was almost a significant negative correlation ($p < .10$) between the crime rate and the risk of conviction in Scotland.

In order to avoid this methodological problem, we correlated the recorded crime rate with the risk of conviction based on the survey crime rate for burglary, vehicle theft, robbery, and assault. However, this approach may be disadvantageous where we believe that the recorded crime rate is not a good measure of the true crime rate (e.g., because of changes in the probability of recording). This is likely to apply when there is a low correlation between the survey crime rate and the recorded crime rate.

There was a low correlation (less than .40) in six cases: burglary in Sweden; vehicle theft in the Netherlands; robbery in the Netherlands, Switzerland, and Scotland; and assault in the United States. In at least three of these cases (vehicle theft and robbery in the Netherlands, assault in the United States), this low correlation was probably caused by changes in the probability of a reported crime being recorded, and the recorded crime rate is probably less accurate than the survey crime rate. In these three cases, the correlations between survey crime rates and the risk of conviction were more in accordance with the deterrence hypothesis. (Netherlands vehicle theft: survey = −.60, recorded = .28; Netherlands robbery: survey = −.75, recorded = .85; United States assault: survey = −.49, recorded .79).

III. Conclusions

We have documented changes in crime rates in four countries, making rigorous efforts to collect comparable data across time and across countries. We found many differences both in crime levels and in crime trends. More efforts need to be made in the future to repeat these kinds of analyses in different countries. In particular, there is a great need for more countries to carry out large-scale annual victimization surveys to provide national estimates of crime rates.

We have also reported correlations between crime rates and possible causal factors across time and in different countries. Apart from the negative correlation between crime rates and the probability of an of-fender being convicted, few of these results proved to be replicable across different countries. However, we were not able to measure and control for numerous factors that might influence national crime rates.

There is a great need to measure more national indicators of possible causal factors in different countries and to carry out multivariate, multi-country analyses to try to isolate the effects of particular factors on crime rates. These analyses might aim to explain not only crime trends over time but also differences between countries in levels of crime.

It seems quite likely that causal influences may be different for dif-ferent types of crimes in different countries in different time periods. For example, it was argued that one reason why vehicle theft decreased in Switzerland was because wearing crash helmets on motorcycles, mopeds, and scooters became compulsory, thereby making it more risky to take one of these vehicles (by potential offenders who were not wearing crash helmets). Another reason was because the ownership of these vehicles decreased as car ownership increased, and cars were much harder to steal.

It may be that specific, rather than general, explanations are needed for many of the crime trends shown in figures 1–6.

We know much less about factors that influence national crime rates over time than about factors that influence individual offending. Co-ordinated, collaborative cross-national research, incorporating serious efforts to achieve comparability between countries and across time, is needed to advance knowledge about this very important issue. We need to know why crime increases and decreases, what the effects of different economic and criminal justice policies are, and what steps governments can take to decrease crime.

REFERENCES

Cook, Philip J., and Nataliya Khmilevska. In this volume. "Cross-National Patterns in Crime Rates."

Farrington, David P. 1986. "Age and Crime." In *Crime and Justice: An Annual Review of Research*, vol. 7, edited by Michael Tonry and Norval Morris. Chicago: University of Chicago Press.

Farrington, David P., Bernard Gallagher, Lynda Morley, Raymond J. St. Ledger, and Donald J. West. 1986. "Unemployment, School Leaving, and Crime." *British Journal of Criminology* 26:335–56.

Farrington, David P. and Darrick Jollitte. In this volume. "Crime and Punishment in England and Wales, 1981–1999."

Farrington, David P., Patrick A. Langan, and Michael Tonry, eds. 2004. *Cross-National Studies in Crime and Justice*. Washington, D.C.: U.S. Bureau of Justice Statistics.

Field, Simon. 1990. *Trends in Crime and Their Interpretation*. London: H.M. Stationery Office.

Killias, Martin, Philippe Lamon, and Marcelo F. Aebi. In this volume. "Crime and Punishment in Switzerland, 1985–1999."

Langan, Patrick A., and David P. Farrington. 1998. *Crime and Justice in the United States and in England and Wales, 1981–96*. Washington, D.C.: U.S. Bureau of Justice Statistics.

Smith, David J. 2004. "Scotland." In *Cross-National Studies in Crime and Justice*, edited by David P. Farrington, Patrick A. Langan, and Michael Tonry. Washington, D.C.: U.S. Bureau of Justice Statistics.

Wikström, Per-Olof H., and Lars Dolmen. 2004. "Sweden." In *Cross-National Studies in Crime and Justice*, edited by David P. Farrington, Patrick A. Langan, and Michael Tonry. Washington, D.C.: U.S. Bureau of Justice Statistics.

Author Index

Subject Index